Primary Prevention of Psychopathology
Volume I: The Issues

Primary Prevention of Psychopathology

VOLUME I: THE ISSUES

EDITORS

George W. Albee
Justin M. Joffe

Published for the University of Vermont
by the University Press of New England
Hanover   New Hampshire   1977

The University Press
of New England

Brandeis University
Clark University
Dartmouth College
University of New Hampshire
University of Rhode Island
University of Vermont

This volume is dedicated to James and Faith Waters. They, together with their children, Barbara and Richard, are Trustees of The Waters' Foundation, which supports efforts directed toward primary prevention, environmental modification, emotional education, and improvements in psychotherapy. James and Faith Waters attended every session of the Conference and participated actively in the discussions, both during the scientific sessions and during the informal gatherings at other times. Without their active financial and organizational support, the Conference could not have taken place. We look forward to a continuing collaborative relationship with them, and we acknowledge our gratitude and admiration for this selfless couple.

Contents

Preface

The First Vermont Conference on the Primary Prevention of Psychopathology was a consequence of a number of converging determinants. Chance, good luck, and careful planning all played a part. A major factor was the sense of social responsibility of James and Faith Waters, which led them to establish the Waters' Foundation, which supports efforts to improve the mental health of both children and adults. When it was decided, after many conversations with the Foundation, to hold an integrative conference designed to bring together a group of persons around a specific issue affecting the mental health of people, a Planning Committee of faculty members at the University of Vermont proposed the topic Primary Prevention. We felt that this subject was in the air, waiting to be precipitated.

The past three decades have been a time of ferment, debate, conflict, and excitement in the field of mental health. The work of the Joint Commission on Mental Illness and Health in the late 1950's represented a turning point, away from custodialism and pessimism. A special message to Congress in 1963 from the late President John F. Kennedy urged a new and massive attack on mental retardation and mental disorder. The subsequent development of the Comprehensive Community Mental Health Centers has been called by Nicholas Hobbs the Third Mental Health Revolution. (The first revolution began with Philippe Pinel's striking off the chains that bound mad persons in the dungeons of Paris in 1792; the second was the Freudian revolution in the first decades of this century, which emphasized the lawfulness of all human behavior, but especially emotional disturbances, and resulted in the recognition of the continuity between sanity and insanity).

In all three, as so often happens in revolutions, powerfully entrenched forces with rigid patterns of thinking blunted many of the new insights, and some of the hard-won gains were lost. But each revolution has changed things enough so that after a period of consolidation, the forces of decency, humanity, and social responsibility have been able to gather for a new attempt, a new struggle against the forces of reaction and inhumanity.

What has been gained in the two hundred years since Pinel? Basically, an important idea has taken root and has been growing, despite all efforts to destroy it. This idea holds that the many forms of mental disturbance have natural causes, that these causes can be untangled and unsnarled and, in some cases at least, counteracted, so that the process leading to disturbance can be reversed. It is a short step from here to the belief that prevention itself may be possible.

Other ideas took root as well. We gradually became aware of the self-fulfilling nature of some of our traditional pessimism. We learned that reacting with fear, repulsion, and rejection to the insane, particularly to the insane poor, locking them up in so-called asylums, accentuated their isolation and often turned them into zombie-like oddities. We gave diagnostic names, high-sounding and scholarly labels, to the behavior that our rejection itself produced. We mutilated the insane psychologically and then did careful studies to determine the amount of deficit they showed in comparison with the non-mutilated. But we also began to do epidemiological research and were surprised to discover differences in prevalence among social classes, between the sexes, across cultures, and across societies at different stages of industrial development. We began to suspect that mental disorders are primarily a social phenomenon, that social factors drive people crazy. We learned that people most often become neurotic or psychotic in relation to other people. So for the past decade or two, ideas of prevention have been germinating; some are finding fertile soil, some are not.

What is primary prevention, and how does it differ from other contemporary enthusiasms? How is it different, for example, from social psychiatry, community psychiatry, community mental health, and community psychology, all of which are evolving foci of efforts in the mental health field?

Primary prevention is a concept borrowed from the field of public health. It involves action taken to prevent the occurrence of disease or disability in large populations. Public health measures like vaccination against smallpox, chlorinating drinking water to make it safe, putting iodine in salt to prevent goiter, forbidding the use of carcinogenic substances used as food additives or pre-servatives—all are aimed at groups rather than at specific individuals, and have as their purpose the prevention of illness at the source.

What are primary prevention measures in the field of psycho-pathology? Treating primary syphilis prevents the appearance, twenty or thirty years later, of general paresis. Where the mental illness is a genuine illness and has an organic cause, things can be done to prevent the occurrence of the disease. But what about mental and emotional problems that are not "diseases" but learned patterns of social maladjustment and emotional distress? Here we get into issues involving less clear-cut empirical relation-ships between early experiences and later disturbance. Clearly, efforts at primary prevention of psychopathology engage a more amorphous problem and involve a much wider range of actions than public health prevention of disease. Our speakers were chosen to represent this wide range of approaches, at both the theoretical and the practical levels.

The dimensions of the problem of psychopathology become more clearly outlined as a result of epidemiological research, but the very limited human resources currently available to deal with people in mental trouble seem destined not to be reinforced by recruits. The federal government is reducing funds that support training of mental health professionals, and that provide staffing grants for mental health centers; yet the number of retarded and mentally deficient children increases as medical science applies new skills to save the lives of damaged infants who in earlier times would have perished, and the dramatic increase in the number of separations and divorces means that many more children are being raised in broken homes or in single-parent families, a situation known to be conducive to later emotional problems. Chronic and widespread unemployment and other kinds of malaise in our industrial society cannot help people to grow in strength. The problem of defining psychopathology is exceedingly complex.

It is our expectation that this volume will be the first in a series of Conference Reports devoted to the primary prevention of psycho-pathology. A second conference was held in June 1976, and Vol-ume II is in press. Further conferences are on the drawing board.

In the first conference, which was meant to provide a general background for more specialized approaches later, we made a serious attempt to enlist persons representing a diversity of views and approaches to the subject of primary prevention. Although a few notable experts were unable to attend, we believe that the present volume contains a range of thoughtful presentations from persons generally recognized to be leaders in the field. The papers represent a mixture of the theoretical and the practical, of conventional and unconventional approaches. Genetic and biological factors are considered, although our belief in the importance of the childhood origins of psychopathology led to a heavier emphasis on papers concerned with interventions in childhood.

The Appendix of this volume, by Kessler and Albee, examines some of the dimensions of this field. We have not limited our conception of psychopathology to the conventional categories included in the American Psychiatric Association's Diagnostic and Statistical Manual II—indeed, we believe that sexism and racism are as psychopathological as the more conventional diagnostic categories. We hope that future conferences will focus on these damaging conditions as psychological disturbances which lend themselves to primary prevention efforts.

Future conferences, like the first and second, will be organized by the faculty of the Department of Psychology at the University of Vermont, with support and collaboration from James and Faith Waters and their Foundation. The current conference committee included, in addition to the editors of this volume, Robert B. Lawson, Richard E. Musty, and Jon E. Rolf. It had active participation and help from other members of the department, some of whom are identified in the volume as authors. We also had the assistance of a number of graduate and undergraduate students and staff in the department. We would particularly like to thank Janet R. Forgays, Dianne M. Maughan, and Ira D. Turkat for their help.

George W. Albee
Justin M. Joffe

Burlington, Vermont
November 1976

I
Introductory Papers

Introductory Notes

As we planned this first Vermont conference on the Primary Prevention of Psychopathology, we became increasingly aware of the complexity of the field. Problems of definition of primary prevention were important but were overshadowed by problems of agreement on appropriate methodology, and problems of deciding which areas of human interaction were the most fruitful points of entry for our efforts at prevention. There were also problems of identifying target populations at risk, and problems of defining clearly the behaviors to be prevented. Most people who write or work in the field of primary prevention have a developmental orientation. That is, nearly everyone believes that later psychopathology is to be understood in terms of earlier life experiences. Inevitably our first conference took on a developmental flavor.

We invited a large number of distinguished people to talk at the first conference. To our knowledge this conference was the first attempt to bring people in the field together in an open meeting focused exclusively on primary prevention. Most of our participants appeared to be preoccupied with the urgency of primary prevention in psychopathology. They all seem to subscribe to the public health view that mass disorders afflicting humankind are almost never brought under control by attempts to treat affected individuals.

In various ways and at various intervention points our conference speakers had been struggling to establish programs in primary prevention. The conference turned out to be stimulating, exciting, and frustrating. We tried to pack so much into three days that both the participants and the audience often felt saturated with ideas and information. As we have received feedback about it, it has become clear that future conferences should each examine a specific theme, in terms of both method and content.

This first volume begins with an overview of the field, its failures and successes and its directions for the future. The following papers have a developmental sequence. Speakers examine genetic, prenatal, and perinatal factors and then move to the problems of identifying high risk children and adolescents, and of intervening with these groups. Papers are concerned with both practical and theoretical issues. We move to a group of papers concerned with the prevention of adult psychopathology. We hear from a commissioner of mental health in a state, and from a program planner at the federal level discussing ways that efforts in the direction of primary prevention interact with the practical worlds of state and federal agencies. Most of the conference reports are concerned with aspects of psychopathology prevention, but we did not entirely neglect the other side of the coin: factors associated with good mental health. The last paper deals with this issue, focusing on the experience of well-being. Finally, in an appendix we reproduce a thorough review of the literature in the field and a lengthy bibliography.

Part I is made up of papers that introduce the topic of the conference. They deal with definition and show the complexity of our subject. James G. Kelly was Keynoter. He is Dean of the Lila Acheson Wallace School of Community Service and Public Affairs at the University of Oregon. Dean Kelly was formerly professor of psychology and urban planning at the University of Michigan, where he also directed the graduate program in community psychology, a field in which he is recognized as a national authority. For some years he was Chief of the Community Project Section of the Mental Health Study Center of the National Institute of Mental Health. He is a former President of the Division of Community Psychology of the American Psychological Association. His address started the conference off with a thoughtful analysis of practical research approaches to primary prevention, with some intriguing suggestions and observations about the unexpected and beneficial side effects of such research.

Stephen E. Goldston is Coordinator for Primary Prevention Programs at the National Institute of Mental Health. Dr. Goldston was helpful in the planning stages of our conference, and we prevailed upon him to deliver a talk during one of the evenings of the conference. Many of those attending had expressed a wish to hear him speak about the federal government's present and future activities and plans in this area. Dr. Goldston later agreed to prepare a paper based on the talk he gave, and on the questions and answers that followed his presentation. When his paper arrived, the editors took the liberty of dividing it into two parts. The first section, which is part of this introductory series of papers, is Goldston's attempt to define primary prevention as a field. This section should be especially useful as an orientation. In a later section we carry Dr. Goldston's discussion of primary prevention at the federal level.

Eli M. Bower is Director, Health and Medical Sciences, University of California, Berkeley. Dr. Bower has been a consultant and research coordinator in problems of emotionally disturbed children, working for many years with the California State Department of Education. During the 1960's he spent several years at the National Institute of Mental Health as a Consultant in Mental Health Education. He has written extensively on the subject of prevention and is the author of widely quoted research studies in this area. In the paper he prepared for the conference, he instructs us in the differences between healing and prevention, employing some illuminating Greek mythology; he then goes on to make some very practical suggestions about things we can do for and with children in the area of primary prevention.

Arnold J. Sameroff is professor of psychology in the Departments of Pediatrics and Psychiatry at the University of Rochester. Prof. Sameroff was in Greece the month of our conference and circumstances made it impossible for him to join us, but he sent along his prepared paper, which is a carefully reasoned, well-documented reminder of how easily certain biases and beliefs cherished by professionals can interfere with an understanding of research. Taking a developmental approach, Sameroff reminds us of the startling fact that "there has yet to be demonstrated a causal connection between a constitutional variable and any personality or intellectual developmental outcome." We continue to read journal articles reporting on retrospective research which implicates early trauma or early defective functioning as causal to later intellectual and emotional difficulties; but prospective research invariably establishes, as

Dr. Sameroff points out, that people with the same sort of early problems and experiences often reach adulthood without these negative consequences. Dr. Sameroff brings to the reader an important message: Data are critically important, but we must constantly guard against forcing them into our own preconceived beliefs and prejudices.

1

The Search for Ideas and Deeds That Work

JAMES G. KELLY

In my opinion, the topic of primary prevention is a most exciting and overdue challenge for psychology. It is exciting because understanding what it takes in the way of ideas, knowledge, and personal commitment to prevent prychopathology increases our chances of contributing to an integrative force within psychology. Primary prevention requires the best efforts of all varieties of psychologists, and can help psychology to select new topics for research and new ways of doing research. What study of primary prevention may do in the long run is to bring psychology closer to the concerns and hopes of both citizens and professionals who wish to have an impact upon our social and physical environment and to improve the quality of life. Working on unconventional topics, developed outside the mainstream of psychology, however, requires, in my opinion, changes in the way we think, the way we work, and the choice of topics for our work. If we psychologists take seriously the topic of primary prevention, we ourselves will be changing. This is my message: if we seriously believe in working in the field of primary prevention, we will not be doing psychological business as usual.

As I view it, understanding the cultural, social, and economic forces that affect human behavior puts us in daily contact with other professionals and citizens. In unraveling the impacts of the family, social groupings, and the immediate community upon people's day-to-day lives, we will be doing research in the field as well as the laboratory over long periods of time, and we will be creating methods that adapt to the local context rather than looking for subjects to do our research in. We will be spending more occasions like this integrating our ideas and pooling our intellectual resources to understand our accomplishments, rather than parade them so as to be one up on our colleagues. We will also be worrying in new ways about how what we learn can be tried out by our consumers. It may be that psychology will have a consumer research foundation to sift our ideas and findings and test them out for quality control for popular consumption. If we know important things, we increase our influence, our respect, and the fears about us. As I see it, as we begin to understand more and more about human behavior, a consumer research enterprise formed not to protect the public from psychology but to work with psychology to learn how to communicate our work for maximum usefulness, will be an asset for both psychologists and consumers. Certainly, understanding how and what to do to prevent psychopathology will earn us both respect and fear, and the need for consumer protection.

I would like to offer a few suggestions for changes in our behavior if we are to take seriously the challenge and the exhilaration of working in the field of primary prevention. The suggestions are offered to accelerate our search for ideas and deeds that work.

EXPANDING THE TIME PERSPECTIVE

How can we know about prevention if we do not understand the psychological processes that are related to development over time? We can all recall from our professional and personal experience an event, unplanned and unwanted, that has created a personal or social crisis. What are the characteristics of the persons, the situations, the circumstances that accelerate the positive, emotional, and intellectual growth that makes us more integrated people? Does the successful management of a crisis help us cope with the next event? We need to know more about these everyday events in people's lives and how they can be congealing and developmentally enriching. More important, we will need to know more about the cyclic patterns of growth. If we do not know the characteristics of persons and events that aid social development, and we do not know more about the stages of the growth process, how do we know enough to intervene in order to prevent?

Thinking about people longitudinally and doing research from a longitudinal perspective requires a commitment in life goals of the researcher and learning competences in the administration of research, as well as the ability to obtain grant funds for that research. Such activities have not been recognized as necessary for our research training or research careers. If we wish to understand behavior in relation to primary prevention, we will do more work with people over time. Even if we carry out cross-section research on how to make an impact upon public policy, we will adopt a longitudinal perspective; I believe that it takes extra effort over time to see that results have an impact. For example, I am personally interested to find out more about the impact of Head Start. One of the exciting consequences of working from a longitudinal perspective is to be a part of the positive and unanticipated consequences of social policy research. It has certainly taken ten years for some of the tangible effects of the educational programs to be observed in the behavior of the children. It has also taken ten years to see that Head Start is influencing the way in which educational and health agencies respond to the poor in their communities.

Edward B. Fiske in the *New York Times* cites one example of the consequences of work done at an earlier period which has improved the quality of life in an unanticipated way (Fiske, 1975). To quote Mr. Fiske: "The reformers' goal of fundamentally changing public school structures has clearly gone unfulfilled, but in some cases parents' experience in governing Head Start has changed their relationship to schools. To quote a parent, Mrs. Rinaldo, 'Parents are no longer afraid to go to school and ask the teacher why their child doesn't have homework . . .'." That illustrates the long-term but tangible effects of action research, effects that are increasing the awareness of citizens and their competence to be advocates for their own development—a just and valid outcome of the Head Start experience. Expanding the time perspective creates the opportunity for us to consider secondary benefits of research and service to be as valuable and as valid as the initial purpose.

In the process of conducting a longitudinal study of coping preferences of boys from the eighth to the twelfth grade in two Detroit area high schools, I was impressed with the unanticipated consequences of research findings and the relationship of research with the collaborating schools. Both results and relationships contributed to educational policy for the high schools. We began to worry about the fact that our primary personality variable, exploratory preferences assessed at the eighth grade, did not show any relationship at the ninth or tenth grade level to expected differences with such variables as level of self-esteem, satisfaction with school, and psychological involvement with school. Staff who were buying into a more straightforward, deductive approach to research proclaimed the early death of another personality construct. By the 11th grade, however, significant differences appeared which were sustained over the 12th grade. We were not prepared to believe in the developmental process, even though we were doing a longitudinal study. It appears that within these two high schools the differences in the impact of school environment upon the students does not show up until the junior year—in retrospect, a reasonable finding. We were finally converted and began to pay attention to our own theoretical pronouncements.

In our research we were interested in learning about the social competences and self-confidence of the junior high school student. We had made a major error in believing that eighth-grade boys were miniature versions of graduate students in psychology. Early in the research, we discovered that boys in the eighth, ninth, and even tenth grade received almost all their sense of self-esteem from their participation in athletic activities. The fact that only about 4 percent of their reported competences were related to interpersonal skills, while 70 percent of reported personal competences were related to athletic skills, surprised us. Our surprise motivated us to discuss our findings with the high school faculties and administration. In both of these schools, athletic activities were restricted to varsity sports programs. There were no intramural sports. Our findings, our concern, and the concern of the high school administration led to the creation of intramural coed sports programs at both schools. I am still pleased that an unanticipated finding sparked a change in the educational program of the high schools, so that all students could have more opportunity to develop self-confidence and self-esteem through learning athletic skills and participating in athletic programs.

From this personal experience, I am convinced that expanding the time perspective keeps us honest as researchers and allows more opportunity for our research to contribute to the positive development of both persons and the social organizations in which we work.

LEARNING FROM NATURAL SETTINGS

Primary prevention means for me changing the local conditions within a community or an organization in order to improve positive development of persons or reduce negative reactions to stress. Carrying out these tasks means more understanding of the natural history of disorder, within an emphasis of the word "natural."

To know what does not work means getting at the problem as experienced by those in the situation. I believe this because I have seen much social science carried out primarily for the education of other social scientists. One example of doing social research that meets the standards of intellectual and research procedures, but which may miss an understanding of phenomena as expressed in the daily lives of people, is the research on Social Indicators. A recent commentary by Eleanor B. Sheldon and Robert Parke offers a sober reminder of laying on research methods without improvising or creating methods that get behind the experiences and variables. To quote Sheldon and Parke:

> *The notions of social indicators and social accounting, expressed by analogy with the natural economic accounts, generated excitement in the 1960's, and the interest continues to grow if we may judge from governmental activity and the publication of programmatic and research papers. But the concepts which focused much of the early enthusiasm gave exaggerated promise of policy applications and provided an unproductive basis for research. The essential theoretical prerequisites for developing a system of social accounts—defining the variables and the interrelationships among them—are missing. It is now realized that evaluation research, particularly experimentation, must be relied on for evaluation of government programs. (Sheldon and Parke, 1975)*

We have maintained a tradition of doing scholarly work for our colleagues; our reference groups have been our disciplines and our professions. This has been important for us to do as psychologists and desirable for the development of the science and profession of psychology. Primary prevention, however, challenges the design of scholarly work to be tangible and useful for taking positive action.

The exciting challenge for psychology's affiliation with the cause of primary prevention is that we can be intellectually vital, analytical, and rigorous while we are directly involved with the contexts of our informants. Involvement with the contexts of our informants means that we will change our view of ourselves and our informants and change the way we work. Learning from natural settings means that we spend time and begin to develop an appreciation of the life styles and values of our informants. It means working with them to define what is important to study and, if we do research, how it can be least harmful and most beneficial. The relationship of investigator and subject evolves to roles of consultant and client, with more equality, more reciprocity, and more clarification of the impact of the research process and knowledge upon the client. With these steps, psychology moves closer to developing guidelines for the hows and whys of public policy.

I hope that there will be an accelerated development of new research methods that can encourage us to learn more directly from the conditions we hope to intervene and change. Developing inquiries that unfold from the local condition can increase the opportunity to establish quality control for our preventive programs. We will be making fewer pronouncements as scholars, but we will be focusing upon those variables, topics, ingredients, and findings that contribute to our own betterment as members of society. We will also earn more credibility from being participants with those for whom we are working.

The word "natural" stimulates fantasies of skinny dipping, partaking of herbs, a life of virginal purity. Bending our research tradition to the requirements of natural conditions is a complex task filled with experiential anxiety that what we have learned from our scholarly past is not enough or is not appropriate. This is troublesome because the premises we make about human behavior do not always hold true now, under new and natural conditions.

Not only is there the gigantic challenge of creating observational methods, of new statistical procedures, of worrying about how and what to select for intensive analysis, there is also the need to rethink our relationship as investigator and client. Historians, novelists, anthropologists, and journalists have created some accommodations to allow inquiry to be done with the informant remaining intact and on occasion helped. Some psychologists, including yourselves, along with Erik Erikson, Roger Barker, Carl Rogers, and Jean Piaget, have made useful contributions for all of us and for those specific persons with whom they have learned.

There *are* increasing opportunities for future psychologists to learn how to do quality work that is useful. We who value this activity can applaud, for example, the work of George Fairweather and colleagues at Michigan State University, where doctoral students can learn to do research that has impact (Fairweather, 1967; Fairweather et al., 1974; and Fairweather, 1975). A few of their dissertation topics suggest both role relationships and content that directly relate to primary prevention. For example: "An Evaluation of Two Drug Abuse Treatment Programs in Lansing, Michigan"; "The Role of Reading, Speaking Dialect and Associative Bridging in Behavioral Achievement and Attitude Change," with black and white school students; "An Evaluation of a Community Based Delinquency Prevention Program on the Basis of Group and Individual Employment"; and "The Application of Small Group Techniques to Training in Community Participation: A Field Experiment." Each of these pieces of work has adhered to the criteria of incisive design, and also has redefined the relationship between inquiry and utility. Persons have received benefit from the research, even when the findings were inconsequential. Whether the research methodology is the field survey, the interview, participant observation, combinations of these methods, or the creation of new ways to assess, count, or test out ideas, the relationship of the investigator with the community undergoes change when the inquiry goes to the people. This is a sine qua non for primary prevention.

In the research I previously mentioned, the study of coping preferences of high school students, our staff spent several years doing reconnaissance with the school officials and the students, discussing the rationale for the study, exploring and defining expected benefits of the research, and building a working relationship between our staff and the schools. In looking back, our entré process was limited by the mutual false beliefs that we shared about each other. We, at the University of Michigan, believed that high school faculty and administration were uninterested in research and interested in the status quo of keeping problems quiet. The high school administration believed that we were only interested in them as guinea pigs, and that whatever we did would have very little benefit for them or the students; not only would we intrude upon their time, but we would leave them in a worse situation than when our work began. We would be pollutants. We were both partially right.

During the six years of our work, while we learned a lot about socialization of high school youth and contributed to changes in policies regarding education in these two schools, we also learned something equally valid. We learned that organizations that are responsive as research collaborators can be less interested in the impact and use of research, while collaborators who are initially antagonistic and suspicious of research can become willing to improve the quality of life of their high school environment. We learned something about the dynamics of social research that I believe has direct significance for doing research for impact. In one high school we were elated in the beginning of our work when the faculty member assigned to help us, along with the school principal, worked very hard to ease data collection and to ensure faculty and parental collaboration. We had an optimum relationship as scientist and subject. The subjects were punctual, pliable, courteous, and cooperative to the point of being dutiful. We were boosted in our view of ourselves as eminent. In the second high school we found ourselves being hazed. We found the faculty member assigned to our project balky, and a principal who insisted that we develop elaborate safeguards to ensure the written approval from parents for their sons' cooperation in every phase of the research. Faculty and administration carefully screened our materials. We believed that we were put upon and put down. The eminence we gave ourselves from the experience in the first school was washed out when we came to the second school. During the six years of our collaboration, we worked to improve our relationship with the second school, but did so with reluctance and self-righteousness.

When it came to catching the attention of both high schools in order to translate what he had learned so as to benefit the schools, we found the faculty and administration in the first school less than enthusiastic in taking what we found and putting it to use. We had to exert firm and persistent efforts to receive their attention. We finally managed to help the counselors and administration develop additional insights concerning developmental changes in their students. Afterward, we learned that the major reasons for letting us do the research were that the principal liked me and that collaboration with the University of Michigan was a personal and political plus for the principal and the school. The thrill was creating the contract; once we were coupled, there was less interest in a deep relationship.

In the second school, there was an agitated, persistent inquiry about what we learned and a propulsion to pull out facts and data from our report which could help the school understand the causes of low faculty morale and disinterest in students. We learned that the suspicion about our research was partially the result of the belief that we would find out the whole story. But behind the anxiety about the research process was a genuine interest to receive help. As this revelation began to dawn on us, we felt a sense of guilt, then enthusiasm, and then humility as we began to see again the multiple processes involved in doing good. We learned that compliance is not necessarily cordiality, and resistance does not necessarily represent opposition to new ideas.

Over time the insights accumulated as a result of understanding the differences in response to research as inquiry and research as action have been as important as the detailed findings on adolescent development which we accumulated. If we can get ourselves up for the challenge of relating our work directly to our clients, by understanding their settings and their contexts, we can enrich ourselves, contribute to psychology's growth, and help earn the respect of citizens who pay the taxes for many of us for the privilege, and the freedom for our minds to work.

I'd like to talk more about ways to increase the validity and transfer of our ideas for the goals of primary prevention. Two are perhaps enough, but before I close, I must mention one research topic that I think offers a great deal of promise for understanding contemporary society and for designing community-based prevention programs. This is research on the impact of television viewing for the American community, as well as experimentation with the use of television programming for community development. I am just becoming familiar with this type of research, and I have been impressed with the implications of recent research. For example, Douglas Cater in writing about television viewing, quoted Robert T. Bower's work on *Television and The Public*, to the effect that the educated viewer "watches the set as much as others, during the evening and weekend hours . . . Even when he had a clear choice between an information program and some standard entertainment fare, he was just as apt as others to choose the latter" (Cater, 1975). One implication for me is that American communities are being increasingly deprived of contributions of all people, including the educated, to contribute their ideas, energies, and talent to their locales.

A recent report by Joseph Klapper, Office of Social Research at CBS, as reported in *Behavior Today*, reveals that a Saturday morning show, "The Harlem Globetrotters' Popcorn Machine," has had success in getting prosocial messages across to kids. Although the show is not pedagogical, it does aim to entertain and to convey prosocial messages. Klapper reported that 87 percent of the children received at least one prosocial message from the program they saw. He also reported that the interview itself served as a teaching experience and that the study picked up a lot of interview effects. The implications of that are important, he believed, since the interview was just an organized chat. What would the effect be, he wondered, if parents and children talked about the programs? How's that for primary prevention?

I have also been intrigued with Peter Goldmark's efforts to apply his television engineering talent to increase participation of Americans in their communities by arranging the use of television for discussion, feedback, and large group participation (Goldmark, 1973). If we are at home watching T.V., can we also be taught to listen to each other over T.V., to increase the latent talent in our communities so that we may serve as resources for one another?

Research and demonstration activities with television and the media seem compelling and apt work for primary prevention. I am pleased to note that the motivation which propelled us to first look at T.V. primarily in terms of its impact upon violence has now moved us to consider the potential of television as a resource for the development of children's positive behavior. I am excited as well that intellectual and personal resources can be activated in our communities through television.

CONCLUSION

The search for ideas and deeds that work is a plus; the search can do little wrong and can contribute many benefits. The effort to understand and adapt more purposefully the intellectual traditions of psychology to the overwhelming and compelling needs of citizens to understand and improve the quality of life is a worthy goal for psychology. We psychologists have been accepted, we are bountiful in numbers and variety, and our changing values are encouraging us to improvise, to participate in new ways with citizens to make psychology work for ourselves and for society. Besides, primary prevention has attracted a lot of people's attention, is tempting curiosity and arousing hope. Developing a longer time perspective for both our observations and our expectations for impact, and getting ourselves in the midst of natural situations, may do some good for people and may help us learn something of ourselves.

REFERENCES

Cater, D. The intellectual in videoland. *Saturday Review*, May 31, 1975, pp. 12-16.
Fairweather, G. W. *Methods for experimental social innovation.* New York: Wiley, 1967.
Fairweather, G., Sanders, D. H., and Tornatzky, L. G. *Creating change in mental health organizations.* New York: Pergamon Press, 1974.
Fairweather, G. W. Personal communication, May 8, 1975.
Fiske, B. Head Start: After 10 years, planning experiments. *New York Times,* June 8, 1975, p. 40.
Goldmark, P. C. *Maverick inventor: My turbulent years at CBS.* New York: Saturday Review Press, E. P. Dutton, 1973.
Kelly, J. G., et al. *The high school: An exploration of students and social contexts in two midwestern communities.* Community Psychology Series 4, New York: Behavioral Publications, 1976.
The Professional's Newsletter. *Behavior Today,* June 16, 1975, *6*, No. 24.
Sheldon, E. B., and Parke, R. Social indicators. *Science*, 1975, *188,* 693-699.

2

Defining Primary Prevention

STEPHEN E. GOLDSTON

INTRODUCTION

This chapter presents a point of view about primary prevention—an idiosyncratic perspective based upon my fifteen-year involvement with the national mental health program. An early interest in primary prevention, kindled in the 1950's while a graduate student at a school of public health, subsequently became reinforced through continued doctoral studies in education and clinical psychology and led to an abiding career commitment. Two decades ago there were no convenient, succinct labels to describe the scope of primary prevention, other than to fumble and mumble about a concern with "mental health/public health issues"; indeed, no one spoke of an "interface" between two fields, nor had the term "community psychology" come into professional vocabularies. This somewhat personal historical note has several purposes: first, to present my credentials; second, to point out that in spite of the unparalleled current interest, primary prevention as related to mental health is not recent but has been around for quite some time (though of professional interest to all too few persons); and third, to offer my judgment that, conceptually and experientially, the roots of primary prevention are grounded in the soil of public health and that to understand primary prevention requires some familiarity with public health philosophy and practice.

In my opinion, primary prevention is the most misunderstood, undersupported, and neglected aspect of mental health work. Nonetheless, its allure, excitement, and promise tend to reinforce the graphic analogy in which primary prevention is compared to the Okefenokee Swamp: "If one explores and survives, the area becomes compelling, even addictive" (Kessler and Albee, 1975). Accordingly,

I offer the views of a primary prevention addict as seen from the federal level.

THE MYTHS ABOUT PRIMARY PREVENTION

Until the last two years there were few dissenters from the prevailing sentiment in the mental health field that primary prevention is unrealistic, virtually impossible to achieve short of total social revolution, illusive, beyond conceptualization, and too difficult to verify. I refer to this view as the myth *about* primary prevention. The literature is replete with broadsides on one hand and homilies on the other directed toward primary prevention. For example, primary prevention has been described as "benevolent gambling" (Panzetta, 1971), "more cost than benefit" (Cumming, 1972), "our Holy Grail" (Brown, 1970), "corraling a cloud" (Isbister, 1975), and a "magical notion," a "woolly notion," and "an illusion" (Henderson, 1975). These phrases are cited to illustrate the rhetoric that has been utilized in place of funds for primary prevention research and practice. Rhetoric aside, primary prevention is neither smoke nor a cloud, nor a rosy vision of a happier tomorrow, but *specific* actions directed to *specific* populations. Before presenting specific primary prevention program activities pursued at the federal level, however, some definitions and a framework for understanding program development and operation are necessary.

DEFINITIONS AND CONCEPTUAL FRAMEWORK

In public health terminology, *prevention* is an all-embracing concept having three distinct levels: primary prevention, referring to actions taken prior to the onset of disease to intercept its causation or to modify its course before man is involved; secondary prevention, meaning early diagnosis and treatment; and tertiary prevention, indicating rehabilitative efforts to reduce the residual effects of illness (Leavell and Clark, 1965). In this conceptualization primary prevention has two aspects: *Health Promotion*, referring to measures concerned with improving the quality of life and raising the general level of health in a population, and

Specific Protection, denoting explicit procedures for disease prevention—for example, immunizations, prevention of cretinism by adequate iodine intake, and prevention of the sequelae of German measles by vaccination of females prior to pregnancy. Unfortunately, critics of primary prevention are quick to seize on the virtual absence of Specific Protection activities, since the etiologies of most mental illnesses are unknown; these same critics are even more apt to ignore, or be unaware of, Health Promotion as an integral aspect of primary prevention.

This multilevel definition of prevention provides both a broad and a convenient framework for accommodating almost all the activities of health workers as well as a justification for collectively including diagnostic, treatment, and rehabilitative functions under the rubric of prevention. The terminology is confusing and misleading, however, and contributes to the continued neglect and misunderstanding of primary prevention. Some standard meaning of the term *prevention* is needed to avoid semantic difficulties. Accordingly, this writer advocates that *prevention* be used solely to refer to actions which aim either to (1) anticipate a disorder or (2) foster optimal health. In short, only activites that deal with health promotion or health maintenance, or what in the mental health field has been called positive mental health, should bear the label of prevention; the term prevention, then, would be synonymous with primary prevention.

As a function of professional practice and a recognized need for conceptual clarity I have evolved the following definition of primary prevention:

> *Primary prevention encompasses activities directed toward specifically identified vulnerable high risk groups within the community who have not been labeled psychiatrically ill and for whom measures can be undertaken to avoid the onset of emotional disturbance and/or to enhance their level of positive mental health. Programs for the promotion of mental health are primarily educational rather than clinical in conception and operation, their ultimate goal being to increase people's capacities for dealing with crises and for taking steps to improve their own lives.*

Conceptually, this definition is grounded in crisis theory, which provides a construct for presumptions maintaining that interventions keyed to critical life points can allay the onset of emotional disturbances. These presumptions argue in favor of such primary preventive activites as mental health education, anticipatory guidance, a variety of forms of mental health consultation, and the training of vital caregivers. Within this framework the issue is no longer one of whether what you are doing will prevent mental illness, but a recognition that mental health workers need to view primary prevention efforts and to evaluate them in much broader terms (Bower, 1972):

> *Prevention and promotion in mental health have in the past been so tightly tied to mental illnesses that any foolhardy or misguided adventurer who stumbled into this arena was continually plagued by the question—does what you do prevent mental illness? Unfortunately, mental illnesses are only one of many end points in human failure . . . The modes and roads to human failure are many and varied. Preventive and promotion programs need to be tied into the human condition in all its manifestations.*

Within this public health/crisis theory approach, the stated objective of primary prevention efforts is not the prevention of mental illness. Rather, the goals of primary prevention are twofold: first, to prevent needless psychopathology and symptoms, maladjustment, maladaption, and misery regardless of whether an end point might be mental illness; and second, to promote mental health by increasing levels of "wellness" among various defined populations. The concept of health promotion connotes a socio-psycho-cultural-educational model distinct from a medical model, and the overriding question becomes one involving social competence, coping ability, and ego-strengthening measures rather than criteria of psychiatric symptomatology. The key question becomes, "How well is the individual or community?" rather than "How sick?"

In this connection, the Conference Planning Committee acted astutely when they designated the focus of this meeting in theme and content on the primary prevention of *psychopathology* rather than on mental illness. Clarity of labels, foci, and objectives are necessary in order to facilite primary prevention activities and to advance this critical sphere of mental health work.

PRIMARY PREVENTION: AN IDEA WHOSE TIME HAS COME

The past two years have witnessed an unparalleled interest in primary prevention among professional mental health workers and human services groups. This interest has been translated into program activities, conferences, publications, sessions at professional meetings, and the identification of relevant training and research issues—all directly focused on primary prevention. To a large degree, Victor Hugo's famous words of over a century ago could be applied to primary prevention: "Greater than the tread of mighty armies is an idea whose time has come!"

A varied field of forces would appear to be related to the "emergence" of primary prevention as a respectable area for consideration by mental health workers. From a federal perspective, some of the causes and effects that have served to provide primary prevention its present unprecedented prominence include:

(a) The public consumer movement, which has been characterized by a greater sharing of information previously restricted to professional workers and the raising of questions and issues heretofore either ignored or overlooked.

(b) Growing awareness that primary preventive activities can be a major vehicle for eventual reduction of health care costs—for example, hospitalization, etc.—an "ounce of prevention" philosophy with economic considerations.

(c) Genuine interest and growing commitment in the field about translating into action community mental health principles dealing with primary prevention, particularly the notion that community mental health practice implies responsibility for the mental health of an entire population and not merely for the casualties that appear at the doors of the mental health facility.

(d) The identification of prevention as one of five program emphases in the DHEW Forward Plan for Health over the next five-year period. Such official high priority for prevention has been reflected in considerable support for prevention being expressed by key policy-planners and decision-makers within the federal health and mental health establishment.

A more favorable climate for primary prevention is still evolving. Only the sanction has been forthcoming—not the mandate for action. The future directions of primary prevention, from the federal perspective, will be influenced by past events and present activities.

REFERENCES

Bower, E. M. K.I.S.S. and kids: A mandate for prevention. *American Journal of Orthopsychiatry*, 1972, *42*, 556-565.

Brown, B. S. *Mental health and social change*. Austin, Texas: Hogg Foundation for Mental Health, 1970.

Cumming, E. Primary prevention—more cost than benefit. In H. Gottesfeld (Ed.), *The critical issues of community mental health*. New York: Behavioral Publications, 1972.

Henderson, J. Object relations and a new social psychiatry: The illusion of primary prevention. *Bulletin of the Menninger Clinic*, 1975, *39*, 233-245.

Isbister, J. Speech before the Southern Branch, American Public Health Association, Houston, Texas, May 1, 1975.

Kessler, M., and Albee, G. W. Primary prevention. *Annual Review of Psychology*, 1975, *26*, 557-591.

Leavell, H. R., and Clark, E. G. *Preventive medicine for the doctor in his community* (3rd ed.). New York: McGraw-Hill, 1965.

National Institute of Mental Health, Biometry Branch. *Consultation and education services: Federally funded community mental health centers 1973*. (Publication No. (ADM) 75-158). Rockville, Maryland: U.S. Department of Health, Education and Welfare, 1974.

National Institute of Mental Health, Biometry Branch. *Consultation and education services: Federally funded community mental health centers 1974*. In preparation, 1975.

Panzetta, A. F. *Community mental health: Myth and reality*. Philadelphia: Lea and Febiger, 1971.

3

Mythologies, Realities, and Possibilities in Primary Prevention

ELI M. BOWER

It is almost axiomatic that as one gets into the unstructured spaciousness of primary prevention, one searches for places to grab or stand. Since the field of primary prevention has as yet no restricted turf (no one makes or loses money doing it), it is still a friendly and virtuous territory of high abstraction and low practicality.

Although it did not spring full-grown out of the head of Zeus, much of mythology gives form and substance to its concepts. If one accepts human mythology as basic structures a la Lévi-Strauss (1966), then the song of Asclepius and Hygeia has a nostalgic and haunting melody.

MYTHOLOGIES—ASCLEPIUS AND HYGEIA

One can surmise that the professional healers back in the days of ancient Greece and Rome were—as they are today—part savant, part mystic. The chief of the lot was Asclepius, the God of Medicine or Healing, whose father was Apollo, the sovereign God of Healing, the sender and stayer of plagues, the protector or destroyer of mice, and the God of Light. Asclepius' mother was Karoni, about whom little is known except that her soon-to-be-famous son was plucked from her womb while sye lay on her funeral pyre. Asclepius married Epione, about whom also little is known, and had five or six children, two sons and three or four daughters. There is a votive relief of the Asclepius family (Kerenyi, 1959, p. 72) which shows the two sons, Machaon and Podaleirios, and three daughters, Iaso, Panakeia, and Hygeia. In this relief, Hygeia is standing directly behind her father but is barely visible. Asclepius' children served as apprentices to his healing chores and, as their names indicated, provided an enlargement of the healing concept. Hygeia, however, was noted by her father as the daughter who was worth as much as all the others (Edelstein and Edelstein, 1945). She was always close to her father and was often called his wife. Conceptually, however, Hygeia differed from her father in one contentious aspect of health. Health, to healers, was a process of restoration; to Hygeia, it was a process of living which resulted in an expanding and enhancing of self. The healer was the active agent in restoring health; the person himself was the active agent in hygienic health.

Iaso (healing) and Panakeia (cure-all) were much preferred by father as apprentice healers. At one point, Asclepius curtly chided his rebellious daughter with a line anachronistically stolen from *King Lear:* "Striving to better, oft we mar what's well" (Lear to Cordelia, I, 2, 371).

What was well in those days was Asclepius' widespread popularity and support by the populace. The worship of the healing God went far beyond its medical significance and came to play a large role in the people's religious life. Indeed, as the Edelsteins point out, in the final stages of paganism, Asclepius, of all the Greek gods, was judged the foremost antagonist of Christ (Edelstein and Edelstein, 1945).

Houses of healing called Asclepias soon dotted the landscape. In recent years these have been carefully restored and studied as "health centers" (Caton, 1900). The Asclepias were replete with hotels or motels, theaters, spas, and priests and healers. Included on the staff were a Hierophant, a physician or nonphysician head official, key bearers, receipt and payment bearers, basket bearers, and carriers of mysterious and holy things. Daughters Iaso and Panakeia also developed a priesthood and a following, but Hygeia could barely attract a small crowd. And so, the poor girl was left Cinderella-like in the back wards of history to find some identity when paired with "dental" or "mental."

Asclepius in time became a god so good at healing that without any malpractice insurance he began to "heal" the dead. This was seen as an invasion of the turf of Pluto, the guardian of Hades, who raised the devil with Zeus, complaining that healing the sick was one thing but mucking around in hell was quite another. Zeus was amused; but when Pluto suggested the possibility that Asclepius would soon get around to resurrecting Hippolyta, the Queen of the Amazons, Zeus dispatched the great healer into hell with a characteristic thunderbolt.

We cease our mythological narrative at this point to explore the structure of our own narrative. Health to the Asclepions was a state of perilous balance between an organism and his environment which, when upset by disease, accidents of birth, or other homeostatic problems, could be restored by the faith and skill of a healer. To Hygeia, the balance between an organism and his environment was an opportunity for growth; the balance might be restored by a healer but health growth was a process of increasing reasoned and knowledgeable behavior of persons related to themselves and their more effective relationship to the environment.

Hygeia may have been conceptually correct, but she was dramatically ineffective. We still respond with higher concern and action to disease and death than to notions of growth and fitness. As Dubos (1959, pp. 132–133) points out, schools of public health have in the past played, and continue to play, second string to schools of medicine.

Consider these facts in appraising the status of Asclepius and Hygeia in the modern world. Asclepius' disciples are the most prestigious, most economically rewarded of all professions. Aided by Panakeia, medicine persons and allied groups practice the healing arts by doing something to someone else, usually someone discomforted or in pain. Hygeia has no designated hitter except perhaps a few brave souls who seek ways of preventing specific diseases. Here again Hygeia is grateful but clearly differentiates between solving the problem of specific infections or nutritional diseases and the processes and goals of healthful living. Moreover, it becomes apparent that as Asclepius' skills increase to conquer and control specific diseases, others often emerge. Certainly with all our medical knowledge, technology, and health-care systems, we seem no closer to being a healthy society. Our Asclepian resources seem more able and useful in keeping the very young and very old alive, but often with severe and overwhelming constrictions on healthy and productive living. Hygeia faces these problems with reason and dignity but with eggs and tomatoes on her optimistic countenance.

REALITIES: PUBLIC HEALTH

It seems impossible for Asclepius and Hygeia to have come from the same philosophical family despite their filial relationship. Certainly their goals appear to be the same. One wonders if "health" maintained and enhanced by one's conduct is the same "health" that is restored after illness. One ballpark which allows both father and daughter to play is that of public health.

The notion and applicability of prevention first found both theoretical and practical payoffs in public health concepts. Initially public health was divided into three levels of activity. Man fights disease when it is full blown (tertiary prevention), when it is getting started (secondary prevention), and when conditions can be managed so that it won't get started at all (primary prevention). Some practicioners, especially those in preventive medicine, have expanded the three levels to five, as follows: (1) health promotion, (2) specific protection, (3) early diagnosis and prompt treatment, (4) disability limitation, and (5) rehabilitation.

The public health paradigm of prevention has paid off in some spectacular jackpots, such as the prevention of diphtheria, measles, pellagra, tetanus, typhoid, plague, polio, phenylketonuria, Down's syndrome perhaps, and other nutritional and genetically related diseases. In the case of our plaguing microorganisms we have been highly successful in identifying some of the pathogenic culprits, tracing their ecological habits and finding ways of blocking their noxious effects. Yet it is interesting to note that the adaptation processes that allow man to develop preventive mechanisms in response to specific diseases often produce greater vulnerability to other illnesses.

For example, large numbers of blacks and some whites with southern Mediterranean ancestry carry sickle-cell genes. Persons having a pair of such genes have only about one chance in five of surviving, so that about 16 percent of sickle-cell genes should be lost in every generation. Epidemiologists find, however, that this does not happen—a fact that suggests some other survival advantage to the carriers. Recent discoveries demonstrate the high degree of resistance of children with sickle-cell traits to malaria. Apparently, the trait "developed" as a healthy response to heavy malarial infestations. What happens when a sickle-cell population moves to a noninfectious area where the trait is no longer a necessary preventive health resource? The incidence of sickle-cell trait among North American blacks has now fallen far below the prevalence in prevailing parts of Africa. Public Health researchers are not at all surprised, then, to find that many of man's adaptive responses to disease are not permanent but situational and temporary.

Despite the present attempts to shake its ancestral heritage, there are still enough Asclepian genes in the public health phenotype to keep it specific-disease-oriented. If there were no diseases to prevent, it might be difficult to justify the need for clean air, unpolluted water, uncontaminated food, well-baby clinics, and primary care nurses. It is still man's discomfort and difficulties that keep public health schools and services financially and professionally healthy. It is like the cabin passenger who wrote in his diary a parody of Descartes: " 'I feel discomfort, therefore I am alive,' then sat pen in hand with no more to record" (Greene, 1961, p. 9).

Living is apparently getting riskier by the day. There are only a few gulps of air, water, and foods, only a few families, that can be given a clean bill of health. The various agencies and professions in public health complain, with overwhelming evidence to back them up, of a 168-hour week on present problems alone. Despite all this, public health needs to find ways of activating health promotion conceptually and operationally. Public health must enter the somewhat strange lands of behavioral and social sciences with more than a bar of soap or a stethoscope in hand. It must begin to invent and activate ways in which basic societal institutions can enhance and support growth encounters between living organisms and the environment.

POTENTIAL AREAS FOR PREVENTIVE PUBLIC HEALTH

There are two possibilities among many for such public health trials. One is the programs being developed around child and family development (The Child Development Act): Early Childhood Education, Head Start, Family Planning Programs, Family Support Programs; the other is the program sanctioned and mandated by federal legislation under the Social Security Act amendments (Title XIX) called EPSDT (Early Periodic Screening Diagnosis and Treatment) and other programs of early intervention.

Early Effective Screening and Interventions

Much preventive activity in public health has rallied around two basic concepts: the causes of psychopathology and the effectiveness of early intervention. Garmezy (1971) and Rolf and Harig (1974), for example, have documented the absence of scientific knowledge about the causes of psychopathology. Yet lack of knowledge alone does not seem to deter action; all kinds of halfway or inadequately documented therapies are visited upon the mentally ill—perhaps because the need is critical and the person is hurting. It is humane to try to help the ill despite our doubts about what we are doing. One cannot make such a case for primary prevention.

The mentally ill certainly have little need or concern for primary prevention for themselves; the mentally healthy already have it. In fact, as quite a few professional and volunteer workers in the mental health field point out, there is so much to do in our institutions and communities for people who are suffering that it may be wasteful to channel our limited resources and manpower in chasing butterflies down the yellow brick road.

Part of the problem of obtaining knowledge related to the prevention of psychopathology is our metaphysical rigidities. Having identified a host of behaviors as end games of maladaptive development, we then give them names as specific diseases—schizophrenia, manic-depressive psychosis, involutionary melancholia, and so on. I would like to re-emphasize, as others have before me, that the genetic and experiential factors which interplay to give individuals free and easy reality testing and good feelings on the one hand or poor, inadequate, or limited reality testing and bad feelings on the other, follow multidimensional pathways. One who is said to have "schizophrenia" is as loosely diagnosed as one who is found to have a temperature reading of 104.5. All persons with 104.5 temperatures are warm and ill; yet the pathways to this condition may vary from heat exhaustion, pneumonia, food poisoning, or bee stings to dehydration.

Some years ago we were able to investigate the immediate backgrounds and interpersonal histories of a group of young men all of whom were hospitalized at a veterans hospital with the clinical diagnosis schizophrenia (Bower et al., 1960). Under the guise of doing a vocational follow-up of high school graduates we obtained behavior ratings and personal histories of these patients and a randomly selected group of peers with whom the patient had attended high school. Most of the patients were shy and dreamy, peculiar, or unable to concentrate, but some had qualities of leadership in athletics or academics and appeared to be well integrated and moderately popular. This group of "reactive" schizophrenics when seen at the hospital wereas severely ill and disturbed as any of the "process" schizophrenics. Later, when we divided our 88 adolescents into 4 groups of 11 experimentals and 11 controls and gave their high school protocols to judges to rank from "least likely to be hospitalized as a schizophrenic" to "most likely," we obtained some interesting results: quite a few of the controls were judged as likely to be hospitalized as were our patients!

I am reluctant to bewail the fact that our lack of information pins anything on baselines, such as the schizophrenias. Confounding this further is the fact that there are schizophrenic-like persons complete with withdrawal, voices, and word salad who hold jobs, get along, and somehow prosper. I am also reminded of our ephemeral mathematics on incidence and prevalence of so-called hospitalized schizophrenics in the state hospitals of California. A personal letter from the director of the department of mental hygiene to a hospital superintendent asking questions about the rate of discharge of mental patients inevitably produced a higher rate of discharge. The number of hospitalized "schizophrenics" rested not on the nature of the illness but on the number of available families and homes in which the patients could be placed.

Schizophrenia is not a single disease but a concatenation of many factors. I agree with Garmezy (1971, p. 112) that we need to "turn away from a premature fixation on global theorizing about the etiology of schizophrenia and engage in the search for relevant behavioral parameters that can differentiate high risk maladaptive from high risk adaptive children."

The High Risk – Low Risk Parable

There is an old saying that if you want to reap the benefits of a medication or drug, take it when it is first marketed. Early intervention with high risk children has gone beyond the first blush of the goddess Panacea. Bronfenbrenner (1974) reviewed seven projects that he felt were significant and scientific and came to the conclusion that such programs work best when they are family-centered rather than child-centered, have continuity over time, and utilize primary agents of socialization (parents, siblings, peers, school personnel). Caldwell (1974) asked the same questions about early intervention with somewhat similar responses. For example, in commenting on the Westinghouse study often cited as showing that Head Start programs had no effect on children, she points out that in urban areas serving predominantly black families in the southeastern parts of the United States, summer-only programs in fact yielded little effect, but full-year programs—examined separately by geographic regions, urban-rural locations, and the racial composition of the children—produced significant differences in measures of cognitive growth. We cannot, she adds, promise the eradication of poverty, mental illness, and delinquency through early intervention programs; but there is promise and hope somewhere in its conceptual mists and political possibilities.

Institutional Effectiveness

Primary prevention is not primarily conceived as a special intervention program only for children in need. Cannot such ingredients be included within the normal life space of children and communities so that interventions are lasting, positive, and conceptually significant for all children?

The two preventive program possibilities which follow are based on an ecological epigenetic concept of human institutions that need some specification (see Bower, 1972).

Some years ago Abraham Kardiner proposed the phrase *key integrative systems* to describe those primary institutions that give pattern and meaning to the basic personality of the individual and to the society in which he lives. I have added *social* to the phrase to make it into an affectively laden acronym (KISS) and to re-focus the field of preventive action on four key arenas: (1) health services, especially to prospective mothers and young children; (2) families; (3) peer-play arrangements, both formal and informal; and (4) schools. Consider that each of these KISS arrangements is primarily and in most cases wholly man-made, that each is lashed to the other with strong ecological chains, and that the KISS quartet is mandated on children with almost no alternatives. After birth, the essential confinements of a child's living space are family, peer-play groups, school (including religious instruction), music lessons, and *Sesame Street*.

We are well aware that not all children thrive at all times within

KISS. Some require occasional social first aid, usually as a result of a health, family, peer, or school problem. When they do, they go to general hospitals, night hospitals, homes for children, special schools, social agencies, county jails, juvenile courts, behavior and learning disability clinics, and the like. As a general rule, these institutions can be described as AID (Ailing-In Difficulty) institutions for children who are unable to function adequately in the KISS arena. The interplay between the KISS and AID institutions depends to a great degree on the flexibilities and supports available in the KISS group. For example, in families where a mother of a young child becomes ill and the father needs to work, the child may need to be cared for outside the home if home care services are not available within the geographical and economic boundaries of the family. Before about 1950, families of trainable retarded children who reached school age had no choice but to place their children in private schools or institutions. This usually required that the children leave their homes and give up their prospective schools. With the advent of special programs within the school and community, these children were now able to live within the KISS life space. Thus, the need for AID institutions is a function of the range of services or degrees of freedom of the KISS institutions, as well as the children they serve.

KISS permits and in some cases encourages the greatest degree of personal freedom and functioning. Styles of living may range from the Amish to the Yippee, with more problems always present at the extremes. In any case, within this range there are choices and consequences. In AID institutions the choices are limited and life becomes more rigidly circumscribed by role and behavioral expectations. The major function of the AID institutions is to act as a temporary haven for dropouts from KISS and, where possible, to restore health, economic viability, and social and emotional competence, utilizing a variety of restorative, health, rehabilitative, and therapeutic interventions. However, it is often difficult to differentiate between the child for whom the temporary haven is indeed temporary and the child for whom the haven is only the first step toward more guarded and restricted fortresses. Such strongholds can be considered our ICE (Illness-Correctional Environments), represented by state and federal prisons, 24-hour training schools, mental hospitals, and the like.

Such ICE institutions as prisons and mental hospitals are supposedly correctional, rehabilitative, and/or therapeutic; practically, they can do little but serve as depositories for reinforcing human failure.

The Mediating Parent

There are probably at least a few thousand definitions of a healthy, child-enhancing family. Let me add one of my own. A family, or reasonable facsimile, exists to provide children with the best chance of experiencing a mediating adult. Such an adult is able to lower and connect affective bridges with children over which all kinds of important cognitive-affective traffic can pass. The earliest traffic helps the child begin to separate himself out of the environment; once the bridge is down, however, the rush hour is on. The child seeks, explores, touches, tastes, bites, smells, eats, listens, and grasps. The mediating person provides the conceptual glue by which the child joins these sensory data to affective-cognitive concepts. Thus, in the confusing kaleidoscope of objects, events, and feelings, the child is helped to see similarities in things that differ and differences in things that are alike.

The mediating function of the family has always been there, camouflaged by economic, protective, health, and consumer functions. As these functions disappeared or were displaced into other institutions, one tended to see the family as declining or dissolving. But as Ogburn (1953), Parsons and Bales (1955), Vincent (1967), and other sociologists have pointed out, the loss of functions may strengthen an institution by allowing it to concentrate more fully on its essential purpose. But to do so it may need a new constellation of supporting services.

If the family is not able to mediate "future" in a hopeful and enhancing way, where are the incentives for growth? Women no longer see the mother role as a full-time five-year stint, or at any rate they want alternatives to household chores without in any way reducing the importance of their job. I think families can be happier, freer, and more effective if we can help them exercise options by making quality child care, home care, and related services available as part of the KISS arrangements.

Play and Imagination

The mediating person in the family is followed by a succession of other mediating persons. These may be close relatives, nursery teachers, teachers, and other adults. But between the family and the school "there comes a pause in the day's occupations that is known as the children's hour." Unfortunately, this hour has been chopped down and eroded to a few minutes. I am referring to the informal and formal arrangements by which children get to play. Play begins in the family and moves into a peer social system, where it is formalized into more structured play, often called games. The basic goal of play is not therapy, ego rehearsal, or release of hostility, but having fun. The possibilities for such fun are predicated on learned mediated skills of inner safety and separation between the physical external world and the inner world of imagination. The child learns to step into and out of play at first somewhat sloppily but with increasing control and differentiation.

The differentiation between the "as if" quality of play and games and the real qualities of the external world circumscribed by time, space, and cosmic constrictions is crucial. Not all fun in life is in play. To be fun, play must be serious but not real. I do not choose to characterize life as a game; it has its realities, its lighter and darker moments, its boring and exciting interludes. When I play games I want the opportunity to enter and leave this domain of my own free will.

For children, the world that follows play will be geared mainly to the rational and the real. Unfortunately, play itself—embedded as it is in the Puritan tradition—is often but not always seen as an interlude of nothing between *Sesame Street* and dinner. True play has no purpose except play. Occasionally some of us dip down into this world with other goals: we want children to play language games to help develop language, math games for math competence, Monopoly for careers in real estate, sensory games to sensitize the senses, and bridge to help solidify the family.

Many community planners and political statesmen see space for play as a grudging compromise between houses, roads, and money. Our housing authorities, architects, landscape gardeners, park commissioners, playground developers, and toy manu-facturers see play as something children do when parents have not adequately planned their TV viewing time. Consequently it is not surprising that the children's hour is down to a few minutes.

The school stands last in the epigenetic line and is geared to serve children who have experienced the mediating person, have a wide variety of cognitive-affect skills and sets of symbols, have learned to enter their imagination and return, have learned to accept and modify rules (as in games), and can seek goals outside themselves. These are assumptions that even Professor Pangloss, in his best of all possible worlds, would find difficult to accept. Nevertheless, we act as if all children enter school through the same door with the same inner and outer push and preparation.

Education, to be significant, requires a sparking, an emotional charge between learner and idea. It is, as Freud describes, "an incitement to the conquest of the pleasure principle and to its replacement by the reality principle" (1911/1959, p. 19). But Freud goes on to say, "the substitution of the reality principle for the pleasure principle denotes no dethronement of the pleasure principle but only a safeguarding of it" (p. 18). The schools of today require a new working metaphor—an ego-integrative one, perhaps—which can begin to tie primary symbolic processes (emotion) into secondary symbolic processes (cognition) so that each has access to and can enhance the other. Let us teach and reward imagination and bisociative thinking along with math, science, and English. Cultivating imagination and the legitimacy of emotional thought does not imply a dethronement of cognitive processes but a safeguarding of them.

TITLE XIX: EARLY PERIODIC SCREENING DIAGNOSIS AND TREATMENT

Title XIX, the 1967 Amendments to the Social Security Act, placed into the Medicare-Medicaid program a requirement that the states take steps to screen, diagnose, and treat children with health and mental health difficulties early and effectively. The act makes such action mandatory on the states, with penalties for inaction. Some states, like California, have implemented the legislation by removing the Medicare-Medicaid restrictions, thus making such screening and early assistance available to all children.

What has happened in this program since 1967 would make a play by Samuel Beckett seem to be an action packed thriller. The process of early screening and assistance where needed for physical and dental health problems are clear enough. Mental health screening and help is another matter.

A major block to effective mental health screening is the persistence and tenacity of medical metaphors, which see screening as a series of graduated sieves through which pass smaller and smaller units—be they grains of sand or children. Emerging as an end product is someone more prone to disability, abnormality, or disease and in need of help to avert this outcome. Take into consideration that we have large populations of children who are in dire need of help without a single sieve to fall through, plus a host of cultural, economic, and developmental disparities among groups.

Suppose one were to reverse the screening metaphor and pay attention to the sieves rather than the stones that fall through them —that is, develop screening procedures that stimulate the positive passage of children through the four KISS institutions. Adopting this metaphor, however conjectural, produces the following effect: children are assessed not by professionals in offices but by persons involved in the institutions mentioned above. (Remember, this is screening, not diagnosis; mental health and/or development, not genetic or somatic disease.) We are looking at behavior related to functioning within specific institutional prescriptions and settings and at the same time institutional behaviors related to individuals. To run through this or that checklist of 75 specific items, which from "not at all" to "all the time" identify a list of horrors indicating that the child is or is not a risk or close to a diagnostic label, is an interesting exercise in futility. Such data collection wouldn't be half bad if what was generated could assist the key people in the institutional setting in which the data were collected to do something with them. But in most cases all that remains is to dispose via referral. This means that someone beyond key persons will be asked to apply his professional skills and negate or confirm the truth. The myth still exists that someone, somewhere, somehow, knows how to assess developmental behavior or mental health independently of the social and cultural context in which the child is attempting to function. This is in no way meant to disparage the training or competence of mental health professionals. They can and often do add significant increments of understanding and insight to what might be done to help the child and his family. After all this activity has cleared, however, we are left with prescriptions of varying degrees of do's and don'ts, some realistic and some idealistic, for persons in the key management roles of KISS institutions.

One way to look at data-gathering on behalf of children is to ask how one can find ways to modify the ongoing relationships in the KISS institutions that are attempting to serve the child and in which the child is striving to be competent. This means that in learning all there is to know about the child/institution relationship (and there may not be much), one finally comes to a corner which requires positive direction. Finding what is wrong does not automatically suggest how to make things better, unless one is willing to consider that not making things worse is improving them.

The notion dies hard that somehow it is economical and meaningful to put vast screening operations into high gear to find "cases" early. One of my close colleagues accompanied me on several site visits to budding screening programs many years ago. It seemed to me he was less than enthusiastic about such efforts. One day what was on his mind emerged. "Why in the hell do you propose all this activity on screening and early identification of emotionally disturbed children? We've got enough cases right now. We don't need these programs to find more for us!"

The "case" is still the goal of much of screening. The "finding" of cases earlier rather than later may be a neat trick but the rabbit is still in the hat. It isn't at all clear why one would want to screen for cases, delinquents, autistic children, or retarded children. Of what possible positive use is it to collect a gigantic array of data on, let us say, fourth-grade children for predicting adolescent delinquents? If, inherent in this kind of statistical crystal ball gazing, one or two solid and effective interventions could be made that related to the school's attempt to help the child learn (and ease his struggle to learn better tomorrow), a case could be made. But more often than not, it is not.

Enough of what is wrong with our screening metaphors. What are some better possibilities?

Going back to the KISS model, screening locations are best situated at points of transition between one institution and the next. Where they are best placed depends on what institutional resources can be mustered at the transition point. Three possibilities are a mother with a newborn baby, a child nursery school, or kindergarten. I like the kindergarten or first grade junction because parents are nervously anxious to assist in any endeavor to get their children off to a good start on a journey of no less than ten years and often twenty or more. Moreover, it is a natural, positively perceived rendezvous for the two major administrators of children's growth: teachers and parents.

A number of years ago a few graduate students in school psychology, a district psychologist, a speech therapist, and a school principal invited all the families whose children were about to enter kindergarten to participate in a two-week preschool experience. This was planned and communicated early enough so that almost all such families participated. The children were enrolled in a three-hour play program in which they were observed and occasionally videotaped. All parents were seen twice for about an hour and a half each time. The first session focused on two questions: "What are your expectations and wishes for your children that the school can build on?" and "What can you tell us about your child which would be helpful in his/her education?" Also at that time, we discussed our purpose in observing their child and sharing our data with them at the end of the two weeks. We sought positive linkages to healthy and creative development in four areas: (a) relationship to adults, (b) ability to communicate in speech, (c) ability to use body, muscles, and self, and (d) ability to play, take turns, express and control impulses, and have fun. All of these functions were assessed by the staff in their interaction with the children on scales which ranged from "ragged" to "ratty." We did, however, as a staff, gather and share a lot of data about children. One or two were obviously in need of professional help. This came as no surprise to the parents. Even as we discussed the utilization of other resources, we planned for their effective entrance into kindergarten. At this point, teachers who were returning for the fall term were brought into the discussions. Parents, staff, and teachers were present and developed an operational set of joint expectations and proposals. Some parents returned for two sessions in the final week after having a chance to digest the first session.

Any teacher, parent, principal, or school psychologist can fill in the blanks in this brief description of what I would describe as effective Early Periodic Screening (omitting the Diagnosis and Treatment) program. Note that our goal in the two-week preschool experience was not to screen mental health problems, developmental laggards, or predelinquents, but to find positive linkages in child and parent on which to build school success. There is nothing new or earth-shaking in this. It can be done and has been done: see, for example, Newton and Brown's (1967) description of a more extensive and better researched program in Sumter, South Carolina.

Possibly one productive action for Hygeia's sake would entail reconceptualizing the balance and interaction of the KISS institutions. For example, suppose we locked up the health, family, play, and cognitive functions into one care unit called a Growth Center. Instead of a child being mandated to school at age four or five, he would be relegated to school when it appeared he had undergone the experiences and taken on the functions necessary to deal with group activity and curriculum as prescribed by the school. In such a Growth Center would be a core group of health professionals, parents, or parent surrogates who could be identified and used by children as mediators and sufficient play space and opportunities for all levels of development. A child could move through aggressively and regressively as he chose, experience as he wished, but would be guided by a plan which helped develop the more integrative and maturing aspects of personality. Early cognitive learning would be available, much as it would be in a good kindergarten or early grade school, but in suitable doses and exposures. All children could be served in the Growth Center until age nine or ten, or could be dispatched to a more formal school when deemed to have a 51 percent chance of success.

Some of the children in the Growth Center might require special assistance in the form of various therapies, special programs (as for the deaf, blind, retarded, and so on), or family support. Such resources would all be coordinated and administered through professional staff in accordance with the needs of the child and his family. Moreover, the relationship between Center staff and parents would remain stable as the child moved out to include teacher and other school personnel. With such a KISS agency, children would require screening only for planning and programming services. No child would be excluded or screened out. All actions and most programming would be variations of services already provided within the Growth Center by Center staff or allied community resources.

Such a growth center is neither expensive, revolutionary, nor unrealistic. The professionals to do this job are mostly in place. Yet it would take years and a few of Zeus's mighty thunderbolts to move professionals onto a team to begin this task.

We have no choice. The economic, social, and human toll of inadequate and unhealthy children is rapidly reaching flood stage. Such floods cannot be quelled by mighty dams located at the mouths of rivers. "A little fire is quickly trodden out; which, being suffered, rivers cannot quench" (*Henry VI, Part III*).

REFERENCES

Bower, E., Shellhamer, T. A., and Daily, J. M. School characteristics of male adolescents who later became schizophrenic. *American Journal of Orthopsychiatry*, 1960, *30*, 712–729.

Bower, E. M. K.I.S.S. and kids: A mandate for prevention. *American Journal of Orthopsychiatry*, 1972, *42*, 556–565.

Bronfenbrenner, N. Is early intervention effective? *Day Care and Early Education*, November 1974, pp. 15–19.

Caldwell, B. A decade of early intervention programs: What have we learned? *American Journal of Orthopsychiatry*, 1974, *44*, 491–496.

Caton, R. *The temples and rituals of Asklepios*. Liverpool: University Press, 1900.

Dubos, R. *Mirage of health*. New York: Harper and Row, 1959.

Edelstein, E. J., and Edelstein, L. *Asclepius, a collection and interpretation of the testimonies* (2 vols.). Baltimore: Johns Hopkins, 1945.

Freud, S. Formulations regarding the two principles in mental functioning. In *Sigmund Freud: Collected papers* (J. Riviere, trans.), Vol. 4. New York: Basic Books, 1959. (Originally published, 1911)

Garmezy, N. Vulnerability research and the issue of primary prevention. *American Journal of Orthopsychiatry*, 1971, *41*, 101–116.

Greene, G. *A burnt-out case*. New York: Viking, 1961.

Kerenyi, K. *Asklepios—archetypal image of the physician's existence*. (R. Manheim, trans.). New York: Pantheon, 1959.

Lévi-Strauss, C. *The savage mind*. Chicago: University of Chicago Press, 1966.

Newton, M. R., and Brown, R. D. A preventive approach to developmental problems in school children. In E. Bower and W. Hollister (Eds.), *Behavioral science frontiers in education*. New York: Wiley, 1967.

Ogburn, W. The changing functions of the family. In R. Winch and R. McGinnis (Eds.), *Marriage and the family*. New York: Holt, 1953.

Parsons, T., and Bales, R. *Family socialization and interaction process*. New York: Free Press, 1955.

Rolf, J., and Harig, P. Etiological research in schizophrenia and the rationale for primary prevention. *American Journal of Orthopsychiatry*, 1974, *44*, 538–553.

Vincent, C. Mental health and the family. *Journal of Marriage and the Family*, 1967, *29*, 18–39.

4

Concepts of Humanity
in Primary Prevention

ARNOLD J. SAMEROFF

The concept of primary prevention of mental disorder seems clear enough in its meaning and is certainly clear enough in its humanitarian concern for the welfare of society. It is possible, however, that certain common interpretations of the notion of primary prevention may actually interfere with its goal.

In a recent conversation with a friend who was in psychotherapy, I asked how he was doing. He replied that he didn't think much of his therapist, who seemed to spend valuable therapy time raising questions about such simple issues as why the patient was late for every session; he thought the therapist should be spending his time discussing the specific problems that had brought the patient into therapy. Listening to my friend's report, any of us would have used our psychodynamic sophistication to make the appropriate interpretations—that the patient was unwilling to deal with his own relation to his therapist and instead focused on what he felt to be the more pressing issues in his life. Shortly thereafter he terminated therapy as a luxury he could not afford.

Concerning the problems we are facing here of preventing mental illness, similar problems arise. In the same way that the individual in psychotherapy must step back to place his immediate concerns into the context of his more general mode of interpersonal existence, we must step back to put our concerns with human suffering into the more general frame of our own social existence.

A discussion is needed to accomplish this goal, based not on academic philosophy, which may have divorced itself from its origins in the real world, but a philosophy that arises from our own attempts to place ourselves and the individuals with whom we are concerned into a common context. For this purpose, I will focus on one central issue in the following discussion. The question is, "What does it mean to be a person?" I will show that how this question is answered determines our views not only of mental illness and therapy but also of ourselves and the world. I will contrast two different answers to the question and show how they lead us to two different views of what we will see and what we do. One answer is that a person is a "thing." The second answer is that a person is a "human being." One would think that the answer is self-evident, since none of us would admit or support the idea that people are merely things. Yet it is surprising that those who would reject the view of people as things when it is clearly labeled accept many concepts not so clearly labeled which tend to place people in "thing" categories. The two concepts of thingness which I will explore in the following presentation are (1) that if a thing does not work right, it is wrong, and (2) that things do not change.

Let us begin by considering where psychopathology is thought to come from. There are a number of ways in which we can understand how people turn out the way they do. The simplest way of understanding disorder is to say that people were born that way or that some significant trauma occurred early in their lives which so altered them that in effect they were born that way. Some genetic theories of intelligence or schizophrenia are of this variety: blacks are not as smart as whites because they were born with a genetically limited capacity to do abstract thinking; people become schizophrenics because they were born with a genetically limited capacity to deal with stress. Another area, which has generated less controversy but probably could use some, is the role of pregnancy and delivery complications in producing behavioral disturbances, including hyperactivity and mental retardation. A review of some of these studies will give us a clearer perspective on the sources of pathology.

CONTINUUM OF REPRODUCTIVE CASUALTY

It has been estimated by Babson and Benson (1971) that 300,000 children are born each year who will have learning disorders ranging from mild to severe retardation. This large number of general learning disorders is of great concern to clinicians. In most cases, either a lack of a clear genetic basis or signs of clear anatomical damage in these children has been puzzling to investigators who believe in the traditional *medical model.* From this point of view, if a disorder exists, there should be some clear factor in the patient's history, preferably biological, which led to this disorder. If such a factor could not be found, it was presumed that the diagnostic techniques were not yet sufficiently sophisticated to detect it. Such reasoning led Gesell and Amatruda (1941) to propose the concept of minimal cerebral injury as the perinatal cause of the learning disorder effect. The reason for not being able to show the existence of such injury is that by definition it is minimal, that is, undetectable. Pasamanick and Knobloch (1961) expanded the range of deviant developmental outcomes thought to result from minor central nervous system dysfunctions caused by damage to the fetus or newborn child. Their results led them to propose a *continuum of reproductive casualty.* The term *casualty* referred to a range of minor motor, perceptual, intellectual, learning, and behavioral disabilities found in children. In a review of their own studies, Pasamanick and Knoblock (1966) reported that five additional disorders were significantly associated with greater numbers of complications of pregnancy and prematurity: cerebral palsy, epilepsy, mental deficiency, behavioral disorders, and reading disabilities. In the comparisons between a group of children with these disorders and a control group, those having the most serious condition—cerebral palsy—were more sharply differentiated from control groups in the number of obstetrical complications than were those with the milder disorders, for example reading disabilities.

Such retrospective studies have implicated at least three factors in early development as related to later disorder: anoxia, prematurity, and delivery complications. The major question is, How can these pregnancy variables play a role in producing later abnormalities? The most obvious—the biological possibility—was some damage to the brain. The most obvious brain damage was oxygen deprivation, in the form of either anoxia or asphyxia. As early as 1861, Little proposed that asphyxia was a cause of brain damage in the child. It seemed reasonable to assume that a generalized deficit in brain functioning could be related to cerebral oxygen deprivation early in development. This view was reinforced when it was shown in studies of animals that oxygen deprivation led to learning deficits and brain damage (Windle, 1944). Human research on asphyxia was stimulated by a report by Schreiber (1939) that 70 percent of a group of mental retardates had histories of anoxia at birth.

Most of these earlier studies used retrospective approaches to study the problem. In a typical retrospective study, people are identified who already have the disorder and then the investigator looks back into their early history to find some etiological cause. Retrospective approaches, however, entail serious problems in subject selection, since only those subjects who have the later disorder are ever studied. By contrast, prospective research permits the selection of subjects with early characteristics thought to be implicated in the etiology of the later disorder. If indeed asphyxia led to brain damage and mental retardation, then it should seem obvious that if a group of subjects who had asphyxia at birth were followed up, a significantly greater amount of retardation would be found in this group as compared with a control group of infants who did not suffer from the anoxic experience at birth.

In one of the better of these studies, Graham and her associates (Graham, Pennoyer, Caldwell, Greenman, and Hartman, 1957) tried to overcome the inadequacies of most previous studies resulting from either poor measures of anoxia at birth or poor measures of intelligence at the follow-ups. They argued that if a large variety of measures, including neurological, personality adjustment, and perceptual-motor tasks, were utilized, the significant differences between the affected and control groups should be revealed. In many prior studies, control groups had not been adequately matched and the criteria of anoxia had not been carefully defined. These investigators proposed a longitudinal study beginning at birth with multiple assessments of anoxia and its effects on newborn behavior, followed by assessments during later years.

Several hundred infants in St. Louis were seen in the newborn period (Graham, Matarazzo, and Caldwell, 1956) and followed up at three years (Graham, Ernhart, Thurston, and Craft, 1962) and again at seven years (Corah, Anthony, Painter, Stern, and Thurston, 1965). As expected, when examined during the first days of life, anoxic infants were found to be impaired on a series of five measures: maturation level, visual responsiveness, irritability, muscle tension, and pain threshold (Graham et al., 1957). When the performance on these measures was compared with a prognostic score based on the degree of anoxia experienced by the children, those infants with the poorest prognostic scores performed most poorly on the newborn assessments.

The same infants were seen again at three years of age and tested with a battery of cognitive, perceptual-motor, personality, and neurologic tests (Graham et al., 1962). The group of anoxic infants scored lower than controls on all tests of cognitive function, had more positive neurological findings, and showed some personality differences. There were, however, no differences on tests of perceptual-motor functioning. At seven years of age, the children were again tested (Corah et al., 1965). Significant I.Q. differences had disappeared between the anoxic group and the control population; and of the 21 cognitive and perceptual measures, only vocabulary and one perceptual task appeared still deficient. Corah et al. concluded that anoxics showed minimal impairment of functioning at seven years and that efforts to predict current functioning on the basis of the severity of anoxia were highly unreliable.

Other studies have found similar developmental patterns among anoxics. In terms of personality differences there was little evidence in the three-year follow-up that any personality constellation could be related to brain injury. By the seven-year follow-up, Corah et al. (1965) found no data to support the existence of a hyperkinetic personality syndrome in their anoxic group, although they did find some impairments in social competence. The anoxic subgroup with the better newborn prognostic scores were rated as more impulsive and distractable than the controls but, paradoxically, the subgroup having the poorer prognosis was found to be significantly less distractable than were the normal controls.

I have given the details of only one study here, yet there have been many which show essentially the same findings. Gottfried (1973) in a review of 20 studies of the longitudinal effects of anoxia came to similar conclusions, among which were (1) that the intellectual consequences of perinatal anoxia are more prevalent in infants and preschoolers than in older children and adolescents; (2) that anoxic subjects as a group are not mentally retarded; and (3) that whether anoxic subjects are deficient in specific intellectual abilities is not known as yet. Sameroff and Chandler (1975), in a more extensive review of the effects not only of anoxia but also of prematurity and a variety of other perinatal complications, were even more dubious about the developmental effects of anoxia.

How is one to explain the later disappearance of the effects of a severe trauma to the early physiological functioning of the brain? Moreover, how is one to explain the retrospective data which tended to show that children with a variety of deficits did have more perinatal complications in their histories than children who did not suffer from these disorders? A major clue to the answers can be found in another study of perinatal complications. Werner, Bierman, and French (1971) reported on the development of all 670 children born on the island of Kauai in the Hawaiian Islands in the year 1955. The multiracial nature of Hawaii and the total sampling of social class involved in the Kauai sample permitted the investigators to provide ample controls for both racial and social-class variables. During the newborn period each infant was scored on a four-point scale for severity of perinatal complications. At twenty months and again at ten years of age, these scores were related to assessments of physical health, psychological status, and such environmental variables as socioeconomic status, family stability, and the mother's education.

As in the St. Louis study, at twenty months of age infants who had suffered severe perinatal stress were found to have lower scores on the Kauai investigators' assessments. In addition, however, a clear interaction was found between the impairing effect of perinatal complications and environmental variables, especially socioeconomic status. For infants living in a high socioeconomic environment with a stable family structure or with a mother who was well educated, the I.Q. differences between children with and without complication scores was only five to seven points. For infants living in a low socioeconomic environment, with low family stability or with a mother of poor educational background, the difference in mean I.Q.'s between infants with and without perinatal complications ranged from nineteen to thirty-seven points. The results of the Kauai study seem to indicate that perinatal complications taken alone do not appear to be consistently related to later physical and psychological development; only when combined with and supported by persistently poor environmental circumstances do such infants show later deficiencies.

The infants of the Kauai sample were again examined when

they reached ten years of age (Werner, Honzik, and Smith, 1968). There was no correlation between the perinatal stress score and the measures at ten years. Some correlation was found, however, between the twenty-month and ten-year data, especially when socioeconomic status and parents' educational level were taken into consideration. The stability of intellectual functioning was much higher for those children who had I.Q.'s below 80 at the ten-year testing period. All of these children had twenty-month scores of 100 or less, with almost half below 80, and the majority had parents with little education and low socioeconomic status. The Kauai study seems to suggest that risk factors operative during the perinatal period disappear during childhood as more potent familial and social factors exert their influence. Werner and her associates (Werner et al., 1971) extrapolated their findings to predict that of 1,000 live births in Kauai, by age ten only 660 would be functioning adequately without a recognized physical, intellectual, or behavioral problem in school. Of the 34 percent of children who had problems at the age of ten, only a minor proportion could be attributed to the effects of serious perinatal stress. The authors concluded that "ten times more children had problems related to the effects of poor early environment than to the effects of perinatal stress."

How are we to understand a situation where perinatal complications influence later development only in children raised in poor environmental conditions? Even the retrospective data of Pasamanick, Knobloch, and Lilienfeld (1956) found that the proportion of infants having some complication increased from 5 percent in the white upper social class stratum, to 15 percent in the lowest white socioeconomic group, to 51 percent among all nonwhites. These data imply that the biological outcomes of pregnancy are worse for those in poorer environments. They are clearly not the result of the delivery complications themselves, since children with identical complications raised in good environmental situations show no consequences of such problems. Also, the environmental situation is clearly not responsible, since the children without complications raised in the poor environments did not show the same deviant outcomes evidenced by their affected neighbors.

Sameroff and Chandler (1975) proposed a *transactional model of development* to describe the dynamic process by which children with poor constitutions, such as those having delivery complications, enter into an interaction with their environment which leads ultimately to developmental abnormalities.

TRANSACTIONAL MODEL

The distinctive feature which differentiates the transactional model from the medical model described earlier is that the role the child can play in modifying its environment is recognized. The common-sense understanding of how children are raised is that society takes them in hand through the agency of their parents or the school system and shapes them to fit current norms. Many recent studies have demonstrated, however, that in the process of trying to shape the children, the caretakers are shaped themselves. The specific characteristics of the individual child transact with the caretaker's mode of functioning to produce an individualized, ongoing miniature social system.

A clear example of this situation is found in the work of Thomas, Chess, and Birch (1968) in their New York longitudinal study. These investigators were able to classify infants into two major categories of temperament, the difficult child and the easy child. The easy child slept and fed regularly, was able to approach and adapt to new situations, had a high threshold to stimulation, and expressed positive mood for the most part. The difficult child was characterized by low threshold to stimulation, high intensity responses of negative mood, irregularity of sleeping and eating, and withdrawal and poor adaptiveness to new situations. The mothers in the New York study were all white, educated, and middle class, with normal child rearing attitudes. When confronted with a difficult infant, however, their behavior toward the child was negatively influenced. Most of them became either anxious over their ability to control the child's crying and irregularity or hostile through frustration. The difficult child had converted a formerly normal mother into an abnormal one. The outcome of this disturbed relationship was that nearly three times as many of the infants identified as difficult required professional help during childhood as compared to nondifficult infants in the New York study.

Of great importance for the conclusions we will come to later were the difficult infants who did not have developmental problems. The later normalcy of these difficult infants appeared to result from their parents' ability to make allowances for their temperaments: rather than becoming anxious or hostile, they regarded the infants' colicky behavior as part of a passing stage that the child would grow out of. Thus, the fate of the difficult infants appeared to depend on the context in which their behavior was understood by their parents.

Sameroff and Chandler (1975) were also able to use the transactional model to interpret the mechanisms behind child abuse. A great deal of research has been devoted to identifying retrospectively the characteristics of parents who abuse their children. Other parents with very similar characteristics do not abuse their children, nor do the abusive parents mistreat all their children. It appears that certain children are selected for battering, or rather that certain children tend to elicit abusive behavior from their parents. Klein and Stern (1971) studied a population of abused children and found that most of them either had been born prematurely or had significant medical illnesses during infancy which may have served to deplete their parents' positive emotional resources. The fact that abusive parents are less intelligent, more aggressive, impulsive, immature, self-centered, tense, and self-critical than nonabusive parents (Spinetta and Rigler, 1972) nevertheless does not ensure that they will abuse their children. It appears that only when this kind of parent transacts with a child who is seen as making greater than ordinary caretaking demands that the parent becomes abusive. The child with the appropriate characteristics is necessary to complete the system.

What I have tried to demonstrate in the two examples above is that knowing the characteristics of either the parent alone or the child alone does not permit us to make reliable predictions of developmental outcome. In the New York longitudinal study, parents with normal attitudes were led to behave nonadaptively when confronted with a difficult child. In the case of child abuse, parents identified as batterers were able to respond normally to children who made minimal caretaking demands. We are beginning to see the germ of an answer to our question, Why is it that some children with delivery complications show no later effects while others show strong signs of retardation?

ROCHESTER LONGITUDINAL STUDY

At the University of Rochester, Melvin Zax and I (Sameroff and Zax, 1973a, 1973b) have been engaged in a longitudinal study of the offspring of women with a variety of psychiatric disorders. We wanted, first, to determine if the psychiatric status of the mother had any effect on the constitutional characteristics of the offspring and, second, to identify characteristics of these offspring which would be predictive of later emotional disorders in the children. The women in the study were seen at a psychiatric interview followed by a psychometric testing during their pregnancy. After delivery, the newborn infants were examined in the newborn nursery with a variety of neurological, psychophysiological, and behavioral tests. At four and twelve months of age observers went into the homes of the infants and, using a time sampling technique, recorded the mother-infant interactions for periods of from four to six hours. At four, twelve, and thirty months of age the infants were brought into our laboratory and tested with the Bayley Developmental Scales as well as a number of other psychometric procedures. Of the 300 children in the study, about 100 have passed through the thirty-month assessment. The observations to date will serve as a concrete example of how the transactional model relates to the development of the child.

The temperamental characteristics of the child are the most important variables to emerge. When the infants were four months old their mothers filled out questionnaires (Carey, 1970), which have been used to identify the variables that Thomas and his associates used in their longitudinal study of the effects of infant temperament. The children were scored on the basis of how closely they approximated the difficult child. We then attempted to discover the antecedents in either the infant or the mother of the difficult temperament. Our first effort was to discover if the psychiatric characteristics of the mother played a role. Four groups of women having diagnoses of either schizophrenia, neurotic depression, personality disorder, or no disorder were matched for age, race, socioeconomic status, and marital status. The temperament scores for these women were compared, and no significant differences were found in the temperaments of their infants. To sharpen the psychiatric distinction, only the schizophrenic women were compared with the normal controls, and again no differences were found. It was apparent from these data that psychiatric diagnosis was not a primary determinant of infant temperament.

In an earlier study of perinatal complications, Melvin Zax and I (Sameroff and Zax, 1973a) had compared the same groups of women to determine if there were any differences in birth or delivery complications. As with our temperament data, no differences were found; the study did, however, reveal differences when the women were divided on the basis of severity of mental illness rather than specific diagnosis. A high-pathology group of women who had had many hospitalizations and psychiatric contacts were compared with a group having few psychiatric contacts and no hospitalizations, and the more chronically ill group showed a greater number of pregnancy and delivery complications.

This same breakdown was then applied to the temperament data. The scores of the offspring of a high-pathology group consisting of neurotic depressives and schizophrenics were compared with the scores of a low-pathology group of women having situational and personality disorders and with a control group of normal mothers. Significant differences were found between the groups. Severity of mental illness appeared to be a contributor to difficult temperament in the infants; but the major differences were between the normal controls and the two psychiatric groups, not between the two pathology groups. Psychiatric diagnosis appeared to be a weaker differentiator than we had suspected. Fortunately, data on other variables were available that could be related to the level of difficult temperament of the child. Anxiety and maternal attitude, as revealed in our questionnaires, along with the demographic variables of race and social class, were found to correlate reliably with the temperament of the child. In order to differentiate which of these factors was making the largest contribution to the child's temperament, multiple regression analyses were performed. The results showed that the mother's anxiety score measured before the child's birth had the greatest influence on his temperament at four months of age, with social class and race close behind. The analysis implicated a fourth factor: the more children a woman had had, previously, the more her current child tended to have a difficult temperament. When examined alone, each of these factors—high anxiety, black race,

low social class, and high number of children—correlated positively with difficult temperament at four months of age. What is
of sociological interest is that while these characteristics taken
separately all contribute to producing difficult temperaments
during infancy and thereby increasing developmental risk, they
are usually found in combinations—low socioeconomic status,
poor education, many children, and black race—which may be
regarded as producing extreme risk.

Let us now examine some of the consequences of difficult
temperament. At four, twelve, and thirty months of age the
children in the study were tested with the Bayley Developmental
Scale, and the results were intercorrelated with the temperament
scores. An interesting pattern appeared. The correlation between
the scores on the Bayley at four months and thirty months was
.18, typical of the low correlations found between these age
periods in other studies (Lewis and McGurk, 1972); but comparison
of the four-month difficult temperament scores with the thirty-
month Bayley scores revealed a highly significant negative correlation of .49. Our other thirty-month psychometric assessments
—the Peabody and Binet Vocabulary Tests—also showed strong
negative correlation with the four-month difficult temperament
assessment.

Again we performed a multiple regression analysis to determine
what were the most significant contributors to the thirty-month
Bayley scores. Socioeconomic status and race still were very high
on the list. But the mother's prenatal anxiety score, which had
contributed so much to the child's difficult temperament at four
months, made no significant contribution to the thirty-month
developmental score; instead, it was replaced by the difficult
temperament itself. What we can conclude from these results is
that if one wants to predict an infant's I.Q. score at thirty months
of age from his behavior at four months, a much more reliable
prediction can be made from a report of the child's temperament
than from his actual functioning.

What sense can we make out of this relation between difficult
temperament at four months and poorer performance on I.Q.
tests at thirty months? Is temperament a precursor of intelligence?
Is it a more reliable precursor than the child's own intellectual
capacities, or whatever it is we are measuring at four months? A
more rational explanation can be made using the transactional

model. The child's temperament at four months influences how the mother is going to treat him in the future. The mother of a child with a difficult temperament withdraws from that child and as a consequence does not provide the stimulation and caretaking that would lead the child to perform competently at thirty months. Is there any evidence to support such speculation? In our longitudinal study at both four and twelve months of age, intensive home observations were made of the mother-infant interactions. There were many behaviors at the twelve-month home observation which were related to the child's performance on the Bayley scales at thirty months. Mothers who stayed close to their infants and spent a great deal of time looking at them and socializing and playing with them at twelve months tended to have children who scored higher on the Bayley scales at thirty months of age. There were also significant correlations between the child's temperament at four months and the mother's behavior at twelve months: mothers of children with difficult temperaments tended to stay away from them more, to look at them less, to socialize and play with them less.

Although the ultimate analysis of the data will provide a much richer and more complex picture of the transactions that occur between infant and mother which produce developmental outcomes, these preliminary data demonstrate the efficacy of the model and appear to confirm the hypothesis that difficult temperament in an infant elicits negative behavior in the mother which, in turn, reinforces the temperament and is related to poorer scores at the child's thirty-month assessment.

PARENTS' UNDERSTANDING OF THE CHILD

Our longitudinal data appear to have identified chains of mother and infant behaviors that produce the diversity found in the competence of growing children. A major factor in this diversity has been the variety of ways in which parents react to their children. Can we find some shortcut to identifying the more negative of these interactive claims early in development? Can we identify the behavior of more maladaptive parents and act to ameliorate it? Surely an assessment of parents' attitudes and personalities should be of some value. But the vast research literature on efforts to relate parents' child-rearing attitudes to the behavior of their children has come up with surprisingly few answers (Becker and Krug, 1965). Why do the children of parents with very different attitudes turn out the same, while children of parents with the same attitudes turn out very different? Predicting outcome from child-rearing attitudes of parents without knowing the characteristics of the child to be reared appears futile. Extremes in rearing practices would seem to be detrimental to any child, yet reports have appeared of cultures with normal adolescents who spent the first two years of their lives in dark cupboards (Kagan and Klein, 1973).

The typical child-rearing-attitude questions used have focused on specific caretaking practices: "Should children be taught about sex?" "Is early toilet training beneficial?" and the like. A different approach (Sameroff, 1975a, 1975b) focuses less on the specific practices of parents and more on their general understanding of the process of child development. Research on the cognitive development of the child has shown that the infant must go through a number of stages before achieving the logical thought processes that characterize adulthood (Piaget, 1960). Similarly, the mother must recapitulate many of these stages in her relationship to the child, and mothers whose understanding of the child is restricted to more primitive levels may have great difficulty in dealing with what they consider to be deviant children.

For this analysis I have utilized Piaget's stages of development as a framework for the description of the cognitive levels. These stages represent the best current description of how one goes from the immediacy of perceptual experience to successively removed levels at which abstractions are made from our here-and-now experiences while at the same time placing these experiences in a larger and larger context.

For present purposes I will describe only two of these levels. At the lower, which might be called the *labeling* level, parents are able to see their children and themselves as independent actors; the children's actions and characteristics are viewed as manifestations of their intrinsic nature. A consequence of this objectification of the child is that he can be labeled. A mother who has had a successful experience with her child assigns positive labels—for example, the good child, the pretty child, or the bright child. Once labels are assigned, they are thought to belong to the child. Just as the two-to-five-year-old labeling child thinks that the label *cup* is as much a part of the object as its color or shape, so the labeling mother considers the label *good child* as much a part of the child as his blue eyes or brown hair. This device can be very adaptive, for when the good child occasionally acts bad—crying too much, breaking a few dishes, throwing a tantrum—the mother will still think of him as the good child; it can also be very maladaptive, as when the mother, because of early negative experiences with the child, labels him as the difficult child, the bad child, or the ugly child. Even though the infant may outgrow the behavior that caused him to be labeled as difficult, the perceptions and reactions of the labeling parent may continue to be dominated by the original label.

At advanced levels of understanding the child, parents are able to view their children as existing independently of the labels they give them by relating the behavior of the child to his age. Infants cry, toddlers are hyperactive, adolescents brood. The positive achievement at this higher level is that the parent sees the infant's behavior as age-specific and recognizes that he will probably behave quite differently at later ages. This parent is able to use a much broader context for evaluating the child (beauty can compensate for lack of brains, and vice versa). No single label can typify the entire range of the child's behavior. Additional context is provided when the parent can place his own child and his own child's caretaking situation into a hypothetical context relating all kinds of children to all kinds of caretaking situations, so that the specific situation of his or her own child is only one of a multitude of possibilities. The parent is able to see the child's behavior as stemming from his individual experience with his specific environment; if that experience had been different, the child's characteristics would be different. Deviancies in the child can be perceived as being deviancies in the relationship of a particular child to a particular environment, rather than as concrete expressions of the intrinsic nature of the child. Moreover, remediation can now be proposed through an alteration in the current experience of the child through environmental changes.

One might ask, What are the influences that determine this level of understanding which parents might have toward their children? One of the most obvious answers would be the educational level of the parents. One would suppose that the more education an individual has, the greater would be his capacity to place his child and himself into broader context. Anthony Costello and I have recently attempted to test this hypothesis using a questionnaire designed to assess an individual's level of developmental understanding. We administered the questionnaire to a group of 50 mothers with a high-school education and a second group of about 50 professionals with advanced eduction—psychiatrists, psychologists, and social workers. The results completely contradicted our hypothesis: the professional group was significantly lower in their developmental understanding than the group of mothers. For example, while none of the nonprofessional women agreed with the statement "Premature babies will have a lot of problems later on," 24 percent of the professionals did. On the face of it one can understand this result, since many studies support the statement; a more complete reading of the literature, however, would show that deficits of premature babies are related to poor social environments or other physical disorders and not to the prematurity alone (Sameroff and Chandler, 1975). Such reading would lead one to agree strongly with the item "With good care premature babies turn out the same as babies born on time." These issues have been dealt with quite extensively in the work of Marshall Klaus (reported elsewhere in this volume). Here we have a good example of a little knowledge being a dangerous thing, since the professionals—who did more poorly on these items—are the ones who advise the nonprofessionals with the better attitudes.

Another hypothesis we tested was that the more experience one had with child rearing, the higher would be one's level of understanding development. We compared the questionnaire results from a group of women having only one child with those of a group of women having more than one child. Surprisingly, the second hypothesis was also contradicted: women with more children, instead of scoring at a higher level than women with only one child, scored lower. The multiparous women had a significantly more nativistic orientation than the primiparous women. Clearly more research is necessary to explicate these complex findings fully, but in the meantime I suggest a possible explanation. Women appear to approach a single child primarily with the environmentalist attitudes they learned in school. Our society generally believes that we can influence the development of our children. Once a woman has had more than one child, this simplistic view is contradicted by the different experiences she has with each child. As with the professionals, the little knowledge the mother gains from having a second child seems to regress her rather than advance her. She moves from an environmentalist position of seeing herself as omnipotent in influencing the child's development to a nativistic position where she sees herself as far less effective in the face of the constitutional givens with which she is confronted. Both groups, the professionals and the multiparous women, require a still more advanced level which can integrate both environmental and constitutional elements. The mother must come to see that if she can adapt her behavior (the environmental side) to the individuality of each of her children (the constitutional side), each child can reach a positive outcome. Such an advanced level of understanding is expressed in the transactional model discussed earlier, in which developmental outcomes are seen as the mutual effects between parent and child as they change each other by virtue of their continuing experience together.

CONTINUUM OF CARETAKING CASUALTY

The continuum of reproductive casualty, which was earlier thought to explain significant aspects of later developmental deviancy, has been shown to be an empty concept unless related to the subsequent caretaking environment in which the child is raised. Sameroff and Chandler (1975) have proposed that a new concept, which they have labeled the *continuum of caretaking casualty*, is necessary to appreciate fully the developmental implications of perinatal complications. The continuum of caretaking casualty refers to a range of environments into which infants are introduced. At one end of the continuum, the environment is so adaptive to the needs of the child that even the most distressed infant can achieve an adequate developmental outcome, while at the other extreme the environment is so disordered through emotional, financial, and social distress that even the best of infants can come to a bad end. The mother who can appreciate her child's development at a high level of sophistication is better equipped to make qualitative changes in her treatment of the child as the child's activities and requirements change with age. The mother who is restricted to more primitive levels of viewing her offspring enmeshes the child at later stages in obsolete social and affective relationships formed during infancy.

The picture becomes more complex when one considers the source of such constitutional factors as "difficult" or "colicky" or even the delivery complications themselves. The view espoused by Thomas, Chess, and Birch (1968) is that infants with a random assortment of temperaments were born into environments with a random assortment of adaptive capacities. Actually, however, a number of researchers have noted that women with emotional problems tended to have not only more reproductive complications (MacDonald, 1968; Ferreira, 1969) but also more difficult infants (Carey, 1968; Sameroff, 1974). Thus, it would appear that the same mothers who, through their emotional difficulties, tend to have the most trouble adapting to infants with caretaking problems are those most likely to produce infants with caretaking problems.

One of the major stumbling blocks to studying the separate effects on development of prenatal delivery, or neonatal variables, is the compounding of these variables in real life. The mother who begins her pregnancy under stressful emotional conditions starts the cycle which ultimately leads to a poor attachment after delivery. Her prenatal stress tends to be associated with more delivery complications. Delivery complications tend to be associated with a higher incidence of difficult temperament in the offspring. Difficult temperaments place more demands on the mother's adaptive ability and caretaking skill. The increased demands on the mother tend to result in reduced affection and attachment to the child. Major questions remain before we can identify points in this negative cycle where intervention should occur and the kinds of intervention that would be the most effective.

In contrast to the stress-laden situations described above is the positive reciprocal cycle of the mother who has prepared for her pregnancy, suffers a minimum of stress, trains for her delivery, requires a minimum of obstetrical intervention, immediately begins caretaking for her good-tempered child, feels effective in her caretaking, and is able to enter a responsive, affectionate relationship with her infant.

CONCLUSIONS

Now let us return to our initial philosophical question, "What is a person?" I suggested two possibie answers: that a person is a thing, and that a person is a human being. How is it possible for us to confuse these two definitions? How is it possible to treat what we would all consider to be human as a thing?

The above presentation has been aimed at providing an explanation. When a person is treated as if a constitutional or genetic deficit remains as an unchanging characteristic, he is being treated as a thing. When any abnormality in functioning is treated as intrinsic to that person and taken out of the social and cultural context in which he is living, that person is being treated as a thing. The ethical considerations of such depersonalization can be left to the humanists. Of concern here are the hard data of medical and psychological research. There has yet to be demonstrated a causal connection between a constitutional variable and any personality or intellectual developmental outcome. This may sound like a strong statement, but it characterizes the developmental data from myriads of longitudinal studies. Whenever retrospective research has indicated a variable thought to be causal to some adverse behavioral outcome, prospective research has shown that individuals with exactly the same characteristics or experiences have not had the adverse outcome. Whether the variable be poor genes, birth complications, or even psychosexual trauma, other individuals with these same characteristics have shown not only a lack of later deviancy but often an increased competence (Garmezy, 1974). Why is it, then, that in the face of these negative indications we continue to believe that premature children, difficult children, or handicapped children will all have poor developmental outcomes? I would suggest it is because we do not have the necessary developmental perspective. As long as we believe that labels are received rather than given, we will be confronted with this problem. Only when we come to see that the label is not only something we have attributed to the child but also the initial ingredient in a self-fulfilling prophecy, will we come to the heart of primary prevention.

The transactional model I described earlier has permitted us to obtain the first realistic view of the developmental process. It is not original here, but has a rich history running through Piaget in cognition, Waddington in embryology, Marx in economics, and Schneirla in animal behavior. The model is obvious to anyone who has attempted to see people as living creatures whose characteristics are the consequences of a series of mutual effects between what they started with and what environments they experienced.

When change is seen to be the rule of development rather than the exception, then a new perspective can be given to prevention. If a child is viewed as doomed because of a poor genetic, reproductive, or caretaking history, we are left only with the problem of defining an optimal institutional setting for him. On the other hand, if a child's characteristics are seen as the consequence of an ongoing adaptation to a particular set of life circumstances, then we are offered a multiplicity of possibilities for changing those circumstances and thereby changing the prognosis for that child. Frequently, the effort required may exceed the energies of parents, educators, or professionals, but that does not entitle us to shift the responsibility for the condition to the child. It is only through a clear view of the developmental process that future hope for a genuine primary prevention can be derived.

REFERENCES

Babson, S. G., and Benson, R. C. *Management of high-risk pregnancy and intensive care of the neonate.* St. Louis: Mosby, 1971.

Becker, W. L., and Krug, R. S. The Parent Attitude Research Instrument—a research review. *Child Development,* 1965, *36,* 329-366.

Carey, W. B. Maternal anxiety and infantile colic. *Clinical Pediatrics,* 1968, *7,* 590-595.

Carey, W. B. A simplified method for measuring infant temperament. *Journal of Pediatrics,* 1970, *77,* 188-194.

Corah, N. L., Anthony, E. J., Painter, P., Stern, J. A., and Thurston, D. L. Effects of perinatal anoxia after seven years. *Psychological Monographs,* 1965, *79* (3, Whole No. 596).

Ferreira, A. *Prenatal environment.* Springfield, Ill.: Thomas, 1969.

Garmezy, N. The study of competence in children at risk for severe psychopathology. In E. J. Anthony and C. Koupernik (Eds.), *The child in his family: Children at psychiatric risk* (Vol. 3). New York: Wiley, 1974.

Gesell, A., and Amatruda, C. *Developmental diagnosis.* New York: Hoeber, 1941.

Gottfried, A. W. Intellectual consequences of perinatal anoxia. *Psychological Bulletin,* 1973, *80,* 231-242.

Graham, F. K., Pennoyer, M. M., Caldwell, B. M., Greenman, M., and Hartman, A. F. Relationship between clinical status and behavior test performance in a newborn group with histories suggesting anoxia. *Journal of Pediatrics,* 1957, *50,* 177-189.

Graham, F. K., Ernhart, C. B., Thurston, D., and Craft, M. Development three years after perinatal anoxia and other potentially damaging newborn experiences. *Psychological Monographs,* 1962, *76* (3, Whole No. 522).

Graham, F. K., Matarazzo, R. G., and Caldwell, B. M. Behavioral differences between normal and traumatized newborns: II. Standardization, reliability, and validity. *Psychological Monographs,* 1956, *70* (21, Whole No. 428).

Kagan, J., and Klein, R. E. Cross-cultural perspectives on early development. *American Psychologist,* 1973, *28,* 947-961.

Klein, M., and Stern, L. Low birthweight and the battered child syndrome. *American Journal of Diseases of Children,* 1971, *122,* 15-18.

Lewis, M., and McGurk, H. Evaluation of infant intelligence. *Science,* 1972, *170,* 1174-1177.

Little, W. J. On the influence of abnormal parturition, difficult labor, premature birth, and asphyxia neonatorum on the mental and physical condition of the child especially in relation to deformities. *Lancet,* 1861, *2,* 378-380.

McDonald, R. L. The role of emotional factors in obstetric complications: A review. *Psychosomatic Medicine,* 1968, *30,* 222-237.

Pasamanick, B., and Knobloch, H. Epidemiologic studies on the complications of pregnancy and the birth process. In G. Caplan (Ed.), *Prevention of mental disorders in children.* New York: Basic Books, 1961.

Pasamanick, B., and Knobloch, H. Retrospective studies on the epidemiology of reproductive casuality: old and new. *Merrill-Palmer Quarterly*, 1966, *12*, 7-26.

Pasamanick, B., Knobloch, H., and Lilienfeld, A. M. Socioeconomic status and some precursors of neuropsychiatric disorders. *American Journal of Orthopsychiatry*, 1956, *26*, 594-601.

Piaget, J. *Psychology of intelligence*. Patterson, N.J.: Littlefield, Adams, 1950.

Sameroff, A. J. Infant risk factors in developmental deviancy. Paper presented at the meeting of the International Association for Child Psychiatry and Allied Professions, Philadelphia, July 1974.

Sameroff, A. J. Transactional models in early social relations. *Human Development*, 1975, *18*, 65-79. (a)

Sameroff, A. J. Early influences on development: Fact or fancy? *Merrill-Palmer Quarterly*, 1975, *21*, 267-294. (b)

Sameroff, A. J., and Chandler, M. J. Reproductive risk and the continuum of caretaking casualty. In F. D. Horowitz, M. Hetherington, S. Scarr-Salapatek, and G. Siegel (Eds.), *Review of child development research*. Chicago: University of Chicago, 1975, *4*, 187-244.

Sameroff, A. J., and Zax, M. Perinatal characteristics of the offspring of schizophrenic women. *Journal of Nervous and Mental Disease*, 1973, *157*, 191-199. (a)

Sameroff, A. M., and Zax, M. Schizotaxia revisited: Model issues in the etiology of schizophrenia. *American Journal of Orthopsychiatry*, 1973, *43*, 744-754. (b)

Schreiber, F. Mental deficiency from paranatal asphyxia. *Proceedings of the American Association of Mental Deficiency*, 1939, *63*, 95-106.

Spinetta, J. J., and Rigler, D. The child-abusing parent: A psychological review. *Psychological Bulletin*, 1972, *77*, 296-304.

Thomas, A., Chess, S., and Birch, H. *Temperament and behavior disorders in children*. New York: New York University Press, 1968.

Werner, E., Honzik, M., and Smith, R. Prediction of intelligence and achievement of ten years from twenty months pediatric and psychologic examinations. *Child Development*, 1968, *39*, 1063-1075.

Werner, E. E., Bierman, J. M., and French, F. E. *The children of Kauai*. Honolulu: University of Hawaii Press, 1971.

Windle, W. F. Structural and functional changes in the brain following neonatal asphyxia. *Psychosomatic Medicine*, 1944, *6*, 155-156.

II
Genetic, Prenatal, and Perinatal Factors in Primary Prevention

Introductory Notes

As we have indicated, primary prevention often falls into a logical order that begins with efforts before birth, or even before conception, and proceeds along the developmental sequence. Following this organization, we begin with papers on genetics and on prenatal and perinatal interventions.

L. Erlenmeyer-Kimling is principal research scientist in the Department of Medical Genetics of the New York State Psychiatric Institute and Associate Professor in the departments of psychiatry and of human genetics and development at Columbia University. Her paper deals with the present state of research knowledge in the genetics of mental disorder with special attention paid to schizophrenia and manic-depressive psychosis. She analyzes thoughtfully the possibility of genetics counseling for potential parents of children who might be negatively affected by the interaction of the parental genes and reviews many significant studies done throughout the world on the inheritance of these and other mental conditions. Clearly, if our goal is the primary prevention of psychopathology we must begin with what is known about genetic factors.

This section continues with a paper by Thomas F. McNeil and Lennart Kaij. Dr. McNeil is associate professor in the department of psychiatry at the University of Lund in Malmö, Sweden; Dr. Kaij is on the same faculty. Dr. McNeil is also on the staff of the Lafayette Clinic in Detroit and for the past five years has been engaged in research in Sweden, examining factors occurring during pregnancy and throughout the neonatal period as they affect later behavior. He describes the Swedish system of providing complete prenatal care, excellent delivery facilities, and state-supported baby clinics. Despite the resulting low infant mortality, Dr. McNeil identifies a number of potential problem areas that are a consequence of the system itself.

5

Issues Pertaining to Prevention and Intervention of Genetic Disorders Affecting Human Behavior

L. ERLENMEYER-KIMLING

There can be no basis for primary prevention of psychopathology unless we understand the etiology of the disorders that we hope to prevent and are able to identify individuals at risk for succumbing to those disorders. We need to know *what* to prevent —what constitutes vulnerability and what causes it to develop into a disabling condition—in order to know how to evolve specific interventions for specific kinds of mental aberrations.

GENETIC RISKS

I have been asked to review a part of etiology—the genetic risks for various disorders. Some psychiatric conditions, of course, have no apparent genetic involvement: for example, conditions arising from reactions to trauma, drugs, toxins, or viral infections or those associated with certain vitamin deficiencies. It is possible, however, that genes play a part in differential vulnerabilities and tolerances to some of these environmental insults. For other disorders, a genetic basis is clearly prominent, although here too it is (or ultimately should be) possible to demonstrate how the genetic defect interacts with some aspect of the environment. For the major forms of psychopathology, however, there has been a continuing controversy over the relative roles of heredity and environment. Indeed, it has frequently been questioned whether genes make *any* contribution to schizophrenia or the affective disorders, for example.

There are many reasons for the dislike of genetic hypotheses in

*Preparation of this paper was supported in part by a grant (MH-19560) from the National Institute of Mental Health and by the Department of Mental Hygiene of the State of New York.

the social sciences and mental health fields (Erlenmeyer-Kimling, 1972; Rosenthal, 1971), but probably none is so salient as the fear of inevitability that the idea of heredity so often excites. The confusion centers mainly around the distinction between genotype and phenotype—or, rather, around the failure to make such a distinction. Thus, many people, in the behavioral sciences as well as in the public at large, continue to hold to the notion that characteristics with a hereditary basis are inherited full-blown and ready-made to follow a fixed, unalterable course. Viewed in this way, of course, genetic theories seem threatening at a personal, as well as a professional, level. As Gottesman (1965, p. 72) has observed, "There is a natural reluctance to accept the supposed determinism that is associated with views that human behavior is genetically influenced. The former is especially true when one thinks of oneself. The ego defenses aroused are in part due to the values placed on free will and equality which are part and parcel of our democratic way of life"—and, he might have added, in part due to "the pessimistic belief that heredity is incompatible with possibilities for modification or amelioration" (Erlenmeyer-Kimling, 1972, p. 6).

The notion that psychiatric disorders with a genetic basis are neither treatable nor preventable with environmental measures is echoed in the misconception that a high heritability of I.Q. is synonymous with noneducability. It is not, of course. Individuals with high or with low potential benefit from educative efforts to develop their abilities to the fullest—when and if such efforts are made. The potential for genius is squandered if there is no opportunity for learning, while persons with less fortunate combinations of genes, as well as those damaged by birth trauma, infectious diseases, and other environmental agents can frequently achieve normal autonomy of functioning and do very well.

There is a growing list of so-called hereditary disorders that are treatable or symtomatically preventable as a result of an understanding, or at least a partial understanding, of the interaction of genetic and environmental factors. They include diabetes, cystic fibrosis, hemophilia, Wilson's disease, phenylketonuria, maple sugar urine disease, galactosemia, and galactokinase deficiency—the latter four involving inborn metabolic errors whose clinical manifestations are prevented or relieved through nutritional control. The list is short compared to the catalogue of human disorders that have both genetic and environmental components. It can be lengthened.

The genetic risks for some of the most important of the psychiatric disorders are not fully understood and the underlying mechanisms of gene action are not yet clear. But neither are environmental risks and environmental causes understood, although numerous hypotheses exist about them. We can learn more about the genetic and the environmental sides of the coin if we study them together than we have learned heretofore by considering them separately.

I will review, briefly, some of the genetic risk data for schizophrenia and the affective disorders—the major psychoses—and will refer to some other conditions, clearly genetically based, which result in psychiatric disturbance or may do so.

Schizophrenia

Schizophrenia has undoubtedly been the most intensively studied of all the mental illnesses. The earliest genetic study of schizophrenia was reported in 1916 by Ernst Rüdin. Since then, family and twin studies and, more recently, the methodologically sophisticated work on adoptive samples have investigated well over 50,000 individuals in total. The cumulative evidence supports a general hypothesis of hereditary involvement in the predisposition to schizophrenia, although it is currently not possible to determine which best fits the data—a polygenic threshold model, a monogenic model allowing for reduced penetrance of a dominant gene, or a genetic heterogeneity model involving several genetic mimics. In any event, it also seems clear that environmental factors have an important, though possibly nonspecific, role in the development of a genetic predisposition into an overt illness. Environmental factors may perhaps be responsible, too, for buffering vulnerable individuals against the development of psychiatric disorder.

The incidence of schizophrenia in most populations where it has been studied is usually estimated as ranging from slightly under 1 percent to about 2 percent, although in some population groups the incidence appears to be higher or lower. The lifetime risks for first-degree relatives of a schizophrenic proband are very substantially higher. I will focus on the risk data for the

Table 1. *Schizophrenia risk estimates in the general population and in offspring of schizophrenic parents. Definite schizophrenia only.*

	Number of studies	Bezugsziffer[a]	Risk estimates Range of values	Risk estimates Mean of values
General population[b]			0.4–2.4	1.2
Offspring of:				
(1) One schizophrenic parent[c]	14	2083.5	6.8–19.4	11.5
—Paranoid dx in parent[d]	1	118	——	6.8
—Simple dx in parent[d]	1	57	——	1.8
—Hebephrenic or catatonic dx in parent[d]	1	194	——	13.4
—Mother affected[e]	3	327	2.7–14.9	10.9
—Father affected[e]	3	250	7.6–15.4	9.2
(2) Two schizophrenic parents[f]	6	225	32.0–55.3	36.0

[a] Number of subjects after correction for age. Not all studies age-corrected.
[b] After Zerbin-Rüdin, 1967.
[c] Expanded from Hanson, 1974. The studies are: Hoffman, 1921; Oppler, 1923; Gengnagel, 1933; Kallman, 1938; Garrone, 1962; Heston, 1966; Reisby, 1967; Lindelius, 1970; Fischer, 1971; Bleuler, 1972; Rosenthal, 1972; Reed et al., 1973; Moskalenko, 1973; Tsuang et al., 1974.
[d] Kallmann, 1938.
[e] Kallmann, 1938; Bleuler, 1972; Reed et al., 1973.
[f] Expanded from Erlenmeyer-Kimling, 1968. The studies are: Kahn, 1923; Kallmann, 1938; Schulz, 1940; Elsässer, 1952; Lewis, 1957; Erlenmeyer-Kimling, unpublished.

children of schizophrenic patients because they are the only first-degree relatives for whom primary prevention is a possible issue.

Children of schizophrenic parents have been investigated in 14 studies. The age-corrected risk estimates for definite schizophrenia, excluding borderline and questionable diagnoses, range from 6.8 to 19.4 percent, with a mean of 11.57 percent (see Table 1). In most of the studies, a substantial number of the remaining offspring were classified as borderline or questionable cases of schizophrenia or as showing other psychiatric disorders.

In Kallmann's (1938) study, separate risk figures were reported according to the parent's diagnostic subtype (Table 1). When the other parent was psychiatrically normal, the risk to children of hebephrenic or catatonic parents was 13.4 percent, compared to only 6.8 percent in children of a paranoid parent and only 1.8 percent (!) in children whose ill parent had a diagnosis of simple schizophrenia. Some discrepancy among studies may therefore be due to different compositions of parental samples.

Three studies (Bleuler, 1972; Kallmann, 1938; Reed et al., 1973) allow comparison of schizophrenia risks in the offspring of schizophrenic mothers and normal fathers versus the offspring of schizophrenic fathers and normal mothers. For the three studies combined, no differences are to be found (see Table 1). Moreover, in none of the studies does the risk for the offspring of schizophrenic women exceed that for the offspring of schizophrenic men when the other parent is psychiatrically normal. A reanalysis of the Reed et al. data by Hanson (1974) suggests, however, that husbands of schizophrenic women may be more likely to display other psychiatric disturbances than the wives of schizophrenic men. As the risk to the offspring of schizophrenics is generally somewhat higher when the second parent has another psychiatric disorder, the rate of affected children may thus *seem* to be higher for schizophrenic mothers than for schizophrenic fathers if no attention is paid to the psychiatric status of the other parent.

In most of the reported studies, it is not possible to evaluate differential rates of risk for children of schizophrenic x normal matings in contrast to those for offspring of a schizophrenic parent and a parent who is not considered to be psychiatrically normal, or even the children of two schizophrenic parents. In Kallmann's (1938) study,* children with one schizophrenic and one normal parent had a schizophrenia risk of 9.5 percent, compared to a slightly higher rate of 15.1 percent when one parent had another disorder, and to the much higher rate of 55.3 percent when both parents were schizophrenic. The risk for illegitimate children born to schizophrenic women in Kallmann's sample was 24 percent, suggesting that some of the unknown fathers may have been schizophrenic or latent schizophrenic individuals also. Unfortunately, there have been no attempts to replicate either the size or the detail of this study, and many of Kallmann's findings— which have some important implications for ongoing prospective studies of schizophrenics—have been overlooked or forgotten.

Five studies (Elsässer, 1952; Kahn, 1923; Kallmann, 1938; Lewis, 1957; Schulz, 1940) have yielded data on children of two

---

*All figures cited here referring to the Kallmann (1938) study are for definite schizophrenia only. The expectancy rates for children of one schizophrenic parent and for illegitimate offspring are calculated from Tables 34–37 (pp. 106–111). The other figures are taken from Tables 57 (pp. 154–155) and 38 (p. 157) respectively.

schizophrenic parents. The age-corrected risk figures for definite schizophrenia in the offspring range between 36.1 percent and 55.3 percent, with an average of 39.2 percent (see Erlenmeyer-Kimling, 1968). If cases of questionable schizophrenia are included, the average for the offspring in the five studies rises to 44.4 percent. Elsässer et al. (1971) have recently published a follow-up of almost twenty years on one of these samples (Elsässer, 1952), with little change in the morbidity risk figures originally reported for them.

A new sample of children of two schizophrenic parents has been described by Moskalenko (1971) in the Soviet Union: 57.8 percent (uncorrected for age) of the children were reported to have developed schizophrenia, but because the sample includes families identified by illness in the *children*, as well as those identified by the illness of the parents, this investigation may not be compared directly with the earlier studies.

New investigations of offspring of two psychotic parents (all diagnoses) by Kringlen (1971) in Norway and by Gottesman and Fischer (1974) in Denmark include small numbers of children whose two parents are schizophrenic. We (Erlenmeyer-Kimling and Rainer, 1970) have been following a sizable group of children with two schizophrenic parents for several years (See Erlenmeyer-Kimling, 1968; Kallmann et al., 1964).* Although most of these subjects are only in their early to middle twenties, a preliminary calculation of schizophrenia risk yields a figure of 32 percent for the group. The estimate may be, on the one hand, inflated by the procedure of age-correction on the relatively young sample and, on the other hand, underrepresented because of the difficulties in tracing some of the subjects.

Finally, studies of children reared away from their biological parents show that a specific cultural transmission of schizophrenic behavior cannot be responsible for the elevated risk of the disorder in the offspring of schizophrenic parents. In Heston's (1966) investigation of children separated at birth from their schizophrenic mothers, the age-corrected schizophrenia rate in adulthood was close to 16.6, while among matched children, who had been separated at birth from their psychiatrically normal parents, there

*This study is supported by a grant from the Benevolent Foundation of Scottish Rite Freemasonry, Northern Jurisdiction, U.S.A.

was no schizophrenia. Again, in the investigation conducted by Rosenthal and colleagues (Rosenthal, 1972) in Denmark, adopted-away children of schizophrenic parents were compared to matched adopted-away children of normal parents; 6.8 percent of the adoptees whose biological parent had a definite diagnosis of schizophrenia were also given a blind diagnosis of schizophrenia, while none of the control adoptees were considered to be schizophrenic. In Karlsson's (1966) study in Iceland, 29.4 percent of the children reared away from their schizophrenic parents developed schizophrenia (25 percent when reared by relatives and 33 percent when reared by nonrelatives), compared to 11.8 percent of the children who were reared by their schizophrenic parents. The large family study of psychotic patients carried out by Reed et al. (1973) in Pennsylvania gives similar results: 28.6 percent of children separated from schizophrenic parents before age six, and 17.5 percent of those who were not separated, developed a schizophrenic psychosis. Mednick and Schulsinger (1968) have also reported—in their prospective examination of children of schizophrenic mothers—that those who were separated early from their mothers seemed to be at highest risk. Reed et al. (1973), commenting on their own and other investigators' findings, suggest that the parents who had to give their children away were more severely ill than those who were able to keep their children, and that the more severely ill parents presumably transmitted a heavier genetic loading for schizophrenia to their children.

To summarize the genetic risk data for the children of schizophrenic parents: (1) the evidence is that children with one schizophrenic parent have a risk for a schizophrenic psychosis which is some 7 to 19 percent higher than the schizophrenia risk in the population at large; (2) the risk is the same regardless of the sex of the schizophrenic parent, but increases somewhat if the other parent is psychiatrically disturbed, and is elevated to about 39 percent if both parents are overtly schizophrenic; (3) risks are probably higher for children of hebephrenic and catatonic parents than for paranoid parents; (4) separation from the schizophrenic parent does not reduce the risk of disturbance in the offspring and, indeed, may be associated with a higher rate of risk because the more severely ill—and hence more genetically loaded—parents are the ones who give up their children.

Affective Disorders

For the affective disorders, as for schizophrenia, we still do not have a clear picture of the mode of genetic transmission, although it seems certain that heredity is importantly involved. A multigenic model is supported by some investigators, a single dominant gene model by others. Several studies recently have provided evidence supporting the hypothesis of an X-linked dominant gene in the bipolar (manic-depressive) form of the illness, though clearly not all bipolar cases follow this mode of inheritance. The analysis of the cumulative genetic data is complicated by the fact that earlier workers did not distinguish between the bipolar form, with both manic and depressive phases, and the unipolar depressive form of the disorder. Recent studies indicate that both unipolar and bipolar cases are found in high frequency among relatives of bipolar probands, but that many families ascertained through unipolar probands contain only unipolar members (Angst, 1966; Mendlewicz and Fleiss, 1974). Thus it seems likely that at least two separate genotypes are subsumed under the rubric of "affective disorders." One of these may be expressed as either a bipolar or a unipolar disorder, while the other genotype is evidently expressed only as a unipolar depression (Mendlewicz and Fleiss, 1974).

Despite the uncertainty about the appropriate genetic model, there is less controversy over the degree to which genetic factors are implicated than is true of schizophrenia, and it is generally expected that an understanding of the biochemical nature of mania and depression will come before the key is found to schizophrenia.

The incidence of affective disorders in the general population is variously estimated as lying between 0.4 and 2 percent (Slater and Cowie, 1971). A review of the older literature, in which no distinction was made between bipolar and unipolar probands, shows risk figures for children with one affected parent ranging between 6 and 24.1 percent (see Zerbin-Rüdin, 1967), with substantial increases in all studies if doubtful cases and suicides were included. Schizophrenia, however, does not appear in these children, and the kinds of "other psychiatric disorders" that are described in them are usually different from those reported in children of schizophrenic parents. The large discrepancies between studies may be attributable to different proportions of unipolar and bipolar parents in the different samples, so that it is probably not worthwhile to calculate a mean risk figure for the children based on the old data. Most of the recent family studies show higher rates of psychoses in the first-degree relatives of bipolar probands than in the families of unipolar cases, although there are few data on children of either category.

Mendlewicz and Rainer (1974) reported a morbidity risk of 66.7 percent in the offspring of bipolar probands but they noted that this figure is probably artefactually high because of the small sample size and the application of age-correction to relatives of young ages.

In the Danish adoption study conducted by Rosenthal and colleagues (Rosenthal, 1972) one out of seven, or 14.3 percent, of the adopted-away offspring of manic-depressive parents received the same diagnosis. This figure is about the same as the average of 15.3 percent for the older studies in which children were reared with their psychotic parents. Other adoption studies focusing primarily on the affective disorders are now being carried out, though no data have yet been reported.

In short, while there is substantial and strong evidence for genetic predisposition to the affective psychoses—perhaps especially so for the bipolar disorder—the expectable range of risk in the offspring of affective disorder parents is not clear. The risks of unipolar and bipolar psychoses in the children of bipolar parents with affective disorders are probably not less than the risk of schizophrenia in children of schizophrenic parents, and very likely are considerably higher.

Rare Single-Gene Defects with Psychiatric Implications

Several single-gene conditions have severe effects upon neurological and mental functioning. I would like to consider four of these. Each is rare in itself, and together they make up a very small part of the total of psychopathology. They are of interest, however, because, although they are all clearly much more simple matters than the functional psychoses, they each show a different stage of advancement in our understanding of etiology, in our understanding of ways in which heredity and environment interact, and in the present status of our ability to do primary prevention.

The first two are inherited as autosomal dominant conditions and do not usually become manifest until adulthood. They are Huntington's disease (HD) and acute intermittent porphyria (AIP). In neither disease are environmental variables known to influence the development of symptomatology, although both disorders show clinical variability in severity and in age of onset that may represent responsiveness to environmental stress. HD has probably received more attention, but both disorders can be traced back through history.*

HD is a progressive disorder of the brain which begins to manifest itself, usually in middle age, as a change in personality and which then progresses to choreic movements, usually passing to complete loss of muscular control and complete mental deterioration. Offspring of affected parents are at 50 percent risk, and the gene is apparently fully penetrant. The biochemical action of the gene is not yet understood, nor is it possible to recognize carriers before the illness appears. Recent research, however, is promising with respect to both the possibility of early detection (Klawans et al., 1971) and the effectiveness of palliative drugs in retarding symptoms.

In AIP, almost all patients show some degree of behavioral disturbance and, indeed, a frank psychiatric disorder may be the initial presenting picture (Levere and Kappas, 1970). Abdominal pain and neurological disturbances are also characteristic of AIP. The genetic lesion apparently results in an overproduction of a specific enzyme, although the precise nature of the metabolic abnormality is not certain. While there are environmentally induced forms of porphyria, it is not known exactly how environmental factors interact with the genetic lesion. The variability of expression seen in porphyria, however, suggests that gene-environment interaction is probably important. Prevention, treatment, and early detection remain to be achieved.

The third genetic disorder in my list of examples – the Lesch-Nyhan syndrome – is inherited as an X-linked recessive condition and is found exclusively in males. It is due to the reduced activity of an enzyme. The syndrome is characterized by neurological abnormalities, mental retardation, aggressive

*AIP may have been the cause of the American Revolution. It has been speculated that King George III of England was a victim of this disease and that his behavior and critical judgment suffered accordingly.

behavior, and—most striking—by compulsive biting that leads to severe self-mutilation. A drug (allopurinol) can control the over-production of uric acid resulting from the enzyme deficiency, but the brain dysfunction so far appears to be irreversible (Friedmann and Roblin, 1972). It is, however, possible to identify heterozy-gous women who are clinically normal but have a 50–50 chance of having affected sons, and the disorder can also be diagnosed prenatally by culturing cells from the amniotic fluid surrounding the fetus (cf. Milunsky et al., 1970). Thus, both genetic counseling and therapeutic abortion are possible.

The tale of the fourth single-gene defect—Wilson's disease—appears to be a modest success story, where research has paid off fairly quickly in terms of the goals of early detection and preven-tion. Wilson's disease is attributable to an autosomal recessive gene which must be inherited in double dose for an individual to be at risk. The basic defect is an error of copper metabolism. As with phenylketonuria, where the basic defect is an inability to metabolize phenylalanine taken into the body in food, Wilson's disease plainly shows how a genetic defect and the nutritional environment may interact adversely. Personality changes, some-times mimicking a schizophrenic psychosis, and neurological im-pairment are frequently a part of the clinical course. Fortunately, victims of Wilson's disease can now be identified early in families whose history warrants screening for the disease, and heterozy-gotes too can frequently be recognized. With the administration of penicillamine, which acts as a chelating agent and therefore decreases tissue copper storage, it appears to be possible for the identified homozygotes to remain asymptomatic. In individuals affected before penicillamine treatment became available, some of the symptoms have actually been reversed with treatment (cf. Thompson and Thompson, 1973).

There have been speculations about the possibility that a number of other recessive genes, involving metabolic errors and usually leading to mental retardation when in the homozygous state, may present as psychiatric disturbances in heterozygotes. Heterozygotes for phenylketonuria and homocystinuria have been the chief targets for speculation, and, in fact, a few studies have reported an elevation of schizophrenia-like psychoses in families of phenylketonuric and homocystinuric patients (see reviews in Larson and Nyman, 1968; Welch et al., 1969). Other investigators, however, have been unable to confirm these findings (Larson and Nyman, 1968; Welch et al., 1969). Nevertheless, it is possible that heterozygotes for some of the rare metabolic disorders may be at heightened risk for mental illness and that such conditions may represent a fraction of the psychiatric disorders.

Sex Chromosome Anomalies

There are indications also that the sex chromosome anomalies may be more common among the mentally ill than they are in the general population. Several surveys of mental hospital patients have turned up a higher frequency of Klinefelter syndrome (XXY) cases than is expected in the population at large (cf. Jarvik et al., 1973). Other sex chromosome anomalies, with the exception of Turner's syndrome (XO), also appear to be overrepresented in psychiatric populations. Even if this is true, the sex chromosome anomalies would make up a very small portion of the mentally ill.

One condition—the XYY syndrome—has received a great deal of attention in an atmosphere of increasing controversy. When first described, the XYY syndrome was reported to occur with higher incidence in the criminally retarded than in the general population (Jacobs et al., 1965). XYY males were described as being unusually tall, of borderline intelligence, and subject to episodes of violent aggressiveness. Subsequently, it has become clear that the majority of men with an extra Y chromosome do not exhibit violence, are probably of normal intelligence, and may not even be tall. As a consequence, some workers have challenged the notion of any increased pathology associated with the XYY karyotype (cf. Kessler and Moos, 1969). The weight of evidence, however, does continue to support the view that there is increased risk of violent behavior associated with the extra Y. As Jarvik et al. (1973) pointed out in a review of the XYY investigations, the frequency of men with this syndrome in the criminal population amounts to nearly 1.9 percent, or 15 times the rate (0.13) percent) of XYY individuals found in newborn males or in normal adult men.

Disorders of Uncertain Genetic Involvement

Finally, I will mention some more common disorders of uncertain genetic involvement. Alcoholism, criminality, and delinquency, specific learning disabilities (e.g. dyslexia), and minimal brain dysfunction (MBD) are aspects of psychopathology that cause a growing amount of public concern. All have recently been claimed to involve a hereditary factor, though both genetic and environmental data on each of them are still quite sparse.

For MBD, present findings are reasonably suggestive of the role of genetic factors, possibly of a polygenic nature—although Wender (1973) and Omenn (1973) have both stressed the need to consider genetic and environmental heterogeneity of MBD. Taking into account the behavioral and neurophysiological observations of MBD patients, as well as the pharmacological evidence, Wender (1973) and Omenn (1973) have suggested a biochemical basis for MBD involving the dopaminergic systems that may also be associated with schizophrenia.

If MBD is recognized as being a heterogeneous and still poorly defined diagnostic grouping, alcoholism and criminality are even looser. Each encompasses a variety of different phenotypes—and undoubtedly a variety of different genotypes, some of which may play a part in predisposition to the problem and many of which may not. Until clearer definitions are established within these two broad labels, the best motto would seem to be: "Proceed with caution."

IDENTIFICATION OF RISK

Understanding etiology is the first prerequisite for primary prevention. The ability to recognize a disorder before it becomes manifest is the second. What we know about the role of genetics in some areas of psychopathology should help to make risk identification easier. What we learn further about the characteristics and development of children and adolescents at risk for a disorder such as schizophrenia, for example, may in turn help to shed more light on the etiological process.

Prevention can be truly primary for a growing number of hereditary disorders, in the sense that individuals who would suffer from crippling and tragic conditions need not be born at all. Primary prevention of this sort is made possible by the expansion of methods for heterozygote detection and by prenatal diagnosis of biochemical and chromosomal defects (cf. Milunsky et al.,

1970). The assumption underlying the development of techniques for heterozygote detection is that screening programs will make it possible for two carriers to avoid marrying, to avoid having children, or, more likely, to have each pregnancy monitored by amniocentesis, presumably with abortion of affected fetuses. In practice, however, very little routine screening of heterozygotes is done, and amniocentesis is of course not done unless there are a priori reasons to suspect that genetic risk is involved, as is the case for example when one affected child has already been born. Additionally, some parents are unable on moral grounds to accept fetal abortion, or even contraception, recommended in genetic counseling as solutions. Thus, many children affected with detectable and preventable disorders will slip through the net.

Postnatal screening can be carried out for a number of metabolic errors and for chromosomal anomalies. Screening of newborns for phenylketonuria and a few other genetic conditions is now mandatory in many states. The goal of mass screening programs is to introduce therapeutic intervention—such as the low phenylalanine diet in phenylketonuria—as early as possible in development, before irreversible damage to organs and the central nervous system has had a chance to take place.

Neonatal screening for the XYY syndrome, however, has been viewed adversely by sectors of the scientific community and lay public who were ultimately able to bring sufficient pressure to bear on the research to cause its termination (Culliton, 1975). It is true that there is no immediate and obvious therapy to be offered in the case of early-detected XYY males; it is true also that the association between the extra Y chromosome and behavioral risk has not been clearly established. The opportunity to clarify this question, as well as a valuable opportunity for devising and testing means for helping in the psychological development of males who may be vulnerable to aggressive impulses, appears to have been lost with the shutting down of Walzer's prospective study at Harvard (Culliton, 1974).

The issue of "labeling" was part of the objection to the Harvard study. Whether labeling is the bugaboo that many people believe remains questionable. Labeling applies in some measure to all of the methods of risk identification and perhaps especially to the endeavors to identify prospectively subjects who are at risk for various kinds of psychopathology. Extreme care must by all means be taken in such research to avoid creating expectations of, or anxieties concerning, future mental difficulties. If prudence is exercised, it seems to me that the value of prospective research far outweighs its possible harm.

Early identification of individuals at risk for the major psychoses is unfortunately not yet possible, although over 20 studies (see Erlenmeyer-Kimling, 1975; Garmezy, 1974) are attempting to make beginnings in this direction with respect to schizophrenia. Prospective investigations of affective disorders are also being initiated. For simplicity in the following discussion, I will refer to schizophrenia only, although most of the same points refer to the affective disorders as well.

Most of the studies take as their high risk subjects the children of schizophrenic parents for whom risks are already known to be greater than for the general population. The prospective studies are thus dealing with groups of individuals of whom only a fairly small percentage are actually expected to develop schizophrenia. A major goal is to determine the early psychological, biological, and/or social characteristics of the members of the risk group who will later break down. The hope is that once the early indicators of vulnerability are pinpointed in the limited but accessible population of children of schizophrenic parents, the same indicators can be used in mass screening of the general population to identify other children at risk whose parentage does not flag them so readily. Only 10 to 15 percent of people who become schizophrenic have had an overtly schizophrenic parent. It is essential, therefore, that findings generated in studies of children of schizophrenic parents be made applicable to the entire population of individuals at risk for future schizophrenia.

Because of the foregoing problem, some investigators are attempting to use criteria other than relationship to a schizophrenic patient as a means of establishing high risk populations. Such criteria are based on hypotheses—and sometimes data—about the premorbid characteristics or social backgrounds of schizophrenic patients. Commonly held notions about premorbid characteristics may be misleading, however. For instance, as Gottesman et al. (in press) point out, a common assumption is that a large percentage of schizophrenics were characterized in childhood by extreme shyness and withdrawal; but follow-up studies comparing shy, withdrawn children and children with mixed signs of introversion and extroversion show the highest occurrence of adult schizophrenia in the mixed group and the lowest in the shy, withdrawn subjects (Michael et al., 1954). Similarly, Watt (1974) found little evidence of the characteristics usually ascribed to adult schizophrenics in their follow-back study of school records of individuals who later became schizophrenic. That social class is not a predictor of behavior disturbance in adulthood is ably demonstrated by Robin's (1966) follow-up study of deviant children. It is therefore difficult at present to know what criterion for selecting individuals at high risk for schizophrenia will yield as high a payoff as the genetic criterion.

Another approach to risk identification is suggested by environmental hypotheses about the etiology of schizophrenia. For example, if hypotheses about parental variables that have been claimed to "cause" schizophrenia are correct, it should be possible to generate a high risk group by studying children whose parents are not overtly schizophrenic but possess characteristics that some investigators (cf. Lidz, 1973) attribute to parents of schizophrenic patients. Whether such children would in fact prove to be at unusually high risk in the course of a prospective investigation remains a matter for empirical verification, of course. The study would at least put the hypotheses to a test that has so far not been rigorously applied by providing double-blind (as to parental group and as to outcome of the children) evaluations of the supposed high-risk group and a comparison group of children whose parents do not exhibit the characteristics in question.

PREVENTION

Primary prevention of mental illness is something for the future. I have mentioned the identification of heterozygotes, prenatal diagnosis, therapeutic abortion, postnatal screening, and the institution of therapeutic regimens for individuals discovered to be genetically vulnerable. These methods are available, and they are tremendously relieving for parents and children who carry a variety of genetic defects. But they do little more than scratch the surface as far as mental retardation is concerned and far less than that in regard to psychiatric disorders. If we can unravel the biochemistry of schizophrenia and the affective disorders—if we can find genetic markers—then the methodology of prenatal and neonatal detection may some day become feasible.

Genetic counseling is sometimes proposed for members of families in which a psychiatric disorder appears. Prime candidates for counseling are the children of Huntington's disease patients who are themselves at 50 percent risk of manifesting the same condition by middle life. If they do become ill, each of their own children will again be at 50 percent risk. One might suppose that with the horror of HD most members of these families express, individuals at risk would choose not to become parents; on the contrary, however, the reproductive rate of HD families is relatively high (though not as high as for members of the general population). Interestingly also, it is higher for those individuals who later become ill than for their siblings who remain unaffected (Reed and Chandler, 1958). Thus, genetic counseling is evidently not highly effective.

At present, genetic counseling with respect to schizophrenia and the affective disorders is of limited use in terms of its potential for reducing the frequency of illness in the population. Most parents whose children will eventually be diagnosed as psychotic will not have been identified before that event and will therefore not have been exposed to the possibility of genetic counseling. Usually, all of their children will have been born long before any one of them shows signs of becoming ill.

In general, neither a relationship to a known schizophrenic nor specifiable individual characteristics serve to identify preschizophrenic individuals as being at risk. Thus, genetic counseling is not indicated for most persons until after a breakdown has occurred; the target group for counseling is pretty much narrowed down to those who have already become ill.

I do not think there is usually much question about the direction that genetic counseling should take in advising persons (or their spouses or prospective spouses) who have already experienced a schizophrenic breakdown. Parenthood and schizophrenia tend to mix poorly. In addition to the genetic risks to the children of schizophrenic parents, there is considerable likelihood that any children of such parents will be exposed to a disrupted and often grossly unsuitable home environment. The birth of a child often exacerbates the patient's illness, and the responsibilities of bringing up the children tend to trigger further difficulties. Prospects for the nonschizophrenic spouse's happiness are not good, either; it is difficult to be mother and father, wage-earner and homemaker, sometime mate and companion, and, increasingly, part-time nurse and attendant to a departed mind. Most counselors would probably agree that schizophrenic patients should be advised against parenthood, or having further children, and probably against marriage if they are not already married (Erlenmeyer-Kimling, 1973).

But, to reiterate: although genetic counseling is indicated for identified psychosis, it will do little to reduce the overall incidence of mental illness.

There are many hypotheses about the environmental variables that interact with a genetic predisposition in the development of schizophrenia. Some of these hypotheses are the basis of the prospective studies of children at risk: they have to do, for example, with family interaction patterns, hyperarousal and psychophysiological responsiveness, the ability to filter stimulus input, the development of coping skills, perinatal factors, and other fairly specific and testable ideas (see Erlenmeyer-Kimling, 1975; Garmezy, 1974). Fortunately for the problems of sample size, replicability, and so on, some of the investigators are beginning to adopt each other's measures and allow for more than one type of hypothesis to be tested. Thus in a few years it may be possible to evaluate the various hypotheses and to draw up profiles characterizing children at risk. Then, in a few more years, it should become possible to say with more certainty which of these characteristics describe the children who will eventually break down. We will then have a better idea of the environmental factors that we have to prevent—or encourage.

Intervention might then take the form of working with perceptual deficits, helping to restructure parental behaviors, enhancing children's coping skills, behavioral modification for specific types of problems, or, perhaps, teaching high risk individuals to recognize and defend against stimulus overloads. Which, if any, of these will be appropriate we do not yet know.

Huessy (1973) has emphasized that, while an understanding of causes is important for prevention, it is less necessary for treatment. I have been focusing only on prevention. I do not mean to dismiss traditional approaches to psychotherapy or the newer work in family therapy, ongoing work in behavior modification, the role of schools, the training of parents to deal more effectively and rewardingly with their normal (Becker, 1971) or abnormal (Kaufman and Hagamen, unpublished; Kozloff, 1974; Thomas et al., 1969) children or any of the other avenues that help to alleviate the symptoms and suffering of mental illness and to promote health.

ENVOI

There is a tendency nowadays to be impatient with research, to call for action now. This is true in education as well as in the mental health fields. Efforts at prevention will not succeed, however, unless we establish specific interventions that work on the causes of specific kinds of psychopathology. As Arnhoff (1975) recently pointed out, the body of evidence that we now have about the psychoses "does not support the belief that treatment, intervention, and policy formulations can be meaningfully addressed, in a nonspecific global manner." Without an understanding of causes, we are in the position of relying on serendipity—surely a poor substitute for the solid knowledge that research can provide—or relying on vague hopes that broad, often unsubstantiated social action programs will automatically decrease the rate of mental illness by correcting social woes and increasing the general psychological well-being. Arnhoff noted, "Somewhere along the line, a problem as old as man, that of mental illness, was absorbed into the pursuit of global mental health" (p. 1281). It is this confusion of objectives that has led some workers to formulate the issue of primary prevention in terms of eliminating poverty, slums, and economic insecurity—among other commendable but nebulous proposals.

In the Scandinavian countries, which are exemplars of birth-to-grave social security, however, schizophrenia, depression, alcoholism, suicide, and other forms of psychopathology have not been eliminated or in fact even reduced. The goal of improving the lot of all our citizens, all our children, is praiseworthy, extremely important, and quite probably a step toward improving global mental health. But it is apparently not a goal that will lead to the disappearance of mental disorder.

It is true that we cannot simply bide our time until solutions are found, often with great slowness. There are many relatively specific kinds of interventions that may in the meantime help at least to alleviate some of the pain of mental disorder and a few that may actually decrease the frequency of some types of conditions. I have indicated a few of them. We need to recognize that it is only with continued efforts in basic and clinical research that we will ever find answers to our problem. We need to re-create the atmosphere in which research can be successful; we need to see to it that our resources are not so heavily diverted to stopgap measures that research is underinvested.

REFERENCES

Angst, J. *Zur Ätiologie and Nosologie endogener depressiver Psychosen.* Berlin: Springer, 1966.

Arnhoff, F. N. Social consequences of policy toward mental illness. *Science*, 1975, *188*, 1277-1281.

Becker, W. C. *Parents are teachers.* New York: Research Press, 1971.

Bleuler, M. *Die schizophrenen Geistesstörungen im Lichte langjähriger Kranken- und Familiengeschichten.* Stuttgart: Thieme, 1972.

Culliton, B. J. Patients' rights: Harvard is site of battle over X and Y chromosomes. *Science*, 1974, *186*, 715-717.

Culliton, B. J. XYY: Harvard researcher under fire stops newborn screening. *Science*, 1975, *188*, 1284-1285.

Elsässer, G. *Die Nachkommen geisteskranker Elternpaare.* Stuttgart: Thieme, 1952.

Elsässer, G., Lehmann, H., Pohlen, M., and Scheid, T. Die Nachkommen geisteskranker Elternpaare. *Fortschritte der Neurologie, Psychiatrie, und ihrer Grenzgebiete*, 1971, *9*, 495-522.

Erlenmeyer-Kimling, L. Studies on the offspring of two schizophrenic parents. In D. Rosenthal and S. S. Kety (Eds.), *The transmission of schizophrenia.* New York: Pergamon Press, 1968.

Erlenmeyer-Kimling, L. Genetics, interaction, and mental illness: Setting the problem. *International Journal of Mental Health*, 1972, *1*, 5-9.

Erlenmeyer-Kimling, L. Schizophrenia: A bag of dilemmas. Paper presented at Workshop on Genetic Counseling in Psychiatric Disorders, Indiana School of Medicine, Indianapolis, May 1973.

Erlenmeyer-Kimling, L. A prospective study of children at risk for schizophrenia: Methodological considerations and some preliminary findings. In R. D. Wirt, G. Winokur, and M. Roff (Eds.), *Life history research in psychopathology* (Vol. 4). Minneapolis: University of Minnesota Press, 1975.

Erlenmeyer-Kimling, L., and Rainer, J. D. Behavioral and environmental analysis of children with a high risk of schizophrenia. Grant from the Scottish Rite Committee on Research in Schizophrenia (The Benevolent Foundation of Scottish Rite Freemasonry, Northern Jurisdiction, U.S.A.), 1970.

Friedmann, T., and Roblin, R. Gene therapy for human disease? *Science*, 1972, *175*, 949-954.

Garmezy, N. Children at risk: The search for the antecedents of schizophrenia. Part II: Ongoing research programs, issues, and intervention. *Schizophrenia Bulletin*, 1974, No. 9, pp. 55-125.

Gottesman, I. I. Personality and natural selection. In S. G. Vandenberg (Ed.), *Methods and goals in human behavior genetics.* New York: Academic Press, 1965.

Gottesman, I. I., and Fischer, M. A long term follow-up of children born to two Danish psychiatric inpatients. Grant from the Scottish Rite Committee on Research in Schizophrenia (The Benevolent Foundation of Scottish Rite Freemasonry, Northern Jurisdiction, U.S.A.), 1974.

Gottesman, I. I., Shields, J., and Heston, L. L. Characteristics of the twins of schizophrenics as fallible indicators of schizoidia. *Acta Geneticae Medicae et Gemellologiae*, in press.

Hanson, D. R. Children of schizophrenic mothers or fathers compared to children of other psychiatric controls: Their first eight years. Unpublished doctoral dissertation, University of Minnesota, 1974.

Heston, L. L. Psychiatric disorders in foster home reared children of schizophrenic mothers. *British Journal of Psychiatry*, 1966, *112*, 819-825.

Huessy, H. R. Some historical antecedents of present American mental health dilemmas. Paper presented at IXth International Congress of Anthropological and Ethnological Sciences, Chicago, August-September, 1973.

Jacobs, P. A., Brunton, M., Melville, M. M., Brittain, R. P., and McClemont, W. F. Aggressive behavior, mental subnormality and the XYY male. *Nature*, 1965, *208*, 1351-1352.

Jarvik, L. F., Klodin, V., and Matsuyama, S. S. Human aggression and the extra Y chromosome: Fact or fantasy? *American Psychologist*, 1973, *29*, 674-682.

Kahn, E. Schizoid and Schizophrenie im Erbgang. *Monographien aus dem Gesamtgebiete der Neurologie und Psychiatrie*, 1923, *36*.

Kallmann, F. J. *The genetics of schizophrenia*. New York: J. J. Augustin, 1938.

Kallmann, F. J., Falek, A., Hurzeler, M., and Erlenmeyer-Kimling, L. The developmental aspects of children with two schizophrenic parents. In P. Solomon and B. C. Glueck (Eds.), *Recent research on schizophrenia*. Washington, D.C.: Psychiatric Research Report No. 19, American Psychiatric Association, 1964.

Karlsson, J. L. *The biological basis of schizophrenia*. Springfield, Ill.: Thomas, 1966.

Kaufman, K., and Hagamen, M. Sagamore Children's Center programs for parents. Sagamore Children's Center, Melville, N.Y. (Unpublished).

Kessler, S., and Moos, R. H. XYY chromosome: Premature conclusions. *Science*, 1969, *165*, 442.

Klawans, H. L., Jr., Paulson, G. W., Ringel, S. P., and Barbeau, A. Use of L-dopa in the detection of presymptomatic Huntington's chorea. *New England Journal of Medicine*, 1971, *186*, 1332-1334.

Kozloff, M. A. *Educating children with learning disabilities*. New York: Wiley, 1974.

Kringlen, E. Children of two psychotic parents. A preliminary report. *Proceedings of the 4th International Symposium on Psychotherapy of Schizophrenia*, Turku, Finland. Amsterdam: Excerpta Medica, 1971.

Larson, C. A., and Nyman, G. E. Phenylketonuria: Mental illness in heterozygotes. *Psychiatria Clinica*, 1968, *1*, 367-374.

Levere, R. D., and Kappas, A. The prophyric diseases of man. *Hospital Practice*, 1970, *5*, 61-74.

Lewis, A. J. The offspring of parents both mentally ill. *Acta Genetica et Statistica Medica*, 1957, 7: 349-365.

Lidz, T. *The origin and treatment of schizophrenic disorders*. New York: Basic Books, 1973.

Mednick, S. A., and Schulsinger, F. Some premorbid characteristics related to breakdown in children with schizophrenic mothers. In D. Rosenthal and S. S. Kety (Eds.), *The transmission of schizophrenia*. New York: Pergamon Press, 1968.

Mendlewicz, J., and Fleiss, J. L. Linkage studies with X-chromosome markers in bipolar (manic-depressive) and unipolar (depressive) illness. *Biological Psychiatry*, 1974, *9*, 261-294.

Mendlewicz, J., and Rainer, J. D. Morbidity risk and genetic transmission in manic-depressive illness. *American Journal of Human Genetics*, 1974, *26*, 692-701.

Michael, C. M., Morris, D. P., and Soroker, E. Follow-up studies of shy, withdrawn children. II: Relative incidence of schizophrenia. *American Journal of Orthopsychiatry*, 1954, *27*, 331-337.

Milunsky, A., Littlefield, J. W., Kanfer, J. N., Kolodny, E. H., Shih, V. E., and Atkins, L. Prenatal genetic diagnosis. *New England Journal of Medicine*, 1970, *283*, 1370-1381, 1441-1447, 1498-1504.

Moskalenko, V. D. A comparative study of families with one and two schizophrenic parents. *Zhurnal Nevropatologii i Psixiatrii*, 1972, *72*, 86-92.

Omenn, G. S. Genetic approaches to the syndrome of minimal brain dysfunction. *Annals of the New York Academy of Sciences*, 1973, *205*, 212-222.

Reed, S. C., Hartley, C., Anderson, V. E., Phillips, V. P., and Johnson, N. A. *The psychoses: Family studies*. Philadelphia: Saunders, 1973.

Reed, T. E., and Chandler, J. H. Huntington's chorea in Michigan. I. Demography and genetics. *American Journal of Human Genetics*, 1958, *10*, 201-225.

Robins, L. N. *Deviant children grown up*. Baltimore: Williams and Wilkins, 1966.

Rosenthal, D. A program of research on heredity in schizophrenia. *Behavioral Science*, 1971, *16*, 191-201.

Rosenthal, D. Three adoption studies of heredity in the schizophrenic disorders. *International Journal of Mental Health*, 1972, *1*, 63-75.

Rüdin, E. Studien über Vererbung und Entstehung geistiger Störungen. I. Zur Vererbung und Neuentstehung der Dementia praecox. *Monographien aus dem Gesamtgebiete der Neurologie und Psychiatrie*, 1916.

Schultz, B. Kinder schizophrener Elternpaare. *Zeitschrift für die Gesamte Neurologie und Psychiatrie*, 1940, *168*, 332.

Slater, E., and Cowie, V. *The genetics of mental disorders*. London: Oxford University Press, 1971.

Thomas, A., Chess, S., and Birch, H. *Temperament and behavior disorders in children*. New York: New York University Press, 1969.

Thompson, J. S., and Thompson, M. W. *Genetics in medicine*. Philadelphia: Saunders, 1973.

Watt, N. Childhood roots of schizophrenia. In D. F. Ricks, A. Thomas, and M. Roff (Eds.), *Life history research in psychopathology* (Vol. 3). Minneapolis: University of Minnesota Press, 1974.

Welch, J. P., Clower, C. G., and Schimke, R. N. The "pink spot" in schizophrenics and its absence in homocystinurics. *British Journal of Psychiatry.* 1969, *115*, 163-167.

Wender, P. H. Some speculations concerning a possible biochemical basis of minimal brain dysfunction. *Annals of the New York Academy of Sciences,* 1973, *205*, 18–28.

Zerbin-Rüdin, E. Endogene Psychosen: Schizophrenien (pp. 446-513). Manisch-depressive Psychosen (pp. 513-544). In P. E. Becker (Ed.), *Humangenetik* (Vol. 2). Stuttgart: Thieme, 1967.

6

Prenatal, Perinatal, and Post-Partum Factors in Primary Prevention of Psychopathology in Offspring

THOMAS F. McNEIL AND LENNART KAIJ*

The topic we are addressing here is primary prevention of psychopathology in offspring based on factors in the mother during pregnancy, delivery, and the postpartum period. We touch upon a variety of areas: general preventive medical systems and lessons from the Swedish system, individuals' needs within the formal system, the particular needs and characteristics of mothers with histories of mental disturbances, and further needs for research on primary prevention. We have based our presentation on published literature, on experiences (our own and others') within the Swedish obstetric-psychiatric-pediatric system, on our series of retrospective studies on psycho-obstetrics and obstetro-psychiatrics,† and our ongoing prospective study of the offspring of psychotic women and never-psychotic control women.

If the question were asked, "What factor during the pregnancy-postpartum period has most often been shown to be associated with subsequent psychopathology in the offspring?" the best answer would probably be, "obstetric complications" (OCs). The series of studies by Pasamanick and Knobloch (1961) led to their positing a continuum of reproductive casualty extending from death through varying degrees of neuropsychiatric disability. OCs were found to be related to subsequent cerebral palsy, epilepsy, tics, mental deficiency, behavior disorders, and reading disabilities.

*Our research has received support from NIMH Grant No. 18857, Grant No. 3793 from the Swedish Medical Research Council, and the Grant Foundation Inc. We wish to thank the following people for their help in providing information for this presentation: Lennart Jacobson, Ylva Laurell-Borulf, Bengt Bjerre, Signe Jansson, Iris Hugoson, Bertha Katz, and Lars Svanberg.

†By the term *obstetro-psychiatrics* we mean the study of the effects of obstetric factors on the mental (psychiatric) condition of the offspring and mother.

Other researchers have provided evidence for the association between OCs and epilepsy (Churchill, 1959, 1966), cerebral palsy and spastic paraplegia (Plum, 1956, 1962), and broader ranges of mental or behavioral disorders (McNeil et al., 1970; Pollack, 1967). A number of studies have found positive OC histories for schizophrenics (Bender and Faretra, 1961; Gittelman and Birch, 1967), especially as compared with their normal siblings (Vorster, 1960; Whittam et al., 1966), with their nonschizophrenic monozygotic twins (Pollin et al., 1966), with matched controls and siblings (Taft and Goldfarb, 1964), and with neurotic children (Osterkamp and Sands, 1962). Other studies show high OC rates in the histories of autistic children (Kanner, 1957; Keeler, 1957; Knobloch and Pasamanick, 1962). Not all empirical studies have found positive OC histories for mentally disturbed samples (Terris et al., 1964; Pasamanick et al., 1956; Eisenberg and Kanner, 1956; Lotter, 1967; Rimland, 1964; Schain and Yannet, 1960), but the general conclusion may be drawn that an important factor in primary prevention of psychopathology is the prevention of OCs. The presentation and evaluation of an existing system for primary prevention of OCs is thus relevant.

Furthermore, existing systems for primary prevention is obstetrics have considerable value as models for early attempts at primary prevention of psychopathology. Obstetrics has made considerable progress even in prevention of conditions (e.g. toxemia) whose etiology is not necessarily fully understood (Page, 1972; Brody, 1970); and primary prevention of psychopathology will often have to contend with a similar uncertainty about etiological factors. In addition, existing systems provide lessons regarding the behavior of both patients and staff within a preventive system. Reproduction is a topic of great emotional loading—as is psychopathology—and human response to medical systems regarding primary prevention within obstetrics may give some clues to anticipated human response regarding primary prevention of psychopathology.

SWEDISH PRENATAL AND CHILD HEALTH CARE SYSTEM
(Socialstyrelsen, 1970)

The Swedish system for health care of women during pregnancy and postpartum and of children from birth to school age has been established by law since 1937. The system has broadened over time: approximately 80 percent of all pregnant women were covered in the beginning of the 1960's, compared with 95 to 98 percent since 1970. The purpose is "to prevent, through both physical and mental health care, the development of diseases and disturbances in mothers and children" (p. 5). All examination and care related to the system during this period are free of charge, as is delivery and postpartum care at the obstetric departments. Participation is voluntary; but, though both outpatient prenatal and pediatric examinations are available from a number of private physicians (in many regions), the vast majority of pregnancies and children are cared for through the standardized system.

Prenatal and OB System

All deliveries are performed at the centralized hospitals. Prenatal care is given through the Prenatal Clinics (PNCs), which are associated either with the hospitals (in large cities) or with district physicians (in smaller cities and the countryside). The pregnant woman's entry into the system is very simple: she calls the clinic on the telephone and makes an appointment. Her primary contact with the PNC is through highly trained midwives (RNs) or, in some cases, district RNs with special training in prenatal care. The scheduled prenatal care for normal cases includes three examinations by a physician: usually once in the third month, once after quickening (fifth month), and once in the eighth month. From quickening through the eighth month, examinations by midwives are conducted every other week at the PNC, and, from the eighth month until delivery, once a week. Thus, for the normal pregnancy the mother is examined approximately 15 times at the PNC.

Women fitting into the established risk categories, as described below, or showing other complications are referred to specialists in OB/GYN. Hospitalization is suggested currently for a broad spectrum of risk cases: multiple pregnancies, toxemias, premature labors, bleeding, and so on. The extent of hospitalization varies in different areas, but in Malmö (population 250,000, with about 3,000 deliveries per year) approximately half of all beds in OB are occupied by nonterm pregnant women (B. Bjerre, personal communication, 1975). This means that more than 10 percent of all pregnant women are prophylactically hospitalized at some time during pregnancy (L. Jacobson, personal communication, 1975). The policy concerning legal abortion has been liberal in Sweden since the early 1960's. But since January 1975 a pregnant woman has been given the sole right, through the eighteenth week of pregnancy, to decide whether she will have an abortion. Prior to the thirteenth week, only a physician's examination is required, and from the thirteenth through the eighteenth week consultation with a social worker is an additional requirement. (Legal abortions after the eighteenth week are approved only by the governing medical board and only on grounds of serious physical or mental illness.) All legal abortions are free of charge.

By law, parent education classes are made available, taught by midwives, covering information about pregnancies, deliveries, and fetal development and including preparatory physical exercises. In recent years, methods of psychoprophylaxis (Lamaze, 1956) have been taught in many areas.

All deliveries take place at centralized hospitals. Normal deliveries are performed by midwives. Complicated cases are handled jointly by the midwives and the physician on duty at the delivery department. Strong emphasis is placed on natural delivery; in 1974, for example, 84.4 percent of the deliveries at Malmö General Hospital were vaginal noninstrumental deliveries. The remainder consisted of 6.6 percent by Caesarean section, 8 percent by vacuum extraction, and 1 percent by forceps.

The pediatrician or physician on duty is called to attend any delivery where problems are anticipated in the neonate (as with premature births, Caesarean sections, or ablatio placentae); and the physician is, of course, available when such additional problems as respiratory difficulties are encountered. The newer hospitals have placed infant intensive care units contiguous to the delivery departments. About 7 percent of newborns are transferred to the pediatric department for care or observation, 5.5 percent of these being premature.

The mother and baby typically remain at the delivery department until two hours postpartum, and are then transferred to the puerperal ward, where the usual stay is four to six days before discharge home. A number of rooming-in, self-care puerperal units are available at many hospitals and are very popular among mothers, especially I-parae. Pediatric examinations of the baby are typically conducted on the first day after birth and on the day of discharge, with additional examinations if problems arise during the stay at the puerperal unit.

Given the extensive schedule of examinations for all pregnant women, not every woman can be examined by obstetric "specialists."* The following 20 criteria have been established to provide guidelines for choosing obstetric risk groups to receive specialist care: (1) 35-year-old or older O-para; (2) woman with more than 8 years since last delivery; (3) woman with 4 or more deliveries; (4) woman with previous child with birthweight more than 4,500 grams; (5) woman with history of involuntary infertility or repeated miscarriages; (6) woman with history of complicated pregnancy or delivery (premature infant, stillbirth, toxicosis, Caesarean section, etc.); (7) multiple pregnancy; (8) breech presentation after thirty-fourth week of pregnancy; (9) woman undelivered by 14 days after expected term; (10) contracted pelvis; (11) Rh-immunization; (12) chronic medical disease (diabetes, circulatory illness, kidney disease, etc.); (13) uterine or vaginal malformation; (14) toxicosis (at least one among proteinuria, noteworthy oedema or quick weight gain, and blood pressure more than 140/90); (15) bleeding during pregnancy; (16) previous bleeding or coagulation disturbance; (17) hydramniosis; (18) abnormal fetal position; (19) anemia of $\leq$ 10 g percent (65 percent) which is unresponsive to iron supplement; (20) other conditions: allergies, suspected drug effects on the fetus, large discrepancy between fetal development and length of pregnancy, notably poor psychosocial conditions, unusual attitude toward delivery, and so on.

Our contact with obstetricians and midwives has led to the following observations regarding these obstetric risk criteria and their use.

(a) In practice, these 20 criteria are supplemented by other risk-group criteria, for example premature labor; and criteria indicating fetal risk, such as growth retardation and signs of placental insufficiency, are increasingly used.

(b) The 20 criteria are effective in identifying women with higher somatic risk; few other categories could be suggested, and some might well be modified or further restricted.

*All pregnant women are examined by physicians who may be general practitioners in the smaller towns and countryside or not yet specialized physicians working in the departments of obstetrics in the centralized hospitals.

(c) The criteria should be used as a preliminary screening device to identify women needing further evaluation on an individual level. "Once at risk" defined by a general criterion is not necessarily "always at risk," and a comparable formal system may be needed for removing individuals from risk groups.

(d) The designation "at somatic risk" in terms of the 20 categories places a relatively large proportion of mothers at risk; estimates of this proportion range from about 20 to 40 percent, and the more extensive the screening, the higher the proportion of mothers found to be at risk.

(e) The designation "at risk" according to the 20 categories calls for varying degrees of intervention. For example, category 9, "post-term pregnancy," usually results in initiation of labor. Other categories, for example 1 through 5, generally call for increased observation of the woman during pregnancy and at delivery. Being "at risk" does not necessarily call for intervention but rather for further observation and evaluation.

(f) The twentieth category, which provides the possibility of defining risk in terms of psychosocial or psychic conditions, is very seldom used as compared with the other nineteen. In our opinion, women deserving special consideration during the pregnancy-postpartum period are very young mothers, those without a stable relationship with the biological father, those with an abnormally strong fear of the delivery, those with a history of serious mental disturbance (as discussed below), those with an openly negative or ambivalent attitude toward the pregnancy, and especially those who desired an abortion but were unable or unwilling to obtain it. Some data suggest that these groups have an increased risk for OCs (Brody, 1970) and for widespread disturbance in the offspring (see Forssman and Thuwe, 1966, regarding the offspring of women refused an abortion), but further systematic study is needed regarding the risk-increasing properties of psychological and social situations surrounding this period. The steps taken to help women defined as risk cases on these bases need, of course, to be appropriate to the existing problems, which may be of a completely different nature from those embodied in the somatic risk criteria.

(g) The specialists who care for women designated as "at somatic risk" do not feel that labeling the mother as at risk has caused any problems for the women; most women either are unaware that they are in a special risk group or seem to appreciate the extra care and attention they receive.

Well-Baby Clinics

Upon birth of the child, the Well-Baby Clinic covering the residential area of the child is automatically informed of the birth and engaged in the care of the child. A personal relationship is established between the parents (mother) and the pediatric nurse in the district where the parents live. The nurse visits the home on a number of occasions to become familiar with the baby's home environment and give advice and support to the parents. Health check-ups for the baby are performed by a pediatrician a recommended four to seven times during the first year of life, twice during the second year, and once per year thereafter up to seven years of age, when school health services take over responsibility for health care of the child. The parents have 24-hour reference service through the emergency services of the pediatric departments. The Well-Baby Clinics have regular telephone hours for advice and consultation regarding the child and its care. The health system described here concerns normal cases; sick babies are not brought to the Well-Baby Clinics. The identification of health problems requiring treatment leads to referral of the mother or infant to the relevant facility—the department for obstetrics, pediatrics, ENT, child psychiatry, or whatever is appropriate. The system described can thus be considered to represent routine attempts to identify incipient problems or situations and take steps against the problems before they become worse; and it thus has the essential characteristic of a structure for primary prevention of illness and disturbance.

LESSONS OF THE SYSTEM

The Swedish prenatal system described above provides a good opportunity to make the following observations about standardized systems and people's responses to them.

(a) The system is extensively used. Between 95 and 99 percent of all pregnant women receive prenatal care. All women come to the delivery departments for births. On a nationwide basis, at least 95 percent of all children are taken to the Well-Baby Clinics during the first year of life and 85 percent continue with the scheduled health check-ups during the second year of life (A. Baude, personal communication, 1975).

(b) The system is both expensive and inexpensive. The prenatal clinic in Malmö cost $325,000 (1.3 million kronor) in 1974, which gives an approximate per-pregnancy cost of $110—quite inexpensive considering the large number of examinations. The cost of the Well-Baby Clinic in Malmö in 1974 was $1,150,000 (4.6 million kronor); again, this is reasonably inexpensive considering the service for approximately 18,000 children up to seven years of age (about $65 per child per year). On the other hand, prophylactic hospitalization of nonterm pregnant women was used extensively in Malmö and cost about $1.5 million (6 million kronor) for 1974, or more than the cost of the prenatal and Well-Baby Clinics combined.

(c) In terms of perinatal mortality,* the system is among the best in the world (Brody, 1970). The mortality figures in Malmö for 1974 were 1.06 percent. Perinatal mortality statistics are obviously not the only relevant measure of the effectiveness of the system, and primary preventive systems that take such mortality as the ultimate criterion may unintentionally cause a great number of psychological and social problems (see below regarding twins).

(d) Since participation is voluntary, the very relevant question may be raised whether those who most need help are those who use the services of the system. Whereas at least 95 percent of all pregnant women receive somatic prenatal care, acceptance of other services offered appears to be more selective. By law, mothers who should be given the most attention in parent education classes are the young and the unmarried. Roughly 50 percent of all women registered at the PNC in Malmö in 1974 chose to attend parent education classes (I. Hugoson, personal communication, 1975). The women who do not take advantage of the classes are to a large extent the very ones who need the most help—the young, the poorly informed, and foreigners (S. Jansson, personal communication, 1975).

(e) The production-line approach to prenatal care has functioned

---

*Perinatal mortality is here defined as fetal-neonatal death from the twenty-ninth week of gestation through the first seven days after birth.

reasonably well in providing a large amount of somatic screening for all pregnant women. At the same time, the experience has led both patients and medical staff to desire smaller, decentralized units with the opportunity for more personal contact between patient and staff, such as is possible in the small countryside units. In the large city clinics, the psychological needs of the patients (and staff) have often not been met by the production-line approach, and as a result a number of helpful changes have been made in the necessary compromise between cost, amount of contact, and quality of personal contact. In Malmö, mothers have been assigned to a given midwife so that there is continuity of contact, however brief, on each occasion. A social worker assigned as a permanent staff member at the prenatal clinic is a helpful reference person for mothers with social and psychological problems and need for additional personal contact. Thus, providing adequate somatic examination and care for the vast majority of pregnant women may be the first goal in the primary prevention of OCs, but this needs to be supplemented at some level by opportunities for meaningful personal contact.

(f) The effects of preventive measures need to be viewed in their totality. In Malmö, for example, prophylactic hospitalization for all women with multiple pregnancies is standard practice from the thirtieth through the thirty-sixth week of pregnancy, the gestational period bearing the highest risk for premature births with nonsurviving fetuses. With a twin frequency of one per 80 births, this means that in about 37 cases a year the policy results in a guaranteed six-week separation of the woman from her family, often including small children.* Estimates of the number of twin infants saved in Malmö range from 1 to 5 per year; as yet, no systematic evaluation has been done of the psychological and intrafamilial consequences of this separation. And multiple pregnancy is only one of the indications for such extensive hospitalization. Cases have been seen where marginal marital adjustments have been ruined by the separation; where the woman and her family cannot cope economically or practically with the separation; and where the woman's psychological balance has

*It should be noted that the mother is not completely isolated from her family during this period; she has opportunities for living at home on the weekends and receiving frequent family visits (including small children) at the OB department.

been seriously (if temporarily) endangered by guilt feelings about her family and by the experience of being in a monotonous hospital environment concentrated solely on her preganancy. Perinatal mortality figures are definitely thought to be served by extensive prophylactic hospitalization, but the total costs and benefits to the families have not yet been weighed.

(g) The broad use of nondoctor medical personnel has allowed a preventive system that would be entirely impossible if doctors alone were to conduct prenatal examinations and check-ups and deliver babies. About four midwives can be hired for the cost of one obstetrician; this provides considerable economic savings, since 80 to 90 percent of all deliveries are conducted by midwives, as are 80 percent of the scheduled prenatal examinations.

(h) Use of the psychoprophylactic method (PPM) can make an important contribution to prevention of OCs and postpartum problems. Systematic studies of the effects of PPM (Enkin et al., 1972; Huttel et al., 1972) suggest that PPM is associated with reduced use of medications during labor and delivery, less operative intervention, more favorable parental experience of labor and delivery, and less maternal depression postpartum. The studies also stress the very helpful effect of the father during the labor and delivery. The preliminary results of a Swedish study (Jansson et al., 1975) support the earlier findings. PPM can be effective both on a somatic basis and on a psychological level as a supportive part of the labor-delivery program. Given that PPM is effective in reducing OCs, important topics for primary prevention of OCs are the questions of why certain parents cannot effectively use PPM in spite of considerable advance practice, how these parents can be identified during pregnancy, and what kind of extra help or intervention may allow them to profit from PPM during labor-delivery.

(i) Effective primary prevention of psychopathology on a large scale is likely to require some type of primary screening of individuals regarding risk characteristics (psychologic, somatic, social) associated with higher risk for psychopathology. This primary screening would probably have to be done by teachers, nurses, and social workers rather than by psychiatrists or psychologists. The extent of systematization and thoroughness of such screening is undoubtedly going to vary from area to area; but both primary screening and effective management of incipient problems require theoretical and practical knowledge of psychopathology, of the criteria to be used for identifying risk cases, and of the potential benefits of primary prevention.

Lack of education and understanding can easily frustrate all attempts at primary prevention (a) by a resulting increase rather than decrease in the dangers to the individual through such screening and (b) by the inability and/or unwillingness to identify the relevant conditions or problems. Taking examples from the prenatal-postpartum period, a history of mental disturbance for the mother can lead delivery personnel, because of their own fear of mental illness, to overmedicate the mother during labor and/or to terminate the delivery as quickly as possible through medical or operative intervention. In some cases such practices may be justified, but the decision should be made after careful consideration of the mother's and fetus' current condition and should not be based solely upon her mental history (sometimes rather ancient history). To cite another example, psychologically enlightened delivery personnel feel emphatically that they could profit from knowing which mothers have an unusually strong fear of the delivery, so that they could be aware of the mothers' need for extra support and consideration; the information should be contained in the medical record that is sent in advance from the prenatal clinic to the delivery department. But the midwives at the prenatal clinics are generally unwilling to "mark" a mother by writing anything in the record about her fears or psychological condition. Our experience is that if a mother communicates fears and apprehension to the personnel at the PNC, she is seeking help and is not opposed to the delivery midwife's knowing about her fears and giving extra help. Thus, the potentially effective use of a preventive system may be frustrated as a consequence of unwillingness to record important psychological conditions.

Similar examples may be taken from the puerperal wards. We have received reports that some women cry all day long for several days and that the personnel ignore it or dismiss attempts to call it to their attention, saying, "Everyone feels a little blue the first days after delivery." We have observed other mothers with clear perceptions of changed sex ("I feel like a man") and with the highly unusual behavior of walking all night with the baby in her arms; when we asked whether the mother might need special help, the response was that "the mother is just a little tired."

Such inability or unwillingness to recognize problems not only hinders effective care of mothers and infants during this period, but will hinder effective primary prevention when such prevention is theoretically possible. Education of professional workers and society in general must be given very high priority by those interested in promoting primary prevention.

(j) We may learn something about difficulties of primary prevention by considering the rate of success in preventing unwanted pregnancies—an easily diagnosed somatic condition with known etiology and highly developed methods for primary prevention. Sweden, by contrast with other countries, has had a very liberal attitude toward disseminating sexual information and education; contraceptives are available everywhere and are even free in certain areas. As a result, one might expect to find an effective birth control rate. The real figures, however, suggest that primary prevention of unwanted pregnancies is not very successful. In Malmö in 1974, for the roughly 3,000 births and 300 spontaneous abortions, 1,200 legal abortions took place; thus, 1,200 (26.6 percent) among 4,500 identified pregnancies were terminated deliberately. A recent prospective study by Nilsson (1970) in Lund showed that of 151 women who did not terminate their pregnancy, 39.4 percent reported during pregnancy that the pregnancy was not desired and 57.3 percent said it was not actively planned. These figures accord with an earlier study by Nilsson et al. (1967) showing 30 percent with undesired pregnancies, as reported postpartum. Thus a general estimation of the rate of unwanted and intentionally terminated pregnancies is 65 percent. This should lead us to consider the difficulties of preventing psychopathology, where the causes are less well known and most probably multifactorial and the particular measures are less specific or available.* It is well to remember in this context that real progress has been made in primary prevention (for example, the control of cholera and typhoid fever) through societal and political implementation

---

*One is tempted to imagine a future where one can buy a "contra-psychotic" from a vending machine for 25 cents or get an IHD (Intra-Head Device) fitted by the family physician. The question would still remain whether people who apparently wished to avoid mental disturbance would actually use the preventive measures as inefficiently as they currently use contraceptives.

of preventive procedures and not by the mere development of appropriate techniques and procedures.

SPECIAL CONSIDERATIONS REGARDING WOMEN WITH HISTORIES OF SERIOUS MENTAL DISTURBANCES

We wish to share a number of ideas and observations regarding reproduction among women who have had psychoses or other serious mental disturbances. The topics discussed are: (1) criteria for designating such women as obstetric risk cases, to receive extra care during reproduction; and (2) problems associated with postpartum mental disturbances.

Criteria for Designating Women as Obstetric Risk Cases

Should women with a history of serious mental disturbance be considered obstetric risk cases and receive extra somatic care or attention during pregnancy and birth? We can find four different bases upon which such women might be categorized as at obstetric risk.

Criterion I: If They Have Increased Rates of OCs. Since premorbid identification of future mental patients is, as yet, impossible within the context of OB systems, the relevent question concerns whether women already identified as having (had) serious mental disturbance have increased rates of OCs during subsequent reproductions. A great many data exist regarding OCs in all reproductions for mental patients, but few exist comparing reproductions of already identified patients as against reproductions of controls. We therefore review the three types of empirical studies which bear relevance to this criterion.

i. Comparison of controls vs. all reproductions of patients. Studies including reproductions both before and after onset of illness show complex results, with some studies of schizophrenics and other psychotics showing significantly increased rates of OCs (Sameroff and Zax, 1973; Paffenbarger et al., 1961; Wiedorn, 1954; Mura, Mednick, Schulsinger, and Mednick, 1973; Mednick and Schulsinger, 1968), while others show none (Mizrahi Mirdal, Mednick, Schulsinger, and Fuchs, 1974; Mednick et al., 1971;

Soichet, 1959; McNeil and Kaij, 1973a, 1974). Sameroff and Zax (1973) found increased rates of OCs in reproductions of neurotically depressed women. Our own study (McNeil and Kaij, 1974) of all hospitalized female patients showed no significant increase in OCs for all patients or any diagnostic group. The results of these studies thus provide no uniform answer. Even different studies by the same authors on the same diagnostic groups (for example, Mednick and Schulsinger, 1968, compared with Mednick et al., 1971) or on subgroups of the same sample (for example, Mizrahi Mirdal, Mednick, Schulsinger, and Fuchs, 1974, compared with Mednick and Schulsinger, 1968) show different results. Within the context of the clinical question raised here, it must be remembered that findings based on all reproductions may be unrepresentative for reproductions after onset of illness (of interest here), especially since some diagnostic groups—process schizophrenics, for example—appear to have proportionally few reproductions after onset.

   ii. Within-group comparisons of patients before vs. after illness onset. One position recently taken (Mednick and Lanoil, 1975; Mednick, 1975) is that schizophrenics have more OCs in reproductions before, as contrasted with after, onset of illness. A close look at the studies that have presented within-group comparisons shows that currently available results are very complex and contradictory. Wiedorn (1954), studying samples with almost unparalleled rates of toxemia (from 22.2 percent for controls up to 83.3 percent for O-parae schizophrenics), found significantly higher rates of toxemia for schizophrenics before, as contrasted with after, the first psychotic episode. (There appears to be no basis in this study for comparison to the other studies cited in terms of obstetric background and psychiatric diagnostic practices.) Mednick, Mura, Schulsinger, and Mednick (1971, p. S110) found that although "character disorder" mothers showed more pregnancy and delivery complications after than before onset of illness, schizophrenic mothers showed more pregnancy complications before than after onset of illness (data unpublished, statistical significance unstated). In contrast, the original Mednick-Schulsinger schizophrenic sample, as studied by Mizrahi Mirdal, Mednick, Schulsinger, and Fuchs (1974), showed no significant difference in mean OC score, mean severity of OCs, or mean number of OCs before as against after onset of illness.

Our own research showed similar complexity of results among different OC variables. We found significantly more prenatal developmental deviations in reproductions *before* than after first psychiatric hospitalization for endogenous psychotics (McNeil and Kaij, 1974) and for process schizophrenics (McNeil and Kaij, 1973a) but significantly more neonatal disturbances *after* first hospitalization for both endogenous psychotics and all psychiatric patients (McNeil and Kaij, 1974). Schizophrenic-like psychotics, as a specific diagnostic group, showed significantly more birth complications and neonatal disturbances plus a trend toward more pregnancy complications *after* first hospitalization (McNeil and Kaij, 1973a). Age- and parity-matched controls did not show the same significant results in our study, thus hindering simplified explanations of the above results.

Within the clinical perspective of the current question, it must be noted that within-group comparisons of type "before vs. after onset" do not necessarily indicate the absolute magnitude of OCs after onset nor their relevance for disturbance in the offspring. Existing differences of a before-after-onset nature, whether statistically significant or not, may be of little clinical importance. To take one example, Mizrahi Mirdal et al. (1974) stated that there was a tendency toward more complicated births in the birth-before-breakdown group, but there may be little clinical relevance in an average of 0.23 points more severe OCs in births before illness onset. OCs exist in abundance for reproductions during all life periods in the studies cited, and clinical efforts should be aimed at reducing these.

iii. Direct comparison of controls vs. patients in reproductions after illness onset. Sameroff and Zax (1973) found that small samples of both schizophrenic and neurotically depressed mothers had significantly more OCs than did controls. Schachter (according to Garmezy, 1974) found significantly more birth complications for 23 schizophrenic women as contrasted with controls; no significant differences were found between the groups in pregnancy complications or offspring birthweights. A number of current prospective studies, including our own, should in the future provide more data regarding this specific comparison, which is most relevant to the question raised here. Data existing now appear contradictory, but the safest conclusion (from a clinical point of view) is perhaps that enough studies have shown significantly increased OC rates to justify considering such women as "at somewhat increased risk for OCs."

Criterion II: If OCs Associated with Such Reproductions Are Especially Damaging to the Fetus. The theoretical position underlying this criterion is that an OC of a given type and degree may have varying effects on different fetuses, and that fetuses of psychotic mothers may have selective sensitivity to OCs. For example, in the Mednick-Schulsinger study (Mednick and Schulsinger, 1974, p. 110) of the offspring of schizophrenic and normal mothers, OCs were found to be significantly associated with short latency of the galvanic skin response (GSR) in the schizophrenics' offspring but not in control offspring. These data suggest an interaction between genetic risk and OCs, while other data from the same study suggest an additive effect (for example, on GSR amplitude) of genetic risk and OCs. These findings are very interesting, but far more data are needed, and independent replication of the results should be awaited before drawing extensive theoretical conclusions.

Criterion III: If the Mother and the Family Are Not in a Good Position to Accept and Support a Perinatally Damaged or Preterm Infant. A perinatally damaged or premature baby can be a considerable stress for even the most adequate, trouble-free family. The integration of the baby into the family is hindered by premature birth, which results in at least some separation of the baby from the family. In families already having to contend with current or threatened recurrent mental disturbance in the mother, all steps should be taken to reduce problems in the offspring. Furthermore, although most parents tend to blame themselves for reproductive problems and failures, the mother who needs psychopharmacological drugs during pregnancy and at delivery and is aware of their potentially harmful effect on the fetus (as are almost all Swedish mothers) is put in a special conflict between her own needs and those of the baby; this conflict increases her guilt feelings when something goes wrong with the reproduction.

Reversing the argument, one can say that the perinatally damaged or preterm infant may not be in a good position to enter a disturbed family. A study by Drillien (1964) showed that prematurity appeared to render children more vulnerable to the effects of family stress and difficulty, thus resulting in increased

108 Thomas F. McNeil and Lennart Kaij

behavioral disturbance in the children. Even in the absence of genetic risk for disturbance, children entering families with a psychotic parent should be provided as good a start as possible.

Criterion IV: If the Mother Is Psychologically (or Somatically) Less Able to Withstand the Effects of OCs With our focus upon the effects of OCs on the fetus-infant, we must bear in mind that OCs often mean the mother is sick or at least very concerned about the course of the pregnancy or delivery. Many OCs and the resulting treatment procedures are stressing, irritating, frightening, tiring, or depressing, not to mention endangering to the mother's general somatic health. Preventing OCs is advisable for the mother's own well-being, which is presumably relevant to the prevention of psychopathology in the offspring.

In combination, these four criteria suggest that women with histories of serious mental disturbances should receive fully adequate (extra, that is, if what is usual would fall short) somatic examination and consideration during pregnancy and delivery. Although the scientific evidence that would define these women as "at obstetric risk" is still ambiguous, such extra care may be indicated on the basis of the general "at risk" situation surrounding the women and the offspring.

Certain practical considerations should be mentioned in association with extra care for such women.

(i) Judging from the difficulty of finding large samples for research, treating these women as obstetric risk cases is not going to place an enormous burden on prenatal care resources.

(ii) How is one to identify the women needing this extra service? In one of our retrospective studies (McNeil and Kaij, 1973b), about 50 percent of women who had been psychiatrically hospitalized withheld this information from the medical history given to the prenatal clinic. If further research provides more sophisticated criteria for judging which disturbance histories (diagnostic type and severity, for example) indicate real obstetric risk and which do not, the question of obtaining relevant anamnestic information becomes even more pressing.

(iii) We must consider the effects of labeling a pregnant woman in this way. We have seen many cases of entirely normal maternal behavior which were interpreted as abnormal because the medical

personnel were aware of the mother's previous mental disturbance. Also important is the effect on the patient's self-perception.
A number of women with whom we have had contact have been
hesitant to accept extra benefits—however attractive—that they
feel identify them as deviant or unusual. Furthermore, many are
reluctant to have any contact with medical personnel, and their
attendance at the regular prenatal examinations is irregular. If such
women are to accept extra care, they must be convinced of its
importance; and this, in turn, raises the possibility that telling a
woman she or her offspring is at risk will actually increase the risk.

(iv) Many of the patient's problems uncovered in the process of
considering a history of mental illness as an OB risk criterion are
not somatic but psychological, intrafamilial, economic, or the like.
Facilities are needed for dealing with these problems, but our
experience from Sweden suggests they are not typically available
within routine prenatal and obstetric systems. Identifying problems
without having the capacity to deal with them may be frustrating
for both patients and personnel.

Problems Associated with Postpartum Mental Disturbances

As mothers are well aware, the postpartum period carries an
increased risk for maternal mental disturbance of varying degree.
Women with psychosis histories have often had mental disturbances associated with previous reproductions, and fear of
recurrent psychosis is well founded: whereas the general population
risk for postpartum psychosis is about 1 per 1,000 reproductions,
the risk is about 1 in 7 reproductions for women with a previous
postpartum psychosis and 1 in 4 for those with previous psychosis
both postpartum and in other life periods (Arentsen, 1966;
Kaij and Nilsson, 1972).

Many mothers with previous psychotic episodes are afraid not
only of recurrent disturbance but also of being separated from
the baby and thus missing a period which is of great importance
to them. Separation of mother and baby for any reason during
the early period is problematic for the relationship; but where
the cause is mental illness, the mother is at a special disadvantage
on two counts. The disturbance itself interferes with the emotional
relationship; and she feels guilty because she cannot take care of
the baby. Many of our subjects with postpartum psychoses have

expressed the feeling of irreparable loss. They feel inadequate as mothers and say they "never got off on the right foot" with the child. Where relatives are able to care for the baby, the mother is spared having it placed in an institution, but she still must live with her own maternal inadequacy. She feels the baby is not really hers. Well-intentioned relatives who rush in to take over the care of the baby—leaving the cleaning and household chores to the mother—reinforce these feelings. Our own bias is toward separating mothers and babies as little as possible: hospitalizing the baby with the mother, supporting the mother substantially in the home, and intruding as little as possible on the mother-baby relationship.

Fear of recurrent mental disturbance in the mother is also a serious concern for the father. If the mother must be absent, he is responsible for her, for himself, and for the baby. And if he cannot cope with the baby and must place it temporarily in an institution, both he and the mother can develop feelings of guilt and failure. We have seen a number of postpartum disturbances in fathers which may be related to this problem of paternal adequacy, and the threat of mental disturbance in the mother exacerbates the problem.

The important question arises whether to initiate discussion of the topic with expectant parents who have histories of mental illness and what to tell them about postpartum risk. Should the same principles apply at all periods—before pregnancy, during the early weeks when legal abortion is possible, and after the legal abortion period is past? Some practical examples may help to illustrate difficulties.

One of our subjects with a previous postpartum psychosis consulted her psychiatrist before she became pregnant about her chances of becoming ill again. According to her, the psychiatrist assured her she would not get sick again, and so the pregnancy was initiated. But after delivery, she did become seriously depressed and was hospitalized for four months, while her baby was cared for in an institution. At our most recent contact, she and the baby were at home but she was unable to cope with anything beyond feeding the child.

Another of our subjects had lost custody of a child during divorce proceedings on grounds of her mental illness; and in a new marriage she became pregnant in order to replace her lost baby.

The psychiatrist told her early in pregnancy that whether or not she would be allowed to keep the new baby depended upon whether or not she remained mentally healthy postpartum. By the time of our contact with her during pregnancy, she was extremely paranoid toward the researcher and broke down with our project midwife because of the tremendous pressure to stay healthy.

In contrast, another subject had developed a "catastrophe plan" with her family, relatives, and neighbors in the event she became ill again; she had also received assurance from the psychiatric clinic that she was welcome if she needed help. As a result, she was unusually calm about the possibility of becoming ill again. This example strongly suggests that a realistic approach to coping with the practical difficulties of recurrent disturbance may contribute to the mother's mental health during pregnancy and postpartum.

IDEAS REGARDING RESEARCH RELATED TO PRIMARY PREVENTION

Careful, methodologically sound research on the effects of preventive or interventive efforts must be given high priority. Much of the work we have seen is done unsystematically and with some apparent resistance toward evaluating the effects of the prevention. Unless the work is evaluated, important side effects will be missed, resistance toward all prevention will increase, and costs will be extended beyond what is necessary for the most effective elements within generalized preventive efforts. Control groups are of great importance, both for obtaining evidence of possibly positive effects and for guarding against the spurious apparent increases in deviation that result from increased evaluation for mental deviation. Effective primary prevention makes good financial sense, but we need sound evidence that it *is* effective if we are to compete against current, manifest problems to obtain funds for prevention of events or conditions which after all are not certain—only highly probable.

In the service of effective primary prevention, research needs to develop adequate scoring and interpretation systems for risk-identifying characteristics and events. Even the type of risk characteristics obtained from such fascinating studies as Pollin and

Stabenau's (1968) compilation of characteristics of monozygotic twins discordant for schizophrenia begin to pale in the face of contact with subjects in prospective studies. In our current prospective study of high- and low-genetic risk children, few subjects—including controls—go through the pregnancy-birth-neonatal sequence without showing some event or characteristic that would have been highly interesting if seen retrospectively in a schizophrenic patient. The more complete the data, the more critical the problem of adequate scoring, weighting, and interpretation. Multivariate studies are crucial both because they tend to reflect better the complexity of reality and because they provide the possibility of finding combinations of characteristics and factors which enable us to identify groups needing primary prevention.

REFERENCES

Arentsen, K. *Om psykoser opstået efter fødsler med saerligt henblick på prognosen* (On psychoses beginning after childbirth with special consideration of prognosis). Odense: Andelsbogtrykkereit, 1966.

Bender, L., and Faretra, G. Pregnancy and birth histories of children with psychiatric problems. *Proceedings of the Third World Congress of Psychiatry*, 1961, *2*, 1329-1333.

Brody, S. *Obstetrik och gynekologi*. Stockholm: Almqvist and Wiksell, 1970.

Churchill, J. A. The relationship of epilepsy to breech delivery. *Electroencephalography and Clinical Neurophysiology*, 1959, *11*, 1-12.

Churchill, J. A. On the origin of focal motor epilepsy. *Neurology*, 1966, *16*, 49-58.

Drillien, C. M. *The growth and development of the prematurely born infant*. Edinburgh: Livingstone, 1964.

Eisenberg, L., and Kanner, L. Early infantile autism, 1943-55. *American Journal of Orthopsychiatry*, 1956, *26*, 555-565.

Enkin, M. W., Smith, S. L., Dermer, S. W., and Emmett, J. O. An adequately controlled study of the effectiveness of PPM training. In *Psychosomatic medicine in obstetrics and gynaecology*. Basel: Karger, 1972.

Forssman, H., and Thuwe, I. One hundred and twenty children born after application for therapeutic abortion refused. *Acta Psychiatrica Scandinavica*, 1966, *42*, 71-88.

Garmezy, N. Children at risk: The search for antecedents of schizophrenia. Part II. Ongoing research programs, issues, and intervention. *Schizophrenia Bulletin*, 1974, No. 9, pp. 55-125.

Gittelman, M., and Birch, H. G. Childhood schizophrenia: Intellectual, neurological status, perinatal risk, prognosis, family pathology. *Archives of General Psychiatry*, 1967, *17*, 16-25.

Huttel, F. A., Mitchell, I., Fischer, W. M., and Meyer, A. E. A quantitative evaluation of psychoprophylaxis in childbirth. *Journal of Psychosomatic Research*, 1972, *16*, 81-92.

Jansson, S., Kask-Esperi, I., and Kaij, L. Effekten av den psykoprofylaktiska metoden (PPM) vid förlossningen (Effect of the psychoprophylactic method of delivery). Preliminary manuscript, 1975.

Kaij, L., and Nilsson, Å. Emotional and psychotic illness following childbirth. In J. G. Howells (Ed.), *Modern perspectives in psycho-obstetrics*. Edinburgh: Oliver and Boyd, 1972.

Kanner, L. *Child psychiatry*. Springfield, Ill.: Thomas, 1957.

Keeler, W. R. Discussion of paper presented by L. Kanner. *Psychiatric Research Reports of American Psychiatric Association*, 1957, *7*, 66-88.

Knobloch, H., and Pasamanick, B. Etiologic factors in "early infantile autism" and "childhood schizophrenia." Paper presented at the Tenth International Congress of Pediatrics, Lisbon, Portugal, 1962.

Lamaze, F. Introduction au dernier stage. *Encyclopedie medico-chirugicale*. Paris, 1956.

Lotter, V. Epidemiology of the autistic condition in young children: II. Some characteristics of the parents and children. *Social Psychiatry*, 1967, *1*, 163-173.

McNeil, T. F., and Kaij, L. Obstetric complications and physical size of off-spring of schizophrenic, schizophrenic-like, and control mothers. *British Journal of Psychiatry*, 1973, *123*, 341-348. (a)

McNeil, T. F., and Kaij, L. Obstetric notations of mental or behavioral disturbance. *Journal of Psychosomatic Research*, 1973, *17*, 175-188. (b)

McNeil, T. F., and Kaij, L. Reproduction among female mental patients: Obstetric complications and physical size of offspring. *Acta Psychiatrica Scandinavica*, 1974, *50*, 3-15.

McNeil, T. F., Wiegerink, R., and Dozier, J. E. Pregnancy and birth complications in the births of seriously, moderately, and mildly behaviorally disturbed children. *Journal of Nervous and Mental Disease*, 1970, *151*, 24-34.

Mednick, S. Discussion. WHO Conference on Primary Prevention of Schizophrenia in High-Risk Groups, Copenhagen, 1975.

Mednick, S. A., and Lanoil, G. W. Efforts at prevention in high-risk children. First Vermont Conference on Primary Prevention of Psychopathology, Vermont, 1975.

Mednick, S. A., Mura, E., Schulsinger, F., and Mednick, B. Perinatal conditions and infant development in children with schizophrenic parents. *Social Biology*, 1971, *18*, Supplement, 103-113.

Mednick, S. A., and Schulsinger, F. Some premorbid characteristics related to breakdown in children with schizophrenic mothers. In D. Rosenthal and S. S. Kety (Eds.), *The transmission of schizophrenia*. London: Pergamon Press, 1968.

Mednick, S. A., and Schulsinger, F. Studies of children at high risk for schizophrenia. In S. Mednick et al. (Eds.), *Genetics, environment and psychopathology*. Amsterdam: North-Holland, 1974.

Mizrahi Mirdal, G. K., Mednick, S. A., Schulsinger, F., and Fuchs, F. Perinatal complications in children of schizophrenic mothers. *Acta Psychiatrica Scandinavica*, 1974, *50*, 553-568.

Mura, E., Mednick, S. A., Schulsinger, F., and Mednick, B. Erratum and further analysis. Perinatal conditions and infant development in children with schizophrenic parents. Manuscript, 1973.

Nilsson, Å. Paranatal emotional adjustment. A prospective investigation of 165 women. Part I. *Acta Psychiatrica Scandinavica*, 1970, Supplement 220.

Nilsson, Å., Kaij, H. L., and Jacobson, L. Postpartum mental disorder in an unselected sample. IV. The importance of the unplanned pregnancy. *Journal of Psychosomatic Research*, 1967, *10*, 341-347.

Osterkamp, A., and Sands, D. J. Early feeding and birth difficulties in childhood schizophrenia: A brief study. *Journal of Genetic Psychology*, 1962, *101*, 363-366.

Paffenbarger, R. S., Steinmetz, C. H., Pooler, B. G., and Hyde, R. T. The picture puzzle of the postpartum psychoses. *Journal of Chronic Diseases*, 1961, *13*, 161-173.

Page, E. W. On the pathogenesis of pre-eclampsia and eclampsia. *Journal of Obstetrics and Gynaecology of British Commonwealth*, 1972, *79*, 883-894.

Pasamanick, B., Constantinou, F. K., and Lilienfeld, A. M. Pregnancy experience and the development of childhood speech disorders: An epidemiologic study of the association with maternal and fetal factors. *American Journal of Diseases of Children*, 1956, *91*, 113-118.

Pasamanick, B., and Knobloch, H. Epidemiologic studies on the complications of pregnancy and the birth process. In G. Caplan (Ed.), *Prevention of mental disorders in children*. New York: Basic Books, 1961.

Plum, P. Cerebral palsy: A clinical survey of 543 cases. *Danish Medical Bulletin*, 1956, *3*, 99-108.

Plum, P. Early diagnosis of spastic paraplegia. *Spastic Quarterly*, 1962, *11*, 4-11.

Pollack, M. Early "minimal brain damage" and the development of severe psychopathology in adolescence. *American Journal of Orthopsychiatry*, 1967, *37*, 213-214.

Pollin, W., and Stabenau, J. R. Biological, psychological and historical differences in a series of monozygotic twins discordant for schizophrenia. In D. Rosenthal and S. S. Kety (Eds.), *The transmission of schizophrenia*. London: Pergamon Press, 1968.

Pollin, W., Stabenau, J. R., Mosher, L., and Tupin, J. Life history differences in identical twins discordant for schizophrenia. *American Journal of Orthopsychiatry*, 1966, *36*, 492-509.

Rimland, B. *Infantile autism*. New York: Appleton-Century-Crofts, 1964.

Sameroff, A. J., and Zax, M. Perinatal characteristics of the offspring of schizophrenic women. *Journal of Nervous and Mental Disease*, 1973, *157*, 191-199.

Schain, R. G., and Yannet, H. Infantile autism. *Journal of Pediatrics*, 1960, *57*, 560-567.

Socialstyrelsen. *Normalreglemente för mödra- och barnhälsovården* (Regulations for prenatal and child health care). Stockholm: Kungl. Boktryckeriet, 1970.

Soichet, S. Emotional factors in toxemia of pregnancy. *American Journal of Obstetrics and Gynecology*, 1959, *77*, 1065-1073.

Taft, L., and Goldfarb, W. Prenatal and perinatal factors in childhood schizophrenia. *Developmental Medicine and Child Neurology*, 1964, *6*, 32-34.

Terris, M., LaPouse, R., and Monk, M. The relation of prematurity and previous fetal loss to childhood schizophrenia. *American Journal of Psychiatry*, 1964, *121*, 475-481.

Vorster, D. An investigation of the part played by organic factors in childhood schizophrenia. *Journal of Mental Science*, 1960, *106*, 494-522.

Wittam, H., Simon, G. B., and Mittler, P. J. The early development of psychotic children and their sibs. *Developmental Medicine and Child Neurology*, 1966, *8*, 552-560.
Wiedorn, W. S. Toxemia of pregnancy and schizophrenia. *Journal of Nervous and Mental Disease*, 1954, *120*, 1-9.

III
Identifying High Risk Children and Adolescents and Intervening for Primary Prevention

Introductory Notes

This third section includes a series of papers dealing with high risk children and adolescents and reporting on attempts at intervention with them.

Jon E. Rolf and Joseph E. Hasazi are both faculty members in psychology at the University of Vermont. Their paper reports on current research projects with high risk children in a small, relatively rural state.

A paper by Sarnoff A. Mednick and Georgia Hope Witkin-Lanoil, with a similar focus, follows. Professor Mednick is Director of the Psykologisk Institute, Kommune Hospital, in Copenhagen and professor of psychology at the New School for Social Research in New York. Georgia Hope Witkin-Lanoil is on the faculty of Westchester Community College. Because Professor Mednick was out of the country at the time of the conference, Professor Witkin-Lanoil read the paper and led a spirited discussion of this whole area of intervention. In addition to discussing some of Mednick's findings and observations based on more than fifteen years of research in this area, the paper contains the first preliminary discussions of a new project Mednick is conducting in Mauritius, a densely populated island country in the Indian Ocean.

E. James Anthony is currently the Blanche Ittleson Professor of Child Psychiatry and Director of the William Greenleaf Elliot Division of Child Psychiatry at the Washington University School of Medicine. He is active as a training, teaching, and supervising analyst of the Chicago Institute of Psychoanalysis and is consultant to numerous hospitals. He is one of the most widely known research child psychiatrists and is a member of the Board of the Foundation Fund for Research in Psychiatry; he chairs the Child Psychiatry Section of the Group for the Advancement of Psychiatry;

and he has received a lengthy series of awards for his work in the field of psychiatry. Dr. Anthony is widely recognized for his efforts at intervention with the high-risk children of psychotic parents. In this paper, reporting on a clinical study that attempts various intervention efforts with disturbed children and their families, he has tried to bring order into an exceedingly complex area. He recognizes the methodological shortcomings of such clinical research but suggests some intriguing findings and prepares the way for further, more carefully controlled studies.

Thomas Gordon is President of Effectiveness Training Associates in Pasadena, California. One of the early group of students trained by Carl Rogers, Dr. Gordon has written a popular and widely respected book on parent effectiveness training that has had a national impact. His organization trains people to train others to be effective parents; this clearly places Dr. Gordon in the area of primary prevention. Here, he discusses candidly how he has been able to build a national organization which has reached over a million parents with a 24-hour training program designed to improve their parenting skills.

Dr. Marie Skodak Crissey was a leading member of the group of young researchers to come out of the University of Iowa in the 1930's. She got her Ph.D. in developmental psychology there in 1938. For many years she was Director of the Division of Psychological Services in the schools of Dearborn, Michigan, and was a lecturer at the University of Michigan. She received the Joseph F. Kennedy, Jr., award for research in Mental Retardation in 1968 and the Distinguished Service Award of the Division of School Psychology of the APA in 1972. A past president of the APA Division of Consulting Psychology and Division of Mental Retardation, she is now enjoying a working semi-retirement while consulting and lecturing throughout the world.

Her paper elicited a large amount of discussion and enthusiasm at the conference. In it she reports her dramatic findings on the effects of stimulating environments on children who, to all appearances, would otherwise have been doomed to a life of serious mental retardation.

7

Identification of Preschool Children
at Risk and Some Guidelines
for Primary Intervention

JON E. ROLF AND JOSEPH E. HASAZI

INTRODUCTION

The purpose of this chapter is to describe the Vermont Child Development Project (VCDP) and to present it as an example of applied research investigating the etiology of behavior disorders in early childhood. The long-range goals of the project have been to increase our understanding of the multiple causes of these disorders and to test several early intervention procedures which some day may prove useful for purposes of primary prevention of psychopathology. In planning the project, we have attempted to justify these remote and perhaps elusive long-range goals by applying research strategies that should have shorter term payoffs. These strategies include epidemiology, intervention, and follow-along studies of very young children at risk for behavior problems.

This chapter describes the rationale, the epidemiological survey methods, the intervention procedures, and the means of identifying children at varying degrees of risk. A sampling of the descriptive data about the structure and the incidence and prevalence of developmentally determined psychopathology is also presented. Finally, the cultural and institutional impediments we have encountered in the past two years are reported so that those who wish to travel similar research paths may be forewarned and thus forearmed.

The Theoretical and Practical Origins of the VCDP

If one attempts a logical approach to research intended to test the feasibility of primary prevention of behavior disorders among children, the first proposition one must face is that there can be no intentional prevention without identifying various types of children who may be considered at high risk. Second, there can be no identification program without first defining the concepts of vulnerability and risk for psychopathology. These concepts in turn depend both upon empirically observed probabilities of disorder and upon theoretical formulations about the etiological mechanisms underlying the psychological disorders. If one looks at the historical roots of early identification and intervention, one is struck by the confusion between theoretical assumptions and empirical data in developmental psychopathology.

Theories hoping to identify and explain the etiology of behavior disorders in children have usually focused on either the crucial importance of experience or the constitutional vulerability of certain genotypes. Rarely have theories attempted to integrate the environmental and behavior genetic theories—especially rarely when the intended target is the vulnerable young children in the community. There has, however, been a notable shift in the attitudes and dogma in the field of developmental psychopathology. This probably reflects a recognition that it is futile to create straw men, dressed in either behavior genetic or environmental risk cloaks, for the sole purpose of embarrassing scientific and professional champions from the opposing camps. There appears instead to be an awakening and an acknowledgment of the legitimacy of a multitude of theoretical positions based on data which have come from the general area of life history research in psychopathology and the prospective high risk sample method in particular.

Predicting the Outcome and Life History Research

Persons interested in the etiology of psychopathology have attempted to prove various theories empirically by obtaining data on the life histories of the psychologically disordered. The healthy competition for such empirical proofs soon brought into question many typically applied research methods. The clinical retrospective method, for example—which had been the most convenient, if least rigorously scientific—was put out to pasture as being suitable for generating hypotheses but otherwise inappropriate as a strategy for empirical validation of theoretically based predictions. Studies achieved higher status if they could cite long-term facts: follow-up data on the outcome of disordered and normal youngsters, or follow-back data on already disordered adults obtained from records kept on premorbid childhood adjustment. As the quality of follow-up and follow-back research studies improved, the list of life history variables with recognized etiological significance began to grow rapidly. Today, the list is a very formidable one, for it includes variables from both constitutional and experiential aspects as well as their interactions. A representative outline of them is presented in Table 1, showing etiological factors that must be considered when one attempts to develop and demonstrate primary prevention programs.

As the list of sources and indicators of risk for young children increased, it became more difficult to find control subjects who, when matched retrospectively, had the same intensity of risk as the target children. The obvious solution to this (and other sources of uncontrolled error variance) was to adopt a prospective research design in which children with different degrees of identified risk were followed in their development, so that the emergence, course, and duration of psychopathology could be measured concurrently. Children with similar degrees of baseline risk could serve as reciprocal controls for each other because not all of the cohorts, in all probability, would be judged as disturbed at any one time.

A superb review of this prospective research strategy has been written by Garmezy (1974), with particular attention to the etiology of schizophrenia. The high risk sample prospective-research strategy has in fact had its most thorough application with children believed to be at genetic and/or environmental risk for schizophrenic outcome in adulthood. Studies of these children began to yield short-term information on the development of childhood psychopathology in general. It was this more immediate payoff that led Garmezy (1971) to discuss the implications of the concept of vulnerability among children for research in primary prevention; it also prompted Rolf and Harig (1974) to present the rationale for including primary intervention procedures in etiological prospective research projects on children at risk. There are more differences than semantic ones between the terms "prevention" and "intervention" as applied to these projects. Early intervention remains a less ambitious concept than primary prevention, and it is a more definable and more compelling need as one follows the course of breakdown among vulnerable children in a research project's high risk sample.

Table 1

Sources and Indicators of Risk for Young Children

I.   PRESENCE OF PHYSICAL OR MENTAL DISABILITY
a. Record of PBC's and Unspecified Brain Dysfunction
b. Report of Sensory or Motor Handicaps
c. Report of Intellectual Retardation
d. Report of Abnormal Temperament

II. DEMONSTRATION OF DEVELOPMENTAL LAG
a. Failure to Acquire Milestones within Normal Age Range
b. Failure to Abandon Immature Behavior Patterns

III. CURRENT PROBLEMS IN SOCIAL BEHAVIOR
a. Clients of Child Care Professionals
b. Non-Clinic Disturbed Children (Discovered Through Epidemiological Survey)
c. Children Failing to Cope Successfully Within Elementary School

IV. "PATHOGENIC POTENTIAL" IN FAMILY BACK-GROUND
a. Genetic High Risk for Psychopathology
b. Psychopathology in One or Both Parents
c. Absence of Adequate Competence Promoting Parenting Skills

V.   PATHOGENIC FACTORS IN PHYSICAL ENVIRONMENT
a. Greater Exposure to Physical Injury, Malnutrition, and/or Severe Illness
b. Living Within Severely Impoverished Socioeconomic Strata
c. Acculturation within Deviant Subcultural Neighborhoods and/or Schools

THE VERMONT CHILD DEVELOPMENT PROJECT

As a result of this reasoning, the Vermont Child Development Project was initiated. Its purpose was to put into effect the theory of early intervention studies, to parallel a prospective high risk sample research project.

It is not a simple matter to describe the project concisely, for its scope ranges widely. It has been attempting to maximize the usefulness of data collected by joining the strategies used in two different types of studies: epidemiological surveys in natural settings, and developmental psychology studies of group differences among preschool-aged children in natural and laboratory settings. To do this, it has employed within-subject, cross-sectional, and prospective research designs. Thus, unlike most laboratory or developmental studies, it has studied target groups of children who are known or inferred to be at risk. In addition, it has attempted to determine the base rates of behavior disorders in the preschool-age child population of the general community, to provide a background against which to compare the relative competence of target children at varying degrees of risk.

The scope of the project grew from our opinion that adequate research in the etiology, the intervention, and ultimately the prevention of behavior disorders in young children must be based on the following considerations.

1. More information is needed on the development and duration of behavior pathology in children before one can assess the relevance of childhood antecedents to adolescent or adult psychopathology.

2. The best strategy to accomplish this goal is to do prospective studies of target children with known disorders or inferred vulnerabilities.

3. The most vulnerable children—according to current risk studies, follow-up studies, and behavior genetic work—are (a) children with deviant parents, especially those with schizophrenic or other types of psychotic parents; (b) children with chronic unsocialized aggressive behavior disorders; (c) children with severe social, cultural, economic, and nutritional deprivations in their environments; and (d) children with physical, temperamental, or intellectual handicaps.

4. Questions concerning the etiology of specific behavior

disorders cannot be answered unless there is regular close observation and measurement of vulnerable and nonvulnerable children during their early years when rapid social, intellectual, and physical maturation is to be expected.

5. Long-term prospective studies cannot be successfully completed unless one chooses a geographical area having a sufficiently representative but nonmobile population.

6. Close observation of children who experience significant degrees of disorganization and psychological distress cannot ethically be sustained unless vigorous and legitimate attempts are made at therapeutic intervention.

7. One should not undertake such an intervention and service research program unless one has access to an already operating and funded day care center or equivalent intervention setting.

8. Intervention programs cannot be assessed unless they are compared with parallel epidemiological surveys, covering a sufficient number of target and control children all of whom could not be offered treatment for early signs of behavior disorder (whether because of the community's limited intervention resources or because of their parents' lack of motivation to seek treatment for them).

The current project, then, was conceived and implemented with the belief that it could contribute significantly to primary prevention of behavior disorders in children at some future time. In order to avoid the magical thinking and speaking found in many research efforts purporting to demonstrate the effective of primary preventive interventions, we have attempted to divide our research products into two groups. The first involves the hoped-for long-term goals of primary prevention strategies, while the second speaks to the more realistic issues of short-term data produced from our research surveys and interventions.

The Goals of the VCDP

The long-term and perhaps ultimately elusive goals of the current project are to put into proper developmental perspective (1) the emergence and incidence of competent behavior and symptoms of behavior pathology in preschool-age children; (2) the response of children with behavior disorders to therapeutic intervention or to no treatment at all; (3) the relationship of preschool-age competence measures to the school-related variables of social and academic abilities; and (4) the relationship of empirically determined patterns of preschool and early elementary school incompetence to the relatively better defined precursor signs of serious adult psychopathology.

To achieve the long-term goals, the project for the past few years has set the following short-term goals: (1) to collect epidemiological data on the prevalence, incidence, and severity of behavior disorders in preschool-age children; (2) to collect empirical data on the children's success in attaining age-appropriate competence skills in their physical, social, and intellectual development as related to their family background and socioeconomic status; (3) to describe the development of children from certain target groups of vulnerable children (those with psychotic and neurotic parents; those from severely deprived backgrounds; those with recognized serious behavior disorders; and those with physical, temperamental, or mental handicaps); (4) to create a risk-profiling system for identifying preschool-age children at risk, for early preventive intervention; (5) to develop effective and intensive therapeutic day care intervention techniques in treating behavior disorders with already disturbed preschool-age children; and (6) to quantify the effects of a preschool child's experience in home care or day care settings as they relate to his adaptation to public schools in terms of academic and social competence criteria.

The Structure of the Project

To attain the goals described above, four major VCDP components were created. (1) An *epidemiological surveys* section samples a cross-section of preschool-age children living in one county in Vermont. The survey has a repeated-measures design, using the Vermont Behavior Checklist and Family Background Information Form to discover the incidence, prevalence, and duration of both competent and disordered behavior of preschool-age children who spend their days in their homes and/or in day care settings. (2) A *controlled high risk family studies* section examines the social, intellectual, and pre-academic work competence of several groups of vulnerable children as they relate to their parents' personality and family structure. (3) An *intervention studies* section tests the effectiveness of therapeutic day care

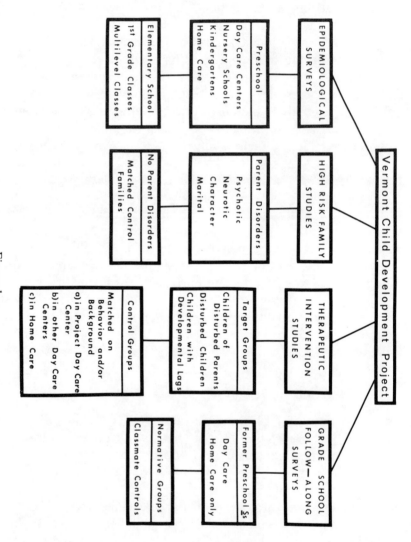

Figure 1

experience for already disturbed or vulnerable children. And (4) an elementary school *follow-along survey* section studies the academic and social competence in school-age children in order to provide normative data and follow our preschool-age sample. The structure of the project is displayed in Figure 1.

THE WHO, WHAT, WHY, AND HOW OF OUR INTERVENTION PROGRAMS

We now turn our attention to a detailed discussion of the Vermont Child Development Project's intervention strategies and their relationships with the current epidemiological surveys. Persons interested in obtaining information on the other aspects of the project are referred to Rolf and Hasazi (1973–1976), Klemchuck, Rolf, and Hasazi (1975), and Miller (1975).

Why Intervention? The Epidemiology of Risk or the Necessity of Intervention

Clinicians working with disturbed preschool-age children have been handicapped by a lack of empirical information concerning normal preschoolers. Without information on the incidence, prevalence, and severity of their problem behaviors, it is not possible to develop accurate diagnostic classification systems for young children, to select the most vulnerable from the large number of children presenting problems to their parents, or to make accurate predictions about symptom remission with or without therapeutic intervention. The diagnostic criteria for determining symptomatic behavior in adults has not proved appropriate for children. In fact, the difficulties in validly defining behavior disorders actually increase as the age of the target population decreases until the reliability of pathology criteria reach their most ambiguous and ephemeral status—at the preschool-age level.

The classifications of preschool children's behavior disorders currently in the clinical literature are handicapped by two sources of sampling error. First, parents are less inclined to bring a very young child to a clinic for diagnosis of, or treatment for, a problem behavior; they believe (often correctly) that the child will outgrow it. Second, unlike older children who are screened by teachers and guidance officers in public schools, those preschool-age children with serious and chronic deviant behaviors will not be referred by a concerned nonrelative for psychological evaluation. Consequently, estimates of the incidence and prevalence of behavior disorders among preschool-age children are based solely on data drawn from retrospective record searches on a very limited number of clinic cases. Extrapolating from the frequency of the symptoms written in these clinic records to expected rates in the general population of preschoolers would be scientifically unsound.

Recently published studies (Kohn and Rosman, 1972; Behar and Springfield, 1974) have not only successfully sampled large groups of children in day care centers but have also applied factor analytic techniques to the obtained teacher-rating data in order to determine empirically syndromes of behavior disorders in early childhood. These studies are important in that they demonstrate the existence among preschoolers of two major factors which have already been consistently identified among symptomatic behaviors of older children: externalizing (unsocialized-aggressive) behavior and internalizing (socially withdrawing) behavior. They have not, however, reported the incidence, prevalence, and severity of these symptomatic behaviors in day care or home care settings. In contrast, the VCDP has gathered these data as a function of sex and of day care or home care experience, and by source of rating (teacher or parent). The data (Rolf and Hakola, 1976) have not only proved useful for basic epidemiological purposes but have also provided a background against which one can measure the effectiveness of our intervention programs. In the latter case, curves showing both the rates of acquisition of developmental skills and the rates of abandonment of behavior problems can be compared between intervention subjects and no-treatment controls drawn from our large-scale surveys.

The Concept of Early Intervention

The project has been attempting to assess the therapeutic effectiveness of two related types of intervention strategies. On the one hand, we are assessing the impact of day care and nursery school experiences in general on various samples of children considered at risk for behavior disorders, as compared to control children who remain in their homes. On the other hand, we are specifically defining, developing, and assessing the therapeutic effectiveness of specialized day care intervention programs for a selected subsample of already disordered preschool-age children. The concept of early intervention has a theoretical history dating back at least to 1949 with the publication of D. O. Hebb's book *The Organization of Behavior*. As a result of Hebb's work, the relationship of early environmental stimulation to behavioral development became the subject of considerable experimental interest in the decade following its publication. The implications of this research for child development theory and practice were presented in J. McV. Hunt's (1961) book *Intelligence and Experience*, which in turn served as impetus for such broad-scale early intervention programs of the 1960's as Head Start.

Most early intervention programs have been concerned primarily with cognitive development. In general, the rationale for these earlier interventions has been the assumption that preschool-age children who failed to develop adequate social and emotional skills are very likely to be the same ones who lose "learning time" by failing to adapt early to the elementary school routines. Closely associated with the therapeutic educational viewpoint is Albee's (1967) strongly voiced opinion that most emotional disorders are defects in social participation and social interaction. He believes that the origins of these defects are to be found in the first few years of life in the social interaction with significant adults and peers who must interact and cope with the stresses of economically and socially deprived neighborhoods. Thus, the appropriate intervention would be to provide these children with "enriched environments" and more adequate social models of behavior. Indeed, it has been the intention of most federally funded day care and Head Start programs to provide such an intervention environment.

Therapeutic Day Care and Primary Prevention

The concept of a nursery school or day care center specifically designed for therapeutic intervention is not a new one, but because available funding, supportive cultural context, and sufficiently trained staff have not been adequate, it has rarely been implemented. The therapeutic day care center typically employs traditional day care programs with the addition of certain therapeutic modifications. The teacher's or therapist's task is to shape the child's behavior from self-centered, unsocialized, aggressive, or dependent behavior toward more acceptable patterns of social interaction. As might be expected, there has been no concensus of what type of intervention has proved most successful with emotionally disturbed children in general. While the major thrust of one center's programs may have a particular theoretical bias, it seems that a combination of various methods has generally proven to be most useful in working with disturbed preschool-age children.

Perhaps the most compelling argument for intervention with children considered to be at high risk for more serious psychopathology is that such early interventions may be both therapeutic and prophylactic. The argument has been articulated by Garmezy (1971):

> *The questions for study are these—can we adapt such methods (for example, behavior modification) for use with our high risk children? Can we use our schools and clinics as centers for training the children in more effective ways of coping? Can we use participation in successful play to increase the flexibility of response repertoires of these children?*

The questions raised by Garmezy are those to which our early intervention program has been addressed.

The Vermont Child Development Project has chosen a somewhat atheoretical approach in order to assess—as objectively and in as controlled a manner as possible—the relative contributions made by day care programs in general and by the specific, individualized therapeutic interventions to the ultimate acquisition of social competence among children selected for intervention. We have selected children from several high risk groups and are investigating the effects of varying levels of intervention on selected aspects of social, cognitive, and behavioral development. The experimental protocol we have devised includes naturalistic and manipulative strategies, large numbers of children, and a variety of outcome measures. The remainder of this report is divided into sections in which key aspects of the study are described in detail. We discuss first the relationship between our epidemiological survey and the intervention program, and then the specific intervention protocol.

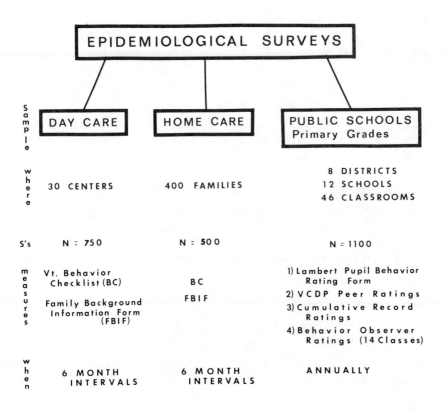

Figure 2

THE INTERVENTION PROGRAM

VCDP Epidemiological Surveys

Figure 2 presents the structure of the surveys for the preschool and grade school surveys. The families of approximately 750 children drawn from 30 day care centers have given written consent for their children's participation in our project. For each of these children, we have at least one 1 20-item Family Background Information Form (FBIF) and one or more 90-item Vermont Behavior Checklists (VBC), which have been administered at roughly six-month intervals. In addition, the home care sample now includes children from about 500 families randomly selected from school census records, birth records, and town clerk residence directories. These families have also provided written consent and have completed the FBIF's and VBC's. During the past year, for all day care center children, VBC's have been completed by both the parents and the children's classroom teachers on a similar schedule (N = 300 dual-rated children).

The VBC asks the rater to check the frequency with which a child was observed to emit specific cognitive, perceptual, language, motor, and social behaviors. Scaling varies from three points (for motor skills, for example) to seven points (for example, for social behavior). The overall reliability of the VBC was indicated by the exact concordance rates of .76 between teachers, .79 between teacher and day care parent, and .86 within teacher for a test-retest interval of two weeks.

To provide feedback to day care teacher and parent raters, as well as to track the progress of our intervention subjects, we have drawn up what we call a developmental profile program, which analyzes and presents normative data on development for any sample or selected reference group of children. Individual behavior checklist items, rationally determined clusters of items, and factors of items (derived from verimax rotations) have all been used to produce age by sex group means for any specific time and for mean changes over time. This profile program permits both cross-sectional and longitudinal examinations of the developmental data and thus also permits both between- and within-subject comparisons.

The developmental program is obviously a very valuable tool for

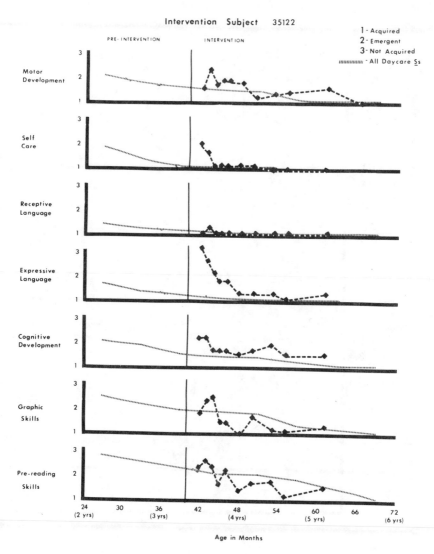

DEVELOPMENTAL PROGRESS

Intervention Subject   35122

1 - Acquired
2 - Emergent
3 - Not Acquired
⎯⎯ - All Daycare Ss

Figure 3

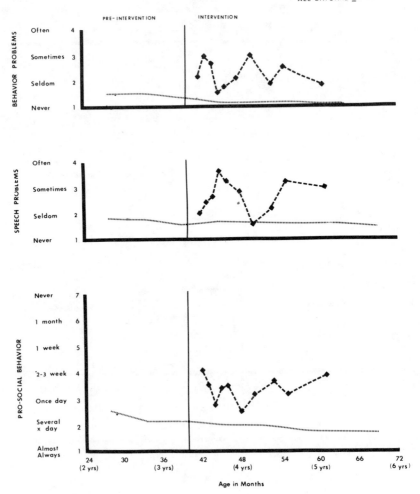

Figure 4

our intervention program. The stage of development of any intervention subject at any time can be compared to that of controls (drawn from our epidemiological surveys) who have been statistically matched on significant family background variables and/or to any relevant baseline behaviors. Thus we can plot changes in our intervention subjects over time and compare the changes to those of the controls or to any cross-sectional reference group of children. A variation on this program has permitted us to begin calculating the duration of problematic behaviors for any single child or any group of children.

Figures 3 and 4 provide examples of how normative cross-sectional data can be used to present and contrast the developmental progress of a specific child in our intervention program. The figures show the developmental progress of one intervention subject as compared to that of day care children in general. The checklist items have been divided into rational categories (motor development, self care, and so on) which are detailed in Table 2. Note that as age in months ascends, the curves tend toward 1, the point at which the skills are rated as "acquired" and become visible on a daily basis.

A brief review of this case should provide a better context in which to interpret the figures. The child (subject 35122) was referred for intervention by a social service agency after an investigation of possible abuse and/or neglect. Both of his parents have been institutionalized for emotional disorders, and in addition the father has been imprisoned for over a year. The child was three-and-a-half years old at the time of the referral, but social skills were typical of children half that age, toileting and self-care skills were absent, and language was almost nonexistent. Given the urgency this case represented, intervention was begun immediately. (This explains the absence of pre-intervention data in the graphs.) The child's difficulties in the self-care and expressive language areas are clearly reflected in the initial data points for these dimensions in Figure 3. It can also be seen in this figure that the child has made significant progress in these and other key developmental areas over his first eighteen months in the project. A comparison of his performance to the dotted line representing those of day care children in general reveals that at age five (one-and-a-half years after the start of therapeutic interventions) he is performing at or close to his age level in all areas. His initial difficulties in socialization are most clearly seen in Figure 4. The presence of speech problems, which is also clear in this figure, is not inconsistent with the data of Figure 3, since this category takes into account articulation and other speech dimensions that the earlier categories did not. Unlike the performances seen in Figure 3, two things are apparent in Figure 4. First, it is clear that the child significantly deviates from the typical performance of other children of the same age. Second, his performance is marked by significant variability. We believe this variability reflects the serious episodic family crises and the chronic attendance problems we have encountered with this child. His mother is heavily self-medicated and has had repeated difficulty awakening early enough to consistently get the child to the Center. Given his erratic attendance pattern, it is not surprising that socialization areas have been the most seriously affected. After trying in a number of ways to overcome the chronic attendance problem, we have finally resorted to hiring his day care teacher to phone the subject and his brother (also in the intervention program) early in the morning and also to pick them up and bring them to the Center.

Forgetting for the moment the nature of intervention with this child, Figures 3 and 4 both demonstrate the way in which the project makes use of developmental profiles as an ongoing evaluative device. The graphic procedure illustrated has as its major advantage the representation of the child's performance against the context of what is typical of other day care children at each age level.

Other comparisons with an intervention subject—or any child—also incorporate factor scores that have been empirically determined for 2, 3, 4, and 5-year-old subjects in our sample. These scores are based on factor analyses that have been compiled for all age levels. We have tentatively labeled the factors as (I) Basic Cognitive and Perceptual-Motor Skills; (II) Basic Motor and Self-Care Skills; (III) Externalizing Symptoms; (IV) Communications Skills; and (V) Internalizing Symptoms. As one might expect, the factor loadings for each age level differ; so the factor score loadings have been determined for each age level separately. It is also significant that the internalizing and externalizing factors are present for all age levels and represent an important downward extension of these empirically determined behavioral syndromes, which have been observed in school-age clinic samples by Achenbach (1966) and others.

Table 2
Rational Categories and Primary Factor Loadings* of the Vermont Behavior Checklist Items

Basic Cognitive and Perceptual Motor Skills	Basic Motor and Self-Care Skills	Externalizing Behaviors	Communication Skills/ Problems	Internalizing Behaviors	Rational Categories
I	II	III	IV	V	
					CATEGORY: MOTOR DEVELOPMENT
	+				—Can walk
					—Can run well without falling or bumping into things
					—Walks up and down steps alone one foot to a step
					—Can skip
					—Can balance on one foot
					—Can pick up small objects with thumb and forefingers
					—Can use scissors
					—Can catch ball against body
					—Can catch ball with hands only
					CATEGORY: SELF-CARE BEHAVIORS
	+				—Feeds self without help
					—Dresses self partially with help
	+				—Dresses self fully without help except for winter wear and shoes
	+				—Goes to the bathroom without help
					CATEGORY: RECEPTIVE LANGUAGE
			+		—Understands two-step directions
					—Understands directional concepts (in–out, up–down)
			+		—Knows own name when spoken
					CATEGORY: EXPRESSIVE LANGUAGE
			+		—Communicates what he wants by putting words together
			+		—Speaks so that he is understood even though the words may not be spoken clearly
			+		—Speaks words clearly and distinctly
			+		—Can name objects
					CATEGORY: COGNITIVE DEVELOPMENT
			+		—Can name objects
+					—Knows the names of colors
					—Can match colors
+					—Knows the names of shapes
+					—Can count from one to ten correctly
			+		—Can identify parts of the body
					CATEGORY: GRAPHIC SKILLS
+					—Can copy own first name
+					—Can write own first name without copying
					—Can draw using scribbles and lines
+					—Can draw using recognizable shapes (circles, squares, etc.)
+					—Can draw a partial figure
+					—Can draw a whole figure

*Primary factor loadings greater than .40 for 4- and 5-year olds combined.

Table 2 (continued)

I   II   III   IV   V

CATEGORY: PREREADING SKILLS

I	II	III	IV	V	
+					—Reads pictures (tells about them)
+					—Shows interest in words (through books)
					—Can read
+					—Can answer questions about stories
+					—Can recite alphabet
+					—Recognizes capital letters
+					—Recognizes small letters
+					—Can tell the sounds of the letters
+					—Recognizes own name when written

CATEGORY: BEHAVIOR PROBLEMS

—Wets pants or bed after being considered toilet trained
—Soils self, moves bowels in pants after being toilet trained
—Has a noticeable twitch of face or body, or mannerism
—Masturbates or stimulates self physically
—Seems more intelligent than most other children his or her age

CATEGORY: SPEECH PROBLEMS

I	II	III	IV	V	
	—				—Speech difficulties
					—Hesitates when speaking, involuntarily pauses between words
					—Stutters
					—Chatters, talks a lot, most of it not related to what is going on
	+				—Voice seems louder than the voices of other children
		+			—Voice seems softer than the voices of other children

CATEGORY: HYPERACTIVITY PROBLEMS

I	II	III	IV	V	
					—Loses energy and needs to rest often
	+				—Has overabundance of energy and has trouble being in one place for a period of time
					—Chatters, talks a lot, most of it not related to what is going on

CATEGORY: ORAL BEHAVIOR PROBLEMS

—Eats too little (rejects many foods)
—Eats too much, gorges self with food
—Sucks thumb or fingers
—Vomits
—Feeds self without help
—Bites nails so much that it causes bleeding
—Sucks thumb or fingers so much that it causes pain or bleeding

CATEGORY: PROSOCIAL BEHAVIORS

I	II	III	IV	V	
		—			—Plays and works well with others
					—Plays alone
		—			—Mixes freely with people
					—Refuses affection from other children and adults
			+		—Avoids contact with others; bashful
			+		—Is overly afraid of everyday situations and people
					—Is easily influenced or used by other children and not in his/her own interest
	+				—Misuses other children to his/her advantage in a selfish way
	+				—Struggles or picks fights with another child or adult
	+				—Demands constant adult attention
	+				—Refuses to do things when asked
					—Cries or whines for no apparent physical reason
	+				—Destructive, breaks and throws things on purpose
	+				—Has temper tantrums, outbursts of rage
					—Runs away from home or out of day care center
	+				—Has trouble coping with frustration
	—				—Pays attention to an activity
		+			—Gets upset if daily routine is changed

Table 2 (concluded)

I   II   III   IV   V

+	−Disrupts ongoing activity
	−Initiates activities or play and leads others
−	−Cooperates with others, goes along with another's suggestion in an activity or play

The factor analysis of the behavior checklist items, as well as clustering of the Family Background Information Form data, are steps toward one of the major goals of the project—to develop an empirically derived *risk profile* whereby outcome is predicted from the continuous reciprocal influences of a child's behavior and his environment (taking into account the particular developmental state in which these interactions occur). Having obtained standardized factor scores for each child, we will be able to identify those children who are statistically deviant from their peers on the social behavior variables and on skills variables. These variables, used in conjunction with those from the child's family background, will become the data by which we can begin to examine both the simple and the complex interactions of the hypothesized sources of risk. We will then attempt to determine whether we can reliably predict the later development of, and recovery from, pathological behaviors. For example, initial data on a small sample of children exhibiting externalizing behavior problems indicate that we can predict recovery from these *social* problem behaviors during the preschool years on the basis of the acquisitions of developmental, *nonsocial* skills. Such findings as these would, of course, have significant implications for the development of effective intervention programs.

Selection of Children at Risk

Our primary interests to this point have been in children drawn from the following risk groups.

(a) Children with demonstrated behavioral disturbances, particularly those of an unsocialized aggressive or socially withdrawn sort. So far, we have not had specific behavioral criteria for selecting children who show these characteristics, but have been guided by the pattern of referrals for service we receive as well as by clinical judgment. Now, however, we are in the process of developing specific behavioral risk criteria from the factor analysis of the behavior checklist used in the epidemiological component of the project as described earlier. In the future, children will be selected primarily on the basis of their scores on the Externalizing and Internalizing factors of the checklist.

(b) Children with serious developmental lags. In this category, we have relied primarily upon the Portage Project Checklist as a selection device. Our criteria specify children with developmental delays of at least six months below age level; the majority have shown delays of one year or more.

(c) Children whose parents have experienced significant emotional or behavioral disturbances. At least one parent must have been hospitalized for a psychiatric problem, as evidenced by hospital records of admission and diagnosis.

It should be emphasized that these risk criteria are not mutually exclusive, and it has been our experience that most of the children in the project qualify on the basis of more than one risk index. Consequently, our original experimental design calling for statistical comparisons of the three groups separately has not been attainable. Our high risk children are currently considered partly as a single group but primarily on a within-subject basis.

It seems wise to continue to seek children on the same basis as before; but the fact that some *are* subject to more than one risk index suggests that partitioning them on the basis of factor scores will be a more meaningful procedure. Beyond this, use of factor scores will facilitate including subjects who may be deviant in terms of risk indices but otherwise do not display significant problems in cognitive or social areas.

Measures and Test Schedule

Our selection of dependent variables has been guided in part by tradition and in part by specific project objectives. We take the usual measures of intelligence, social maturity, and the like to provide continuity with the early intervention literature. We also use the following tests, checklists, and behavior rating scales to examine particular areas of development in greater depth.

(a) *Family Background Information Form.*

(b) *Vermont Behavior Checklist.*

(c) *Portage Project Checklist,* which consists of several hundred age-norm items divided into five rational categories: cognitive, language, perceptual-motor, self-help, and social. Items are completed by the child's teacher with a provision for direct testing of questionable items. This measure provides more detailed information in key developmental areas.

(d) *Stanford-Binet Intelligence Scale (L-M).* This measure gives a general index of cognitive development and provides continuity with the many other studies of early intervention which used it as an outcome measure.

(e) *Vineland Social-Maturity Scale,* which measures the child's level of social development as seen by the parent.

(f) *Social Interaction Rating Scale.* This scale measures the child's social behavior in free-play situations. Three general categories of play are observed: solitary, parallel, and cooperative. The scale also records aggressive behavior. Based on a time-sampling procedure, 200 observations of the child's behavior are obtained over a one-week period.

With the exception of the Stanford-Binet Intelligence Scale, which is administered at six-month intervals, all other measures are obtained every three months during a two-week testing period of all target children.

The current data collection system evolved in large part to facilitate the coordination of intervention planning for target children. The data collected for target children are not necessarily taken on all control children. Such measures as the Behavior Checklist, which are the least obtrusive and the most cost-efficient, are used consistently across subjects. Others, such as observations of play, are currently restricted to children within the day-care facility housing the program.

Design of the Experiment

The project is designed to compare high-risk children under three intervention conditions: home care, day care, and enriched day care. The enriched day-care program is the target experimental condition: children in this program—the target children—receive the services routinely provided by the staff of the Ethan Allen Child Care Center, in which they are enrolled, and in addition they are given other therapeutic and remedial services by the project staff. The target children are compared with children under day care or home care none of whom receive additional services from the project staff. Target children are matched with children in the other group by family background and by their rated behavior. Comparisons are then made between the target children and the other children on these three bases: (a) target children versus those matched by family background; (b) target children versus those matched by rated child behavior; and (c) target children versus randomly selected children.

The experimental design has also involved a good deal of within-subject analysis. We have developed the previously mentioned system of profiles based on rational groupings of items obtained from the Behavior Checklists. Each target child's progress in developmental areas is plotted against normative data obtained from the epidemiological survey. One can determine at a glance the progress the child is making in the context of what is typical for other children within the area. This system allows us to evaluate and also to continuously monitor program effectiveness in major developmental areas. In addition, it also provides us with a method for terminating or phasing out services.

Intervention Planning

The intervention program for children in the target group is broadly conceived and involves services to them as well as to their families. Intervention goals are determined individually for each child based on the assessment process described earlier. About a week after a testing period has ended, a staff conference, attended by project staff as well as the child's teachers, is held for each child. All of the test data are reviewed and a series of behavioral objectives for the next three-month period are established. The objectives specify behavioral goals, goal attainment criteria (where appropriate), and the educational-therapeutic plans specific to each.

With the objectives as a frame of reference, intervention can be approached in several ways. First, we determine whether the child will already be routinely receiving some experience which should promote development in a given target area; if so, we merely monitor the child's progress. At this level, we are concerned as much with physical, medical, and nutritional experiences as we are with strictly educational ones.

A second level of intervention involves consulting with the child's classroom teachers to help them deal with particular problem areas. Such help may take the form of suggesting learning activities and materials or developing behavior modification programs for use in the classroom.

A third level of intervention involves referring the child for specialized services, such as speech and language therapy. A fourth level involves direct contact between child and project staff on a one-to-one or small-group basis to facilitate the initial shaping of skills that could not be achieved in another context. For example, several subjects have perceptual motor impairments that cause them to avoid practicing a skill—say, drawing and painting—in the presence of their peers. To smooth the approach to the frustrating task, the child is given the relative privacy of a room remote from his peers.

In general, direct contacts may involve intensive remedial work in key developmental areas. Here we rely heavily on specialized learning materials, instructional devices, and motivational techniques. The focus of direct contacts with the child is on socialization processes. Our approach to socialization has been strongly influenced by work in behavior modification areas; but we have tried to avoid a behavior management emphasis. Instead, we have followed Garmezy's advice to use behavioral technology for fostering coping skills and social-interpersonal development.

The use of behavioral methods is most evident in the small group situation and manifests itself in several ways. Since we consider modeling to be a key aspect of social development, we construct small groups with one target child and one or more children selected for their social competence and their positive history of interactions with the target child. We emphasize natural, social consequences of behavior rather than other types of reinforcers. Group leaders (project staff people) select toys, games, and activities which increase the probability that the target child will have satisfying social interactions, and follow these with consistent positive feedback. Finally, group leaders focus their attention on behaviors of interpersonal significance—assertiveness, expression of feelings, and responses to stress and conflict, for example.

Despite the child-directed emphasis of our programs, the intervention program was designed to include parent participation. When a child enters a program, the parents must agree to meet with project staff at least once a month to discuss his progress and his behavior at home. Some parents have been seen as often as once a week for counseling and support in child-rearing techniques. The staff designed and developed a program of parent education to facilitate parental involvement. Ten weekly meetings were planned and a curriculum was developed based on Adlerian and behavioral child-rearing methods. Success was indifferent. All parents of target children indicated interest in the group, but only one actually attended the first meeting. A few who were particularly motivated have been seen frequently by project staff or referred to other community mental health facilities. But as a whole, the weakest component of the intervention project has been the parent component.

A second brief case history will illustrate our intervention planning process. The child (subject 13472) had been enrolled in the day care center for several months prior to his referral. He was not markedly deficient in key developmental areas, but was still somewhat below age level in self-care, receptive language, and cognitive and graphic skills. The major reasons for referral, however, were concerned more with social behavior; he rarely interacted socially with peers and spent the vast majority of his time with adults. Figures 5 and 6 present the child's progress in key developmental and social areas. Of particular interest is the area of prosocial behavior shown in Figure 6. It can be seen that at the point the intervention began, prosocial behavior was infrequent compared to other children the same age. More than six months elapsed before any significant change was observed; but his progress since then has been rapid. To all intents and purposes, the child is now at a level where we felt that intervention was no longer necessary, and direct services to the child and family have been discontinued.

The effective intervention components for this child are impossible to determine on a post hoc basis. Since he was enrolled in day care in the pre-intervention period, it is unlikely that this experience alone produced the observed results; in fact, the child was referred by the day care staff because the child had begun to

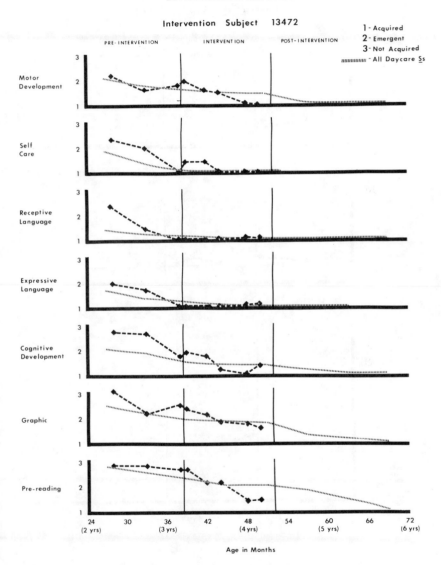

DEVELOPMENTAL PROGRESS

Intervention Subject 13472

1 - Acquired
2 - Emergent
3 - Not Acquired
▒▒▒▒▒ - All Daycare S̲s

PRE-INTERVENTION   INTERVENTION   POST-INTERVENTION

Motor Development

Self Care

Receptive Language

Expressive Language

Cognitive Development

Graphic

Pre-reading

Age in Months

Figure 5

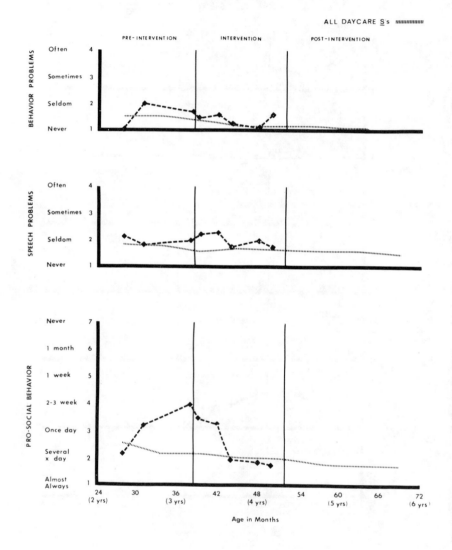

Figure 6

show progressively more negative behaviors at the center. Yet intervention has involved so many separate components that one cannot evaluate them separately or as they interact. For example, beyond routine day care center activities, the child's program involved speech and language therapy twice weekly, individual contact with project staff focusing primarily on cognitive deficits, and small-group play supervised by project staff. Within the small-group situation, the child was literally taught to play with other children and was socially reinforced for doing so. Of course, as a function of the small group he was led into situations and specific activities conducive to cooperative play and was exposed to other children with strong social skills; he was thus able to "try out" social skills in a relatively safe environment. Concurrently, project staff consulted with classroom teachers concerning their approach to the child. As a result, the pattern of teacher responsiveness to social behavior was altered radically. For example, prior to consultation, the teachers responded to the child primarily when he was socially engaged in negative interaction with peers or other adult attention-getting behaviors.

If nothing else, this case illustrates both the advantages and the disadvantages of a broad spectrum approach to intervention. We feel certain that the intervention had a therapeutic influence upon the child but at the same time find it impossible to isolate the aspects of the program that made it most beneficial.

Problems in Program Implementation

Our work over the past two years has taught us that intervening with high risk children presents any number of practical problems. It is impossible to go into all of them in detail here, but we will outline several that have been particularly troublesome.

One of the major difficulties concerns parental involvement. For the majority of children we have worked with, there has been a clear need for parent education, support, and therapy—not surprising, given our selection criteria. But it has been uphill work. Not only have we had small success in attracting parents to formal educational or therapeutic activities. We have had to battle against suspicion and mistrust; deal with the delicate balance between remaining supportive and loyal to the family on the one hand and concern for the child's welfare (particularly when neglect or abuse is involved) on the other; and struggle to impress upon many families the seriousness of their child's difficulties. Unlike many other early intervention programs concerned primarily with cognitive development, ours has had to deal with many parents who are seriously disturbed themselves. Their problems have manifested themselves in a variety of ways, from finding it difficult to wake up in time to get the child to the center to actively resisting project staff. There is no easy way to circumvent these problems.

To a lesser extent, we have found it difficult to plan programs related to the scope of a child's difficulties. Most of our children are handicapped in social behavior as well as in cognitive and physical areas. There is a strong tendency to attack all of a child's problems in one fell swoop, which is not only unrealistic but may actually retard progress. Related to this is the problem of coordinating the child's and family's affiliations with the project, the day care center, and other social agencies. A family may have had a long and unpleasant history with agencies regarding its children. Then when their child is accepted in the intervention program at the day care center, the parents—along with the referring agencies —sometimes believe the child has reached a self-contained healing sanctuary that meets all of his needs. The welfare agency case workers, the therapists from the mental health centers, and the visiting nurses all may promptly terminate active participation in the case they have referred. With the departure of the agency people, the child's parents tend to withdraw to their home and become reluctant to form a working relationship with day care and intervention staff. As a consequence, the work our staff does with the child during the day is often undone at home at night. A further frustration is that the necessary work in parent education often cannot be started because the parents have developed an avoidance reaction to "agency people." Thus, the highest risk children (those who have severe behavior disorders and come from families with multiple problems) in greatest need of therapeutic day care are poor risks for showing steady gains in social and intellectual competence. Lower risk children (those with similar problems but with reachable parents) are perhaps more appropriate intervention cases.

One final issue which is relevant to this and other research projects working with young children is the attitude that children and/or society should be protected from the evils of any kind of research. Fortunately, people holding this view are in the minority; most parents and day care providers are generous in giving their trust to ethical researchers. Perhaps this vocal minority is a necessary check to potentially irresponsible research programs. But we and others who conduct research in the natural settings of day care centers, schools, and homes are often obliged to defend ourselves as *not* being evil, unloving Fagins who are also agents of a corrupt government. This defensive posture depresses us and has from time to time required a great deal of patience and energy.

Associated with the "all research is evil" attitude is the caliber of people attracted to day care and nursery school jobs. Many, to be sure, have superb skills in working with children are are proud of their abilities and relationships with the parents and children. Others, though, choose the work because they believe they will be free to do as they please with the children; and the idea of having their job performance supervised and evaluated by other adults, and especially by authorities (senior child care workers, child development specialists, or others) is not only undesirable but philosophically abhorrent to them. They feel they know what is best for the children. The job philosophy of these workers has important implications for directors of day care centers and especially for early intervention projects working within a day care center.

It is often difficult, if not impossible, to reconcile the approaches taken by different centers or even by different semi-autonomous rooms within the same day care center. For example, the policy of one room may be to allow "fair fights"—thus rewarding the quality of the physical aggression—while the neighboring room in the same center will not permit physical aggression but will isolate combatants until the conflict can be solved in other ways. Anyone wishing to begin intervention studies in an existing day care center cannot expect his treatment programs to be either uniformly accepted or uniformly implemented.

Our intervention staff has encountered some of these problems within the host day care center. Whatever the complications, though, in trying to follow our research design requirements— including such acts of God as blizzards and epidemics of flu and chicken pox—they are trivial in light of the enormous support the center staff has provided to our project. We have been very fortunate to work with so many interesting children, generous child care workers, and interested parents.

152 Jon E. Rolf and Joseph E. Hasazi

We encourage other researchers to join us in testing the effectiveness of other early intervention strategies in other child care centers. To be successful in even maintaining an ongoing program, however, one should seek staff with exceptional abilities to interact gently with people of divergent educational and philosophical backgrounds and to tolerate frustrating delays both in implementing the program and in attaining visible success in treatment outcomes.

REFERENCES

Albee, G. W. The relation of conceptual models to manpower needs. In E. L. Cowen, E. A. Gardner, and M. Zax (Eds.), *Emergent approaches to mental health problems*. New York: Appleton-Century-Crofts, 1967.

Achenbach, T. M. The classification of children's psychiatric symptoms: A factor analytic study. *Psychological Monographs*, 1966, *80* (Whole No. 615).

Behar, L., and Stringfield, S. A behavior rating scale for the preschool child. *Journal of Developmental Psychology*, 1974, *10*, 601–610.

Garmezy, N. Vulnerability research and the issue of primary prevention. *The American Journal of Orthopsychiatry*, 1971, *41*, 101–116.

Garmezy, N., and Streitman, S. Children at risk: The search for antecedents of schizophrenia. Part I. Conceptual models and research methods. *Schizophrenia Bulletin*, 1974, *8* (Spring), 14–90.

Hebb, D. O. *The organization of behavior*. New York: Wiley, 1949.

Hunt, J. McV. *Intelligence and experience*. New York: Ronald Press, 1961.

Klemchuk, H., Rolf, J. E., and Hasazi, J. E. Preschool children at risk: A multilevel approach to developmental psychopathology. Paper presented at the meeting of the American Psychological Association, Chicago, September 1975.

Kohn, M., and Rosman, B. A social competence scale and symptom checklist for the preschool child: Factor dimensions, their cross-instrument generality and longitudinal persistence. *Journal of Developmental Psychology*, 1972, *6*, 430–444.

Miller, R. The assessment of child behavior problems in the school: A preliminary report of a comparison of behavioral observation and trait ratings. Unpublished manuscript, University of Vermont, 1975.

Rolf, J. E., and Hakola, J. The incidence, prevalence, and severity of behavior disorders among preschool children. Paper presented at the Eastern Psychological Association meeting, April 1976.

Rolf, J. E., and Harig, P. T. Etiological research in schizophrenia and the rationale for primary intervention. *American Journal of Orthopsychiatry*, 1974, *44*, 538–554.

Rolf, J. E., and Hasazi, J. E. Epidemiology of and intervention for children at risk. NIMH Research Project progress reports, 1973–1976.

8

Intervention in Children at High Risk for Schizophrenia

SARNOFF A. MEDNICK AND
GEORGIA HOPE WITKIN-LANOIL*

In considering the substantial body of research on the etiology of schizophrenia, the epidemiologist J. N. Morris (1970) points out that "up to now, unhappily, this activity has yielded few new facts; a deficiency somewhat obscured by the communicativeness of psychiatrists and social scientists" (p. 218). It was this questionable record of the traditional research methods that first prompted the adoption of the so-called high risk method. The comments that follow consider the potential long-term goals of the method and its implications for research in primary prevention, particularly as they are embodied in a project being attempted in Mauritius.

LONG-TERM OBJECTIVES OF HIGH RISK RESEARCH

Fifteen years ago at a conference in Ann Arbor, Mednick stated his view of the objectives of high risk research. He planned "to test and interview a group of normal children in the Detroit area. From these tests and interviews we shall predict which of these children will become schizophrenic . . . We have decided to select a group in which the prevalence rates are considerably elevated . . . Individuals who have one or two parents who have been schizophrenic . . . If our predictions prove to be supported, we are then in a position to do research which is aimed at the prevention of schizophrenia. We might observe a normal population with our tests, detect those individuals who are potential schizophrenics and then explore the possibilities of intervention" (Mednick, 1960, page 69).

The first step in implementing the general plan would be the longitudinal study of children of schizophrenics. Such study can provide two useful outcomes. First, it can elucidate a pattern of

* This study was supported by USPHS Grant No. 25325 (Clinical Research Branch).

premorbid variables which distinguishes the high risk individual who later becomes schizophrenic. Such a pattern must then be tested in an unselected population for its predictive ability. If it proves successful in a general population, we have a means of early detection of predisposed individuals in the society. This would be the first step in a specific program of primary prevention. Second, the pattern of variables distinguishing the predisposed individual may suggest a theory of etiology which, in turn, may lead to developing modes of experimental intervention. Goldstein (1975), for example, reports a type of communication disturbance which marks the adolescent at especially high risk for schizophrenia; perhaps corrective training in communication could be tested as a mode of intervention. As another example, in the Copenhagen high risk project, 16 of the children of schizophrenics have not themselves become schizophrenic. In contrast to a variety of control groups, almost all of these schizophrenics were separated from their parents or substitute parents very early in life. This result might also tempt an intervention researcher to test the efficacy of superior foster care as a means of helping prevent schizophrenia. High risk research thus offers the promise of providing means of early detection and suggesting ideas for modes of intervention.

OBJECTIVES OF RESEARCH IN PRIMARY PREVENTION

Universal Screening for Early Detection? A logical public health application of early detection methods is to establish a routine system of universal screening for the specific variables which predispose to psychopathology. It is necessary to screen so as to spare the bulk of the general population from irrelevant intervention programs. The emphasis on specificity of factors or variables reflects the fact that our research will probably yield a number of different patterns of factors each of which may predict specific pathological outcomes. If we continue to look for premorbid indicants of schizophrenia by following children of schizophrenics, for example, we will observe a variety of pathological outcomes in addition to schizophrenia, including neurosis, criminality, and borderline states. The outcomes will hopefully be reflected in a corresponding variety of specific differentiating premorbid characteristics. This differentiated "diagnostic" approach will then make possible equally differentiated intervention programs. For example, in the Copenhagen high risk project, the school behavior of individuals who now are diagnosed as schizophrenic can be contrasted with those diagnosed as psychopaths. The future schizophrenic had no or few friends; the future psychopath had many friends. Interventive work at school age may wish to treat these two groups differently.

Specificity in Screening. The goal of universal screening for specific pathological outcomes suggests that specificity should be built into our observations of high risk children. Measures for counting or timing types of nursery school behavior may be more useful ultimately than overall ratings of levels of adjustment. Since some of these assessment tasks may be time-consuming, such instruments as self-administered questionnaires or behavior checklists for the nursery school teacher may be useful for preliminary rough screening. Techniques like these could narrow the population for more intensive assessment, and risk investigators may consider including one of them in their assessments. Another advantage of specificity of premorbid measures is that specific measures may suggest specific intervention techniques.

EARLY INTERVENTION WITH IDENTIFIED RISK CHILDREN

Goals of Intervention. The major objective of the universal screening, then, is early intervention with identified risk children. In principle, such intervention work is not innovative in medicine. But when preventive work involves malaria, smallpox, or influenza, the intervention touches only those aspects of human existence that are relatively noncontroversial. When we mix into an individual's mental life, we must carefully appraise our intentions and proposed deeds. What do we hope to achieve? Do we wish to shape a more normal adult? If so, toward whose definition of normality do we wish to mold our subjects? Former president Nixon's physician had a definition of normality that he wanted to apply to slum children at high risk for delinquency: his plan called for placing them in isolated training camps. The uncompromising resistance of the United States Public Health Service helped keep this nightmare unfunded. But is your definition of normality to be preferred? The very fact that you are intervening means you are attempting to move the subject toward some explicit or implicit goal of normality, whether it be to adjustment of autonomic nervous system (ANS) recovery rates, blood sodium levels, communication deficits, personality disorders, faulty attitudes, or political and religious views.

In considering means of intervention, it may be advisable to attempt to refrain from shaping children in accordance with specific concepts of behavioral or social normality. Total abstinence from such shaping is impossible by the very nature of the enterprise, but different emphases are conceivable. Perhaps a reasonable goal would be to circumscribe the intervention so as to minimize its interference in the individual's macrobehavioral-social life while maximizing its preventive effectiveness. We might prefer bringing an autonomic nervous system function just a bit closer to the mean over attempts at direct influence on an individual's attitudes toward himself, his peers, and his family. We must repeat that we are dealing with differences in emphasis rather than clear logical differences. By altering an ANS function, after all, we do intend to manipulate social responses indirectly.

Potential Dangers in Intervention. There are potential dangers in specific interventions that must be considered by the researcher. An obvious case is the side effects of drugs. But psychological intervention may also have side effects. Before instituting a specific intervention (such as a change in an ANS function) the investigator must inform himself of the long-term consequences of the intervention. This can perhaps be accomplished only by following an assessed total population for a long time. Perhaps bringing individuals with highly deviant ANS functioning a bit closer to the mean of the population will reduce the incidence of schizophrenia. But what else might it reduce? Creativity? The capacity of some individuals to enjoy themselves? Before we can weigh the gains and losses, we must be aware of them.

Despite the potential problems, specific forms of intervention suggest themselves for public health application. The more specific the interventive technique, the more likely that technicians will be able to administer the procedure. All this emphasis on specific intervention should not discourage less focused interventive

interventive attempts; if successful, however, these should be analyzed and the effective specific components ascertained.

A BONUS FOR CONTROLLED PRIMARY PREVENTION RESEARCH: HELP WITH DETERMINING ETIOLOGY

Some have suggested that an important goal of studying the early characteristics of children of schizophrenics is helping to understand the causes of the illness. Perhaps, but it must be recalled that this method is correlative. We correlate certain early characteristics with adult outcome. In the examples mentioned, can communication disorders or early parental separation be considered possible causes of later schizophrenia? Certainly not in any simple way, since early separation does not seem to have caused any schizophrenia at all in the low risk group. In addition, a dissertation by Edna Hermann (Hermann, 1973) seems to suggest the possibility that the subjects who were separated from their parents at an early age were not selected for this fate by chance only but in part by certain personal qualities that distinguished them from their nonseparated siblings. They were more sensitive and irritable and frightened of strangers and new toys. Thus, instead of separation being a partial cause of schizophrenia, we might argue that, in a sense, schizophrenia is a partial cause of separation. This discussion highlights the well-known difficulties in attempting to deduce causal statements from correlations. The preferred technique for developing causal statements is the experimental-manipulative method. With humans, this method cannot be applied in etiological research since it would involve exposing children to conditions hypothesized to foster schizophrenia. The experimental-manipulative method, however, is the essential nature of interventive research. Perhaps the differential success of various types of interventive procedures may help point to areas of consideration for etiological hypotheses. If foster parent care proves to be more efficacious in prevention than does a biochemical intervention, this information may serve to narrow the field for the search for causes. It is perhaps useful to emphasize that in order to maximize this return from prevention research, careful attention must be given to exact specification of the nature of the intervention procedure.

SOME COMMENTS ON INTERVENTION METHODS

Control Groups. In some writing on intervention research, statements have been made suggesting that all identified risk children should receive treatment. Control groups, it is implied, would be immoral and unethical since they would mean withholding the "optimal" treatment from some selected subgroups. Following such a dictum would simply mean no real research would be done. We should keep in mind the report of Dave Ricks (personal communication). At a leading child guidance clinic, his follow-up study revealed that some therapists seemed capable of immunizing clinic children from later developing hospitalizable schizophrenia. Other therapists seemed to inexorably push frightening numbers of clinic children into schizophrenia. In this situation the children or their parents sought out the clinic services. We will be seeking out our subjects for intervention. How many of us are completely certain that his staff does not house an unknown and unknowing "malevolent" therapist? Since we are far from certain that our intervention will help, we can hardly consider it immoral to withhold this unknown quantity from some subjects. Considering the history of lobotomy treatment, we must examine the morality of *not* evaluating our intervention procedures with proper controls.

When to Intervene? The earliest possible intervention may occur before conception in the form of genetic counseling. In view of relatively low rates of schizophrenia among children with one parent schizophrenic, only two-parent families might be appropriate for such intervention. Since two-thirds of the children of schizophrenic women are born before the schizophrenic woman is diagnosed, however, this procedure is of doubtful utility (Mednick et al., 1971).

Those who consider improving the conditions of pregnancies and deliveries involving schizophrenic parents must also face the fact that they will be able to identify only one-third of the cases at the time of the pregnancy. This would seem a worthwhile goal except for the fact that this one-third, born to women already schizophrenic, have relatively problem-free pregnancies and deliveries (Mednick et al., 1971). Perinatal intervention may be extremely effective, but identification of risk will have to be made by some means other than the diagnostic status of the prospective parent.

The neonatal period suggests itself as a time when society and the investigator have access to the child and the parent. Further, longitudinal research has suggested that neonatal status has predictive value for adolescent behavior (Mednick, 1975). This period, then, has potential for early detection and, conceivably, intervention.

In terms of early intervention, nursery schools have much to recommend themselves. They are in growing demand in western society as more women enter the work force. Children spend from four to eight hours a day at nursery schools being observed by teachers who are potential raters. This gives the investigator ample opportunity to observe and intervene.

In Mauritius and in Vermont, nursery school intervention programs are in progress. We will close this presentation with a brief description of the Mauritius project.

BACKGROUND OF MAURITIUS PROJECT

Mauritius, a densely populated country with about 900,000 inhabitants, occupies an area of about 2,400 square kilometers and lies some 1,000 kilometers east of Madagascar on latitude 20 degrees south. The population is composed of Hindus and Tamils (51 percent), Moslems (16 percent), Creoles (29 percent), and Chinese (4 percent). The economy is not advanced and is largely a monoculture dependent on sugar cane. The annual per capita income is about $220. In spite of this, the infrastructure is quite advanced. Perinatal care is of a relatively high standard. Some 90 percent of the children attend elementary school for several years. Emigration is limited. Infections and parasitic disorders are relatively well under control. Mild malnutrition (hypoproteinemia) is common, but pronounced kwashiorkor and marasmus are rare.

There is one psychiatric hospital bed to about 1,000 inhabitants, a ratio far higher than in other developing countries. The climate is subtropical to tropical. Foreigners manage well with French or English; both are official languages. The indigenous population speak a local patois. In some rural areas Hindi is the major language.

Why Mauritius?

In 1966, a follow-up of the high risk subjects in Copenhagen suggested that the rate of recovery of skin conductance was an important possible premorbid indicant of later pathology. Mednick, as part of a World Health Organization (WHO) panel (1965), reported this finding as well as a description of the high risk method. WHO then proposed that we institute a replication of the high risk work. Since Dr. A. C. Raman, chief psychiatrist of Mauritius, had requested that WHO initiate a program of mental health research in his country, the island nation was chosen for us; we accepted the choice.

In view of the Copenhagen findings, we decided to initiate a new long-term prospective study to determine whether the psychophysiological measures would be useful for early detection in an unselected general population of three-year-olds. Considering the limited number of long-term prospective projects we could still hope to complete, we decided to make a conceptual leap and collect some of the fast-ANS-recovering three-year-olds and controls in nursery schools and observe their behavior closely, then to study the possibility of experimental interventive procedures.

We anticipated certain results from this series of actions. (1) We expected to determine the short-term and long-term life correlates of psychophysiological (and other) laboratory measures in a total population of three-year-old children. (2) Determining these life correlates might help us to estimate the long-term consequences of possible future intervention in ANS functioning. (3) The short- and long-term effects of a superior nursery school on psychophysiologically defined high risk children could be evaluated. (4) Specific interventive actions could be undertaken and evaluated. Under consideration at this time are biofeedback techniques to alter deviant ANS functions, placing risk children with younger children to help them learn adequate social functioning under low-threat conditions, and behavior modification methods. The cooperating investigators are Mednick, Raman, Schulsinger, Sutton-Smith, Venables, and Bell.

Sample and Procedure

In a one-year period beginning in August 1972, we examined 1,800 children who were between 3 and 3¼ years of age on one day of the examination. These children comprise almost all the three-year-olds residing in two Mauritian communities that are representative of the island's population. Dr. Brian Bell, an English psychologist, was on-site director of the assessment.

The assessment consisted of (1) parent interview; (2) social behavior laboratory observation; (3) psychological cognitive assessment; (4) psychophysiology test (skin conductance, skin potential, and electrocardiogram); (5) obstetric information; (6) pediatric examination; and (7) EEG examination (for part of the 1,800). The assessment provides the data base for the longitudinal study of these 1,800 children.

Selection for Nursery School. The project established two nursery schools, each with 50 children. On the basis of the psychophysiological screening of the 1,800 three-year-olds, 54 children were selected with extremely fast recovery and 32 with average speed of recovery. Because of the results of recent investigations by Venables and Christie (1973), 14 children were included who were "non-responders" in skin conductance. These three types of children were then divided evenly between the two nursery schools. Thus in each nursery school, three-fourths of the class were psychophysiologically defined high risk children. For each of the 100 children in the nursery schools, a control was selected who was matched for skin conductance characteristics and area of residence. These "community controls" were simply identified and permitted to remain undisturbed in the community.

Preliminary Results. The nursery school and community control groups total 200 children. Of these, 108 (54 nursery school children and their 54 community controls) are fast recoverers and 64 are average in their recovery function. We compared these two groups on some of the other measures taken in the assessment of the 1,800 in order to see what the behavioral correlates of this deviant ANS behavior might be.

The fast ANS recoverers cried more during the testing and evidenced more fear and anxiety. They are also more disturbing and aggressive in the nursery school. These findings correspond to observations made on fast recoverers in the Copenhagen high risk project.

Behavior in the Nursery School. Since the opening of the nursery schools, the children have been observed in accordance with a system devised by Bell and his associates (1971). The system times, rates, and counts instances of specific behaviors that

Bell found to be reliably observable. The factor structure of the observations and ratings on the Mauritian children has been found to resemble closely that reported by Bell for American nursery school children. The formal analysis of these observations is not complete; but the investigators, who visit Mauritius once or twice a year, have a definite impression regarding changes in the children's behavior. Of course, none of the investigators or staff is aware of the psychophysiological status of any of the children.

When the children first entered the nursery schools, an abnormally large number of them were terribly frightened and had to be held most of the time. This situation continued for the first month. Many of the mothers urged that a sibling be substituted for the selected child, protesting that the selected child would be hopeless since he or she spent most of the day in the closet or under the table or hiding in the sugar cane. This parental report and nursery school behavior was interesting in view of the theoretical interpretation of the significance of the fast ANS recovery (Mednick, 1970, 1974).

At present, the visiting investigators, the nursery school teachers, and the observers agree that there has been a vast change in the behavior of most of the children. They play spontaneously and greet strangers with lively interest and curiosity. They are described by their parents as having become normal, happy children at home.

These positive changes have not yet been related to psychophysiological behavior. It is clear, however, that since three-fourths of the children were selected as psychophysiologically deviant, some of them must have experienced a positive change. The positive effect may be related to any one of the following or to a combination:

1. A good protein-rich nursery school diet.

2. Placement in a group with a high density of other frightened children.

3. A group of warm and enthusiastic young nursery school teachers.

4. The special atmosphere created by the Danish nursery school experts who run the schools and train the teachers.

5. Separation from their home environment for part of the day.

6. Selection for this special experience.

It will be important to ferret out the critical positive aspects of the nursery school experience. But whatever these specific aspects may be, it is possible that our presumably more sophisticated interventions—for example, biofeedback—may have been made unnecessary. Whether this is so will be shown by the data analyses, by observations of community controls, and by the follow-up we are planning in the schools.

REFERENCES

Bell, R. Q., Weller, G. M., and Waldrop, M. F. New born and preschooler: organization of behavior and relations between periods. *Monographs of the Society for Research in Child Development*, 1971, *36*, 1–2.

Goldstein, M. J. *Psychotherapeutic intervention with families of adolescents at risk for schizophrenia*. World Health Organization, Copenhagen, 1975.

Hermann, E. Long range effects of early parental separation experiences in children with high and low risk for schizophrenia. Unpublished doctoral dissertation, Graduate Faculty, New School for Social Research, New York, 1973.

Mednick, B. *Neonatal neurological symptomatology predictive of the minimal brain damage syndrome in preadolescence.* New York: Columbia University Press, 1975.

Mednick, S. A. The early and advanced schizophrenic. In S. A. Mednick and J. Higgins (Eds.), *Current research in schizophrenia*. Ann Arbor: Edwards, 1960.

Mednick, S. A. Primary prevention and schizophrenia—Theory and research. In *Public health practice and the prevention of mental illness*. Copenhagen: World Health Organization, 1965.

Mednick, S. A. Breakdown in individuals at high risk for schizophrenia: Possible predispositional perinatal factors. *Mental Hygiene*, 1970, *54*, 50–63.

Mednick, S. A. Electrodermal recovery and psychopathology. In S. A. Mednick, F. Schulsinger, J. Higgins, and B. Bell (Eds.), *Genetics, environment and psychopathology*. Amsterdam: North Holland/Elsevier, 1974.

Mednick, S. A., Mura, E., Schulsinger, F., and Mednick, B. Perinatal conditions and infant development in children with schizophrenic parents. *Social Biology*, 1971, *18*, 103–113.

Morris, J. N. *Uses of epidemiology*. London: Livingston, 1970.

Venables, P. H., and Christie, M. J. (Eds.). *Research in psycho-physiology*. London: Wiley, 1973.

9

Preventive Measures for Children and Adolescents at High Risk for Psychosis

E. JAMES ANTHONY

It took a considerable time for physicians, preoccupied as they were from the beginning with patients and their pressing demands for treatment, to turn their attention to preventive medicine. The impetus came from the discovery of causal organisms, the conditions under which they thrived, and the artificial immunities that could set up against them. It has taken an even longer period for psychiatry to become prevention-minded, and there are many who believe that the new interest is somewhat premature for the developmental state of the discipline, since we know comparatively little about causation and transmission and certainly nothing about psychological immunization. Nevertheless, psychiatrists and psychologists, separately or hand in hand, have intrepidly entered the field on an exploratory basis guided by only very tentative cause-and-effect notions based on minimal scientific facts. Operating on such ad hoc assumptions, they would make interventions for the oldest experimental reason in science—to see what happened. If things turned out better than chance (which was not unusually the case, since enthusiasm and expectation are potent factors in all intervention outcomes), their causal explanations were strengthened. Others, however, usually found it difficult to replicate the findings.

Of the three levels of psychiatric prevention described by Caplan (1964), the tertiary form (that is, preventing moderate disorder from becoming severe) has had some small success; the secondary form (preventing mild from becoming moderate) has also had slight success; but it is the primary form (preventing nothing from becoming something) that has had the most questionable results. The critical question lay in the area of recognition. It seemed acceptable that the minimal manifestations should be detectable with adequate screening devices as in secondary prevention, but how could one recognize something before it happened? The answer to this was soon adduced: recognition referred no longer to disorder but to disposition, and the search then began for dispositional features.

Genetic studies in the field of psychosis disclosed that children of probands had a much higher than general expectancy for developing psychosis. At first, these so-called high risk subjects were looked at mainly from the viewpoint of final outcome. A certain percentage—the figure varying with different investigators—were apparently doomed to develop psychosis during adult life. They had, it seemed, a latent psychosis that gained manifest expression through reasons of age or conditions of living. The pathway from gene to environment and the relationship between gene and environment remained problematical. In some psychoses, genetic factors appeared predominant, while in others it was the environment that looked more significant.

In the St. Louis study, an intense clinical interest developed in these children at high risk for schizophrenia and manic-depression and 193 of them were fully investigated. They fell roughly into three groups: about 30 percent seemed normally adjusted (10 percent being credited with superior adjustment), about 30 percent had minor adjustment problems not requiring psychiatric intervention, and about 40 percent manifested significant maladjustment. Thus, with any epidemiological screening, about a third would be undetected, a third would be dismissed as being of minor concern, and about a third would be referred for further evaluation, depending on the efficiency of the screening device. The clinical disturbances relating to the maladjustment ranged from severe dedifferentiation, reactive disorders (both internalizing and externalizing), contact disorders as shown in various degrees of folie à deux, and "antecedent" disturbances (so called because they seemed like miniature editions of an adult psychosis reduced in both time and intensity). Those showing no significant adjustment problems nevertheless had a higher score on a checklist of deviant traits than control subjects. The psychotic parents also showed a wide range of psychotic behavior from reactive process, such as manic excitement, schizo-affective disorder, paranoid schizophrenia, psychotic depression, and hebephrenic forms of schizophrenia. What seemed at first a surprising finding was that the two continua of disturbances in child and adult had almost an inverse relationship between severity of disorder in the child and malignancy of psychosis in the parent. Thus schizo-affective and pseudo-neurotic types of schizophrenia produced the most immediately devastating effects, and the younger the child the more noxious did the relationship seem to be. The normal, supernormal, and antecedent disorders, on the other hand, were apparently more related to the process types of psychoses, and it was possible that their influence was postponed into adult life. When the adult psychosis was examined from the point of view of the child's experience, somewhat the same finding emerged: the more included the child was in the psychotic system, the more upset he seemed to be; the more withdrawn the parent was from the child, the less overt disturbance did he display. Two conclusions could therefore be tentatively drawn:

1. That the environmental aspects of psychosis played a more significant role in causing maladjustment in high risk subjects during childhood; and

2. That the genetic aspects of psychosis tended to exert their influence later in the life cycle.

Certain clinical findings lent support to these conclusions. The separation of the child from the reactive parent ameliorated the reactive and contact disturbances in the child, particularly if adequate surrogation was provided. Second, the disturbing effects and their mitigation with separation were more prominent in the case of maternal psychosis. And finally, the so-called antecedent disturbances, such as the development of prepsychotic traits and micropsychotic episodes, continued to increase in intensity, frequency, and duration irrespective of separation from the sick parent. The further fact that the mental health of the other parent is an important factor in determining the degree of disturbance in the child could be interpreted from both genetic and environmental points of view. In practice, it has been clear that whenever it was possible to harness the efforts of the well spouse to the preventive program it not only reinforced improvements in the children but helped to sustain their cooperation.

Another critical finding for the general management of preventive measures has been that casework with the sick parent conducted on a regular and not on a crisis basis, and focusing on the reduction of stresses in everyday living, has been potent not only in keeping the patient out of hospital but in diminishing the level of ,tension and irrational explosiveness in the household. The reality organization of the caseworker has undoubtedly played a guiding and desensitizing role in preserving the emotional equilibrium.

In short, the support system essential to the work of prevention with children who carry the double load of both genetic and environmental risk involves managing the sick parent during phases of remission and mobilizing the coping skills, the caring concerns, and the reality orientation of the well parent. (Unfortunately, because of the operation of homogamous mating, these helpful qualities are not usually distinctive characteristics of the non-psychotic spouse.)

With regard to direct preventive measures for the children at high risk for psychosis, there were a number of complicating and confounding problems.

1. The sample was heterogeneous in many respects: some were manifestly disturbed and some were not; some showed definite antecedent phenomena and some did not; some (two-thirds) were at high risk for schizophrenia and some (one-third) for manic-depression; for some, the fathers were psychotic, for some the mothers; some came from materially good homes and some from impoverished ones; and some had families that were encapsulated and often beleaguered, while others had families that maintained affiliations with the outside community. The encapsulated families were labeled "closed" and the still affiliated families "open." From the standpoint of assessing preventive measures, the "open" families constituted a group that was significantly more amenable to preventive or therapeutic measures; "closed" families frequently showed great resistance to such proposals. With such a melange, it was not possible to establish a common baseline from which to assess change. The only possibility was to use the individual as his own control and match him against his past or future per-formance.

2. The presence of clinically disturbed children made it un-feasible, on ethical grounds, to randomize the group into those receiving intervention and those not. Another problem with regard to randomization concerned the difficulty some of the parents had over treating an apparently healthy child. In the same context, they found it harder to consider probing as compared with ego building or supportive measures.

3. The researchers themselves were not too clear what they were trying to prevent: disturbances during childhood? breakdowns at adolescence? psychiatric disorder or psychosis in adult life?

Eventually, fifty children entered the program. A 20-percent refusal rate included subjects unable to travel the necessary distance, parents who felt the journey was unnecessary, and parents (the more paranoid ones) who were simply resistant to the idea.

With these problems affecting the group as a whole, the focus of the interveners shifted to an evaluation and subsequent re-evaluation of the individual subject.

THE ASSESSMENT OF CHANGE

In all before-and-after studies, there are a number of influences that cannot be controlled: the vicissitudes of development and intervening stressful events. (Comparisons between our experimental group and normal controls on the Life Stress Questionnaire showed that the former group was significantly more stressed, although this could be attributable to exaggerations and distortions of situations. In high risk families, hierarchies of significance are upset so that trivialities are accorded as much weight as matters of great seriousness.) It was therefore decided to ignore such variables—or perhaps treat them with benign neglect—in the hope that they would cancel each other out.

Six areas gradually emerged as having specific importance to a program of prevention with children at high risk for psychosis. Some of these were incorporated into a risk-vulnerability intervention model (Anthony, 1974). The six areas concerned are those where changes would seem to predicate alterations in prognosis.

Area 1. Risk is defined as something affecting the psychological organization from the outside. It is never a single factor but always a combination of factors. Ratings are made on genetic, reproductive, constitutional, developmental, physical, environmental, and traumatic loadings and a total risk score is ascertained. This score can change (but rarely does to any significant extent) because of development, death, disease, impoverishment, or traumatic experiences. The risks are sequential from genetic to environmental, not simultaneous; they represent a mixture of psychological and biological factors; the weighting or predominance of any particular factor is still unknown. Subjects are allocated to categories of high or low risk.

Area 2. Vulnerability is defined as a combination of factors affecting the psychological organization. Unlike the area of risk that covers a spectrum of possible assaults on the organism, the vulnerability this project focuses on is that which pertains to the psychotic disposition or experience. It represents a dynamic state that acquires an unsteady equilibrium, which in turn sometimès generates a state of mind registering a profound feeling of difference or vulnerability. The subject is evaluated in clinical and nonclinical spheres—that is, in terms of weaknesses and strengths. The clinical susceptibility is scored (a) psychiatrically, on a vulnerability rating scale (VRS) gauged on a series of tests for suggestibility, submissiveness, and involvement and identification with the sick parent, and (b) psychologically, on ratings derived from a battery of tests that are summarized to provide a total score of pathology: the sum of clinical disturbance ratings (SCDR). The psychological ratings are based on a battery of tests (WISC, Rorschach, TAT, DAP, and Beery) and on the whole seem more indicative of potential than of actual disturbance. High scores on the VRS are correlated with higher ratings of disturbance across all fourteen of the psychological ratings and with more serious prognostic scores made independently. High SCDR ratings correlated significantly with more frequent hospitalizations of the parent, longer stays in hospital by the parent, lower ages of the children at the time of the parent's first hospitalization, more reactive psychotic disorders, and a more serious disorder in the area of conation. A combined clinical vulnerability score is made.

Area 3. Competence is defined as a capacity to master difficulties, solve problems, and overcome obstacles in an effective way. There are three types of competence: executive, dealing with performance at school and on tests; social, pertaining to the level of interpersonal skills; and representational, referring to the individual's capacity to construct a working model of the problem and understand its dimensions within this frame of reference. (In practice, the children are asked to give an account of the parent's illness in terms of its etiology, diagnosis, treatment, and prognosis.) A total rating of high or low competence can then be made.

Area 4. Maladjustment is assessed on a seven-point rating scale ranging from "superior" to "adjustment difficulties requiring hospitalization."

Area 5. A prediction is also measured on a series of rating scales from one to seven with regard to outcome during childhood, adolescence, and adult life. The prediction is based on the rating scores for risk, vulnerability, competence, and maladjustment. Extreme ratings on the prediction scale occur with high risk, high vulnerability, low competence, and high maladjustment; extreme low ratings are gained with low risk, low vulnerability, high competence, and low maladjustment.

Area 6. Outcome is defined in two ways: (a) changes in test scores, clinical psychiatric and psychological ratings, and ratings of competence; and (b) changes in clinical status as assessed on clinical examination.

It will be noted that both a predictive and a post-dictive model can be elicited from these data.

TECHNIQUES FOR CHANGE

In assessing techniques for bringing about change, the general strategy was examined both quantitatively and qualitatively. The amount of intervention is measured in intervention hours devoted to the family of the child in question, including work with the parents, so that if there were two or three children in a particular family, the parental hours would be added to the intervention scores of each child.

From a qualitative point of view, four types of intervention measures were tried.

1. *Compensatory interventions* involved various nonspecific procedures aimed at building up ego resources, strengthening self-confidence, and bringing the child into contact with benevolent figures and agencies. The opportunities offered included tutoring, camping, "big brother" relationships, outings, and recreational and creative opportunities in addition to a positive alliance with the staff of the research clinic. Most of these activities were carried out by a pair of professionals who were given a general orientation on the need to bolster the child's morale and to inject a sense of reality into his life. A log of

activities recorded the amount of intervention time given to the child.

2. *Classical interventions* were based on individual and group psychotherapy and were carried out by residents in child psychiatry under supervision. The sessions were open-ended and nondirective, so that there was no special focus on the specific human predicament generated by psychosis.

3. *Cathartic interventions* were used mainly during the acute or relapsing phases of the parental illness when defenses tended to be fluid, communications free, and affects highly available. Each child was asked to report his own experiences of the illness as it developed and as it enveloped and influenced him both inside and outside the family. In the course of this intervention, a whole range of affects—fear, shame, guilt, anger, and depression—were abreacted. The wish to drive the psychotic parent out of the house or back into psychosis was often brought up amid a storm of feeling. The family group seemed to provide a more effective atmosphere for catharsis than did the individual situation. The procedure has proven almost useless outside the acute phase of the illness once the defenses were reconstituted.

4. *Corrective interventions* represented attempts to create specific procedures to affect areas vulnerable to the psychotic process. For example, self-differentiation was furthered by courses on self-orientation and nonself-differentiation, starting from the outside (this is my name; these are my clothes; this is my hair, and so on) and proceeding inwardly (these are my thoughts, my memories, my dreams). Object differentiation involved a course of exercises during which the primary and secondary qualities of things were evaluated in terms of sensations, functions, feelings, and associated ideas provoked by them. The rationale for these two interventions was based on the assumption that self-nonself-differentiation required the knowledge of the self and a knowledge of the environment; during development, these two differentiations proceed hand-in-hand. The corrective interventions with regard to unrealistic and magical thinking were based on open-ended stories with multiple choice answers ranging from the unrealistic to the realistic. After the child had made his choice, "reality conversations" were systematically begun with him, covering such topics as his reasons for choosing his answers, his assessment of what smaller or older children might choose, how

his well or sick parent might respond, and, finally, what selection the interviewer might make. The interviewer would then tell the child why he had chosen a particular answer and what realistic thinking governed his choice.

The children of psychotic parents, irrespective of age, tend to be mystified by the incongruities of thought and affect contained in psychotic phenomena. Special demystification sessions were held with the idea of furnishing the subject with a more objective view not only of mental illness in general but of his parent's illness in particular. The underlying agenda aimed at increasing the representational competence of the child and decreasing his natural puzzlement regarding psychotic phenomena to which he was exposed. Organizational competence was taught in small groups in ways that interested and involved the child. He was invited to order and classify his material, schedule his work efforts, bring together parts to construct a whole, carry out problems of reversibility, and restore lawful tidiness in a messy, chaotic field situation. It seemed as if children undergoing the course became more flexible in their thinking, more able to reverse judgments, more able to consider other possibilities, and more able to tolerate ambiguity.

FINDINGS

1. Keeping the quality of treatment constant, there was a significant association at the .05 level between the amount of intervention given and the amount of change produced in the levels of vulnerability and maladjustment. The change in the level of competence was not significant.

2. Keeping the amount of treatment constant, the amount of change generated by the classical intervention measures was greater than for any of the other procedures. The corrective measures came next, followed by the compensatory and the cathartic. The latter interventions produced no significant change.

3. Keeping the amount and type of intervention constant, there was a significantly greater amount of change with the high-risk, high-vulnerability, high-maladjustment, and low-competence group as compared with the low-risk, low-vulnerability, low-maladjustment, and high-competence group. Changes between these and intermediate groups were not significant.

4. Keeping the amount and type of treatment constant, there was a significant difference between "open" and "closed" families, the amount of change being greater with the "open" families.

5. Keeping the amount and type of intervention constant, there was a nonsignificant difference between children of schizophrenics and children of manic-depressives, the change being greater in the children of manic-depressives.

6. Keeping the amount and type of intervention constant, there was no difference between the amount of change in children whose mothers were psychotic as compared to children whose fathers were psychotic.

7. Keeping the amount and type of intervention constant, there were nonsignificant changes between male and female children.

8. The greater the degree of vulnerability and maladjustment the greater the amount of change following intervention, keeping the amount of intervention constant. The differences barely reach significance.

CONCLUSIONS

This experience with intervention measures for children and adolescents at high risk for psychosis, although methodologically weak in parts, has shown sufficient success to warrant a replication with a larger group of children that would include the retesting of control subjects. The last-named is a sad deficiency in the present study. Our experience has taught us that not all areas are equally sensitive to change agents, nor are all change agents effective with all types of cases. When vulnerability and maladjustment are high, prolonged classical interventions seem effective; when they are low, compensatory measures seem highly effective. External behavior appears less resistant than internal behavior. Organizational competence and nonself or object differentiation also seemed to make early and visible gains. Changes in self-concept, sense of identify, and realistic thinking progressed much more slowly. When the family as a whole was reported to be changing, with the sick parent remaining well and the well parent realistically oriented, the changes in the vulnerability and maladjustment scores were dramatic. It is not clear to what extent the generally small but positive findings depended on the fact that those who accepted the invitation for intervention were more highly motivated and therefore change-susceptible from the beginning. The initial expectation had been that the findings would support the use of shorter, more specific, less expensive, and technically simpler procedures; but this was not the case. If further research suggests that the corrective measures are indeed as effective as the longer more complicated ones, an attempt will be made to develop a curriculum for use by paraprofessionals attached to special units at mental health centers and psychiatric hospitals, where it is hoped that the families of the psychotic patients will be screened and helped if necessary and where preventive procedures will be available for the more vulnerable and maladjusted children. We are still far from being satisfied with either our scoring techniques or our intervention procedures and hope to modify and refine them further with experience.

To what extent the intervention work will prevent breakdowns, psychiatric disorders, and psychoses later in life remains to be seen. We have six breakdowns so far in our 18-to-20-year group, but, as mentioned earlier, these are by no means to be equated with psychosis. It would be foolish at this point to be definite about the adult outcome. As Garmezy (unpublished) says, "to attempt to predict ultimate outcomes for a disorder as mysterious and pervasive as schizophrenia (and this holds true for manic-depression as well) requires an ebullience of spirit, a ubiquitous sense of optimism, an overweening confidence, an extraordinary amount of clinical and experimental acumen, and a conceptual clarity which the nature of the disorder tends to obscure."

At the present point in history, we can do little more than acknowledge this with due humility.

REFERENCES

Anthony, E. J.   A risk-vulnerability intervention model for children of psychotic parents. In E. J. Anthony and C. Koupernik (Eds.), *The child in his family: Children at psychiatric risk*. New York: John Wiley, 1974.

Caplan, G.   *Principles of preventive psychiatry*. New York: Basic Books, 1964.

Garmezy, N.   Unpublished manuscript.

10

Parent Effectiveness Training: A Preventive Program and Its Delivery System

THOMAS GORDON

In the early 1960's, an isolated and often lonely psychologist in a small community on the west coast of the United States was strongly influenced by the words of two other psychologists, spoken many hundreds of miles away in the eastern part of our country. I was the isolated psychologist, very much alone professionally because the kind of thinking I was doing as a clinical psychologist in private practice was neither accepted nor valued by my colleagues. I received the words of the two eastern psychologists, both of whom I greatly respected, as supportive and confirming. For this I feel grateful, and today I am able to express my gratitude in person to one of them, for he is the organizer of this very conference. George Albee was one of the first psychologists to challenge openly the wisdom of clinical psychologists' use of the medical model. His prediction of the demise of our psychological profession because its members had chosen the role of the medical doctor was prophetic, viewed in retrospect; at the time it was a reassuring voice in the wilderness to me, for I had become disenchanted with my own efforts to help families by offering "treatment" to children considered by their parents to be sick or emotionally ill.

The second psychologist whose words reached me across the continent was George Miller, who in his inaugural address as president of the American Psychological Association advocated that psychologists must find ways to "give Psychology away to the public." His proposal stressed the need for education to prevent maladaptive behavior. The article, written with considerable courage, reached me precisely when I needed courage to move more decisively from treatment to prevention, from therapy to education, from trying to fix up troubled children to providing "training before trouble."

In working with children and youth, I gradually began to comprehend that these young people were not "sick," nor did they need psychotherapy. Quite the contrary, when I got to know them well, most of them struck me as remarkably healthy and often creatively resourceful in their attempts at coping with the destructive and repressive behaviors of their parents and teachers. Using Bion's simple classification, some of these youngsters had learned to cope through fight, others through flight, and still others through submission. They had to cope some way, so cope they did. It would have been a disservice to them to exert any kind of therapeutic influence that would take away their coping mechanisms.

The parents who brought their "problem children" to me, always with high hopes that I would bring about radical changes in their behavior, were not "sick" either. In fact, most were functioning effectively in their lives—they were successful in their occupations, they had friends, they were active in their community, and many had fairly satisfying marriages. Contrary to what I had been taught in my graduate training, these parents showed very little psychopathology: I never spotted an authoritarian personality, I rarely encountered schizoid or paranoid types, and I never uncovered an oedipus complex.

Instead, most of them were trying hard to be effective parents. They were concerned, conscientious, and eager to raise responsible kids. Usually, they were worried about the youngster or disappointed in the way he was turning out, but they could not be accused of child neglect, nor of failure to discipline their children. Most were doing what they thought best for the child, usually being the kind of parents their own parents were with them (or occasionally deliberately being the opposite).

In addition, the parents were strangely alike in certain ways. With few exceptions, (1) their parental behavior appeared firmly rooted in a belief in the reward and punishment methods used in dog training; (2) their patterns of communication with their children were very similar; (3) they had the same ideas about authority and discipline; and (4) they were almost totally unaware of psychological knowledge relevant to parent-child relationships —for example, self-concept theory, styles of leadership, frustration-aggression theory, modeling theory, transparency or congruence, family communications, empathy and acceptance, conflict-resolution, problem-solving, effects of punishment, and so on. Clearly, these parents were amazingly uninformed in the behavioral sciences—nobody had given away Psychology to this group of parents, although by the usual standards most were quite well educated. My sample of parents included many doctors, lawyers, engineers, college professors, executives, and educators. They seemed prime candidates for education about human behavior. But what kind of education? What type of training?

THE DESIGN OF THE TRAINING PROGRAM

My design for parent training was strongly influenced by my fifteen years' experience in developing and teaching human relations training programs for business and industrial executives. Some of the principles that this experience had validated are:

1. Training is best done in a group.

2. The instructor must model the attitudes and skills he proposes to teach others.

3. Resistance to change must be allowed to be freely expressed and accepted.

4. Awareness or sensitivity is not enough; trainees cannot be expected to come forth with new skills without specific skill training.

5. The classroom climate must be relatively free of threat and evaluation.

6. The power differential in human relationships is the most critical variable.

Incorporated in my training design were certain other features that I felt would maximize its acceptance by parents and increase its chances of reaching large numbers of parents in many communities.

1. It had to be easily transportable to other communities, as well as easily transferable to other professionals who could be trained as instructors.

2. It had to be as brief as possible. The program required 24 hours of classroom time, one three-hour session a week for eight weeks.

3. It had to be divorced completely from the medical model and the language of treatment (doctor, patient, therapy group, diagnosis). The name for the program was deliberately chosen: Parent Effectiveness Training. The language of education was employed throughout (course, instructor, class, students, textbook, assignments, tuition).

4. It had to be much less expensive than therapy. (In California, therapists' fees are often as high as $60 to $75 per hour.) P.E.T., as the course has come to be called, is usually $50 per person and $90 per couple (around $2 per instructional hour).

5. It had to attract fathers, in contrast to most parent education programs in this country. With few exceptions, the P.E.T. course is given at night.

6. It had to be geographically accessible to parents. Hence, P.E.T. classes are held in churches, homes, and neighborhood conference rooms as opposed to universities or college campuses.

7. Rather than depending on grants or subsidies from foundations or from government agencies (funding that is seldom dependable), I decided that the P.E.T. program would be self-supporting. The tuition pays for the instructor's fee and meeting room rental, as well as for the support services of the national headquarters office (Effectiveness Training, Inc.). Of particular interest to those who make a study of the financial and organizational structure of institutions is the fact that Effectiveness Training, Inc., a for-profit organization, is a nationwide network of over 5,000 instructors authorized to teach P.E.T. after completion of special training. Each instructor is an independent agent (as opposed to an employee), affiliated with the corporation by virtue of a written mutual agreement that spells out the obligations of both the corporation and the instructor. The corporation, which maintains a staff of around 25 full-time employees, provides the following partial list of services to the network of instructors:

a. Authorizes the use of the name Dr. Thomas Gordon's Parent Effectiveness Training, with whatever good will and public acceptance it has gathered over fifteen years.

b. Supplies to each student a textbook, *P.E.T.: Parent Effective-*

ness Training (New York, Peter H. Wyden, 1970), and a Parent Workbook.

c. Supplies instructors with brochures, reprints, flyers, and other publicity materials.

d. Publishes a newsletter for instructors, primarily for professional development, instructional improvement, and marketing assistance.

e. Maintains a research library and clearinghouse.

f. Modifies and upgrades instructor outlines and student materials.

g. Administers a speakers' bureau.

h. Refers to instructors the names of parents who write the home office to ask where they may enroll in a P.E.T. class.

i. Develops new courses (Teacher Effectiveness Training, Effectiveness Training for Youth, Leader Effectiveness Training).

j. Produces films, visual aids, and tapes for use by instructors.

The P.E.T. Instructors

Initially, I had hoped to attract many licensed clinical psychologists (like myself) to teach the P.E.T. course in communities throughout the country. I discovered, however, that very few were interested, for a variety of reasons. They wanted to do therapy; or they saw their future in the growth centers which at that time were springing up; or they did not feel there was sufficient financial return; or they found it both difficult and unprofessional to do what was necessary to attract parents into the course (giving speeches, calling on pediatricians and ministers, mailing brochures, and so on); or they felt incompetent as teachers or speakers; or they felt that such a training course could never bring about significant modification of parental behavior.

It has never been difficult, however, to find instructors from other professional groups. In fact, over the years, recruiting new instructors has been one of our easier tasks. In the past three years we have trained between 1,500 and 2,000 new instructors each year, bringing the total number to around 7,500.

By and large, the kind of people who want to be trained as P.E.T. instructors are those who first take the course as parents and discover such rewarding changes in their own families that they want to teach other parents what they learned, sometimes

with an evangelical zeal. Others see teaching P.E.T. as an opportunity to enlarge or enrich their professional roles, which for many
had become limited or stultifying. Other professionals, dissatisfied
with the treatment model they have been caught in, see the P.E.T.
course as a way of moving into the preventive model and having a
far greater impact on their community. Very few of our instructors
are primarily motivated by expectations of financial rewards,
inasmuch as the instructional fees are simply not high enough to
support a person full time.

P.E.T. instructors have been drawn primarily from the following
professional groups: ministers, social workers, school counselors,
marriage and family counselors, school psychologists, nursery
school teachers, parent education teachers, youth workers, and
clinical psychologists. A few of our most active and competent
instructors are housewives with varying amounts of formal education who have wanted to do something constructive and rewarding
in the mental health or human relations field but have been
prevented from doing so by state licensing and certification
regulations requiring academic degrees.

Our training for P.E.T. instructors involves the following
components:

1. Completion of the P.E.T. course as a student (not required
but recommended).

2. Completion of a 5½-day intensive Instructor Training Workshop, taught by one of our six most experienced trainers in various
cities throughout the country and in some foreign countries.

3. Each instructor is furnished a very comprehensive instructor
outline that spells out in great detail his instructional activities in
each of the eight sessions of the P.E.T. course.

4. Instructors become thoroughly familiar with the contents of
the textbook *P.E.T.—Parent Effectiveness Training*.

5. Each instructor is encouraged to co-teach with an experienced
instructor if there is one in his community.

6. An instructor has the option of starting out by practice teaching with a group of no more than ten of his neighbors, relatives,
and friends, who pay only a token tuition fee for this type of class.

7. Instructors get feedback on their instructional performance
from evaluation forms filled out anonymously by all participants
at the end of the course.

8. In many communities instructors form an association, one of

the functions of which is the continuing improvement of its members' instructional skills.

Although this type of training does not ensure that all of our instructors are uniformly competent, of one thing we are certain: most instructors find that teaching the P.E.T. course is one of the most fulfilling and rewarding experiences in their lives. The reasons are clear. Parents are desperate for help; most of them are eager to learn new skills; and a very large percentage report immediate positive results in their family life.

What Parents Learn from P.E.T.

The P.E.T. program in one respect is not unlike a graduate training program for a profession. During a graduate program you acquire certain knowledge and skills, but subsequently you learn much more when you take on a job and begin to apply your knowledge and try out your new skills. In P.E.T. parents also acquire knowledge and skills, but many additional learnings occur when they subsequently use their knowledge and skills with real problems in the home.

That parents learn certain things in the P.E.T. classes is easily ascertained with a rather high degree of certainty, because we incorporate experiences throughout the course in which parents actually perform the skills they have been taught and make use of the knowledge they have been given. A partial list of such learnings reads as follows.

1. Parents learn to think and talk about their children in terms of their discrete existential behaviors (what they are saying or what they are doing) rather than in terms of abstract personality traits or characteristics, ordinarily accompanied by judgments or evaluations: "Jimmy did not say hello to my friend" versus "Jimmy is shy and impolite"; "Kathy left her clothes in the living room" versus "Kathy is sloppy and inconsiderate."

2. Parents learn the importance of responding to the child's behavior consistently or congruently with their feelings, whether their feelings are acceptance or nonacceptance; and they learn how to determine which of these feelings they are actually experiencing. In short, they learn that honesty is the best policy in human relationships.

3. Parents learn to use facilitative communications skills in responding to messages children are sending when they tell their parents their problems. Drawing from my training as a Rogerian therapist, we teach parents to rely heavily on three skills of the professional counselor: *Silence; Door-openers* or *Open-ended Questions:* and *Active Listening* (*Reflective Listening*).

4. Parents learn to confront children whose behavior is unacceptable to them by sending statements limited to their own feelings (leveling, being congruent or transparent) as opposed to blaming, preaching, ordering warning, and the like: "I am too tired to play with you" versus "You are being a pest"; "I need more quiet to read my book" versus "You stop that yelling or you'll go to your room."

5. Parents learn the destructive effects that punishment and power can have on both their children and the relationship.

6. Parents learn the pitfalls of being both permissive (giving in to the child, so child wins and parent loses) and authoritarian (using power to make the child give in to the parent, so parent wins and child loses). Then they acquire an alternative approach to resolving conflicts: namely, a problem-solving method in which a solution is found acceptable to both parent and child (no one loses).

7. Parents learn some new approaches to resolving collisions of parent-child values amicably and with low risk of damaging the relationship.

To ascertain what later happens to parents who continue to apply their new knowledge and skills, we have relied primarily on in-depth interviews with a random sample of parents months or even years after they complete the P.E.T. course. Analysis of the transcripts of these tape-recorded interviews reveals a wide range of outcomes: new awarenesses of the dynamics of the parent-child relationship, redefinitions of their parent role, new insights about themselves and their children, increased trust in the capacities of their children, greater confidence in themselves as parents, deeper and more intimate relationships with their children, and many others. Specific examples give the flavor of what happens when parents put their P.E.T. skills to work:

"I'm more in control of myself."

"I am more relaxed, less uptight, less inclined to come unglued."

"I feel I know what is going on in each specific interaction with the children."

"We've learned to trust each other and appreciate each others' needs."

"I'm more nonjudgmental."

"It has changed my focus from the child as a problem to me and what I'm doing."

"We simply never think of using punishment, of any kind."

"I'm more aware of how important it is to be in touch with my own needs."

"P.E.T. changed my whole outlook—I see our relationships all different now."

"I now feel confident to assert my own needs—to take care of myself, not live my life for my kids or let them walk over me—and all this without guilt."

"We're not afraid any more to talk about feelings."

"A new awareness that parents don't necessarily have all the answers—the kids can be creative and come up with answers."

"An awareness now that nobody has to be in control and calling the shots."

"Now kids can blast at me and I can see that they have a reason to."

"Now we honestly love each other."

"Since experiencing that I have rights and feelings worthy of respect, I have pursued a career, taught P.E.T., got an advanced degree . . . I, who was terrified to speak out loud in an audience, am now giving lectures, teaching classes, doing counseling. Before P.E.T., I really didn't trust myself, my ideas, or even my own judgment of whom I could trust."

"Since P.E.T. training, I am closer to my sons in an intimate way I would never have dreamed of, and at the same time I am happier about their independence."

"The greatest effect in our relationship was having my son come to us and say, 'I really think you love me more than you used to.' "

Further evidence of changes in parents as a result of taking the P.E.T. course is available from ten different research studies, representing a wide quality variation with respect to the measuring instruments utilized, the size of the parent sample, and the experimental control of other variables.

The most carefully designed and controlled studies reported the following statistically significant changes brought about by P.E.T.:

Greater confidence in themselves as parents (Garcia, 1971; Larson, 1972; Lillibridge, 1971).

Greater mutual understanding between parent and child (Garcia, 1971).

Greater mutual trust between parent and child (Garcia, 1971).

Greater parental acceptance and understanding (Hanley, 1973).

Increased trust in children and willingness to allow autonomy (Hanley, 1973; Larson, 1972; Lillibridge, 1971).

Better understanding of children (Knowles, 1970).

Less inclination to use authority (Knowles, 1970; Larson, 1972).

Reduction in authoritarian attitudes (Knowles, 1970).

Children of P.E.T. parents improved in school performance (Larson, 1972).

Increased insight into behavior of children (Larson, 1972).

Improvements in parents' self-concept (Larson, 1972).

Fewer concerns and problems (Larson, 1972).

Increase in acceptance of children (Lillibridge, 1971).

Children of P.E.T. parents perceived parents as more accepting and less rejecting (Lillibridge, 1971).

More distaste for punitive and rigid parental controls (Peterson, 1970).

More willingness to hear problems and complaints of children (Peterson, 1970).

More willingness to accept child's rights to hold different view from parents (Peterson, 1970).

More willing to admit that conflicts can be dealt with directly and openly (Peterson, 1970).

More democratic in attitudes toward family (Stearn, 1970).

Children of P.E.T. graduates increased in their self-esteem (Stearn, 1970).

Children who were designated as underachievers and whose parents took P.E.T. improved one full grade point from the first to the third quarter (Larson, 1972).

SOME LIMITATIONS OF P.E.T.

Obviously a 24-hour educational experience is not going to solve all of the problems in parent-child relationships. Nor will it prevent all of the pathology produced by families in our society. Yet it appears to be a significant and effective beginning in primary prevention focusing on the persons who have the earliest and perhaps the greatest influence on a child's emotional and physical health as well as his social and intellectual development.

Yet P.E.T. reaches only those parents who already have a personal relationship with their children and who desire to improve that relationship. Other preventive methods obviously are needed to counteract the destructive effects of poverty on children, or to help children who have been abandoned, neglected, or ignored by parents. Infanticide and violent child abuse may not be reduced by increased parent effectiveness, although a case could be made for the thesis that such extreme parental behaviors may indeed be related to the strongly authoritarian approach to discipline that is almost universally practiced and sanctioned in our society.

P.E.T. has received virtually no financial support from foundations or government agencies, which obviously makes the program less accessible to low-income parents. Herein exists a paradox. The delivery system for P.E.T., rooted as it is in a self-supporting, independent, entrepreneurial, and cost-accountable organization, is certainly compatible with the American free-enterprise philosophy, and has demonstrated its effectiveness in bringing parent training to over a quarter of a million parents. Yet the fact that Effectiveness Training Associates is not a nonprofit or charitable organization (dependent on others) deters foundations and agencies from offering financial support to subsidize the parents of nearly 5 million children of families living in near poverty in this country.

The P.E.T. program with its focus on parents does not directly influence the "other parents of our children"—teachers, coaches, day care workers, school administrators, probation officers, youth club leaders, and the like. Recognizing the influence of such adults on children and youth, our organization has developed several other effectiveness training courses: T.E.T. (Teacher Effectiveness Training); Effectiveness Training for School Administrators; and Effectiveness Training for Professionals Working with Youth. It is our belief that while primary prevention must begin at home, it must continue in all of the institutions in which adults relate to children and youth.

REFERENCES

Garcia, J. Preventive programs in parent education: A study of P.E.T. Unpublished M.S.W. thesis, University of Southern California, 1971.
Hanley, D. F. Changes in parent attitude related to a parent effectiveness training and a family enrichment program. Unpublished Ph.D. dissertation, United States International University, 1973.
Haynes, S. Altering parental attitudes toward child-rearing practices using parent education groups. Unpublished manuscript, Boston University, 1972.
Knowles, L. Evaluation of P.E.T.: Does improved communication result in better understanding? Chicago State College, 1970.
Larson, R. S. Can parent classes affect family communications? *The School Counselor*, 1972, 261–270.
Lillibridge, M. The relationship of a P.E.T. program to change in parents' self-assessed attitudes and children's perceptions of parents. Unpublished Ph.D. dissertation, United States International University, 1971.
Miles, J. M. A comparative analysis of the effectiveness of verbal reinforcement group counseling and parent effectiveness training on certain behavioral aspects of potential dropouts. Unpublished Ph.D. dissertation, Auburn University, 1974.
Peterson, B. Parent effectiveness training and change in parental attitudes. Unpublished manuscript, University of Santa Clara, 1970.
Schmitz, K. A study of the relationship of parent effectiveness training to changes in parents' self-assessed attitudes and behavior in a rural population. Unpublished Ed.D. dissertation, University of South Dakota, 1975.
Stearn, M. The relationship of P.E.T. to parent attitudes, parent behavior and child self-esteem. Unpublished Ph.D. dissertation, 1970.

11

Prevention in Retrospect: Adoption Follow-Up

MARIE SKODAK CRISSEY

The primary prevention of what is identified in later life as psychopathology will ultimately be governed by the integrated findings from a variety of research efforts. Some of these will emanate from laboratories and some from experimental conditions in defined settings, but perhaps the most significant will come from field observations of people reacting to, and behaving in, real-life circumstances. It is frustrating to experimental scientists that a real-life situation has so many uncontrolled and elusive impacts whose influence cannot be quantified or even identified until after the event, or until their influence has become a part of the individual's behavior repertoire and is in constant modification in response to changing events.

Nevertheless, evidence from real-life situations can lead to general principles, applicable in broader terms to people in similar circumstances. Studies of families in which the individuals experience a generally continuing kind of environment and interpersonal treatment, for example, have shown a continuing thread of similarity in educational and vocational achievement, intelligence, incidence of pathology, and so on. These observations do not, however, give evidence on the modifiability of human development or behavior in response to marked changes in environment or interpersonal relations. One real-life situation in which it is possible to observe the effects of a marked alteration in life circumstances is adoption. Many adoptions, particularly those by step-parents or relatives (which in fact constitute the majority of legal adoptions), do not produce significant changes in life circumstances. One middle-class family functions in general about like another; one that is low in the socioeconomic scale is similar to its neighbor. It is when marked disparity is found between the natural and the adoptive parent and family that evidence regarding human modifiability is uncovered. Intellectually average or superior parents who adopt children from families of distinctly lesser competence can set the stage for a field experiment with implications for primary prevention.

The majority of adoption studies have covered relatively short periods of time, usually one initial and one follow-up observation. They have also been characterized by intensive statistical manipulation of data having dubious validity or reliability. Educational level, occupation, and IQ are themselves dependent on many factors: opportunity, motivation, chance encounters, constitutional differences, or genetic predispositions, to name a few. To leap from data of this kind to controversy about genetic inheritance, or the relative contributions of nature versus nurture, is not only hazardous by virtue of being based on fragile data, but contributes little or nothing that is useful to practices or policies with potentially ameliorative social applications. The state of the art is such that inspecting life histories—studying similarities and differences in outcome, following differences in initial or ongoing conditions—may quite possibly prove more useful than laboratory methods. Pure research methods may not really be applicable to the variability of human beings in real-life situations. This unsophisticated, nontechnical approach is used here to look at data that have been previously reported in other contexts and are now examined with a view to preventing psychopathology, specifically mental retardation.

Most individuals in this country are born into families and remain with them, experiencing a continuity of life style set by their parents and their parents' parents before them. Adoptees, by contrast, have had a different experience. None of the adoptees discussed here remained with their natural families; in fact, few had any contact with them whatever, having gone directly from the hospital ward to an orphanage hospital ward.

I would like to explore with you the life pattern of these children, beginning with information about the natural family and the events that precipitated the changes in family setting, followed by descriptions of the family setting in which the adoptees grew up. Repeated cross-sectional glimpses of the children's development follow them into adulthood. Regrettably, there are gaps in the information, but even so, the data may be useful.

Four groups are discussed. The first group, 13 children, was one in which the natural mothers had IQ's of 70 to 79 and the children were placed in adoptive homes before the age of 6 months. The second group, 11 children, had mothers with IQ's between 53 and 69 and the children were placed in adoptive homes before the age of 6 months. The third group, 13 children, had been identified as retarded in infancy and experienced a planned environment in infancy and preschool ages. The fourth group, 12 children, had been identified as normal in infancy and remained in an orphanage for "normal" children.

Since this conference is directed to the prevention of psychopathology (both developmental delay or retardation, and deviation or mental/emotional disturbance), attention will be paid to evidences of this in the subjects. "Children at risk" are generally understood to be those for whom there is great likelihood of deficit or disturbance based on prediction from present and anticipated circumstances.

The study covers a space of some 40 years. It may be useful to describe the setting in which it began.

Iowa, in the late 1920's and early 1930's, was one of the midwest states suffering from drought and a major economic depression. Though incomes were low and farm foreclosures were frequent, the general life standard of families was not as severely affected as in urban states. Iowans had been used to hard work and home gardens, and chickens and pigs were raised for meat even in cities. Help for neighbors in need had been a long tradition. In many respects the inhabitants of the state suffered less personal hardship and deprivation than people in industrial states to the east or in more drought-stricken states to the south and west. There was little evidence, for example, that more infants were referred for state care than in years preceding or following the Great Depression. It should be recalled that there was no social security at that time, no unemployment supplements or aid to dependent children, no reliable contraceptives or casual acceptance of sex relations. There were few alternatives for out-of-wedlock pregnancies. Some infants were legitimized by marriage; a few were accepted by the maternal family, at great emotional cost to everyone. An unknown proportion, but probably the majority, were placed for adoption. The few private child-placing agencies in the state were selective primarily on the basis of religion, and they tended to reject unwed applicants from the lowest economic and cultural strata and offer care first to girls from "better family backgrounds." Consequently, referrals to the state agency for child care tended to consist mostly of infants no one else wanted. Since no costs to family or local welfare agencies were involved, the majority of these births occurred at the University Hospital, with a direct transfer to the state child caring agency. From there, through a network of essentially untrained placement workers, the children were placed in adoptive homes. The usual stay in the orphanage hospital was two to three months while family selection and the inevitable paper work were completed. In those days before antibiotics, infections and illnesses occasionally delayed placement or removed a child from the placeable list.

Through a liaison between the Board of Control of State Institutions and the Child Welfare Research Station of the State University of Iowa, a series of studies of various aspects of child development were made possible. Among them was a study of the mental development of all children admitted to state care, and specifically all children placed for adoption. Arrangements were made for repeat examinations, and eventually 125 children were followed over a period of nearly 40 years. It was from this latter number that the four groups discussed here were selected.

When the study began, there was no intention of preventing retardation. The infants were simply accepted by the orphanage as dependent children. At that time there were only two alternatives: adoptive placement or retention in the orphanage. Other, more sophisticated child-caring agencies would have looked askance at such histories and would have placed with reluctance if at all, but not so this orphanage.

Adoptive applications, accompanied by medical, ministerial, and financial references and screened locally by untrained field workers, were reviewed by a placement committee and a child was selected on the basis of parental request for sex, coloring, and religion, in that order. The committee—made up of the orphanage superintendent, the head of the state child welfare program, the head nurse of the receiving hospital ward, and later the state psychologist—were influenced primarily by their own impressions of the quality of the baby, as seen in a brief walk through the nursery ward.

The First Group

The first group, of 13 children, had mothers whose IQ's were between 70 and 79, with a median IQ of 76, based on individual 1916 Stanford Binet tests. In addition to the score, comments by the psychologists who gave the tests described the mothers with such comments as "dull, sluggish, with poor memory." All the infants were illegitimate and comments were frequent that the burden of child rearing would be beyond the capabilities of the mothers. Among them were several known to have been promiscuous. The families were not merely "depression welfare" families, but had long records of inadequacy. Although some family members were regarded as slow, the families were not generally labeled as feeble-minded. Other studies, however, have shown that children from such maternal and social backgrounds are at high risk for slow development, poor school progress, and mental ability on the borderline of dull normal levels as adolescents.

Of the 13 infants in this group, all were placed under 6 months of age and most under 3 months. One was placed in a professional (medical services) home, 5 in homes of independent business men or minor professions, 3 in skilled trades or technical homes, and 4 in the homes of farm owners or operators. The contrast in level of families is obvious: the occupational level of all but one of the original families (whether maternal or alleged paternal) was at the unskilled, laborer, or unemployed level. The one exception was a student still in school, and this paternity was not verified.

Examined at age 2, the 13 children had a mean IQ of 121, with none below 102. At age 4, the mean IQ was 108, at 7 years 117, and at 13 years 114. IQ's at age 13, the last formal testing, ranged from 78 and 82 (a pair of twins) to 141. Of the 13, seven had IQ's of 120 to 141 on the 1937 Terman-Merrill test. Interviewed some 20 to 30 years later, it was found that all 13 children, originally qualifying as at high risk, graduated from high school. Four went no further. Of these 4, two are homemakers, one married to a farmer and one to a salesman. One man has made a career in the military service as a cook, with a proud file of commendations for excellence in both quality of meals and sanitation. He has also taken many courses in military law and takes an active role in helping his buddies circumvent unwanted regulations. The fourth high school graduate is a man who had an IQ of 140 at age 13. His family moved to a singularly unstimulating community and he had the misfortune to land in several dead-end military assignments in spite of high aptitude scores. Abandoning a military career short of retirement, he returned to civilian life and within three weeks had advanced to a responsible job in a manufacturing company.

Two others had one year of college and one had two years (one is now a warehouse manager and two are homemakers). One had three years of special training and is now vice president of an advertising firm. One had four years of college and is a specialty salesman, one completed seventeen years' training and is a medical specialist; and one has a two-year master's degree in educational administration.

Of special interest are the two girls who had the lowest IQ's at age 13 and who seemed to be following the pattern that would have been predicted from the natural family background. Throughout their lives they have had spectacular health histories, including near death from ingesting a household chemical, and a fractured skull in a travel accident. They spent a year or two in special remedial classes and in addition had intensive tutoring (two to four hours daily) through elementary school and junior and senior high school. They graduated and attended a two-year college, taking a secretarial course. After working as secretary and receptionist, they subsequently married. The husband of one is now a senior military officer and the other is vice president of a sizable firm. In spite of the stormy beginning—more extensive than this account allows—neither is retarded or maladjusted. Each has three children, all doing well in school.

The singularly successful post-high-school achievement and adjustment would not have been predicted from either the natural family history or the early developmental pattern and educational progress. It does suggest the value of early counseling. When the relative delay of these children was observed, and the educational expectations of the family were clarified, several additional psychological evaluations were arranged and the results and their implications discussed with the parents. Since the children would need additional help to compete with others, this help was arranged at the time it was needed. Instead of being held as a college fund, the investment was made during the earlier years, and with an attitude of help rather than pressure. The supportive nature of the interpersonal relations in the adoptive family was clearly evident in every contact and has implications beyond these two exemplary cases.

There was no evidence of major maladjustment in any of these 13 adults. All were married to people comparable to themselves in education and family socioeconomic level. One (the cook) had a child estimated to be slow or with a learning disability, but all the others were in appropriate grades for their ages, and their report cards (shown with considerable pride) indicated at least average and usually superior progress.

The Second Group

The second group, of 11 children, had mothers whose IQ's were from 53 to 67, with a median of 63. Educational level was commensurate with this degree of retardation. Not only were the mothers described as retarded or mentally defective, but in fact several were, had been, or subsequently became residents of state institutions for the retarded. The general family backgrounds of these mothers were measurably inferior to those of the previous group.

The placement committee was understandably somewhat more cautious in placing these children. Two nevertheless went into the homes of teachers, one into the home of an office worker, 4 into skilled or sales workers' homes, 2 into homes of farmers, and 2 into homes of semi-skilled factory workers. Describing these homes is substantially more difficult, since subsequent to the adoptive placement major problems emerged. The interplay between characteristics of the home and characteristics of the child, and possibly some knowledge of natural family characteristics, becomes too complex to be unraveled on the basis of the information available.

For example, one child had a mother "retarded with psychosis," plus about seven siblings, most of whom have spent at least part of their lives in state institutions. The alleged father was a psychiatric patient. The child was placed in a modest home, where the adoptive mother soon became totally deaf, with accompanying personality changes. The adoptive father immersed himself in his job. As an adolescent, the girl was at loose ends. She married to legitimize a pregnancy, became the mother of four in rapid succession, and broke down, with hospitalization needed for over a year. She has since continued out-patient treatment, with good results; she is an adequate, though slightly demanding, mother and has completed most of a two-year college program. Her husband is a long haul truck driver, her children range from 107 to 135 in IQ, and her home, while disorganized, is full of books, science projects for the children, and a stream of pets which come and go. Erratic and emotionally fragile, she is nevertheless a pillar of the local P.T.A. and a willing helper of the needy in her area.

One child placed in a teacher's home completed a two-year post-high-school technical program. He is married and has two bright children and a fine career as a creative artist. The adoptive father completed a doctorate and the home is comparable to the warmest and most supportive to be found anywhere.

Another child placed in another teacher's home is, to all intents and purposes, psychotic. Unfortunately both adoptive parents are so marginally adjusted that every assessment by the various clinics that have had contact with the family has carried a poor prognosis for the future. "Unworkable" has been the kindest description of them. The adoptee has had about three unsuccessful marriages, has a neurologically involved, maladjusted son, and keeps house for the adoptive parents, who have developed other business and professional activities since giving up teaching. The entire menage is self-sufficient and manages to remain in the community, but hardly qualifies as mentally healthy.

Still another, whose mother had an IQ of 53, is divorced, has been hospitalized, and now lives with her adopted mother in a remote community. Both she and the preceding adoptee had been recognized as seriously disturbed when they were children and had been returned briefly to the agency. Both were reclaimed by the respective adopting parents. Thus the home was reconstituted in spite of the children's poor adjustment and the evident problems of the family; and the adoptees have both gone on to verify the prognosis of poor adulthood made in infancy.

Of the total group of 11 children, two left school at tenth or eleventh grade, but all the others graduated from high school. Six went no further; these are now all housewives. Two had done some office work, two some factory work. One, as mentioned, had two years of specialized training, and two completed college; one of these has since earned a master's degree in education. The other is in a minor profession in which continuing special training is required.

The lot of these 11 children is less neatly successful. On the whole they are not as successful—in middle-class terms—as the children of borderline mothers. At least three have had psychological/psychiatric help and probably three more would benefit from it. None are currently hospitalized; all are doing some useful work. One has not married and two have been divorced. Of the 11, six are known to have good solid marriages.

When success is evaluated, one must ask "Compared to what?" These were indeed high risk children, who went into homes many of which had less than optimum strengths. That 6 of the 11 can be described as at least reasonably well adjusted may still be regarded as speaking for adoption as a preventive measure.

The Third Group

The third group consists of 13 children who had been admitted to the orphanage before the age of three years but were subsequently recognized to be retarded. They were not considered for adoptive placement but were held for observation to determine whether there was some physiological basis for the slow development and whether they might respond to the care available in the orphanage. Medical reasons were not established, and they did not improve in the orphanage.*

In the normal course of events, retarded children were transferred from the orphanage to institutions for the mentally handicapped when space became available for them. Two of these children were regarded as urgently in need of special care, and since no other room was available, each was placed on a ward of older girls and women. Each little girl was the only young child on the ward. To the astonishment of everyone, the two children showed remarkable improvement, not only in appearance, health, and behavior, but in IQ as well. When this improvement endured over a period of two years, a planned program of intervention was

---

*The following two groups have been reported in more detail in Harold M. Skeels, Adult status of children with contrasting early life experiences, *Monographs of the Society for Research in Child Development, 31*, No. 3 (1966).

initiated with the hope that similar gains could be duplicated with other children. Eventually a total of 13 children were involved in a program which removed mentally retarded preschool children from an orphanage for normals to an institution for the mentally retarded with the specific goal of improving their intelligence.

Instead of being placed on wards according to chronological age, which was the usual practice, the project stipulated that the children be placed as individuals on wards where there would be maximum stimulation. On the wards with older girls (ages 15 to 50) these singleton infants received a great deal of attention from both inmates and staff, were played with almost constantly, were talked to incessantly, had a wealth of toys, were given all kinds of extra experiences, and were regarded as highly desirable and eminently successful individuals. In addition to the general attention from all, an individual attachment developed between each child and some particular adult who became a mother substitute.

The children remained in the institution for the retarded for periods of five and a half to fifty-two months. From an initial average IQ of 64 at the age of 18 months all had gained in IQ by the end of their stay from 7 to 45 points, with a mean gain of 28 points. At the end of the "experiment" the range of IQ's was from 70 to 113 with a mean IQ of 92.

The experiment was ended for each child when it appeared that he had attained maximum benefit from the experience in the institution for the mentally retarded. One child who was at the institution when the project closed was returned to the orphanage before she was believed to be ready, and as an adolescent she was again returned to the institution. One remained in the institution for the retarded until adulthood, and later, as an adult, was placed in the community. Five children went directly into adoptive homes. Six returned to the orphanage briefly and then were placed in adoptive homes.

All of these 13 children were reexamined approximately two and a half years after the experimental period closed for them. The interim experience consisted of life in an adoptive home for 11 of the children and continued residential care for two of them.

The follow-up examination showed that on the average the intervention group continued to gain. At an average age of nearly six years, the mean IQ was 96, or a total gain of 31 points from the first examination. Individual gains between pre- and post-placement test ranged from 2 to 61 points (with losses, however, occurring in the two children who remained in institutions and in one child placed in a distinctly below average adoptive home).

After a lapse of twenty to twenty-five years, these children—now adults in their 30's—were again visited. In spite of many moves, and changes of names through marriage, it was possible to locate every member of this intervention group. Either the parents or the child, usually both, were interviewed. Intelligence tests were not given to the "children" (now adults) but tests were administered to *their* children.

All of the 13 members of the experimental group, including the two who had spent a number of years in institutions, are self-supporting and independent. The three men include one in educational administration, one who is a sales manager of a moderately large organization, and one noncommissioned career military service man. Eight of the ten women are married. They include an elementary school teacher, a registered nurse, a beauty operator, a dining room hostess, a nurse aid, and two with no work history except homemaking. Of the two who are unmarried, one is a licensed practical nurse and the other is in domestic service. This latter is one of the two who was in institutional care until adulthood.

The educational record of the 13 is consistent with their present occupations. The two who had been in the institution had completed sixth grade. Three of the adopted had ended school in the tenth or eleventh grade. Eight graduated from high school. Of these, four had education beyond high school, some as much as three years of college, and one had a master's degree—that is, six years beyond high school.

The spouses of all are of educational and vocational status comparable to their partners. The institutional resident who was placed in adulthood as a nurse aid is married to a laborer. The teacher is married to a mechanic, the noncommissioned officer to a lab technician, the nurse to a real estate salesman, the beauty operator to a semi-skilled mechanic, the education professional to an advertising writer, and the clerical worker to a printer.

Nine of the experimental group had a total of 28 children. The IQ's of these children ranged from 86 to 125, with a mean of 104.

Those who were in school were doing well and all are described as attractive, normal children.

Of this group, who began life with a major developmental delay but who experienced a highly stimulating, planned adult-child relationship for some period of their lives, none are retarded or dependent. None have experienced discernible mental health problems and none have had social or emotional problems beyond those encountered in everyday living.

Of the 13 mothers of these individuals, two were described as "psychotic with mental retardation." IQ's of five of the mothers ranged from 55 to 106, with 66 as median. Education ranged from second to eleventh grade, with a median of eighth. Paternity was unestablished in 7 of the 13, and the remaining included printer, salesman, and farm laborer. Even from this meager evidence, the group would be regarded as at high risk for below-average development.

In contrast, the adoptive parents had median educations of twelfth grade or better and were at the farm owner, insurance adjuster, independent trucker level or better. They met the usual criteria for the selection of adoptive homes.

Comparisons of outcome leave little doubt that the children, now adults, more nearly resemble the adoptive families in education, occupation, and life competence than they do their natural families.

The Fourth Group

The final group consists of 12 children who had been normal as infants, but who for one reason or another were not placed for adoption. Most commonly the delay was the product of legal problems associated with commitment, and later exposure to infectious illnesses which interfered with placement. By the time these problems were solved, as much as two to four years had passed and it was found that the child was no longer normal in mental development.

These 12 children remained in the orphanage and in the course of time entered the kindergarten and first grade. Tests given at a mean age of 7 years resulted in a mean IQ of 66, with average gains of 6 points since the next preceding test, a finding consistent with other studies which show a gain in IQ at beginning of school.

Comparison between the 7-year test results and the initial scores, however, showed that losses were still the rule, with one child losing 64 points. This child at age 14 months had been described as a normal infant with IQ of 99. By three and a half years of age he had an IQ of 54, and by five years, 35.

These 12 once normal children showed increasing inability to cope with school or cottage demands, and by the age of eight years, 9 of the 12 had been transferred to an institution for the mentally retarded as residents, not with therapeutic intent. One was paroled to his grandparents, but at eight years of age was still in first grade and was recommended for institutional placement by the school psychologist. Three children continued in the orphanage. One completed kindergarten at six years of age, and one had a delayed school entrance and was nine years old in the second grade.

In contrast to the difficulties in locating the intervention group as adults because of their mobility, it was possible to locate all of the 12 contrast group members through institution records. It was found that 10 of the 12 had spent all, or nearly all, of their lives in institutional care in the twenty-year interval.

One had died in an institution for the retarded at adolescence of complications following surgery for a liver disorder. Four of the surviving 11 (36 percent) have remained institutional residents, unable to adjust in the community at any level. Four others have been "rehabilitated" at considerable expense and over a long period of time, from a life in the institution into jobs as dishwashers or part-time cafeteria helpers in the community. One more is unable to adjust in the community but is employed as assistant gardener in the institution where he lived for many years. None of these are married. One who remained in the orphanage until late adolescence now lives as a floater, working here and there as a handyman or porter. He was married briefly, but deserted his wife and mentally retarded child.

All of these, or 10 of the surviving 11, fit the classical stereotype of the mentally retarded, minimally skilled, unemployed or unemployable individual. They had a singularly barren, affectionless, detached childhood and as adults they are dependent and socially ineffective.

The one remaining contrast group member is consistently the exception. He is the only one who is employed, and employed in a highly skilled and well paying technical specialty. He is the only one with a sound marriage, a home of his own, and four attractive children with IQ's of 103 to 119. He not only graduated from high school, but had some college and trade training, and in every respect is a substantial, well-adjusted citizen and a contributing member of society.

A review of his experiences as compared with the others in the contrast group shows that up to the age of six he, too, had the same barren institutional existence. As a preschooler he had an IQ of 87; by six, his IQ was 67. Then, by chance selection, he was included in an intensive stimulation program as part of a doctoral research that emphasized language training and cognitive development. When he entered the regular school he was found to have a sensory defect. This was no major handicap in everyday life, but it qualified him for admission to a special boarding school. While there, he received personal attention from the dormitory supervisor and became an informal member of her family. In effect (though at a much later age), he experienced the intellectual stimulation and received the emotional acceptance which had been the therapeutic formula for the group previously discussed.

Assessment of family backgrounds suggests that compared with adoptees in general, the members of this group were somewhat more disadvantaged. Maternal IQ's, available for 8 of the 13 cases, ranged from 36 to 85, with a median of 65. Education ranged from less than fifth grade to twelfth, with a median of eighth. Maternal occupations, except for one clerical worker, were either nonexistent or in housework. Natural father occupations, known for 11 of the 13, were all in unskilled labor except for one carpenter.

There were of course no adoptive families to give stimulation, affection, or support.

The orphanage in which these children lived was, at that time, seriously overcrowded and understaffed. There was neither time nor inclination to give affection or attention to individual children. Toys were few and quickly broken. Language development was seriously retarded at all age levels for all children in the orphanage. There was little or no personal contact between children and adults. A more barren or unstimulating existence would be diffi-cult to describe.

If one were to compare only the initial description of the family background and the current adult status of these individuals, it would be easy to claim excellent prediction from the parental data: a high risk family and the expected outcome. Evidence from other studies suggests that children from similar subaverage backgrounds are substantially below the general average in intelligence, school achievement, and vocational success, though not usually to the degree of deficit shown by the 10 individuals. This study goes beyond that and demonstrates that when the environment is singularly restricting, emotionally barren, and the opposite of challenging and supportive, the individual's response adequacy can be so curtailed and become so rigid that he cannot function as a normal adult. Whether mentally retarded or intellectually paralyzed becomes of little significance. He is dependent on society for care.

SUMMARY AND CONCLUSIONS

On the basis of family data—parental education, occupation, social history—all four of these groups of children would be identified as at high risk for retardation and/or maladjustment if they remained in the original parental environment.

All of them experienced a marked change in life setting. For two groups, early placement in adoptive homes moved them into situations offering a great deal of affection, general economic security, and intellectual and cultural opportunities which were above average for the community and in the opposite direction from the offerings of the natural family. The third group, even more at risk in view of initial delays in development, experienced specific programs which effected marked changes in the developmental course and made adoptive placement possible. The fourth group, in addition to adverse family background, had life experiences which accentuated the chances for retardation and adjustment difficulties.

The favorable results of adoption for children from initially disadvantaged family backgrounds when they are placed in homes of average or better opportunities are evident. It suggests the general principle that the home in which the adoptee is placed, the experiences he undergoes, and the reciprocal and ever-changing relationship between the adoptee and the significant persons in his life may be more important than information about his natural family and their socioeconomic status.

The evidence from these four groups speaks for itself. Children in families in which low intelligence, poor school achievement, and social and economic inadequacy are prevalent have repeatedly been shown to follow the same familial pattern. When drastic changes in life circumstances occur early in the formative period, there are marked changes in the subsequent intelligence, educational, vocational, and social achievements of the child, with prevention of inadequacies predictable from the original family history. The responsiveness of the human organism to both facilitative and repressive influences was further underscored in the tragic histories of children once assessed as normal, whose early promise was obliterated by circumstances. The significance of primary prevention needs no further emphasis.

In looking back on these particular adoption follow-up studies, the wisdom of hindsight suggests many things that might have been improved in the interests of scientific purity. Yet, burdened with the constraints of laboratory type research, the studies might never have been made at all. The periodic intrusions into the lives of the children and the adopting parents were friendly, turned out often to be supportive and helpful, and resulted in evidence that has helped influence public policy. Thus it has had a bearing on the lives of others. These studies, it is hoped, will encourage investigators to explore real-life situations and thus augment our knowledge of the modifiability and the responsiveness of the human organism in the direction of happier, more effective, and healthier lives—the true aim of preventive efforts.

IV
Primary Prevention
of Adult Psychopathology

Introductory Notes

This section focuses on primary prevention, and areas of potential intervention, at the adult level. In planning the conference, the committee thought we should take into account the intimate role of poverty in generating a high risk of emotional disorder; we also felt that racism and sexism were important causes of emotional distress, and that they were as much psychopathological problems of the racists and sexists as they were sources of distress for the victims. So we invited two papers in these areas from experts in the field.

Elizabeth Taylor Vance is Associate Professor of Psychology at Cleveland State University. Her paper is a scholarly and stimulating review of the damaging effects produced by various kinds of low-status identity. She pays particular attention to the problems engendered by being black and by being female in the society. Her literature review suggests a number of exciting new areas of research.

Marcia Guttentag is a Visiting Professor of Social Ethics at Harvard University and Professor of Psychology, Graduate School, City University of New York. As persons interested in primary prevention we must be concerned with the prevention of sexism, a form of painful and damaging social injustice. But we must also be concerned with the effects of sexism and racism as stress leading to the development of psychopathology in significant numbers of the people discriminated against. Dr. Guttentag addresses these issues and reports on a study as an example of an attempt to achieve primary prevention of sexism in schools.

The Spring and Zubin paper comes closest to the outer boundary of the area we have defined as primary prevention and raises some interesting questions about the definition. Concerned with people

who have already suffered one schizophrenic episode, they argue
that a single episode of schizophrenia does not define a person as
chronically schizophrenic until death; rather, the illness is a time-
limited state. The task of aborting further episodes in those who
have had a single episode, they maintain, is indeed primary
prevention. Many might like to take issue with their position, but
it certainly deserves a hearing; and their paper is a stimulating
attempt to demonstrate the relevance of their argument.

Professor Joseph Zubin established the Biometrics Research
Unit in the New York State Department of Mental Hygiene
twenty years ago. As editor or coeditor, he has published 28
volumes under the aegis of the American Psychopathological
Association. In 1973 members of the Biometrics Research Unit,
together with outstanding scientists from around the world,
published *Psychopathology: Contributions from the Social,
Behavioral and Biological Sciences* (John Wiley) as a festschrift in
Zubin's honor. He is an honorary life member of the New York
Academy of Sciences and has served as president of the American
College of Neuropsychopharmacology. In short, Professor Zubin is
one of the most distinguished scholars in the field of psycho-
pathology. He is now Professor Emeritus of Psychology at
Columbia University and continues his very active scholarly work.
Bonnie Spring, a student of Professor Zubin's, is a Teaching
Fellow in the Department of Psychology and Social Relations at
Harvard University.

A Typology of Risks and the Disabilities of Low Status

ELIZABETH TAYLOR VANCE

Some of the most desirable strategies in primary prevention —those involving anticipatory techniques of one kind or another—are based on the assumption that we can identify specific characteristics of groups which are related to the types of pathologies we observe in those groups. The belief is not universally shared. Sybille Escalona, for example, has written a cogent paper questioning it (Escalona, 1974). The issue she raises is whether or not the intricate maze of formative events that determine individual personality and pathology can be stated in terms of the empirical generalizations needed for translation into valid interventions for large groups or populations.

The resolution of this issue directly concerns the possibilities of program building for individuals in the target groups discussed in this paper: those whose problems are intimately and complexly derived from their relationship to their society. Social problems always involve complex interactions and, to paraphrase Lee Cronbach, once we attend to interactions we begin looking into a hall of mirrors extending into infinity (Cronbach, 1975). That fact holds many problems for primary prevention.

One purpose of this paper is to provide a conceptual context for primary prevention in which we can consider the problem of interactions. Within such a context the difficulties of interactions may be made less formidable if only because we put some order into them. The concept of risk will apply most directly to the characteristics of pathology and only indirectly to the characteristics of people or groups. In other words, different groups may be at high risk for different kinds of problems which themselves differ in risk characteristics. Second, I would like to present the case of two groups—blacks and females—whose problems in our society, I believe, exemplify the difficulties for analysis which stem from extensive interactions.

A TYPOLOGY OF RISK

I suggest that we think of risk (as this concept applies to characteristics of problems) in terms of a tripartite model. An individual may be at risk if he is a member of a group characterized by an incidence of disorder above the base rates for that disorder in the population at large (Escalona, 1974). But careful observation shows that the discrepancies between base rates and incidence can be rank-ordered for different kinds of problems just as for groups; and to a large extent this variation can be understood in terms of numbers of factors that interact to produce the problem.

When describing problems, the concept of being at risk applies to a gradient of causal factors characterized by an increasing complexity of interactions. For purposes of guiding primary preventive efforts, I suggest there are at least three points on this continuum which make a difference to the analysis of risk and to primary prevention strategies. These loci are distinguished by differences in not one but at least two closely related factors: (a) the extent of interaction involved in the problem, and (b) the magnitude of the discrepancy between population base rates and incidence of the disorder in the target group.

Several practical implications emerge from the resultant typology. I find two of particular relevance here. One has to do with the economy and efficiency of primary prevention strategies. These depend upon the size of the discrepancy between base rates and incidence of disorder in the target group: the greater the discrepancy, the more necessary are population programs and the more wasteful are one-to-one efforts. A second implication has to do with the possibility of using a main-effects strategy for identification and intervention. The possibilities for the form primary prevention takes depend on the scope of the interactions involved and to what extent they can be ignored. The following typology assumes the possibility of differentiating among pathologies in this respect. One meaning for primary prevention is that the greater the number of relevant interactions, the smaller the groupings for which a single treatment will be appropriate.

Type I Risk

Type I risk refers to problems with a genetic or constitutional loading that biases development. The bias is sufficiently extreme to reduce drastically the contribution of moderating social and cultural influences in development.

There is little disagreement today with the belief that the extent of interaction even for these problems is considerable. We all know that, except for conditions with major gene control, the familiar dictum that "heredity sets fixed limits to the effects of environment" is inaccurate. In effect this statement assumes a main effect for heredity. Actually, the influences in phenotypal outcomes are always interactive. In pathology this principle applies even to a child of two schizophrenic parents who himself becomes schizophrenic.

The role of interactions in Type I risks is apparent from the difficulties in using the "At Risk Register" developed by the British (Hersov, 1974). The register was produced by screening and identifying children with birth characteristics thought to play a causal role in later impairment. Once in use, the list of risk categories grew so long that at one point 60 percent of all live births were included! Percentages in this range fall far short of the expressed hope that a high risk group of roughly 20 percent of all children could be identified which would include a large majority of children later found to be handicapped (Lindon, 1961). The considerable amount of discrepancy between at-risk labeling of this kind and actual outcome has motivated several investigators to formulate models or strategies of risk-vulnerability interactions (Anthony, 1974 [a], 1974 [b]; Garmezy, 1974).

It is important never to lose perspective on how deeply interactions are involved in human development. But interaction is generally reduced far below the level required to take it into account in preventive efforts by identifying the polygenic or perinatal influences that preclude an expectable rate or level of development in fundamental human qualities (language, communication, capacity for attachment). Thus interactions in Type I risks may often be treated as nominal with impunity, and interventions may often involve manipulation of single variables, as in the nutritional control of phenylketonuria.

In summary, about Type I risk we can say the following things.

The category includes a group of problems that have as a necessary (though not always sufficient) condition—genetic loading, constitutional biasing, or salient perinatal accident—which places the child at very high risk relatively early in life. The number of factors in interaction are, for all practical purposes, relatively modest and of lower priority than the salient effect. Thus the degrees of freedom in intervention are limited. Ultimately the design of primary prevention will be simplest and most straightforward for these conditions. The politics of professional commitment to, and social acceptability and support for, these programs are likely to be favorable. We have every reason to expect that primary preventive efforts for this group of problems will always have a potential for greater effectiveness and efficiency than those of secondary prevention or treatment.

Type II Risk

A second group of risks is comprised of problems that are eventually manifested largely because the developing child is associated with influences that are psychosocially pathogenic. Siblings of drug users, for example, are likely to be at higher risk for drug use and abuse than other children. Also, as a number of studies consistently demonstrate, there is a strong association between parental conflict and psychiatric disorder in children (Rutter, 1974; Fontana, 1966; Wynne and Singer, 1963 [a], 1963 [b]). Richard Jenkins (1966) has, by computer clustering of 500 children, identified at least five clinical groups each significantly associated with different family background. Excessive rates of personality disorder have been found in mothers of children receiving psychiatric treatment compared with a random sample of children (Wolff and Acton, 1968).

In spite of some reasonably well established relationships of this kind, it is this type of problem for which Escalona has particularly expressed pessimism. She reminds us of the idiosyncracies of individual patterns of experience produced by unique combinations the developing child experiences in his learning conditions and his dispositions and predispositions. In spite of the reality Escalona warns us about, I think we do have a great deal of usable information about associations of this kind and can potentially know a great deal more. Furthermore, I submit that the nature of the interactions in Type II risks will often justify a fairly straight-forward group approach.

We may not yet know whether the processes by which the child becomes disturbed in the association are unique to this category. But I would suggest that learning is saliently involved, as in the case of the child who assumes the delusions of a disturbed mother. Thus, Type II risk is essentially *associative risk*. The nature of human development is such that the large role played by social learning makes these problems relatively simple procedurally. What is or is not learned with respect to socially relevant behaviors and roles can increase the incidence of developmental failure or maladjustment enough above base rates to make it feasible, for preventive purposes, to treat conditions associated with salient social learning as though they had a main effect.

I need remind you of only a few difficulties in designing effective and economical preventive efforts for risks of this type. They are related for the most part to the fact that the interactions are greater than for Type I problems. For example, treating all mothers of preschoolers and school children who have personality disorders is an expedience (though an admittedly expensive one). The more we know about any interactions involved, the safer we are in our assumptions that we can disregard them; in other words, we need to understand what we are doing. Some early education programs may have suffered because the problems they were designed to solve (cultural deprivation, for example) were perceived as associative risk when we have not known enough about the nature and magnitude of the interactions—for example, individual and group differences in learning styles—to justify that approach. We are only beginning to comprehend the extent of interaction in the learning process well enough to build effective early education programs (Cronbach, 1975; Hunt, 1961, 1971). The danger in an over-simplistic, Good-Samaritan, main-effects approach for associative risks is that public support for preventive programs will be lost as resources dry up and programs are viewed as producing questionable returns.

A final point is that primary prevention scientists may need to provide some guidelines and a rationale for assigning priorities among these problems, given a limited public and political commitment to prevention. If no such guidelines are developed, they will be assigned for us. For example, the availability of public moneys for law and order and drug abuse prevention programs is playing a large role in shaping preventive efforts, even while opportunities for school psychologists diminish and food programs for school children are threatened.

Type III Risk

A third group of problems is no less important than those in the first two categories; problems I group under Type III risk, however, pose special difficulties for primary prevention. The category includes the social problems to which the remainder of this paper is devoted.

Social problems result from a network of organismic, psychological, and social influences, both current and historical. Interdependencies are extensive and cannot be ignored. The risks are systemic rather than simply being engendered by association with a particular type of environment. Manipulating a one-dimensional strategy may set in motion different series of unanticipated events in a heterogeneous mix of individuals or may have no effect at all. In many problems, some articulation has been achieved between the ontogeny of the individual and the evolution of his niche in the system. I have described elsewhere a group of diverse clinical and social problems, characterized by common psychological processes, for which I have used the term social disability. Social disabilities, I believe, have as their precursor socialization for roles which are complementary to all positions of low status and powerlessness in our society; and these latter conditions are inherent in the way our system works.

"Ecosystem" problems can range all the way from transient problems—concerned with the dynamics of shifting or evolving relationships between part of the system—to more stabilized internalized problems that develop within the system itself and are intrinsic to it. Intergroup conflict among adolescents is an example of dynamic ecosystem problems (Kelly, 1968).

More insidious are the internalized, stabilized phenomena that are a part of the development and structure of the system and the individual. Any problem intrinsic to an ecosystem has forms that are obscured by its role in supporting the system. Thus a principal consideration with regard to prevention is that many ecological risks are embedded in the interdependencies of the system and its effective values. Many forces in an established social system have a vested interest in maintaining the conditions that place certain of its members at risk. Often the goals of a preventive program would require changes that go right to the roots of the society. In this respect, the problems involved in bringing about change can be likened to the difficulties in trying to change a chronic character disorder.

Another characteristic of these problems is that they almost always involve human potential in some way. Often, failure in fulfilling potential is the only index to the presence of the problem. One of the difficulties this sets for primary prevention is that a focus on human potential is very problematical. It is difficult to get much agreement upon its referents for the species, much less for any group of individuals. To identify and isolate the variables relevant for assessing failure—particularly as these articulate with an entire system—may well be impossible. Yet I hope to demonstrate later in this paper that the question of human potential for specifiable groups is a central, real, and practical kind of problem for primary prevention.

Another difficulty related to those mentioned above has to do with establishing the credibility of these kinds of problems. Preventive efforts with respect to many social problems become ensnarled with politics, fundamental differences in the models of "man," and various other personal resistances. This is well exemplified in the traditional attitudes toward female sex typing. Though we have lots of evidence for the relationship between passivity and pathology, a large portion of society (including many women) continue to idealize passivity as an attractive and desirable trait of femininity and at the very least to view it as benign.

These difficulties are further exacerbated by the fact that one of the effects of being at risk for an internalized and equilibrated ecosystem problem is that one is at risk for a diffusion of effects not only throughout the system but throughout the personality. Thus, not only are the values of the society embroiled, but selective dispositions of the individual come to "cooperate." This fact facilitates what William Ryan has referred to as "blaming the victim" for any manifest maladjustment that ensues (Ryan, 1971).

On the other hand, it is for problems of this type that the concerns recently expressed by Kessler and Albee (1975) are most justified. The issues in the political, social, and ethical implications of doing things to large groups are as yet unresolved. One is confronted by the ethical issues in every parent-child center and in every nursery school with a developmental program.

One implication of this picture is that commitment to the concept of preventive programs for internalized ecosystem problems will always be divided in both society and the profession. After a decade of community psychology and consciousness raising, I find it quite surprising, for example, that I still meet the extent of resistance that I do in graduate students—future psychologists—with respect to attempts at defining some of these social phenomena as legitimate problems for professional and scientific concern. It is quite evident to me that the problems will have relatively low priority in a society not committed to universal human development and that changes in them will require social evolution and other forces over which the mental health sciences have little direct control.

What should be the nature of primary prevention for these problems? My own belief is that any main-effects strategy will be relatively ineffective, at least in the short term, whether the focus is on change in the total system or change in the individual. Preventive efforts will have to be based on principles of human development in combination with the principles governing ecological phenomena as these stabilize over time. We cannot ignore the interactions, so I suggest we begin by looking at some of them.

SOCIAL DISABILITY IN LOW STATUS INDIVIDUALS

I propose, in discussing the social disabilities that evolve in the context of low status, not to approach the subject from the perspective of what society does to certain of its members, but rather to examine such questions as why racism and sexism work. This is one of several possible approaches to identifying the most efficient point of intervention in any ecological risk.

Social Disability in Blacks and Females

In the last two years, while reviewing the developmental literature on women to prepare a book on lifespan development, I discovered that there are many similarities in being black and being female. At first my attention was caught by the risks of pathology in the two groups. But it has become more and more apparent to me that the issues I have been exploring are more fundamentally those of human development and human potential than of variations in clinical magnitudes of pathology. As I plan to illustrate, however, the two issues are inextricably related, as I think they are in all stabilized "ecosystem" problems.

The story that follows is not a straightforward one. Piecing it together hangs not on one crucial, well-designed study but on an integration of diverse sources of cumulative evidence. There are many gaps in the story, particularly with respect to the part played by the black experience. As a strategy for presenting a coherent picture, I therefore rely heavily at some points on extrapolation to blacks from findings with women. The picture is suggestive. Verification of specific parts will require continued research.

I would like to begin by reviewing the findings on symptom variance and prevalence of disorder in blacks, females, and low socioeconomic groups generally. I repeat that the epidemiological knot with respect to ecological problems is a very tough one to unravel. Awareness that if one is poor one's chances of becoming hospitalized for an emotional disorder are 64 times what they are if one is not has unfortunately only served to stir up the old nature-nurture controversy. In a review of comparative studies of blacks and whites in the United States, Dreger and Miller (1968) suggested that the ideal experimental design for analyzing the complexities of epidemiological findings would be a multivariate analysis of variance with interactions reaching to the 25th order.*

In spite of the intimidating picture suggested by Dreger and Miller, I want to try to make some sense of the epidemiological findings. What is to follow are relevant findings on "true" prevalence rates—that is, estimates of pathology in the general population (Dohrenwend, 1974). Also discussed are patterns of symptom variance as observed in several studies conducted with hospitalized clinical groups.

---

*For an analysis of methodological issues and the current status of interpretations of epidemiological research, the reader should see Dohrenwend's 1974 review.

(1) In "true" prevalence studies which include all analyses since 1969, the most consistent result reported is an inverse relationship between overall rates of psychopathology and socioeconomic status. (For example, of 33 communities studied, 28 yielded highest rates in the lowest classes.)

(2) The steepest part of the curve portraying the falloff for severe disorders occurs between the lowest status groups (those below the poverty line) and the working class. That is, the point in the socioeconomic structure which shows the greatest, most precipitous increase in serious pathology demarcates the worst levels of poverty in our culture.

(3) Personality disorders and schizophrenia represent the types of disorders showing the most consistent inverse relationship with economic and social status.

(4) Estimates of the prevalence of pathology among blacks and among white females have been conflicting. To date, Dohrenwend counts 16 studies in which men showed higher rates than women and 27 studies in which women show higher rates than men. In an analysis of prevalence rates in Baltimore, Pasamanick (1962) finds that state hospital rates for blacks (nonwhites) is 75 times that for whites. He nevertheless concludes from an analysis of all institutions (private, state, and federal) that there is no difference in prevalence of disorder for blacks and whites.

From a review of much of the literature, it seems reasonable to draw the following conclusions for the present about prevalence in blacks and in white females:

• With respect to women, there is no *overall* difference in "true" prevalence rates for all disorders when compared with males. There are consistent differences, however, in type and intensity of disorder and in the conditions under which these develop. Also, duration for certain types of disorder is higher among women—thus selectively raising prevalence rates.

• Black prevalence rates vary considerably from locale to locale, in some areas being equivalent to those of whites. In other places, however, particularly in urban high-stress areas, prevalence rates for blacks are as much as three to four times as great as white rates in the same locales. Thus, there is epidemiological evidence for a differential response to high stress.

• Although one reviewer (Malzberg, 1959) has concluded that there are no black-white differences in type of disorder, a comparison of symptom pattern indicates the type of disorder for both blacks and females differs in similar ways from that of white middle class males. The following is a summary of several findings on symptom variance for these groups.

(5) Rates of personality disorder are higher in males. There is, however, significant interaction with such other factors as socioeconomic status and race. Low socioeconomic status or being black account for a large portion of the variance among males.

(6) Neuroses among women are higher than among men in both rural and urban settings. Aside from depression, a large component of the symptom picture tends to be hysteriform in type (for example, conversions and somatization). In rural areas, female psychotics outnumber male psychotics; in urban areas, the reverse is true. (It is my impression that the difference in relative rates is accounted for not by a drop in women's rates for psychosis in urban areas but by an increase in male rates, female rates being relatively constant across locales.)

(7) Among blacks, the largest portion of the difference in rates is accounted for by schizophrenia, which in one study in the New York area was found to be roughly 100 in 100,000, as compared to 33 in 100,000 for whites.

(8) A common description of behavioral differences between males and females given by investigators and clinicians alike is that women patients are much more frequently narcissistic, abandoned, and attacking than male patients (Raskin and Golob, 1966; Weich, 1968).

The following represent differences in characerics of male and female acutely disturbed patients in independent ratings of ward and group therapy behavior (Weich, 1968).

• Males are better organized, more responsive to instruction, more constrained, more intrapersonally and socially organized, less prone to acting out, less "sick," less inclined to scream and cry, less hostile, more inclined to clump in groups, less demanding, and more cooperative.

• Females are more explosive, more violent, more overtly homosexual and acting out, more hysterical, more exhibitionistic, characterized by more physical activity, more overtly hostile, more sexual, more seductive, manipulative, badgering, and talkative, less conventional toward the doctor; they "grab your hand more," do more disrobing, are sillier, are more expressive and more imploring, want more attention, show no "group spirit," exhibit wilder extremes of behavior, are more unkempt, and show more self-neglect. In therapy, the level of noise and activity in women's groups was markedly higher than in the male groups and there were more instances of striking the therapist and other patients.

(9) Remarkable similarities have been observed between the level and quality of symptoms found among women and those among black patients as a group. In a study by Schliefer, Derbyshire, and Brown (1964) in which black and white male and female patients were compared on admission and over the first three days of hospitalization, black patients were generally sicker on admission, with black males rated sickest and white males as least sick. "Sicker" in this study referred to a greater degree of disorientation, irrelevance in speech, and, to a lesser extent, hostility, activity, appearance, and loudness and quantity of speech. At least 40 percent of the females, both black and white, showed symptoms of somatization; relatively few such symptoms were reported in male patients. The investigators noted a fact of particular interest: there appeared to be a faster reduction in symptoms in women than in men over the first three days. This turned out to be due almost entirely to a kind of suggestive hysterical pattern shown in the dramatic reduction in somatization during this period.

Certain findings concerning somatization in black males bearing on the ecology of this symptom are also relevant. There is an interesting reversal of sex differences with respect to somatization in black males and females in southern samples as measured on MMPI (Mosby, 1972). In the south, higher rates of somatization are found among black males than among black females. Northern black males, on the other hand, use this mechanism much less than northern black females—a pattern more common for the population as a whole.

Epidemiological findings indicate that somatization is a common mechanism in the pathology of immigrant and ethnic minorities. Is it reasonable at this point to raise the question of the relationship of status and power and coping mechanisms to these particular *symptom patterns?* Before pursuing that question, I would like to mention two other types of findings that are helpful in interpreting this material.

The first concerns the process-reactive distinction relative to these groups. The process-reactive distinction classifies the schizophrenic according to the level of social competence achieved prior to decompensation. Individuals are classified as process schizophrenic when they have exhibited a wide range of failures on developmental tasks—social development, school achievement, heterosexual relationships, work commitment—throughout the formative years. It is generally assumed that there has been some underlying morbid process present since childhood which has interfered with normal learning. The process does not ordinarily manifest itself in accessory symptoms until maturity. In contrast, individuals are classified as reactive schizophrenics when premorbid adjustment has been good by these standards but accessory symptoms develop suddenly and often in relation to some recognizable stress.

This distinction has been very powerful in that it has reduced some of the behavioral heterogeneity in the schizophrenic group and has also been found to correlate with severity of symptom (or degree of sickness) and length of hospitalization. The problem with the distinction is that it does not hold equally well for all social groups. A particularly consistent finding is that female schizophrenics as a group tend to achieve "healthier" premorbid levels of adjustment than their male counterparts. It is quite difficult to explain the level of decompensation in women on the basis of any simple relationship between degree of socialization and disposition to process pathology. In women, whatever the process is that leads to pathology in adulthood, it has not crippled social development as society defines it for women.

We are faced, on the contrary, with at least the tentative paradox that the behavioral characteristics underlying process decompensation may be the same ones that make women attractive to many males under favorable life circumstances. At the very least we are talking about developmental outcomes that are independent of success or failure in primary socialization or in moving through the few adult social roles available for women.

This fact is quite remarkable to me. I cannot emphasize it enough. It is at the root of the problem of ecological risk. Apparently quite acceptable levels of socialization can proceed as an overlay of a developing incapacity for lifetime growth and of a high vulnerability to stress. The relationship between premorbid ratings and morbid status for blacks is much more consistent with expectations; but this particular difference between black males and white females is only apparent. White females who later become schizophrenic are more successfully conforming to social expectations than are white males who later become schizophrenic. But then so are black males, in that the subcultural social norms of black males just happen to prescribe much of the behavior (narcissim, aggression directed outward) that helps define the process category. The behavior of low status black males is in many respects quite consistent with the pressures of their niche, just as is that of females.

The female paradox and the correspondence of the process reactive dimension with socioeconomic status have been used to criticize the usefulness of the dimension for understanding schizophrenia as such. Ellen Lane (1968) has found that low-status blacks are almost always diagnosed as process schizophrenic on the basis of premorbid history, while white females are almost always diagnosed as reactive. Lane has suggested, as others have, that rather than reflecting a morbid process, both of these categories simply reflect an exaggeration of the norms and values in the culture of white females and black males (aggression directed outward for black males, inward for white females). Yet, given the findings on symptoms and performance for female schizophrenics, this explanation does not account for the phenomenon, since the morbid picture for women *reverses itself* from that of the premorbid rather than exaggerating the normal. In this sense, the reactive diagnosis for women is misleading. This interpretation is further supported by Rosenthal's (1961) finding, from a careful analysis of the literature, that women make up the largest portion of the chronic schizophrenic hospital population—contrary to what is usually predicted for the reactive diagnosis.

It is interesting that Weich (1968), beginning with the decompensated picture rather than with premorbid achievement, has suggested an interpretation of women's pathology opposite to that of Lane. He suggests that the *failure* of the neutralization of impulses in the normal adaptation of women accounts for the extreme and diffuse breakdown in acute states he has observed.

One of the few studies to establish comparable male-female process-reactive groups from which similar predictions could be made was a recent investigation by DeWolf (1973). The criteria he reports for classification were meager, but he appears to have included information about the patient's current status (that is, symptoms). With this as the procedure, the female process group is much more likely to be comprised of women who show a symptom picture comparable to process males, though differentiation of premorbid status remains unclear.

In general, the problematic findings with women schizophrenics underline discontinuity between apparent premorbid resources and morbidity—a discontinuity that does not hold for any other group. A second set of findings provides further support for this observation. There is a differential relationship between girls' and boys' early adjustment and later predictions of pathology. It is well known that girls as a group receive higher adjustment ratings than boys (Weinstein and Geisel, 1960). Rutter, nevertheless, has shown that girls' early adjustment histories do not predict adult adjustment, though certain symptoms in early history do predict for boys: Gardner (1967), for example, found that neurotic symptoms in boys usually predict adult pathology. No such relationship has been found for females. Predictors for girls are not early adjustment attributes at all but presence of pathology in the mother (Rutter, 1974). Rutter has proposed a genetic interpretation for his finding; but it is useful to compare the consistent findings of Heilbrun and others, using nonclinical samples, that when degree of sex role identification is used as a predictor of adjustment in adult males and females, high femininity is more often associated with poor adjustment than any other attribute measured (Heilbrun, 1968).

One other interesting set of findings bears on this story. Ego strength has long been considered among clinicians as a predictor of mental health and as a way of summarizing the potential for resistance to stress. Among other things, it is considered to include the capacity to delay gratification and to regulate and control reactivity, and is generally assumed to involve a high degree of perceptual-cognitive differentiation in the discrimination of external reality, self, and feelings. Using the field dependence technique as a measure of differentiation, Vaught (1965) found that high ego strength is always associated with a highly differentiated perceptual-cognitive system in men—that is, a highly differentiated discrimination and perception of reality. Males with low ego strength, regardless of sex role identification, show poor perceptual-cognitive differentiation. For women, however, there is no such relationship; rather, only masculine sex role identity predicts perceptual differentiation. Women with high ego strength who are also high masculine identifiers are highly differentiated and articulated cognitively. Women with high ego strength who are high feminine identifiers show poor cognitive differentiation. Apparently a behavioral and experiential identification in the masculine mode provides assimilations that lead to such cognitive schemata.

What does this mean about sex role, ego strength, and prediction of pathology? For one thing, it must mean that the structure of ego strength differs for males and females. Further, it would seem that the psychological loading of ego strength is greater for males than for females. Thus, as ego strength develops in women it may reflect little more than the resources required in assuming the feminine role. At the same time, as we have seen, feminine identification is related to poor adjustment. One interpretation of these observations is that ego strength in women is unrelated to quality of coping with stress outside the dictates of social role and bears only upon her comfort with and acceptance of the pressures of primary socialization—*the very factor which places her in great vulnerability for pathology.*

When these findings are combined with the paradoxical findings on premorbid-morbid characteristics, we might almost make the following startling predictions. In white middle-class males, a reasonable predictor of poor adjustment and potential pathology is the deficit in, or excessive demand on, the personal qualities and resources summarized in ego strength. For white females, a predictor of poor adjustment and potential pathology is the ecological fate of the degree to which she has made a feminine identification. Similarly, for black males, a predictor of potential pathology is the degree of assimilation of the social role status of black.

Social Disability and Ecological Risk

Now what is the nature of the interrelationships that define these problems as ecological risks? The common sociodevelopmental and intrapsychic problems of blacks (particularly black low-socioeconomic-status males) and females are rooted in an intricate combination of the power and status characteristics of their social roles and their developing dispositions. Subordinate roles and status are phenomena that are highly institutionalized for blacks and females. Their status, furthermore, is attached to each of their kinds of physical visibilities; therefore status is less negotiable from generation to generation than that of other low-status groups. History as well as ontological change is thus enlisted. But what makes the system work, ostensibly? And why are the risks we speak of so often obscured? Ecological risk refers, after all, to those problems in which vulnerable individuals complement the system's uses of their vulnerability. The answers to these questions lie, I think, in a combination of features that account for adaptation as well as social disability.

The following represents an attempt at a theoretical integration that may help to explain the paradoxes of ecosystem fit, social problems, and pathology. I have used the term social disability to classify a large group of seemingly disparate clinical and social disorders because it seems to me that the evidence strongly suggests they have a unitary ecological as well as developmental character. We must think in terms of some common sociopsychological mechanism, since the disorders are concentrated within the most socially and economically alienated and powerless groups in our society. This statement does not preclude heritability but assumes that the heritability operates—as does any polygenic influence—through the avenues available to it developmentally and through the filters and pressures of one's ecology.

In an earlier paper (Vance, 1973) I summarized the evidence for the relationship between environmental extremity and the development of effectance or competence—a position first formulated by Robert White (1959). Briefly, there is a close empirical and logical relationship between balance and imbalance in power between the child and the physical and social environment and the child's development of resources for dealing with the environment.

"Passivity" is the best term I can think of to summarize the consequences of an overpowering environment. Seligman (1970, 1975) has used the term "helplessness," but I wish to emphasize the perceptual-cognitive rather than the behavioral component. Perceptual-cognitive passivity may be the greatest single source of vulnerability to stress in man. In fact, at the risk of overstating the case, I would not be surprised if, with the fetalization of the brain during the evolution of the human species, an active perceptual-cognitive orientaton had become a major aspect in our survival as a species. Similarly, it has been said that the number of niches a species can fill (and thus by implication increase his survival potential) is a function of the diversity of roles he can actively master by means of his activity and creativity (Wallach, 1970).

The experimental variable *locus of control* (Rotter, 1966) refers to the relationship between the individual and an extreme environment. The variable has been demonstrated to have highly diverse effects in human functioning. I would like to summarize my interpretation of findings with respect to how this diversity of effects is accomplished. The locus of control refers to the belief most people seem to acquire that they can effect or initiate change in the environment. It also appears to be a measure of how much we tend to assume responsibility for the rewards and punishments we receive. Those who characteristically fail to perceive a relationship between their own activity and environmental events are described as "externals." Those for whom this relationship is well articulated are described as "internals."

The diverse behavioral and adaptive effects that have consistently emerged in studies of the locus of control suggest that it must serve as a threshold of some kind. I would guess that its greatest importance lies not in the confident sense of self it must provide but in the feedback it provides to cognition—in the relationship it establishes between the person and information, between the person and his own activity.

There are dimensions of reality that are available only where that feedback relationship exists. When beliefs of this kind are established very early, they sensitize us to information feedback and focus our attention on it. Feedback has turned out to be an extremely important phenomenon, whatever its object. The feedback about activity and inherent in activity provides the base for building differentiated cognitions that maximize the informational value of experience and provide the basis for the self-regulation of behavior.

The person who has no belief in internal causality, who is insensitive to feedback in his own activity and cannot perceive the link between his own behavior and events, is one for whom attention cannot be controlled by memories, images, or internal standards. Poor use of information is a necessary correlate, as is inadequacy in coping with novel, unstereotyped experiences and resolving conflict. The figure on page 226 summarizes the sequence of a chain of relationships between (1) environment, (2) developing organism, (3) response to niche pressures (normative control), and (4) response to stress (social disability).

In the figure, the important chain of relationships describes mechanisms that account for the quality of adjustment and for social disability under high stress. *These mechanisms are the same.* All are characterized by a common level of psychological functioning: pervasive deficits in the central regulation of behavior. Characteristics of personality at the behavioral level are (a) affect mediated behavior (either impulsiveness or inhibition, depending on conditioning); (b) poor modulation of reactivity; (c) deficits in self-mediated delay; (d) difficulties in maintaining a complex set; (e) difficulties in constructing and pursuing plans; and (f) difficulties in using inference to guide behavior, interpretation, and attitude.

One key to understanding the role played by these attributes in so many diverse morbid and premorbid pictures is that they are similar to the dissociative phenomena produced by any depressant drug. For example, animal subjects administered depressant drugs are incurious and incautious; they use problem-solving styles characterized by failure to alternate or withhold responses; they exhibit dissociation of learning; they rapidly learn instrumental and consummatory responses; they are insensitive to information and feedback; and they perform as though attention is poorly controlled by memory (Sachs, 1967). The evidence strongly suggests that underlying both the premorbid adaptations to stress and the morbid reactions to it are common behavioral and cognitive characteristics of this kind. Although symptoms may legitimately be viewed in many ways, the most useful view for understanding these problems is that the symptoms manifested under stress are related to the integrative state of the person. The integrative state of an externalizer is dissociative and basically passive (whether morbid or adjustive). The nature of symptoms-under-stress that express a dissociative and passive mode are exaggerated concreteness (since memory does not support inference), somatization, hysteriform modes of expressing tension, either lability or flatness of affect (depending upon conditioning history), openness to control by stimuli of all kinds, and, in severe decompensation, thought disorder exclusive of coherent delusions. Much of this

226   Elizabeth Taylor Vance

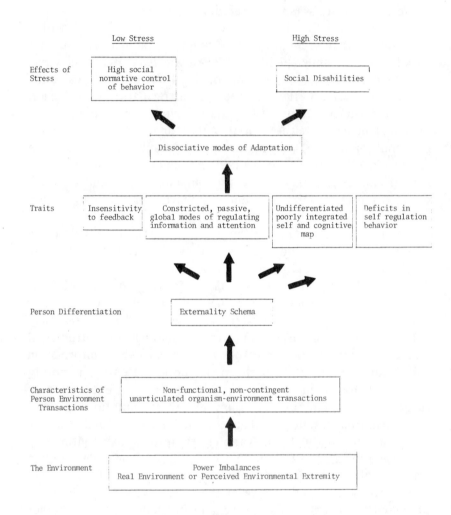

1. The etiology of social disability.

syndrome is consistent with what is observed in process forms of schizophrenia.

On the other hand, in compensated levels of functioning I would expect a high susceptibility to the influence of whatever ecological niche the individual finds himself in. Thus we might expect a considerable range of adjustments by the standards of the larger society; that is, some of the life styles would be recognized as problems and some not. The life styles of many lower-class males are a case in point. Their life styles are quite compatible with their subcultural niches but are considered by the larger society to be maladjustive. We can imagine the social problems generated from niche sensitivities of this kind.

The adjustment of women is seen as much more generally desirable and benign to the society as a whole. A recent discussion of criteria of social competence by Anderson and Messick (1974), however, has suggested that some aspects of social competence must be assessed in terms of attributes that transcend limited niches. Thus, in spite of the differences in the way society views the adjustments and competence of black males and females, these adjustments have some important characteristics in common which in terms of the criteria of social competence reveal their vulnerability and risk. Blacks (males in particular) and white females are minimally distinguished by behaviors which in themselves are prized by "many segments of society and across a large number of situations." Their adaptations are significantly distinguished from those of middle-class males by the fact that they are characterized by behaviors less often universally admired in themselves and their resources are differentially appropriate to different situations.

Furthermore, findings are reasonably consistent that blacks and females and low socioeconomic status groups are external with respect to perceived power or control and that they are less well perceptually-cognitively differentiated than white middle-class males. Among other provocative and related findings are that information in instructions does not affect conditioning in women subjects though it does so for males (Berry and Martin, 1957). Another finding is that low socioeconomic status groups and women remain dominated by empathic identifications rather than cognitive mediations in their moral judgments (Kohlberg and Kramer, 1969; Boehm, 1962). With respect to women's performance on moral dilemma tasks, never at any age measured do women show the level of differentiated, principled thought involved in a generalized ethical orientation in relation to others that over 50 percent of middle-class males are able to exhibit by age 16!

The picture of development and adaptation is far from being as clearcut as this presentation might suggest. For example, achieving a capacity for advanced levels of principled thought and humanism does not seem to guarantee among males a like level of humanistic behavior in interpersonal relations (Kohlberg, 1974). On the other hand, when we consider all the meanings of passivity in women (as in a recent analysis of aggression, dominance, and passivity in males and females by Maccoby and Jacklin, 1974), it is clear that "passivity" in women is not only adaptive in many ways but may mediate some of the most desirable effects of primary and secondary socialization (see Lowenthal, 1971) when the mean level of the general social welfare within the social structure is regarded as the criterion.

The weight of the findings on adjustment, competence, and pathology would nevertheless indicate that the quality of decompensation in blacks and females is a very small index of the debt this society owes to the realization of individual potential in a majority of its citizens.

ECOLOGICAL RISKS AND PRIMARY PREVENTION

Is a society possible in which we can reduce the prevalence of such stabilized ecological risks as those related to social disability? Are strategies of primary prevention—particularly social action that alters power relationships within groups and communities—the most appropriate and efficient way of making these very fundamental changes in society and in human beings? I do not pretend to answer those questions. One major barrier to significant change, however—at least for blacks and females—is the difficulty of incorporating an interaction perspective into a general strategy of interventions.

We cannot maximize human development and increase invulnerabilities to future stress by the elimination of poverty alone. Power, for example, is an element of the structure of all human and infrahuman relationships, deriving in part from the character of the organism in groups ranging all the way from dyads to communities. It is not simply asserted by certain kinds of societies, although unquestionably some types of societies thrive more on imbalances than others.

There are three sources of interactions involved in these social problems based in power imbalances: (1) the varying physical and social environmental parameters (for example, rates of environmental and social change; organization and consistency in the environment; power assertion strategies in families and institutions; (2) intra- and interindividual differences (which often translate into group differences); and (3) age changes. It is seldom that all of these sources of interaction can be incorporated into a single prevention plan.

Any group strategy based on the assumption that power imbalance leads to passive experiencing on the part of the "victim" will have to take into account individual differences and age changes in factors that influence the perception of stress and extremity. For this reason, I provide the following set of examples showing what information is needed about the individual to calibrate social interventions. In the first example I choose the trait reactivity because of what we have learned about the relationship between reactivity and perception. Autonomic reactivity mediates rapid social learning and, within limits, probably accounts for a great deal of developmental flexibility (Vance, 1973). Excess trait reactivity, however, is negatively related to discrimination and use of feedback (Levine, 1969; Denenberg, 1967; Gray, 1975).

There is much evidence for high trait reactivity among blacks, particularly black males (see review by Vance, 1973). If black males and white males differ on reactivity, and if environmental extremity and power imbalances should affect them in different ways, then the interaction between extremity and social disability may be accounted for by the extent to which the two groups are differently reactive.

In a recent study on socioecological stress involving power assertion environments, findings on race and blood pressure supported a hypothesis for an interaction between race, reactivity, and stress (Harburg et al., 1973). Comparing a sample of black and white married males in high-stress and low-stress areas in Detroit, the investigators found that suppressed hostility—a typical pattern for many males in both black and white high-stress areas—was related to high blood pressure levels and hypertension in both black and white males in both areas. Black high-stress males, however, showed significantly higher blood pressure levels and hypertension than any other group. Furthermore, reactivity was highest of all groups for dark-skinned, high-stress black males who suppressed hostility. Is it, then, high reactivity that makes black males particularly sensitive to the perception of extremity?

Reactivity is a survival mechanism which can be viewed as simplifying the discriminations that produce conflict and immobilization, increasing the disposition for physical action and aggressiveness in response to stress. The trait might be quite adaptive in some ecologies. It is relevant here not because of any absolute value of its adaptiveness but because it lowers a threshold for the kind of experience that seems to relate to passive perceptual modes and social disabilities. A similar disposition for white males may be activity level. High activity level, like reactivity, is also negatively related to finely tuned discriminations. Males —particularly white middle-class males—succumb to socialization pressures for modulating gross activity level relatively early in childhood. This fact may account for the finding that the relationship between boys and girls on perceptual-cognitive discrimination (girls exceeding boys in this development prior to four years of age) reverses itself in middle childhood (Coates, 1974).

Women comprise yet another pool of dispositions. There is only equivocal evidence for significant differences in total autonomic reactivity between males and females. If anything, males may be more autonomically reactive than females. But the physiological patterns of reactivity differ for the sexes fairly consistently in ways that suggest differences in perceptual modes for coping with reactivity. Males exhibit a more cortical orienting pattern and females a more cortical defensive pattern in which helplessness (a characteristic of anxiety) may be more acutely experienced (Neufeld and Davidson, 1974; Craig and Wood, 1971; Hare, 1971). Thus in women it may be that the form rather than the level of reactivity facilitates the experiencing of perceived extremity.

Finally, an example of an age-specific factor that can contribute to passive experiencing and trait development has to do with the relationship between sex, race, and the nature of the interpretations of the environment characteristic of the young child. Kohlberg theorizes that children take an active role in interpreting their environments. They attach sex role stereotypes to their own early, highly concrete cognitive categorizations, and for them the entire power dimension we have attached so much importance to *is related to body differences.* Children, then, derive their assumptions of social power from the physical power dimension. Before the age of four, size becomes the basic indicator for all important status differences like strength, knowledge, social power, and self-control. Stereotypes of masculine dominance and social power develop out of body stereotyping (Kohlberg, 1966).

For girls who do not identify with a perceived source of power as an intermediate step on the way to maturity, giving up the promises of power and settling for the perceived impotence in the feminine ideology must operate to obscure diverse and differentiating kinds of experiences as effectively as the extreme environments characterizing urban poverty.

I would also guess that some similar kind of perceptual considerations may operate for black children around color differences in a culture where power is easily perceived to accrue to the color dimension. Interestingly, one recent study tends to confirm the universality of physicalistic power perceptions in children while at the same time confirming the role of cultural specificity and shaping for other attributes of children's experiences—for example, nurturance (Gold and St. Ange, 1974).

This age-specific perceptual-cognitive style may account in part for recent observations that "spontaneous" and persistent traditional sex typing and differentiation appears to be continuing among children even in the face of changes in sex-typing norms by the society as awhole (Emmerich, 1973; Lynn, 1974, pp. 141–142).

It is highly desirable that conclusions following a discussion such as the one presented in this paper should set forth some usable generalizations. Yet generalizations are antithetical to the realities of interactions. Even so, some implications of this review for primary prevention can be noted. The general implications are two. For one, developmentalists have an important contribution to make in the primary prevention of social problems. Second, we must include at least first-order interactions in our prevention strategies. Specifically, we should be concerned with:

(1) *Universal human development.* Social disabilities and stabilized ecosystem problems are negatively related to social competence. Prevention efforts must therefore include knowledge about processes of human development. Furthermore, nothing short of the kind of change in both professional and social attitudes which would facilitate commitment to universal human development will lead to a significant reduction in the kinds of problems discussed in this paper.

(2) *Social competence as a developmental goal.* In most prevention efforts we tend to focus on the pathology we wish to avert. To prevent social problems produced by niche control, we must have a model of "man" that provides us with testable assumptions about social competence and the ecologies that facilitate its development. A good beginning is the recent attempt by a panel of experts under the auspices of the Office of Child Development to define the meaning of social competency (Anderson and Messick, 1974).

(3) *Individual differences.* Prevention strategies must be based on a recognition of the reliability and salience of the individual differences that contribute to developmental outcomes and the mediation of experiences in social contexts.

(4) *The structure of social institutions.* In an earlier paper I reviewed findings showing that various dimensions of poverty contribute to the experience of power imbalance and to social disability (Vance, 1973). The implication, of course, is that prevention requires the eradication of poverty. In this paper, however, we have discussed evidence for power imbalances that are embedded in institutional structures and role relationships. In order to prevent what appears to be a disposition for perceptual-cognitive passivity and its sequelae among blacks and females, for example, there must be a metamorphosis of social institutions into fundamentally developmental institutions. Erik Erikson (1963) has proposed the concept of "mutual regulation" to describe the interdependency between the individual and the institutions of his society. According to Erikson, the structure as well as the content of the relationship between individual and society plays a large role in developing competence. It seems to me that the concept of mutual regulation provides an excellent basis for a model for prevention strategies requiring institutional change.

(5) *Age X institutional interactions.* Primary prevention efforts involving institutional change must focus on role relationships and communication patterns that facilitate effectance experiences in both children and socialization agents. This means designing social institutions of all kinds that will have enough structural flexibility to provide effectance experiences by different means depending on the characteristics of the different age levels with which the institution is in contact.

(6) *Person X institution interactions.* Institutions must also show enough structural flexibility to provide effectance experiences for different individuals or groups. A potential value of personality research is that it can provide information about personality variables that influence effectance experiences in the "interaction space" in person-situation interactions. As a general approach to identifying such variables, Vale and Vale (1969) have suggested that when we know we have something that represents an interaction, we should look for some third underlying variable that mimics the function between the behavior and the environmental variable. When such a variable relates similarly to different characteristics of different individuals, we can do some fine tuning of person-institution relationships. Very frequently, however, we will not have information about personal variables of this kind. For those circumstances, a prevention strategy is suggested by Atkinson and Paulson's (1972) concept of "response sensitive" treatments. Applied to the context of institution X person interactions, creating response-sensitive institutional structures would involve strategies for monitoring responses and roles of individuals in institutional contexts and fine-tuning the roles and relationships according to the nature of the person processes that appear to be influencing the effectance experiences of the individual or group.

REFERENCES

Anderson, S., and Messick, S. Social competency in young children. *Developmental Psychology*, 1974, *10*, 282–293.

Anthony, E. J. A Risk-Vulnerability Intervention Model for children of psychotic parents. In E. J. Anthony and C. Koupernik (Eds.), *The child is his family: Children at psychiatric risk*. New York: Wiley, 1974. (a)

Anthony, E. J. The syndrome of the psychologically vulnerable child. In E. J. Anthony and C. Koupernik (Eds.), *The child in his family: Children at psychiatric risk*. New York: Wiley, 1974. (b)

Atkinson, R. C., and Paulson, J. A. An approach to the psychology of instruction. *Psychological Bulletin*, 1972, *78*, 49–61.

Berry, J. L., and Martin, B. GSR reactivity as a function of anxiety, instructions, and sex. *Journal of Abnormal and Social Psychology*, 1957, *54*, 9–12.

Boehm, L. The development of conscience: a comparison of American children and different mental and socioeconomic levels. *Child Development*, 1962, *33*, 575–590.

Coates, S. Sex differences in field dependence among preschool children. In Freidman, P. C., Richert, R. M., and Vance Wiele, R. L. (Eds.), *Sex differences in behavior*. New York: Wiley, 1974.

Craig, K. D., and Wood, K. Autonomic components of observers of pictures of homicide victims and nude females. *Journal of Experimental Research in Personality*, 1971, *5*, 305–309.

Cronbach, L. Beyond the two disciplines of scientific psychology. *American Psychologist*, 1975, *30*, 116–127.

Denenberg, V. H. Stimulation in infancy, emotional reactivity, and exploratory behavior. In D. C. Glass (Ed.), *Biology and behavior: Neurophysiology and emotion*. New York: Rockefeller University Press, Russel Sage Foundation, 1967.

DeWolf, A. S. Premorbid adjustment and the sex of the patient: implications of Phillips Scale ratings for male and female schizophrenics. *Journal of Community Psychology*, 1973, *1*, 63–65.

Dohrenwend, B. P., and Dohrenwend, B. S. Social and cultural influences on psychopathology. *Annual Review of Psychology*, 1974, *25*, 417–452.

Dreger, R. M., and Miller, K. S. Comparative psychological studies of negroes and whites in the United States: 1959–1965. *Psychological Bulletin Monograph Supplement*, 1968, *70*, 58.

Emmerich, W. Socialization and sex role development. In P. B. Baltes and K. W. Schaie (Eds.), *Life span developmental psychology: Personality and socialization*. New York: Academic Press, 1973.

Erikson, E. *Childhood and society*. New York, Norton, 1963.

Escalona, S. Intervention programs for children at psychiatric risk. The contribution of child psychology and developmental theory. In E. J. Anthony and C. Koupernik (Eds.), *The child in his family: Children at psychiatric risk*. New York: Wiley, 1974.

Fontana, A. F. Familial etiology of schizophrenia: Is a scientific methodology possible? *Psychological Bulletin*, 1966, *66*, 214–227.

Gardner, G. G. The relationship between childhood neurotic symptomatology and later schizophrenia in males and females. *Journal of Nervous and Mental Disease*, 1967, *144*, 97–100.

Garmezy, N. The study of competence in children at risk for severe psychopathology. In E. J. Anthony and C. Koupernik (Eds.), *The child in his family: Children at psychiatric risk*. New York: Wiley, 1974.

Gold, A. R., and St. Ange, M. Development of sex role stereotypes in black and white elementary school girls. *Developmental Psychology*, 1974, *10*, 461.

Gray, A. L. Autonomic correlates of chronic schizophrenia: a reaction time paradigm. *Journal of Abnormal Psychology*, 1975, *94*, 189–196.

Harburg, E., Erfurt, J. C., Hauenstein, L. S., Chape, C. A., Schull, W. J., and Schork, M. A. Socio-ecological stress, suppressed hostility, skin color, and black white male blood pressure: Detroit. *Psychosomatic Medicine*, 1973, *35*, 276–296.

Hare, R., Wood, K., Britain, S., and Frazelle, J. Autonomic responses to affective visual stimulation: Sex differences. *Journal of Experimental Research in Personality*, 1971, *5*, 14–22.

Heilbrun, A. B., Jr. Sex role, instrumental behavior and psychopathology in females. *Journal of Abnormal Psychology*, 1968, *73*, 131–316.

Hersov, L. Introduction: risk and mastery in children from the point of view of genetic and constitutional factors and early life experiences. In E. J. Anthony and C. Koupernik (Eds.), *The child in his family: Children at psychiatric risk*. New York: Wiley, 1974.

Hunt, J. McV. *Intelligence and experience*. New York: Ronald Press, 1961.

Hunt, J. McV. Parent and child centers: Their basis in the behavioral and educational sciences. *American Journal of Orthopsychiatry*, 1971, *41*, 13–38.

Irvine, E. E. The risks of the register: Or the management of expectation. In E. J. Anthony and C. Koupernik (Eds.), *The child in his family: Children at psychiatric risk*. New York: Wiley, 1974.

Jenkins, R. L. Psychiatric syndromes in children and their relation to family background. *American Journal of Orthopsychiatry*, 1966, *36*, 410–457.

Kelly, J. Toward an ecological conception of preventive interventions. In J. W. Carter, Jr. (Ed.), *Research contributions from psychology to community mental health*. New York: Behavioral Publications, 1968.

Kessler, M., and Albee, G. Primary prevention. *Annual Review of Psychology*, 1975, *26*, 557–592.

Kohlberg, L. A cognitive developmental analysis of children's sex-role concepts and attitudes. In E. E. Maccoby (Ed.), *The development of sex differences*. Stanford: Stanford University Press, 1966.

Kohlberg, L. Continuities in childhood and adult moral development revisited. In P. B. Baltes and K. W. Schaie (Eds.), *Life-Span developmental psychology: Personality and socialization*. New York: Academic Press, 1974, pp. 180–207.

Kohlberg, L., and Kramer, R. Continuities and discontinuities in childhood and adult moral development. *Human Development*, 1969, *12*, 93–120.

Lane, E. The influence of sex and race on process-reactive ratings of schizophrenics. *The Journal of Psychology*, 1968, *68*, 15–20.

Levine, S. An endocrine theory of infantile stimulation. In A. Ambrose (Ed.), *Stimulation in Early Infancy*. New York: Academic Press, 1969.

Lindon, R. L. Risk register. *Cerebral Palsy Bulletin*, 1961, *3*, 481–487.

Lowenthal, M. F. Intentionality: toward a framework for the study of adaptation in adulthood. *Aging and Human Development*, 1971, *2*, 79–95.

Lynn, D. *The father: His role in child development*. Monterey: Brooks/Cole, 1974.

Maccoby, E. E., and Jacklin, C. N. *The psychology of sex differences*. Stanford: Stanford University Press, 1974.

Malzberg, B. Mental disease among negroes: An analysis of first admissions in New York State, 1949–51. *Mental Hygiene*, 1959, *43*, 422–52.

Mosby, D. Toward a theory of the unique personality of blacks: a psychocultural assessment. In R. L. Jones (Ed.), *Black psychology*. New York: Harper and Row, 1972.

Neufeld, R. W. J., and Davidson, P. O. Sex differences in stress response: A multivariate analysis. *Journal of Abnormal Psychology*, 1974, *83*, 178–185.

Pasamanick, B. A survey of mental disease in an urban population: VII. An approach to total prevalence by diagnosis and sex. *American Journal of Psychiatry*, 1962, *119*, 299–305.

Raskin, A., and Golob, R. Occurrence of sex and social class differences in premorbid competence, symptom and outcome measures in acute schizophrenia. *Psychological Reports*, 1966, *18*, 11–22.

Rosenthal, D. Sex distribution and the severity of illness among samples of schizophrenic twins. *Journal of Psychiatric Research*, 1961, *1*, 26–36.

Rotter, J. B. Generalized expectancies for internal versus external control of reinforcement. *Psychological Monographs*, 1966, *80* (1, Whole No. 609).

Rutter, M. Epidemiological strategies and psychiatric concepts in research on the vulnerable child. In E. J. Anthony and C. Koupernik (Eds.), *The child in his family: Children at psychiatric risk*. New York: Wiley, 1974.

Ryan, W. *Blaming the victim*. New York: Random House, 1971.

Sachs, E. Dissociation of learning in rats and its similarities to dissociative states in man. In J. Zubin and H. F. Hunt (Eds.), *Comparative psychopathology*. New York: Grune and Stratton, 1967.

Schliefer, C., Derbyshire, R., and Brown, J. Symptoms and symptom change in hospitalized negro and white mental patients. *Journal of Human Relations*, 1964, *12*, 476–485.

Seligman, M. E. P. On the generality of the laws of learning. *Psychological Review*, 1970, *77*, 406–418.

Seligman, M. E. P. *Helplessness*. San Francisco: W. H. Freeman, 1975.

Vale, J. R., and Vale, C. A. Individual differences and general laws in psychology. *American Psychologist*, 1969, *24*, 1093–1108.

Vance, E. T. Social disability. *American Psychologist*, 1973, *28*, 498–511.

Vaught, G. M. The relationship of role identification and ego strength to sex differences in the rod and frame test. *Journal of Personality*, 1965, *33*, 271–283.

Wallach, M. A. Creativity. In P. H. Mussen (Ed.), *Carmichael's Manual of child psychology.* New York: Wiley, 1970.

Weich, M. J. Behavioral differences between groups of acutely psychotic (schizophrenic) males and females. *Psychiatric Quarterly,* 1968, *42,* 107–22.

Weinstein, E. A., and Geisel, P. N. An analysis of sex differences in adjustment. *Child Development,* 1960, *31,* 721–728.

White, R. W. Motivation reconsidered: The concept of competence. *Psychological Review,* 1959, *66,* 297–333.

Wolff, S., and Acton, W. Characteristics of parents of disturbed children. *British Journal of Psychiatry,* 1968, *114,* 593–601.

Wynne, L. C., and Singer, M. T. Thought disorder and family relations of schizophrenics. I. A research strategy. *Archives of General Psychiatry,* 1963, *9,* 191–198. (a)

Wynne, L. C., and Singer, M. T. Thought disorder and family relations of schizophrenics. II. Classifications of forms of thinking. *Archives of General Psychiatry,* 1963, *9,* 199–206. (b)

13

The Prevention of Sexism

MARCIA GUTTENTAG

INTRODUCTION

Sexism abounds. This paper is not addressed solely to overt institutional discrimination, which is best handled through changes in laws and regulations that are systematically enforced. My focus is primarily on the sexism that is an informal part of our institutional and family practices. Based on occupational, familial, and socioemotional stereotypes, this sexism is so much a part of our culture that until recently it has been little questioned.

One can be opposed to sexism on moral and ethical grounds, because it unfairly denies full human opportunities to all. But does sexism do actual damage? Are there any serious mental health effects of sexism? If there are, what kinds of people are most affected?

To begin with, we will consider evidence from mental health utilization rate data, as well as a number of epidemiological studies on the mental health of men and women. The latter work is part of a new nationwide collaborative study on women and mental health which we are doing with the National Institute of Mental Health (NIMH). By integrating data on mental health symptomatology from a variety of sources, we can find out which groups are most at risk. Some of the stresses that correlate with symptomatology are also revealed. Considerable evidence links both the direct and the indirect effects of sexism to symptomatology.

We then turn to the theme of this conference—the primary prevention of sexism. Epidemiological data provide clear pointers about what aspects of sexism must be changed if mental health damage is to be averted. Primary prevention of sexism must occur at an early age. Even as young adolescents, both boys and girls show the damaging effects that sex stereotypes have on their self-concepts and the life possibilities they believe are open to them (Guttentag, 1976). The family is surprisingly powerless to counteract the effects of the sexism that children are socialized to through peer groups, schools, and the media.

Schools probably provide the best institutional setting for the primary prevention of sexism. How can they best be used for this purpose? Does the child's age make a difference? Exactly how can the work be carried out? Who should be the targets of such intervention—should it be directed equally toward boys and girls?

Recently we completed an intervention study in which we attempted—through curricula, teacher training, and peer group involvements—to modify the sex role stereotypes of 5-, 10-, and 14-year-old children in three large school systems. The results were surprising and revealing. What is necessary for primary prevention at different ages, who has to be changed, and how changes can be accomplished are more complex, and yet clearer, than one would have imagined. Data from the study showed a direct relationship to the findings from the study of adult mental health symptoms. Integrating data from these studies of children and adults permit us to make some sharp generalizations about how to effectively implement programs for the primary prevention of sexism.

SEX DIFFERENCES IN MENTAL HEALTH SYMPTOMATOLOGY

Women—especially young women—are more depressed than men. In adolescence, female mental hospital admission rates exceed those of males. In the age group 25 to 44, women's frequency of admission peaks over men's: the figures for 1969, for example, were 766,744 females compared with 666,389 males.[1]

The percentage of men and women suffering from personality disorders, neurosis, and schizophrenia are roughly equivalent,

1. *Socio-economic characteristics of admissions and out-patient psychiatric services, 1969*. National Institute of Mental Health, Department of Health, Education, and Welfare Publication No. (HSM)-72-9045 (U.S. Government Printing Office, Washington, D.C., 1971), Table 7, p. 26.

Table 1

The Three Leading Diagnoses among Male and Female Admissions
to State and County Mental Hospitals and to Community Mental Health Centers in 1970

(From Cannon and Redick, 1973)

	MALES	FEMALES
State and County Mental Hospitals	1. Alcohol Disorders 32.1%	1. Schizophrenia 37.7%
	2. Schizophrenia 24.0%	2. Depressive Disorders 16.9%
	3. Personality Disorders 16.3%	3. Organic Brain Syndromes 10.6%
Community Mental Health Centers	1. Schizophrenia 14.6%	1. Depressive Disorders 20.7%
	2. Transient Situational Personality Disorders 13.5%	2. Schizophrenia 15.6%
	3. Personality Disorders 13.3%	3. Transient Situational Personality Disorders 13.5%

but twice as many women as men are diagnosed as suffering from depressive disorders.[2] These disorders peak in women between the ages of 25 and 44, accounting for 49 percent of total disorders.[3]

In all types of facilities except state and county mental hospitals, depressive disorders are the leading diagnoses for women. This includes community mental health centers, private mental hospitals, general hospital in-patient services, and out-patient services. Only in state and county mental hospitals is schizophrenia the leading diagnosis for women admitted, with depressive disorders second. For men, in contrast, alcoholic disorders, schizophrenia, and personality disorders—in that order—are the leading diagnoses for state and county mental hospital admissions, while in community mental health centers, schizophrenia and personality disorders lead (Cannon and Redick, 1973). For hospital admissions overall, females always outnumber males for depressive disorders, while males always outnumber females for alcoholic and drug disorders.

Throughout the countries of the developed world, mental health utilization figures show a significantly greater number of depressed females than males (Weissman, 1975). Only in a few underdeveloped countries does the rate of depression in women appear to be slightly lower than for men (see Table 2).

Nearly all studies of treated cases of depression in the United States show a marked increase in young females diagnosed as depressed during the past two decades (see Table 2). I recently returned from Hungary—a country that has undergone rapid industrialization during the past two decades—where I was permitted to examine the diagnostic data of the National Institute of Mental Health. These revealed that in Hungary, too, there was a startling increase in the number of treated cases of depression in young females since World War II.

2. As a percentage of total episodes, 9.8 percent males—as against 21.1 percent females—have depressive disorders. *Utilization of Psychiatric Facilities by Persons Diagnosed with Depressive Disorders.* National Institute of Mental Health, Department of Health, Education, and Welfare Publication No. ADM 74-5 (1974), Table 2, p. 7.

3. Ibid., Table 6, p. 16.

Table 2*
Sex Ratios in Depression: Treated Cases
(From Weissman and Klerman, 1977. Reproduced by permission).

TREATED CASES:UNITED STATES

Place and Time	Sex Ratios Female/Male	References
Baltimore, Maryland 1936	2/1 (Psychoneurosis, including depression and manic-depressive)	Lemkau
Boston, Massachusetts 1945, 1955, 1965	Marked increase in young females with diagnosis of depressive reaction.	Rosenthal
Pittsfield, Massachusetts 1946–68	2.4/1 (Patients treated with ECT)	Tarnower and Humphries
New York State 1949	1.7/1	Lehmann
Massachusetts 1957–58	2.5/1 (All depressives)	Wechsler
Ohio 1958–61	First admissions 1.9/1 (White) 2.7/1 (Nonwhite)	Duvall et al.
Madison, Wisconsin 1958–69	Increase in depression for women over decade (patients referred for psychological testing)	Rice and Kepecs
Monroe County, New York	2.1/1 (Affective psychosis)	Gardner et al.
United States	Outpatient Admissions 1.4/1 (Psychotic depression) 1.2/1 (Manic-depression) 1.8/1 (Involutional psychosis) 1.6/1 (Depressive reactions)	Rosen, Bohn, and Kramer
Monroe County, New York 1961–62	1.6/1 (Prevalence) 1.3/1 (Incidence)	Pederson
Northern Florida 1963	26% female and 16% male medical patients were depressed. In the lower class, more men than women were depressed.	Schwab
New Haven, Connecticut 1966	3/1 (All depressions)	Paykel et al.
United States 1970	Admissions to All Psychiatric Facilities 2.1/1 (All depressive disorders)	Cannon and Redick
St. Louis, Missouri 1971	2.1/1 (Excluded bipolar depressives)	Baker

TREATED CASES: OUTSIDE UNITED STATES

Amsterdam 1916-40	2.3/1 Ashkenázim Jews 2.4/1 Gentiles	Gewel
Gaustad, Norway 1926-55	Life Time Risk of First Admission 1.37/1 (1926–35) 1.36/1 (1946–50) 1.33/1 (1951–55)	Odegaard

*References can be found in Guttentag and Salasin, 1976.

Table 2 *(continued)*

Place and Time	Sex Ratios Female/Male	References
Buckinghamshire, England 1931–47	1.8/1 (1931–33) 1.9/1 (1945–47	Lehmann
Basle, Switzerland 1945–57	1.5/1 (approximately)	Kielholz
London, England 1947–49 .	2/1	Lehmann
Scania, Sweden 1947, 1957	1.8/1 (Life time prevalence of severe depression)	Essen-Moller and Hagnell
Hertfordshire, England 1949–54	Neurotic Depression 3.5/1 (Admissions) 2.2/1 (Consultations)	Martin
England and Wales 1952, 1960	1.6/1 (1952) 1.7/1 (1960)	Lehmann
Tanganyika 1954	.5/1	Smartt
Aarhus County, Denmark 1958	2/1 (Endogenous Depression) 4/1 (Psychogenic Depression) 3/1 (Depressive Neurosis)	Juel-Nielson
Salford, England 1959–63	1.9/1 (Depressive Psychosis)	Adelstein et al.
Dakar, Guinea 1960–61	.5/1	Collomb and Zwingelstein
Madras and Madurai, India 1961–63	0.2/1	Venkoba Rao
Tokyo, Japan and Taiwan, China 1963–64	Women have more depressive symptoms.	Rin
Madurai, India 1964–66	0.56/1 (Endogenous Depression)	Venkoba Rao
Bulawayo, Rhodesia 1965–67	1.1/1 (N=76)	Buchan
Baghdad, Iraq 1966–67	1.1/1	Bazzoui
Honduras 1967	1.6/1 (Admissions) 6.7/1 (Outpatients)	Hudgens et al.
New Delhi, India 1968	0.55/1	Teja et al.
Jerusalem, Israel 1969–72	2.1/1 (Affective disorders)	Gershon and Liebowitz
Papua, New Guinea 1970–73	.4/1 (Based on a few cases)	Torrey et al.
Denmark 1973	1.9/1 (First admissions for manic-depression)	Dupont et al.
Bangkok, Thailand	1.3/1 (Far East Orientals) .8/1 (Occidentals)	Tongyonk

EPIDEMIOLOGICAL STUDIES

Rates of treated illnesses must be viewed cautiously. Women are much more likely than men to go to doctors and are therefore more likely to turn up in statistics on treated mental illness. It is therefore important to ask whether there are significant differences in rates of depression for untreated cases. Weissman (1975) has compiled figures from community mental health surveys conducted in the United States and Western Europe during the past twenty years showing that untreated women were indeed significantly more depressed than men in all the developed countries. (See Table 3.)

One must be initially skeptical about such findings, since a number of plausible alternative hypotheses may account for them. Could it not be, for example, that women are more willing to admit distress? Perhaps their response biases make them look more depressed. Perhaps women are freer to express all feelings, or it may be that the same stress has different effects on men and women. After carefully analyzing a number of studies that have investigated these questions, Weissman (1975) concurred with Clancy and Gove (1974) that sex differences "in the degree of symptoms found in community studies appear to reflect actual differences and are not an artifact of response bias" (p. 6).

Interestingly, although the older psychiatric literature has emphasized involutional melancholia as the most prevalent form of depression in women, all of the recent data show that the highest rates of depression occur among young women in the 21- to 44-year age category.

Another source of data on the increase in depression among young women comes from epidemiological studies of suicide attempts. Weissman (1974) reviewed all studies conducted from 1960 to 1971. Throughout the developed world, suicide attempters were overwhelmingly young females, predominantly 20 to 30 years old. The average age has decreased in the past decade, and there has been an increase in suicide attempts among married and separated or divorced women. Several studies of the personality of suicide attempters have found most of them to be clinically depressed at the time of the attempt.

Other studies report an excess of attempters in the lower social classes. Still others have found that such attempts usually take

Table 3
Sex Differences in Depression: Community Surveys
(From Weissman, 1975)

COMMUNITY SURVEYS: UNITED STATES

Place and Time	Sex Ratios Female/Male	References
Brooklyn and Queens, New York 1960	Women were more depressed.	Benfare et al.
Baltimore, Maryland 1968	1.6/1 (Includes wives of blue-collar workers only)	Siassi et al.
Northern Florida 1968	1.8/1	Schwab
Carroll County, Maryland 1968	Women were more nervous, helpless, anxious	Hogarty and Katz
New Haven, Connecticut 1969	2/1 (Suicidal feelings)	Paykel et al.
St. Louis, Missouri 1968-69	No significant sex difference in depression in bereaved spouse	Clayton et al.
New York, New York 20-year period	More referrals for minor depression in female employees in one company	Hinkle et al.

COMMUNITY SURVEYS: OUTSIDE UNITED STATES

Iceland 1910-57	1.6/1 (All depressions)	Helgason
Samsø, Denmark 1960	3.5/1 (All depressions)	Sørenen
Ghiraz, Iran 1964	3.6/1 (N=23)	Bash and Bash-Liechti
Lucknow, India 1969-71	2/1	Sethi
Hertfordshire, England 1949-54	2.4/1	Martin
Agra, India	1.6/1 (Manic-depression)	Dube and Kuman

place "in the context of a recent and serious inter-personal conflict—typically including marital or family discord" (p. 742).

Studies of the suicide attempters indicate which women are the most depressed. Very recent epidemiological work confirms this indication.

One such study, conducted by NIMH (Radloff, 1975; see Table 4) in Kansas City and in Washington County, Maryland, found that the married women and divorced or separated women

Table 4
Mean Depression Score (CES-D):
Sex by Age, Education, Income for Currently Married
(Combined sites, Whites Only)
(From Radloff, 1975)

SEX vs. AGE

		Less than 25	25–64	65+
Male	x̄	9.47	7.38	5.78
	n	62	611	106
Female	x̄	12.41	9.26	8.14
	n	109	747	74

F-test: Sex $p < .01$
         Age $p < .01$
         Interaction Sex x Age $p > .69$

SEX vs. EDUCATION

		Less than HS	HS	Some College	BA+
Male	x̄	7.75	7.79	6.39	6.12
	n	301	254	111	113
Female	x̄	10.92	9.61	7.42	7.54
	n	335	360	151	84

F-test: Sex $p < .01$
         Education $p < .01$
         Interaction Sex x Education $p > .19$

SEX vs. INCOME

		Less than $4,000	$4,000–$11,000	$12,000+
Male	x̄	9.33	7.98	6.47
	n	68	327	342
Female	x̄	11.05	9.81	8.85
	n	84	413	362

F-test: Sex $p < .01$
         Income $p < .01$
         Interaction Sex x Income $p > .77$

in the community were significantly more depressed than men of
similar status. Both working wives and housewives were more
depressed than comparable working married men. The most
depressed women were those who were poorly educated, were
working at low-status jobs, and were married, with children at
home. (As Bernard, 1973, has pointed out, mothers whose children

no longer lived with them were significantly *less* depressed than women whose children were living with them or women who had no children). It is the young married working blue-collar mother who is most likely to be depressed; and the risk has apparently increased dramatically during the past two decades.

Why? A recent study (Warren, 1975) done in urban communities provides some insight into this question. Warren observed where people turned for help when they had problems. She found considerable differences between blue- and white-collar women. Blue-collar men, for example, turned to their wives for help 58.2 percent of the time, whereas blue-collar women turned to their husbands only 40.5 percent of the time. This difference was significantly greater than among white-collar spouses. Again, although blue-collar men could turn to their co-workers for help 34.6 percent of the time, blue-collar women could do so only 18.9 percent of the time. Blue-collar women, in contrast with white-collar women, were also much less able to turn for help to informal neighborhood organizations or professionals.

If depression is indeed related to powerlessness and a sense of helplessness (Seligman, 1974), then it would appear that the blue-collar married young mother has both the greatest number of stresses to cope with and the fewest possible sources of help.

In their review of adult sex roles and mental illness, Gove and Tudor (1972) concluded that role conflicts and demands are probably at the root of these symptoms. During the past two decades, women's entry into the labor force—both blue-collar and white-collar women—has increased markedly (Levine, 1974). However, although the family role demands for white-collar women have changed in a slightly less sexist direction (they can turn to their husbands for help as well as vice versa), the same has not been true for the blue-collar married mother. She is caught within the traditional sexist family role requirements. Her entry into the labor force, in a low-level job, has meant that she must fulfill all of the traditional family role requirements in addition to working at a poorly paid and unsatisfying job. She has few sources of aid (though her husband can turn to her for aid with his problems). No wonder she feels trapped and powerless. The situation of the divorced or separated blue-collar mother is even worse.

If these mental health findings are viewed in relation to sex role stereotypes, the conclusion is inescapable that it is the sex-stereotyped familial and socioemotional roles that women now carry in addition to occupational burdens which are causing the greatly intensified stresses they experience.

THE PRIMARY PREVENTION OF SEXISM

Not only are the effects of sexism damaging; androgynous attitudes apparently are an advantage in problem solving (Bem, 1972; Spence, 1974).

If sex role stereotypes take such a toll in adulthood, especially in the familial and socioemotional areas, can they be eliminated— or at least modified—before they become a part of the adult social expectations of both men and women?

One study made a brief experimental attempt to achieve the primary prevention of sexism in schools We wanted to see whether it was possible, working through curricula, teachers, and peer groups, to modify children's sex role stereotypes in three areas: occupational, familial, and socioemotional.

We chose three large school systems in the Boston area which differed markedly in the social class and ethnic backgrounds of their children. Three age groups were selected in each system: 5-, 10-, and 14-year-olds (kindergarten and fifth and ninth grades). These ages were selected because they represented different stages of cognitive development. We were interested in whether an intervention would have more powerful effects at one age than another. A Solomon 4-groups design showed us that there were no independent or interaction effects of the measurement.

Multiple measures were used to determine the children's stereotypes in the three areas of interest. These included projective questions like "Tell me about a typical day when you are thirty years old"; "Describe a day in the life of a typical woman; a typical man." The answers revealed the child's stereotyping of adult roles and to what extent he felt he would conform to them. We asked the children to tell us about the jobs men and women could have and to describe what men and women were like personally (socioemotional qualities). They also told stories using the characteristics of the opposite sex. On a modified semantic differential instrument, they told us what they thought real boys and girls were like, what ideal boys and girls should be like, and what they themselves were like. They were shown pictures of men and women in stereotyped and nonstereotyped occupations and were asked to tell stories about them. Objective measures were also used, including the Stein sex role preference questionnaire.

The intervention lasted for only six weeks. It consisted of specially devised curricula integrated into regular English and social studies work of the fifth and ninth graders and into the entire day of the kindergartners. The materials were designed to fit the children's cognitive stages. Books, plays, special projects, records, and so on were included. (The complete curriculum is available in Guttentag et al., 1976.)

Before the intervention, teachers received training in nonsexist interaction patterns—that is, maintenance of a high rate of interaction with girls as well as boys regardless of where the girls were physically in the classroom. We also attempted to enlist the peer groups in our work.

Children in control and experimental groups were measured before and after the intervention. Pairs of observers recorded teacher-pupil interactions in each classroom before the intervention, at biweekly intervals during it, immediately after it, and two weeks later. Teachers were also independently rated on their enthusiasm and use of curriculum materials in the classroom.

Intervention and Study Findings

Not surprisingly, the results were complex. Here are some of the most significant findings.

The social classes and ethnic backgrounds of the children made no difference in their initial sex role stereotypes. Having a working mother—even a high status working mother—also made no difference. Even the kindergarten children, regardless of their backgrounds, shared similar views. This suggests that even at young ages children have learned the cultural stereotypes, probably through television and their peers, and these are more powerful than the influence of the family.

At all ages, the children were more stereotyped in their views of opposite sex roles than they were for their own sex roles. This was especially marked for boys' views of girls' roles, and was most pronounced among the 14-year-old boys.

The intervention effort had diverse effects on the three age groups. Initially, the kindergarteners were quite stereotyped about concrete aspects of occupational roles. They emphasized that men and women had different jobs and spent their time doing different things. A woman could not be a mother and an aviator. Fathers always went to work, except on weekends, when they played with the children. Kindergarten girls felt they were just as strong and positive as the boys felt *they* were. After the intervention, the kindergarteners were significantly better able to understand that the same job could be held by either a man or a woman. The girls, more than the boys, were more likely to place men in such inter-personal jobs as social worker, teacher, and sales clerk. But the children did not change their attitudes toward the family and socioemotional roles that men and women could play.

The fifth graders were the least stereotyped of the three groups. They believed that women could have jobs, though might not succeed at them and would then have to desert helpless children and other family responsibilities in order to keep the jobs. Fifth graders nearly always put men and women into sex-stereotyped private routines and hobbies. Boys and men were ascribed particu-larly restrictive socioemotional roles: they never admitted to having any problems and they saw themselves as active in sports and economically successful. Period. Girls readily accepted a socio-emotional emphasis as an important part of their role. They also showed a slight tendency toward negative self-esteem (that is, social desirability). They felt they were not as beautiful as they should be.

At the fifth grade level, the intervention primarily affected the girls. Their belief that women could have varied and successful careers was strengthened. Their perceptions of the qualities of ideal boys and ideal girls converged, denoting a new sensitivity toward nonsexist qualities of personhood. There were also changes in their attitudes toward men's roles. The boys, on the other hand, showed virtually no change on any item.

Ninth graders were the most stereotyped of all. They believed that interpersonal and affective socioemotional qualities were essential for women. Although the girls supported women in occupations, the boys were suspicious of employed women. Girls more often presented women in a dual marriage and career situation. Interestingly, before the intervention, ninth grade girls were privately sure that they were ugly, although they thought women should be beautiful (socially desirable). After the intervention, however, they indicated an improved sense of personal attractiveness and self-esteem. Apparently the intervention succeeded in showing them a variety of alternative ways in which women could achieve status, other than through social attractiveness.

Ninth graders generally reacted negatively to the nonsexist message of the intervention. Most boys' views became more stereotyped afterwards. Peer group support for boys was particularly strong in discounting the importance of the nonsexist issues. Boys were stronger in upholding the stereotypes for girls' roles.

From these results, it appears that a little intervention of a nonsexist type may be worse than none at all for ninth grade boys. Yet a strong, thorough, and intense classroom exploration of nonsexist role possibilities does have a liberating effect even on the sex role stereotypes of ninth grade boys.

Perhaps the most meaningful and relevant finding came from the examination of changes in individual classrooms of all ages. The amount of children's attitude changes in the direction of nonstereotypy was closely correlated with an independent measure of the individual teacher's effectiveness in implementing the curriculum. In other words, the teachers who cared about the issue of sexism in roles and society, and who used the provided curriculum regularly and creatively, were able to change the attitudes of their students even in a brief six-week-long intervention. In a ninth grade classroom where the teacher used the nonsexist curriculum regularly and enthusiastically, in fact, there were significant attitudinal changes, and not only in girls; boys, too, changed to nonstereotyped views in all three areas.

SUMMARY, CONCLUSIONS, AND RECOMMENDATIONS

Although girls at all ages were the most responsive to the intervention, it was boys' sex role stereotypes that were most in need of change. Boys also changed the least after the intervention, as is often the case in any intervention: those who need it the most change the least. Yet, in classrooms where there were active and committed teachers, there were changes in all children, even the boys, and these changes occurred even at the most resistant age.

The greatest changes were apparent in the most peripheral of the three areas: occupational stereotypes. Unfortunately it is the stereotypes about family and socioemotional role requirements, as we noted earlier, that seem to be the most critically in need of change in order to prevent problems from occurring later. These more central stereotypes were more resistant; but even so, we found it *was* possible to change them, even in a brief period of time, in the classrooms where the teachers were the most enthusiastic.

Interestingly, the intervention had some unanticipated side effects on the girls' sense of self-esteem. Apparently exposure to the possibility of multiple job and family choices suggested to girls—particularly the 14-year-old girls—that they need not be so concerned about whether they were socially desirable according to stereotyped notions of attractiveness.

Some recommendations emerge from the integration of these two related but different lines of research. Since males possess the more powerful adult roles in our society, it might be anticipated that male stereotypes, especially of the family and socioemotional role requirements for women, are most in need of change. If we are later to avert the stressful life circumstances that create severe feelings of depression in the young married working mothers, these changes are a first priority.

But we are confronted with a time lag problem. Women's occupational roles have changed more quickly than have their family role definitions. This is particularly true for blue-collar women. Given the rapidly changing labor market participation rates for women, less sexist definitions of male and female family and socioemotional roles could immediately have an ameliorative effect on the stresses many women now experience.

It is clear that the schools can be used in a primary preventive role. Even a brief nonsexist intervention, implemented throughout a school, can have marked effects on sexist stereotypes of children and adolescents. After a short period of training, teachers can radically alter both the content and the quality of their interactions with children. The mental health costs of sexism are high. The schools are a socializing instrument that can serve immediately in the primary prevention of sexism.

REFERENCES

Bem, S. L. Psychology looks at sex roles: where have all the adrogynous people gone? Paper presented at the UCLA Symposium on Women, May 1972.

Bernard, J. *The future of marriage*. New York: Bantam Books, 1973.

Cannon, M. S., and Redick, R. W. *Differential utilization of psychiatric facilities by men and women, U.S. 1970*. (NIMH Biometry Branch, Statistical Note 81), Washington, D.C., 1973.

Clancy, K., and Gove, W. Sex differences in mental illness: an analysis of response bias in self report. *American Journal of Sociology*, 1974, *80*, 205–216.

Gove, W., and Tudor, J. Adult sex roles and mental illness. *American Journal of Sociology*, 1972, *78*, 812–835.

Guttentag, M., Bray, H., Amsler, J., Donovan, V., Legge, G., Legge, W. W., Littenberg, R., and Stotsky, S. *Undoing sex stereotypes: A How-to-do-it guide with tested non-sexist curricula and teaching methods*. New York: McGraw-Hill, 1976.

Guttentag, M., and Salasin, S. Women, men, and mental health. In L. Cater, W. Martyna, and A. Scott (Eds.), *Changing roles of men and women*. Aspen, Colo.: Aspen Press, 1976.

Levine, A. Women at work in America: History, status, and prospects. Unpublished paper, 1974.

Radloff, L. Sex differences in mental health: the effects of marital and occupational status. *Sex Roles*, 1975, *3*, 249–265.

Spence, J., Helmreich, R., and Stapp, L. The Personal Attributes Questionnaire: A measure of sex role stereotypes and masculinity and femininity. *Catalog of Selected Documents in Psychology*, 1974, *4*, 29–39.

Warren, R. B. The work role and problem coping: sex differentials in the use of helping systems in urban communities. Unpublished paper.

Weissman, M. M. The epidemiology of suicide attempts, 1960–1971. *Archives of General Psychiatry*, 1974, *30*, 737–746.

Weissman, M. M. Sex differences and the epidemiology of depression. Unpublished paper, 1975.

Weissman, M. M., and Klerman, G. Sex differences in the epidemiology of depression. *Archives of General Psychiatry*, 1977, *34*, 98–111.

14

Vulnerability to Schizophrenic Episodes and Their Prevention in Adults

BONNIE SPRING AND JOSEPH ZUBIN

Primary prevention of psychopathology refers to eliminating the potentially noxious internal and external factors that might produce deviant behavior as well as fostering the factors of normal development. In a recent paper, Kessler and Albee (1975) compared the field of primary prevention to the Great Okefenokee Swamp. While joining in the tribute they paid to all the investigators who have dared to tread this treacherous ground, we would also like to raise the question of why the early explorers have all devoted their attention to the tiny seedlings and low vegetation that grow there rather than to the full-grown trees that dot the terrain. The last decade's rapid proliferation of research on vulnerability to schizophrenia has almost all been focused on children at risk. Much less research has concerned the problem of identifying and intervening in the lives of adults who are vulnerable to schizophrenic episodes.

In one sense, our concern appears to be outside of the area Caplan (1964) defined as primary prevention. Instead of contending with the problem of how to prevent episodes of schizophrenia from appearing at all, we have decided to confine ourselves to the more focused and presumably more manageable problem of preventing further episodes in those who have already suffered one. But in another sense, we are plunging into the crux of the primary prevention problem. The issue turns on how one answers the question, the primary prevention of what? If one defines schizophrenia as a *trait* which, once manifested, continues chronically until death, then all preventive measures begun after its onset must be regarded as either secondary (aimed at early treatment) or tertiary (aimed at rehabilitating the patient and minimizing long-term damage). If, however, one regards a single episode as a time-limited *state*, which marks those who are vulnerable to transient episodes, then the task of aborting new episodes is one of primary prevention. To grasp this distinction, it is only necessary to understand our premise that the person who has suffered one episode of schizophrenia will not always be schizophrenic. He will, however, always be vulnerable to episodes of schizophrenia. From our point of view, therefore, primary prevention involves blocking only the subsequent full-fledged episodic expressions of schizophrenia—something which may really be possible. We will put off until a much later date the task of eliminating the genetic and acquired bases of vulnerability—something which will certainly be very difficult and may ultimately prove to be impossible except through retroactive birth control.

Thus, we propose that the first step in primary prevention research on adults is to learn how to identify the high risk, vulnerable individual by examining those who have already succumbed once to an episode of schizophrenia. The initial goal of preventive interventions should be to abort a second episode in such individuals. Once we understand the contingencies under which subsequent episodes occur, we may eventually be able to prevent the first one. After overcoming the episodes, we may at last be able to progress toward eliminating or preventing the development of the underlying vulnerability itself.

Having reduced the imponderable problem of primary prevention to a somewhat more ponderable dimension, we face the need for certain definitions and assumptions underlying our task. We must further explore the question of what we are trying to prevent, and what the causes of the episodes may be. Of course it is possible that even though we are ignorant of cause, we may inadvertently do some good preventive work. This was the case with the miasmists who assumed that the swamp miasma was the source of mists and vapor which caused mal-aria (bad air). Although the theory was wrong, it spurred preventionists to build houses higher above the swamp areas. This prevented contact with mosquitoes and pollution, curing the problem by a stroke of good luck. Similarly, obstetrics has found ways of reducing eclampsia even though the origin of the disorder is still unknown (McNeil, this conference). But even the miasmists had some kind of model to guide their efforts. What descriptive and etiological models of schizophrenia are available to us today?

Let us first dispose of the model that mental disorder is a myth.

There are two aspects to scientific investigation: the conceptual framework or model, and testing the hypotheses emanating from it. In the conceptual framework we deal with abstractions in the form of concepts. In testing the hypotheses we deal with ostensible facts to determine the tenability of the hypotheses. About facts or methods for organizing facts, you can only ask if they are useful. That mental disorder is still a useful concept will become apparent in this paper, if it is not already apparent to everyone.

Another problem that merits comment is the rigorous definition of concepts. It is a generally bruited claim that our definitions of diagnostic categories, or even our criteria for the presence of mental disorder, are quite imprecise. True as this statement is, we must not forget that only in mathematics can we find ironclad definitions. Such rigor in behavioral science could lead only to rigor mortis. Even in physical medicine, Feinstein (1967) and Falek and Moser (1975) have reminded us that criteria for the presence of physical disorders leave room for a substantial error margin. Finally, let us not forget that Julian Huxley (1940) found it impossible to give a rigorous definition of species: "There is no single criterion of species . . . a combination of criteria is needed, together with some sort of flair." Instead of striving for a rigorous definition of schizophrenia, therefore, we must seek a description that permits observers to agree about whether the disorder is present or absent. Current studies (Spitzer et al., 1975; Spitzer and Fleiss, 1974) on the reliability of psychiatric diagnoses indicate that considerable inter-rater agreement (for example, kappa = .84 for the presence of schizophrenia) can be achieved by using explicit sets of diagnostic criteria. Thus, if schizophrenia is a myth, at least it is one that doctors can diagnose similarly.

DESCRIPTIVE MODELS OF SCHIZOPHRENIA: CHRONIC CONDITION OR TIME-LIMITED EPISODES?

The history of diagnostic schemas for schizophrenia leaves us a legacy of two main traditions. One is to rely primarily on the clinical symptom picture to diagnose schizophrenia, and to interpret the presence of classic symptoms like hallucinations or thought disorder as evidence for the presence of the disorder.

Eugen Bleuler represented this tradition, and he has been followed by many others, including Schneider, Langfeldt, the staff of the Biometrics Research Unit, and the staff of the WHO Pilot Study of Schizophrenia. In the other tradition are those who argue that such classic symptoms are not in themselves useful as diagnostic criteria since they are manifested by a diverse and heterogeneous group of patients. This latter tradition holds prognosis or actual outcome as the key to diagnostic certainty. Kraepelin, and more recently Feighner et al. (1972) and Kety (1975), are spokesmen for the position that a definite diagnosis of schizophrenia can be made only if symptoms are chronically present for a long time and the patient displays either a deteriorating or an unremitting disease course over time.

If it is correct that once an episode of true schizophrenia has appeared, it runs an unrelenting downhill course, then there appears to be little hope for primary preventive measures aimed at adults. It would seem that unless measures are taken early in childhood, vulnerability will germinate to the point at which chronic mental illness is inevitable and treatment is futile. Those foolhardy ones among us who wish to intervene in the lives of vulnerable adults stand like the fabled little Dutch boy, finger in the dike, trying to hold back the North Sea.

But before we plunge ahead in this pessimistic vein, let us consider the evidence that, in contemporary form, "true" schizophrenia is an ever-present, unremitting disease.

If we first inspect our hospital populations, we find little to support the contention. In the New York State Hospitals, the average length of hospitalization for schizophrenia has fallen from several years in the pre-1950 era to 90 days in 1955 and 37 days in 1975. Parallel trends have occurred in countries all across the globe (for example, Niskanen et al., 1973; Yolles and Kramer, 1969). In the New York State Hospitals three-fourths of the current chronic cases were admitted more than two years ago, and one-half of those have been hospitalized for over 20 years. These statistics suggest that only a small number of current schizophrenic admissions are contributing to the pool of chronic, back-ward patients that Kraepelin spoke of. Indeed, they might make us wonder whether "true" schizophrenia, defined in terms of chronicity, is largely a disease of the past.

But perhaps these statistics do not really tell the whole story.

Maybe the majority of patients are merely caught in the "revolving door" policy and released without any symptomatic improvement. Although this suggestion may often contain a grain of truth, there is also contrary evidence. For example, Glick (1975) has found that schizophrenic patients randomly assigned to short-term therapy lasting only four weeks do show a substantial suppression of symptoms; and Herz, Endicott, and Spitzer (1975) have found similar results. At the discharge point of four weeks, short-term therapy patients function reliably better than other schizophrenic patients who have been assigned to longer term therapy. This finding seems to suggest that a majority of schizophrenics have experienced some remission and, with support, are capable of improved functioning within one month of hospitalization. One might argue, though, that this improvement is only fleeting and perhaps an artifact of the desire to thank or please the therapist.

To truly evaluate the hypothesis that schizophrenia reveals itself in the chronic impairment of a majority of patients, we must examine how the discharged patient functions in the community. It has long been clear that continued phenothiazine medication plays a substantial role in this function. Typical findings are Hogarty et al.'s (1974) data demonstrating that 80 percent of patients receiving placebo medication—compared with 48 percent receiving maintenance phenothiazines—experience significant relapses in the two years following discharge. Still, one might argue that although the drugs help patients to remain out of the hospital, the large majority of schizophrenics never recover fully enough to be functioning and contributing citizens of any wider community.

But the evidence contradicts this premise. Unless patients are already chronically ill at the time of assessment, numerous researchers have found it exceedingly difficult to define a group of newly admitted schizophrenic patients who will experience a poor outcome. Hawk et al. (1975), for example, applied Schneider's first-rank symptoms, Langfeldt's criteria, and Carpenter's discriminating signs to patients at intake in the hope of distinguishing a group of nuclear schizophrenics, but they were entirely unsuccessful in predicting the status of their patients five years later. In fact, 40 percent of them were among the best outcome group when compared with other psychiatric patients on a composite index of symptom severity, duration of hospitalization, and social adjustment. Similarly, of the 208 probands Manfred Bleuler followed longitudinally, 50 percent made an adequate adjustment to the community. Forty percent were hospitalized occasionally but lived most of their lives in the community. Only 10 percent showed the type of disease course discribed as typical in Kraepelin's writings and Eugen Bleuler's early work.

Manfred Bleuler's own observation is apt in this regard:

That which my father had to a certain extent done in cross-section, I have investigated longitudinally. He could stay with his patients only as long as they remained in his clinic. When they left the clinic, they were thereafter out of sight and lost to him, and this was the case with most psychiatrists of his generation. For this reason, an unfavorable picture of the course of illness had to be inferred: the improved and the healed patients disappeared beyond the horizon of the clinic, and he saw above all those who were unimproved or relapsed. (Trans. D. Rosenthal, 1974, p. 92)

To summarize, the bulk of the evidence suggests that chronic, unremitting schizophrenia, especially the catastrophic variety that may have been commonplace generations ago, is becoming increasingly rare. This fact poses a problem for the Kraepelinian model of schizophrenia. Are we to say that only the roughly 10 percent of cases who show no remission are to be characterized as "true" schizophrenics, whereas the other 90 percent are not? As an alternative, let us suggest another descriptive model which at least has the virtue of more widespread applicability.

Specifically, we suggest that schizophrenia, like other mental disorders, appears in time-limited episodes induced when life stressors surpass a threshold set by the patient's characteristic level of vulnerability. Once the episode has ended, a patient resumes functioning either at or close to his premorbid competence level. The hypothesis that schizophrenia is an episodic rather than a continuous phenomenon appears to be consistent with three things we know about these patients. First, as we have already discussed, only a very small group of schizophrenics shows a sharply deteriorating level of functioning over time. Second, the course of this mental disorder is not a continuous one. Just as patients with affective disorders are mentally quite clear between episodes, it is likely that the majority of schizophrenic patients experience periods of normalcy interspersed with their recurring episodes.

Third, our hypothesis may help to explain the well-known fact that in schizophrenia, as in other mental disorders, the good premorbid personalities tend to recover from their episodes, while the episodes of poor premorbids seem to persist endlessly (Zubin, 1974, 1975). Why should premorbid adjustment be so important in recovery? By definition, the good premorbid patient is a competent individual who is adept at coping with everyday life circumstances. Once the stress that triggered his illness is removed and the episode subsides, he should be able to resume his former place in life unless the episode has severely reduced his coping ability. In any event, we should be able to detect clearly the onset and offset of the good premorbid patient's episode, since he plummets from a high level of functioning to a very low one during the episode, and rebounds to his high premorbid level when the episode subsides. These sharp peaks and low valleys punctuating his course of illness make it easy to tell when the good premorbid's recovery has occurred.

What happens in the case of the poor premorbid patient to make him appear to remain endlessly in his episode? There are three possibilities: (1) the episode actually continues indefinitely; (2) the episode ends as in the case of the good premorbid; (3) the episode reduces coping ability. As for the first possibility, there may be a small fraction of cases in whom the episode persists endlessly. We would like to propose, however, that the second and third alternatives—that the episode ends or that it reduces coping ability—describe what happens in the majority of cases. Let us assume tentatively, for the moment, that the episode usually comes to an end in the poor premorbid patient, just as it does in the good premorbid. Think of how one might determine that the poor premorbid's episode has ended, and it is immediately apparent that this is a very difficult task. Even when the patient has recovered, his postmorbid level of adjustment is so low that he cannot cope with life's exigencies, just as he could not premorbidly. The clinical judgment of recovery should be based on a comparison with the patient's premorbid level, but since the premorbid level of adjustment is rarely known this is seldom possible. Consequently, the poor premorbid patient may *appear* to remain debilitated even though the episode has in fact disappeared. A similar problem is evident in detecting episode offset in patients whose coping level has actually been reduced. Loss of coping capacity might come about either directly as a result of the psychopathological process, or indirectly by the iatrogenic effects resulting from hospitalization or Gruenberg's Social Breakdown Syndrome. If the drop in competence has been striking, these patients may also still be mistakenly regarded as ill despite the fact that their episodes have ended.

The unexpected and apparently spontaneous recoveries of some long-term patients may also fall within our explanatory framework. Often a patient remains in the hospital after his episode has subsided because it has not been recognized that he is no longer sick. When the recognition finally comes, either through the patient himself or from those in his surround, he can of course be released from his bondage, and will probably be regarded as a miraculous recovery. In some cases the patient's low premorbid level of competence may even improve as a result of hospital guidance or maturation. These patients too are regarded as manifesting a miraculous and spontaneous remission of disease, when in fact the episode has long since passed and the primary change has been not in the disease process but in the further development of coping skills.

Having begun with the premise that schizophrenia is an episodic mental illness, let us move on to see if we can construct a model that will help us to investigate the causes of the episodes and to identify those who are vulnerable to them.

A MODEL OF VULNERABILITY TO SCHIZOPHRENIC EPISODES

There are of course numerous scientific models for explaining the etiology of mental disorders, and Zubin has previously discussed six of them (Zubin, 1972). The theories can be grouped into two broad categories depending on whether they exemplify a field theory or an atomic approach. In field theory models, the individual is regarded as the target of a field of impinging forces that determine his well-being or illness. The forces may take the form of presently impinging ecological stimuli (ecological model), or more remote events that have influenced developmental maturation (developmental model) or altered the acquisition of response repertoires (learning model). In the atomic approach, each individual is regarded as a discrete unit with individual characteristics

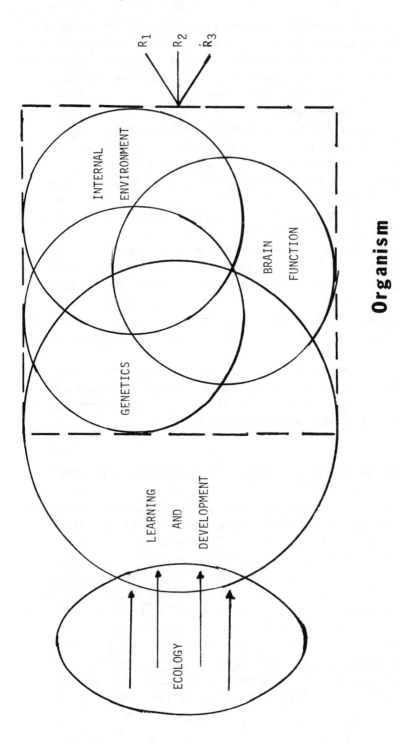

Figure 1. Scientific models for the etiology of schizophrenia

that determine his mental status. The person's relevant constitutional features are reflected in his idiosyncratic genetic makeup and internal biochemical and neurophysiological characteristics. Of course, this bipartite division is something of an oversimplification, since field theories must take account of individual differences in response to impinging forces. Atomic theories, in turn, must consider the fact that the condition and expression of the internal milieu are influenced by the environmental field.

The common thread running through all these models is that each suggests a hypothesis about some ingredient in the etiology of vulnerability to mental illness. Corresponding to the two main types of etiological models, two major causes of vulnerability have been proposed. The first is a genetic component which is laid down in the genes and reflected in the internal environment and neurophysiology of the organism. The second is an environmentally acquired or nongenetic* component of vulnerability. This is a little more difficult to describe. If we consider the evidence that early experience, early exposure to certain stresses, and specific diseases leave their mark and tend to either facilitate or inhibit the development of a disorder in later life, we can metaphorically describe this acquired vulnerability as dependent upon the "memories" of the organism for past experiences, or on the scars such experiences leave behind them. Longitudinal studies of children at risk and retrospective studies of patients have begun to suggest some remote biological, familial, and social events that may be sources of acquired vulnerability. Contributing events may be pregnancy and birth complications, submissive relationships with siblings (Pollin and Stabenau, 1968), disturbed relationship with father, overprotective mother (Kringlen, 1968), or lack of intimacy in adolescent peer group friendships (Kreisman, 1970).

As things now stand, we have a wealth of hypotheses about the etiological sources of vulnerability. What has been lacking, however, is a good operational definition of vulnerability that is not wedded to any single etiological hypothesis. At present our studies of vulnerable individuals are bound by narrow sampling

---

*Strictly speaking, there are no nongenetic causes, since even the response to traumatic happenstances is at least in part dependent upon a genetic proclivity, or the trauma could have no influence. By the same token there are no nonenvironmental causes, since genes cannot work or be evoked in a vacuum.

characteristics that are dictated by the investigator's favorite hypothesis about the etiology of schizophrenia. For example, we never pool samples containing individuals at risk because they have schizophrenic parents together with samples at risk because they were isolated during adolescence. Neither sample is ever compared with a group vulnerable for a different reason—perhaps because of disturbed family communication patterns. What seems to be needed is a more generic measure of vulnerability that would enable us to initially select a more heterogeneous sample of vulnerable individuals, and then to separate out, from the heterogeneous mass, homogeneous subgroups who derived their vulnerabilities by different avenues. With such a strategy, we can study whether the *genetically* at risk individuals are similar to those who *acquired* their vulnerabilities as a result of environmental factors. Perhaps we may yet learn that vulnerabilities derived from different sources are expressed in different forms of schizophrenia.

In the field theory models as well as in the atomic or biological models, the individual is a powerless pawn, at the mercy of ecological forces or in the hands of the fate dictated by heredity. This is hardly a true picture of man. In order to formulate a more acceptable definition of vulnerability, let us begin with an assumption that has won adherents in both the physical and mental health camps. This is that health prevails as long as the individual maintains a dynamic equilibrium against insults from his chemical, physical, infectious, psychological, or social environment. When this equilibrium is pushed out of balance, disease ensues. The dimension of vulnerability–invulnerability describes the degree to which an individual tends to succumb to or resist illness in the face of external and internal threats to his homeostasis. We recognize the existence of individual differences in vulnerability by observing the variability of responses of different individuals to the same environmental stresses. For example, if we inspect patterns of absenteeism for a grammar school classroom, it is clear that a small number of children are most vulnerable to disease and fall ill from germs that rarely affect others in the classroom. Others of more moderate vulnerability succumb only to illnesses that also affect a substantial number of their peers. The least vulnerable rarely miss a day and remain healthy even at the height of an epidemic.

Extending this principle to the study of vulnerability to mental illness, we refer to the well documented role of life event stressors

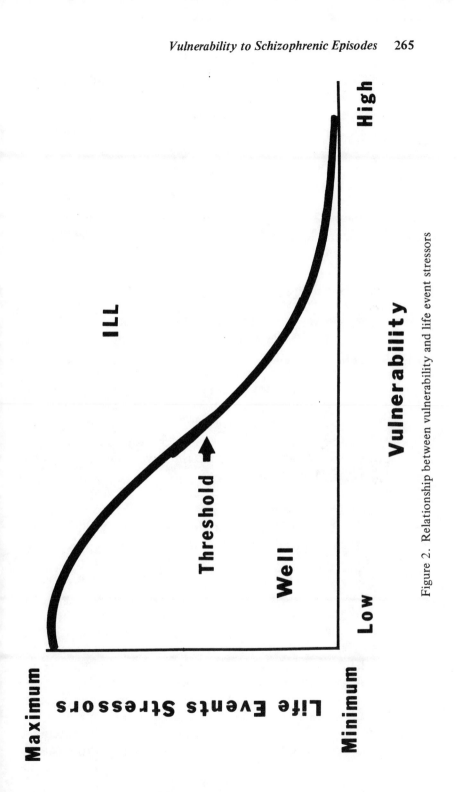

Figure 2. Relationship between vulnerability and life event stressors

in precipitating physical and especially psychological disorders
(Rahe, 1964; Brown, 1968; Dohrenwend, 1972). A life event
stressor is an incident such as bereavement, promotion, marriage,
or divorce which necessitates a substantial amount of readjustment.
The psychological strain induced by a single event or an accumulation of similar prior stressors often precedes and appears to trigger
the onset of an episode of mental illness.

The relation between vulnerability and life event stressors is
shown in Figure 2. It will be noted that as long as the stress is
below the threshold of vulnerability, the individual responds to
the stressor in an elastic, homeostatic way and remains well within
the limits of normality. When the stress exceeds threshold, the
person is likely to develop a psychopathological episode. As stress
recedes below that line—often because the person is removed from
the stressful context and placed in an institution with few pressures
and demands—the episode ends and the person progressively returns to his pre-episode status.

Vulnerability, therefore, is defined in terms of the constitutional factors (internal) that set the threshold at which stressful
life events will catapult an individual into an episode of mental
illness. From this point of view, *life event stressors* can be
regarded as immediate or short-term states of psychological strain
that serve to elicit the encoded long-term engrams or templates of
genetic or acquired vulnerability.

Applying these definitions, we can arrive at a measure of
vulnerability that is not wedded to any single etiological hypothesis and will thus permit us to group patients according to the
degree of their vulnerability without regard to its etiological
source.

Very simply, we know that all individuals who have succumbed
to an episode of schizophrenia are vulnerable to some degree.
Further, individuals for whom relatively minor stresses have been
sufficient to trigger the episode are more vulnerable than those
whose episodes have been precipitated by a major concatenation
of stressful life events. This principle, while enabling us to assess
the vulnerability of those who have already succumbed to an episode, permits only minimal evaluations of vulnerability in those
who have never fallen ill. We can be fairly safe in assuming that
people who have experienced accumulated life event stressors sufficient to elicit an episode in many other people without themselves

falling ill, are relatively low in vulnerability—that is, are relatively invulnerable. But we cannot make any assumptions about the vulnerability of healthy individuals who have not experienced sustained periods of serious stress. Although this is a major limitation, it may be all we can hope for at present. Moreover, understanding this limitation might in itself contribute something to our interpretation of research findings.

For example, the principle might influence how we interpret the well-known statistic that 90 percent of schizophrenic patients do not have a schizophrenic parent, or Kety's finding that there is a low rate of schizophrenia among the biological relatives of acute schizophrenic patients but a high rate of mental illness among relatives of chronic or borderline cases. These data are often mustered to support the contention that genetic factors make either no contribution or a relatively trivial one to vulnerability in most cases of schizophrenia, or at least that their contribution to vulnerability to acute schizophrenia is negligible. This assumption, however, is unwarranted until we know something of the life histories of the probands and their biological relatives. It is possible that the familial genes of the chronic patients set the vulnerability threshold so low that a broad spectrum of ordinary life events is sufficient to trigger an episode. The high familial concordances in these cases would therefore derive from the fact that numerous events present in almost any life history would prove to be pathogenic for such individuals. On the other hand, it may be that the parents and other relatives of the acute patients also possess a genetically based vulnerability to schizophrenia which is of more moderate degree. Thus, unless the life histories of relatives and probands have been concordant for accumulated and severe stressful life events, one would not expect to observe episodes in both despite their shared vulnerability.

We might draw an analogy by comparing schizophrenia to sickle cell anemia. Sickle cell anemia is a severe, debilitating, and usually fatal disease caused by the presence of two abnormal genes that prevent the formation of normal hemoglobin. If only one abnormal gene is present, a heterozygous condition known as sickle cell trait results. Sickle cell trait is a benign, asymptomatic condition that is detectable only under special circumstances, though extensive and sometimes fatal sickling can be evoked even in the heterozygous sickle-cell trait individual exposed to specific stressors such as high altitude, acute alcoholism, or deep anesthesia (Harris, 1963). Perhaps acute schizophrenia, like sickle cell trait, is a genetically linked disorder that achieves full pathological expression only when very severe or specific adverse circumstances exceed the threshold of vulnerability.

Returning to our measure, it should now be possible to categorize our patients according to their degree of vulnerability by measuring the level of stress that was required to precipitate the episode of schizophrenia. Comparing patients of equivalent vulnerabilities, it should be possible to investigate whether the symptom pattern and severity, response to therapy, and disease courses are similar or different depending on whether the vulnerability is genetically or nongenetically based. Perhaps it will be possible to determine therapeutic strategies that are optimally attuned to different subtypes of vulnerables. Moreover, just as the study of individuals who have already experienced an episode of illness can permit us to empirically isolate and test putative causes of vulnerability, the study of individuals who remain healthy even in the face of catastrophic circumstances can enable us to determine some sources of invulnerability.

Competence and Vulnerability

We would like to stress that the problem of discovering sources of invulnerability must be approached empirically. It has long been apparent that the most commonsense assumptions about factors that buffer against or facilitate the development of psychopathology often fail to meet the test of statistical significance. For example, although it seems intuitively reasonable that certain types of family interaction patterns should prove to be schizophrenogenic, Jacob's (1975) careful review of the literature has shown how difficult it is to demonstrate that these patterns occur with greater frequency in the families of disturbed offspring than in families with normal offspring. Just as we insist that the traits contributing to vulnerability to schizophrenia must empirically relate to the probability of developing an episode, so must we insist that traits which intuitively seem to buffer against the likelihood of mental illness meet the test of research validation.

One assumption frequently encountered in the literature is that symptomatology and social competence are inversely related.

In other words, it is often taken for granted that the same skills and dispositions that promote *competence* (defined as success or achievement in day-to-day living) are also sources of invulnerability that reduce the likelihood of developing an episode of schizophrenia. We do not accept the assumption that competence and invulnerability are identical. Instead, we tentatively hypothesize that competence or coping ability is orthogonal to vulnerability. Thus, highly competent individuals can have all grades of vulnerability, and relatively incompetent folk can be highly vulnerable or quite immune to mental illness.

There are several reasons for this suggestion. The first is simply that until we have systematically collected more data specifically investigating the relationship between these variables, it is best to assume the null hypothesis and avoid incorporating unsubstantiated dogma into the literature. The second reason is that there is a small pool of evidence suggesting that the two may in fact be independent dimensions. The third is that measures of competence and vulnerability appear to have distinctly different uses in psychopathology research. Vulnerability indicators measure the likelihood that an individual will succumb to an episode of schizophrenia. By contrast, a sharp dip in a patient's characteristic level of competence permits us to detect the episode's onset, and a return to the premorbid baseline signals the episode's end.

It is difficult to present research findings pertinent to the relationship between competence and vulnerability because, as we will point out, few studies have unambiguously assessed either variable. Although occupational level indexes coping ability in only one of the many domains integral to competence, it is the only measure that has commonly been studied in relation to patienthood. Clark (1948, 1949) in Chicago, Hollingshead and Redlich (1958) in New Haven, Leighton (1963) in Nova Scotia, and Svalastoga (1965) in Denmark have been among the many to show that rates of schizophrenia are highest for the lowest status occupations. There have also been contradictory findings, however, particularly when research is conducted in smaller cities or uses incidence rather than prevalence measures of the frequency of mental illness. In the Hagerstown Study, for example, Clausen and Kohn (1959) presented the following figures on the average annual rates of first hospital admission for schizophrenia per 100,000 individuals between the ages of 15 and 64:

a. professional, technical, managerial, officials, proprietors   21.3
b. clerical and sales   23.8
c. craftsmen, foremen, kindred workers   10.7
d. operatives, service workers, laborers   21.7

In another investigation, Turner (1974) found that fully 67.4 percent of subjects ever hospitalized for schizophrenia were employed. The proportion of employed persons among general population controls who had never experienced a significant hospitalization is only 20 percentage points higher—87.5 percent. Moreover, fully 70 percent of premorbidly employed patients were working at a skilled-manual level or higher, compared to about 68 percent of the general population! Therefore, it appears that high-level job skills, while integral to competence, do not render one invulnerable to schizophrenia. The mentally ill derive from the ranks of the successfully employed as well as the unemployed, and it is far from clear that relatively low-level job skills predispose either to social maladjustment or to episodes of schizophrenia.

One reason why we know so little about the relationship between competence and vulnerability to schizophrenia is that most of our data are derived from health care facilities; and patienthood in a health care facility is a highly inadequate measure of the presence of an episode. As the well-known epidemiological studies conducted in midtown Manhattan and Stirling County have shown, rates of hospitalization probably underestimate the number of individuals in the community at any one time who are troubled by an episode of mental illness. One study that is rather disturbing in this regard was conducted by Lee et al. (1974) on a rural sample in North Carolina. Survey results showed that although psychiatric problems were present in one-half of the homes surveyed, only 50 percent of the troubled families would consider seeking help for them. Moreover, only about 10 percent would overcome the fear of being labeled mentally ill sufficiently to actually seek help at a local mental health clinic that has been in full-time operation for four years and engaged in consultative work for twelve years.

Even if we ignore the attitudinal factors that influence a patient's willingness to seek hospital attention, prevalence studies of psychiatric disorders inflate the percentage of cases from low status occupations, since such patients tend to remain in the hospital longer than cases from high status occupations. There are two possible reasons for this. Either their episodes actually persist longer or (more likely) the patients are poor premorbids so that it is difficult for staff to determine when their episodes have ended. In addition, the poor premorbid patient may have relatively few supports in the community. Coupled with his low competence, his poor premorbid's lack of social supports may make it difficult for a psychiatrist in good conscience to discharge him into the cold, harsh world outside the hospital. In light of these factors, we must conclude that the beginning and end of hospitalization tells us relatively little about the onset, duration, and offset of an episode, since (a) many individuals undergoing an episode do not seek mental health care; (b) many patients continue to be hospitalized after their episodes have subsided; and (c) discharge often bears little relationship to the offset of the episode.

In addition to being a poor indicator of the presence or absence of an episode, hospitalization may reflect and be confounded by a low level of social competence. Meyers and Bean (1968) raised this possibility, noting that lower class psychiatric patients often have less psychopathology than upper class patients even though they are more frequently admitted. Tischler (1975) echoed the idea in a study showing that, particularly for the young, patienthood is primarily determined by factors other than symptom intensity. Individuals who are unmarried, living alone, unemployed, or of the lowest socioeconomic stratum—all of which can be construed as reflecting poor competence in significant role contexts—show a higher tendency to seek and receive mental health care than would be expected from the prevalence of symptoms in these demographic groups in the community. Christensen (1974) has found that low competence rather than psychopathology may be the pivotal factor in hospitalization. In a five-year follow-up study of patients previously hospitalized for schizophrenia, he found that, compared to patients who were readmitted and discharged, those not rehospitalized showed both a better employment record and a more severe level of disturbance at follow-up.*

*In all of these studies, the accuracy and precision of the diagnosis of schizophrenia is quite variable, but the general trends probably hold up despite this source of error.

Competence and Life Event Stressors

In considering the relationship between stresses induced by life event stressors and competence, we must not assume that stressful life events are found more often in those of low competence and hence that we should expect the occurrence of episodes more frequently in the low competence group. Only if the low competence individual is also highly vulnerable will an episode be elicited; and whether high vulnerability occurs more often in those of low competence is not established. It is possible that because the highly vulnerable tend to have more episodes, their competence may wear thin even if it was high to begin with. This downward drift of initially competent patients may contribute to the appearance of a relationship between low competence and high frequency of episodes.

Measuring the Onset, Persistence, and Offset of the Episode

Our two central premises are (a) that schizophrenia appears in time-limited episodes interspersed with periods of remission and normalization and (b) that competence and vulnerability are independent of each other. In order to test them, it is clearly mandatory to arrive at a better strategy for assessing the onset, persistence, and offset of the episode. Changes in an individual's characteristic competence level would provide the ideal markers for the presence or absence of an episode. Patients can be considered in an episode only as long as psychotic symptoms interfere with competence to the extent of impeding the patient's *usual* level of performance in important domains of everyday life. Typically, patients enter a hospital at this point, or they perform other acts which effectively remove them from contexts where their behavior has become inadequate. If they remain in situations where important role performances are still expected, the drop in their usual level of effectiveness should be apparent to their colleagues. The episode can be considered over when the patient is demonstrably capable of matching his own pre-illness level of functioning in these socially significant roles.

Although alterations in competence are optimal criteria for the onset and end of an episode, efforts to determine this variable are beset with all the difficulties that retrospective data suffer from in addition to a few more idiosyncratic problems. Since the patient usually does not come to our attention until after he is well into a full-blown episode of mental disorder, we have a wealth of information on his lack of competence during the episode but very little knowledge of his premorbid competence level. We might describe this as knowing his liabilities but not his assets. Second, it is difficult to know when the episode has ended and the premorbid competence capacities have been restored if the patient is still in the hospital and not exposed to the significant contexts in which his competencies are exercised. Ideally, we should be able to simulate or contrive the important contexts in order to assess competence adequately in still-hospitalized patients. Some progress has indeed been made in this area. For example, following Goldfried and D'Zurilla's behavior-analytic model for assessing competence, Goldsmith and McFall (1975) have experimented with simulated interpersonal contexts to evaluate the effectiveness of patients' social coping strategies. But none of our behavioral assessment techniques has yet achieved the scope necessary to make a full-range evaluation of a patient's competence.

This lack of progress is no doubt partly due to several fundamental quagmires inherent in any process of operationalizing competence. The construct has generally been conceived of as a ladder to make vertical, inter-individual orderings among individuals or groups of people. There are those who argue that competence is a general and uniform property of individuals, quite like the G factor for intelligence. In rebuttal, there are many who insist that the definition of competence must be specific for each particular subcultural group, or even for each important context of day-to-day life, since values and expectations vary so widely across groups of people and types of situations. Moreover, it is quite certain that any given person is likely to show different levels of competence in different situations, something like the horizontal décalage phenomenon that emerges in assessing the Piagetian stages of cognitive competence. These issues, though, while quite substantial in their own right, should really not be major stumbling blocks to devising the type of competence measure we need for research in psychopathology. First, the purpose of designing such measures for use in determining the onset and offset of episodes of schizophrenia is to make not inter-individual comparisons but rather intra-individual ones. Thus, we are interested only in comparing a patient's present level of function with his own premorbid level, not with the performance of individuals in other demographic groups or subcultures that might hold different values and standards.

The problem of one individual's variability in performance across contexts still persists. We regard this as a real and natural phenomenon, however, and not as a form of diagnostic error. This "fact" of nature calls for assessment techniques that cover a full spectrum of contexts evoking significant role performances. The mapping of significant role domains has in fact received considerable attention in recent years, and Weissman (1975) has recently reviewed fifteen scales that are available for assessing performance in occupational, marital, extended family, and community roles. All of these procedures, though, have been designed to assess the social competence of previously hospitalized individuals who are now living in the community. Hopefully, it will still be possible to catalogue each area of role performance into mini-contexts and situational demands that can be simulated to test the specific behavioral competences of hospitalized psychiatric patients.

Perhaps these ideal measures of competence will be available in time to enable prospective researchers of high risk children to evaluate the premorbid level and episode-related fluctuations in competence of their subjects. But most of us who remain completely in the dark about our patients' premorbid coping levels will meanwhile have to seek indicators of the onset, persistence, and offset of an episode of schizophrenia that are not related to competence. The nature of these potential indexes is still an open question. Although it would certainly be opportune to find episode markers of a biochemical or psychophysiological type, such indicators—like our competency change measure—must await future developments. Meanwhile, we must rely on the currently available indexes provided by clinical observation. Even though clinical observations are not initially as valid or reliable as we might like our indicators to be, we could—by continued monitoring of patients—define the clinical features that reliably pinpoint the onset, persistence, and offset of an illness. By moving back and forth from clinical observation to objective indicators in an iterative way (Sutton, 1973) we might ultimately use these clinical observations as criteria for obtaining more objective systematic markers, possibly of a biochemical or psychophysiological nature.

Perhaps we would begin by monitoring the behavioral, bio-chemical, and psychophysiological fluctuations of patients already under observation in a residential ward or treatment facility. Although hospitalized patients probably become adjusted to the hospital routine, medication, and treatment, there will no doubt be flareups of mini- as well as maxi-episodes during their stays. If these episodes could be monitored and measures of behavioral, bio-chemical, and psychophysiological characteristics were compared with baseline measures taken during intermittent periods of tran-quility, we could eventually devise indexes which characterize the onset, persistence, and offset of such episodes. Episodes occurring in hospitalized patients may be of a different variety or intensity from those that initially bring the patient to the hospital, but they can nevertheless serve as a starting point for investigating this important problem. Moreover, we can to some extent investigate the qualitative differences between episodes that begin in the community and those that occur in the hospital by continuously monitoring a subsample of patients beginning with the episodes which are full-blown when they enter the hospital and going through their states of normalization and into the mini-episodes all during the course of a single hospital stay. Of course the great advantage of studying patients under continuous observation rather than only entering patients at the heights of their episodes is that we will be able to observe the *onsets* of the mini-episodes and compare the episode characteristics to the type of baseline pre-morbid data that are never available on newly admitted patients.

As a hypothetical example, let us consider a study that might be conducted on patients at a residential facility. Presumably patients brought to this facility are vulnerable individuals who have just experienced a stressful event that triggered a full-blown episode. After some time, as the acute episode subsides, the patient returns to his pre-episode level of competence in coping with his environ-ment. With the end of the episode that brought him in, he may be regarded as normalized at his premorbid level and consequently not in an episode. Since his vulnerability persists, however, it is possible that some stressful event occurring in the institution will trigger another episode. In this case, it would be useful if we could verify its onset by a technique other than clinical observation, just as the courses of certain physical disorders can be monitored by the patient's blood pressure or EEG.

Of course, the first problem facing us is to determine what kinds of criteria might usefully be examined. Perhaps the best initial procedure would be to study available case records to see what indicators are commonly observed to be associated with the presence, onset, or offset of episodes. Some of these might then be put to use in detecting onset. For example, possible criteria for the start of an episode might be (1) sleep disturbance, (2) eating disturbance, (3) a required change in medication, or (4) attendance at ward functions. At the point when these criteria are met and an episode appears to be starting, a variety of other measures of a psychological, social, and physiological nature could be taken to discover patterns in the new variables that occur at episode onset. An overall criterion based on all these variables could be developed and tested using canonical or discriminant function analyses to compare episode onset versus absence of onset, onset versus offset, or onset and offset with persistence of an episode.

It is of course an empirical question whether such indicators could be used in the community to determine the onset of episodes before they are clinically recognized. But even reseach done exclusively on a hospitalized sample might have important policy implications, by helping clinic staff to plan optimum discharge programs. If it were possible to truly determine the offset of the episode, perhaps earlier release could be facilitated and premature releases avoided. In addition, indicators might be discovered to predict the frequency and severity of future episodes, thereby helping to predict which patients will succeed when released and which will not.

Once the indexes are developed, it might be possible to validate them by manipulating the patient's environment in the direction of eliciting a controlled mini-episode. There have been numerous attempts to simulate mental disorders experimentally, using drugs to evoke an episode: for example, reserpine-induced depression, exacerbation of schizophrenic episode through Ritalin, amphetamine-induced psychosis. Certainly we would not ask patients to ingest these substances, and it may even sound ruthless to subject them to events that might be mildly and temporarily pathogenic. It seems well within ethical boundaries, however, to study reversible episodes engendered by naturally occurring, controlled events. Thus, for instance, if a parent's visit to the hospital or the patient's visit to his home has previously served as a triggering event for the onset of an episode, measurements on the patient might be collected before the visit is announced or expected. Corresponding measures after the visit would determine whether the indexes confirm the presence of an episode.

Summary of the Model

We can now summarize our model of vulnerability to schizophrenic episodes as shown in Tables 1 and 2.

One concept that has been central in our presentation is the distinction between phenomena that are state-determined and phenomena that are traits. We have contended that episodes of schizophrenia are psychopathological states elicited when life event stressors surpass the threshold determined by the individual's characteristic level of vulnerability. Vulnerability, by contrast, is a stable trait that characterizes the individual independently of the presence or absence of the episodes. To paraphrase, a schizophrenic is not a permanently sick individual, but a permanently vulnerable one. There are two models for the course of any disease, the infectious disease model and the chronic disease model. One can apply either model to the study of schizophrenia depending on whether one's focus is the episodic states of illness or the more enduring trait of vulnerability. The infectious model describes disorders like the common cold, in which the course can be pinpointed and initiated or terminated experimentally to learn more about the characteristics of the incubation period. The chronic disease model, which described such illnesses as arthritis or diabetes, may have been appropriate to describe the chronic, nonremitting, deteriorating dementia praecox that was common many generations ago. Now it can be used most fruitfully to describe the fundamental *vulnerability* to schizophrenia rather than the time-limited episodes that intermittently appear.

PROPOSED RESEARCH: DEVELOPING INDEXES OF VULNERABILITY AND EPISODES

If we are to accomplish the primary prevention of episodes of schizophrenia, and ultimately eliminate the underlying vulnerability, we urgently require research enabling us to distinguish between

Table 1

Definitions of Components of Vulnerability Model

1.	Vulnerability	—is the ability to withstand the stresses induced by life events.
2.		—is an enduring trait.
3.	Episodes	—develop when life stress exceeds the threshold of vulnerability.
4.		—are time-limited states of illness.
5.	Competence	—is the ability to achieve success in significant role contexts of everyday life.
6.		—is orthogonal to vulnerability.

Table 2

Therapeutic Intervention in Episodes

7.	Markers of Episodes	—at episode onset, patient's competence drops sharply.
		—at end of episode, patient reattains premorbid competence.
8.	Outcome of Episodes	—Good premorbids return to good pre-episode status—obvious recovery.
		—Poor premorbids return to poor pre-episode status—mistaken as still ill or chronic.
9.	Purpose of therapeutic intervention	—Prevent new episodes from developing by reducing vulnerability and/or stress producing nature of life events.
		—Improve coping capacity of incompetent poor premorbids so they can cope better when episode ends.
		—Modify environment to reduce frequency/intensity of stressful life events so that there will be less opportunity for episodes to develop.

two types of indicators. The first group mark the trait of vulnerability: that is, they stably and reliably differentiate vulnerable individuals from those with immunity to schizophrenia and various other gradations of vulnerability. The second type are those fluctuating, state-dependent markers that can be used to pinpoint the presence and course of the episodes and their termination.

It is important at this point to note the difference between markers of vulnerability and underpinnings or causes of vulnerability. The Wasserman test, for example, is a marker for syphilis but may be neither a cause nor an underpinning of the disorder. We do not know at this time whether the indexes to be discussed below reflect the causes of mental disorders or merely mark the vulnerable individual. We do not even know whether they are stable *traits* or transient *states* signaling the presence of the episode. This is a question we have just begun to investigate.

As we survey the pool of measures that have commonly been found to differentiate schizophrenics and normals, we face a morass of techniques which all too commonly share similar weaknesses. To summarize these sore points as briefly as possible, almost every technique shows that patients perform more poorly than normal controls. Although it is often the researcher's intent to attribute this discrepancy to central nervous system differences or disturbed information processing, other competing hypotheses loom prominently as viable alternative explanations of the data. Rarely can we rule out the arguments that patients failed to understand the instructions, were less attentive or less motivated to perform well, or applied different criteria to determine their responses. The Biometrics Research Unit staff has spent years trying to circumvent these problems by applying four maxims: (1) tasks should be as simple as possible; (2) verbal reports should be avoided wherever possible; (3) forced choice methods should be used to eliminate criterion problems, and signal detection analyses should be used when criteria cannot be eliminated by forced choice methods; (4) tasks on which patients perform "better" than normal people should be preferred whenever they are available.

We have begun with the assumption—emanating from the neurophysiological model—that one etiological source of schizophrenia is to be sought in the way the central nervous system of a schizophrenic processes incoming information. Our psychophysiological laboratory, under the direction of Dr. Samuel Sutton, has been investigating sensory and perceptual responses to energy stimuli for the past several decades. They have limited their investigation largely to the responses to the first 1,000 msec following stimulation in the hope of reducing the influences of past experience, motivation, and so on, as much as possible. Those that have paid off (Burdock, Sutton, and Zubin, 1958) have been the following: (1) cross-modality reaction time; (2) pupillography; (3) sensory integrations in vision; (4) auditory thresholds and masking in audition; and (5) evoked potentials. We do not have the time to present all of these findings but will limit ourselves to a brief description of the sensory-integration and auditory findings.

According to the Bunsen-Roscoe Law or Block's Law, intensity and duration of a stimulus can be reciprocally interchanged and yet leave the response invariant, as long as the total energy of the stimulus (product of intensity times duration) remains invariant. This law holds for only brief periods following the stimulus, that is, for the critical duration in which complete integration takes place. For the particular setup in our laboratory, this critical duration for schizophrenics lasts only from 4 to 6 msecs, while the critical duration for depressives and normals lasts much longer. Only those schizophrenics who have high scores on the dimension of thought disorder show this reduced critical duration. Thus, it appears that thought-disordered schizophrenics show shorter critical durations than the other groups. Moreover, on the specific test procedure that is used, their responses indicate a discrimination that is not possible for normal subjects.

The auditory technique differentiates not between schizophrenics and normals but between affective disorders on the one hand and schizophrenics and normals on the other. First, the auditory threshold under forced choice conditions is higher for the affectives. Second, the reaction time of the affectives is enhanced (shortened) when a 25 db click is followed 15 msecs later by a 10 db click, while the reaction time for schizophrenics and normals is not altered.

Given techniques which are, to the greatest extent currently possible, free of the strictures of lack of motivation or attention, we can set about separating those that index the trait of vulnerability from those that measure the presence of the episode. To do so, we have adopted two simple strategies. The first is to repeatedly monitor the same patients when they are at the height of an episode and when they have entered remission and reattained their premorbid functioning. Presumably the markers for the episodes will be those techniques that show anomalous patient performance during the height of the episode but normalize as the patient regains his premorbid status. It is likely that comprehensibility of speech as measured by the cloze technique would be a good marker of the onset, duration, and offset of an episode, since the patient's disturbed speech is one of the markers signaling the presence of an episode. In contrast, the indicators that stably differentiate patients from normals regardless of the presence of the episode are potential markers of the underlying vulnerability. To cross-validate the indexes of vulnerability, we are testing relatives of probands who share some portion of the genetic and probably also some of the acquired vulnerability to schizophrenic episodes. We predict that a substantial proportion of the relatives will also show anomalous performance on our measures of vulnerability. Some may also display abnormalities on the episode indicators, and our measures of life events will enable us to detect whether these individuals also share a recent history of severe life stress in common with the proband.

What implications does our vulnerability have for prevention? According to our view, the goals of prevention are to prevent any future episodes in individuals of demonstrated vulnerability. This can be accomplished by reducing the person's vulnerability by means of drugs or behavior modification, by controlling the environment to reduce the frequency or intensity of the life events that formerly served as triggering events for an episode, or by reducing the threatening nature of such life events. Should another episode develop in a good premorbid who has a high level of competence, no special intervention needs to be undertaken, since once the episode is ended he will return to his good premorbid status. In the case of the poor premorbid, efforts will have to be exerted in order to uplift his competence, so that when his episode ends, he will be able to cope with life exigencies better than he could premorbidly.

Whether a reorganization of society is necessary (as Commissioner Okin has suggested) before we can deal with mental disorders adequately is debatable, since there are other factors besides the ecological which seem to be sources of mental disorder. Only continued investigation of each of these models ranging from the ecological to the genetic will give us the necessary answers on how to deal with the problem. Any wholesale adoption of one model over the others before the evidence is all in will inevitably lead to false solutions and to increases rather than decreases of pain, suffering, and needless expense.

REFERENCES

Bleuler, M.   Die Schizophrenen Geistesstörungen im Lichte langjähriger Kranken- und Familiengeschichten. (The schizophrenic mental disturbances in the light of long term patient and family histories.) Thieme: Stuttgart, 1972.
Bleuler, M.   The offspring of schizophrenics. *Schizophrenia Bulletin*, 1974, *8*, 93–108.
Brown, G. W., and Birley, J. L. T.   Crises and life changes and the onset of schizophrenia. *Journal of Health and Social Behavior*, 1968, *9*, 203–214.
Burdock, E. I., Sutton S., and Zubin, J.   Personality and psychopathology. *Journal of Abnormal and Social Psychology*, 1958, *56*, 18-30.
Caplan, G.   *Principles of preventive psychiatry*. New York: Basic Books, 1964.
Christensen, J. K.   A 5-year follow-up study of male schizophrenics: evaluation of factors influencing success and failure in the community. *Acta Psychiatrica Scandanavica*, 1974, *50*, 60–72.
Clark, R. E.   The relationship of schizophrenia to occupational income and occupational prestige. *American Sociological Review*, 1948, *13*, 325–330.
Clark, R. E.   Psychoses, income and occupational prestige. *American Journal of Sociology*, 1949, *54*, 433–440.
Clausen, J. A., and Kohn, M. L.   Relation of schizophrenia to the social structure of a small city. In B. Pasamanick (Ed.), *Epidemiology of mental disorder*. Washington, D.C.: American Association for the Advancement of Science, 1959.
Dohrenwend, B. S., and Dohrenwend, B. P.   Social class and the relation of remote to recent stressors. In M. Roff, L. Robins, and M. Pollack (Eds.), *Life history research in psychopathology* (Vol. 2). Minneapolis: University of Minnesota Press, 1972.
Falek, A., and Moser, H. M.   Classification in schizophrenia. *Archives of General Psychiatry*, 1975, *32*, 59–69.
Feighner, J. P., Robins, E., Guze, S. B., Woodruff, R. A., Winokur, G., and Munoz, R.   Diagnostic criteria for use in psychiatric research. *Archives of General Psychiatry*, 1972, *26*, 57–63.
Feinstein, A. R.   *Clinical judgment*. Baltimore: Williams and Wilkins, 1967.
Glick, I. D., Hargreaves, W. A., Raskin, M., and Kutner, S. J.   Short versus long hospitalization: a prospective controlled study. II. Results for schizophrenic inpatients. *American Journal of Psychiatry*, 1975, *132*, 385–390.
Goldsmith, J. B., and McFall, R. M.   Development and evaluation of an

interpersonal skill training program for psychiatric inpatients. *Journal of Abnormal Psychology*, 1975, *84*, 51–58.

Harris, J. W. *The red-cell: Production, metabolism, destruction: normal and abnormal*. Cambridge, Mass.: Harvard University Press, 1963.

Hawk, A. B., Carpenter, W. T., and Strauss, J. S. Diagnostic criteria and five-year outcome: a report from the international pilot study of schizophrenia. *Archives of General Psychiatry*, 1975, *32*, 343–347.

Herz, M., Endicott, J., and Spitzer, R. L. Brief hospitalization of patients with families: Initial results. *American Journal of Psychiatry*, 1975, *132*, 413–418.

Hogarty, G. E., Goldberg, S. C., Schooler, N. R., and Ulrich, R. F. The collaborative study group. Drug and sociotherapy in the aftercare of schizophrenic patients. II. Two year relapse rates. *Archives of General Psychiatry*, 1974, *31*, 603–609.

Hollingshead, A. B., and Redlich, F. C. *Social class and mental illness: A community study*. New York: Wiley, 1958.

Huxley, J. S. Introductory: towards the new systematics. In J. S. Huxley (Ed.), *The new systematics*. Oxford: Clarendon, 1940.

Jacob, T. Family interaction in disturbed and normal families: a methodological and substantive review. *Psychological Bulletin*, 1975, *82*, 33–65.

Kessler, M., and Albee, G. W. Primary prevention. *Annual Review of Psychology*, 1975, *26*, 557–591.

Kety, S. Genetic and environmental factors in the etiology of schizophrenia. Paper presented at the McLean Hospital Symposium on the Biological Substrates of Mental Illness, February, 1975.

Kreisman, D. Social interaction and intimacy in preschizophrenic adolescence. In J. Zubin and A. M. Freedman (Eds.), *The psychopathology of adolescence*. New York: Grune and Stratton, 1970.

Kringlen, F. An epidemiological-clinical twin study on schizophrenia. In D. Rosenthal and S. Kety (Eds.), *The transmission of schizophrenia*. Oxford: Pergamon, 1968.

Lee, S. H., Gianturco, D. T., and Eisdorfer, C. Community mental health center accessibility: a survey of the rural poor. *Archives of General Psychiatry*, 1974, *31*, 335–339.

Leighton, D. C., Harding, J. S., Macklin, D. B., MacMillan, A. M., and Leighton, A. H. *The character of danger: Psychiatric symptoms in selected communities. Vol. III. The Stirling County study of psychiatric disorder and sociocultural environment*. New York: Basic Books, Inc., 1963.

Leighton, D. C., Harding, J. S., Macklin, D. B., Hughes, C. C., and Leighton, A. H. Psychiatric findings of the Stirling County study. *American Journal of Psychiatry*, 1963, *119*, 1021–1026.

McNeil, T. F. Prenatal, perinatal, and neonatal factors in primary prevention of psychopathology. Paper presented at the First Vermont Conference on the Primary Prevention of Psychopathology, Burlington, Vermont, June, 1975.

Meyers, J. K., and Bean, L. L. *A decade later: A follow-up of social class and mental illness*. New York: Wiley, 1968.

Niskanen, P., Jaaskelainen, J., Lohnquvist, J., and Achte, K. A. Duration of hospitalization of schizophrenic patients in 1880-1970. *Psychiatrica Fennica*, 1973, pp. 55-65.

Pollin, W., and Stabenau, J. R. Biological, psychological and historical differences in a series of monozygotic twins discordant for schizophrenia. In D. Rosenthal and S. Kety (Eds.), *The transmission of schizophrenia*. Oxford: Pergamon, 1968.

Rahe, R. H., Meyer, M., Smith, M., Kjaer, G., and Holmes, T. H. Social stress and illness onset. *Journal of Psychosomatic Research*, 1964, *8*, 35-44.

Rosenthal, D. Introduction to Manfred Bleuler's "The offspring of schizophrenics." *Schizophrenia Bulletin*, Spring, 1974, *8*, 91-93.

Spitzer, R. L., Endicott, J., Robins, E., Kuriansky, J., and Gurland, B. Preliminary report of the reliability of Research Diagnostic Criteria (RDC) applied to psychiatric case records. In S. Gershon and R. Beer (Eds.), *Prediction in psychopharmacology*. New York: Raven, 1975.

Spitzer, R. L., and Fleiss, J. L. A re-analysis of the reliability of psychiatric diagnosis. *British Journal of Psychiatry*, 1974, *125*, 341-347.

Sutton, S. Fact and artifact in the psychology of schizophrenia. In M. Hammer, K. Salzinger, and S. Sutton (Eds.), *Psychopathology: Contributions from the social, behavioral, and biological sciences*. New York: Wiley, 1973.

Svalastoga, K. *Social differentiation*. New York: David McKay, 1965.

Tischler, G. L., Henisz, J. E., Meyers, J. K., and Boswell, P. C. Utilization of mental health services. I. Patienthood and the prevalence of symptomatology in the community. *Archives of General Psychiatry*, 1975, *32*, 411-418.

Tischler, G. L., Henisz, J. E., Meyers, J. K., and Boswell, P. C. Utilization of mental health services. II. Mediators of service allocation. *Archives of General Psychiatry*, 1975, *32*, 411-418.

Turner, R. J. The implications of psychiatric disorder for employment: an assessment of the degree and nature of their relatedness. Unpublished manuscript, 1974.

Weissman, M. The assessment of social adjustment: a review of technique. *Archives of General Psychiatry*, 1975, *32*, 357-365.

Yolles, S. F., and Kramer, M. Vital statistics. In L. Bellak and L. Loeb (Eds.), *The schizophrenic syndrome*. New York: Grune and Stratton, 1969.

Zubin, J. Scientific models for psychopathology in the '70s. *Seminars in Psychiatry*, 1972, *4*, 283-296.

Zubin, J. Vulnerability as the common denominator for etiological models of psychopathology. Paper presented at Eastern Psychiatric Research Association, New York, November 14, 1974.

Zubin, J. A biometric approach to diagnosis and evaluation of therapeutic intervention in schizophrenia. In G. Usdin (Ed.), *Dean Award lecture: An overview of the psychotherapies*. New York: Bruner/Mazel, 1975.

V
State and Federal Efforts
in Primary Prevention

Introductory Notes

Dr. Robert L. Okin was invited to discuss primary prevention from his perspective as director of a state mental health program. At the time he delivered the paper, Dr. Okin was Commissioner of Mental Health for the State of Vermont, and he has since then assumed the comparable position in the Commonwealth of Massachusetts. Dr. Okin's paper touches on some of the fundamental questions facing a society that honestly wishes to reduce the rate of psychopathology in future generations. As he points out, commissioners of mental health must often compete for the same state tax dollars which, if spent on family welfare and children's services, might advance the cause of primary prevention more than if they are used to support and intervene with persons already severely damaged. He points to the long-standing relationship between poverty and mental disturbance and expresses concern at society's obvious preference for intervening with sickness rather than spending its resources to reduce or eradicate poverty. The implications of Dr. Okin's message have potentially enormous importance for persons who believe that only through social action and massive, broad tax-supported programs can successful primary prevention come about.

The other paper in this section is part of Stephen E. Goldston's longer paper, described earlier. For several years Dr. Goldston has been the person designated to stimulate efforts at primary prevention working out of the office of the Director of the National Institute of Mental Health. He is perhaps the most knowledgeable person in the country about projects in this area that are completed, under way, or planned. Long a voice crying in the wilderness, Dr. Goldston has seen an enormous increase of interest in primary prevention during the past couple of years. It now appears that his efforts and those of a few kindred spirits have finally penetrated the mental health professions and that at long last everyone is aware that no mass disorder afflicting humankind has ever been successfully conquered by attempts at treating afflicted and affected individuals. Dr. Goldston reviews federal efforts at primary prevention and takes a look at the field from his position high up in the crow's nest of NIMH.

15

Primary Prevention of Psychopathology from the Perspective of a State Mental Health Program Director

ROBERT L. OKIN

Because society so patently neglects and obstructs substantial efforts at primary prevention of psychopathology, it is necessary to justify our collective concern with this subject.

Why should we supplement our exclusive emphasis on techniques of treatment and intensify our search for strategies of prevention? First, there are not now, nor will there ever be, sufficient resources to treat all the human suffering that derives from disorders of the mind. Second, some forms of psychopathology are extremely difficult, if not impossible, to reverse once they have become fully established. Finally, the effect of an individual's psychopathology on his own life, on the lives of those close to him, and on society at large is often both profound and devastating.

Since most people would readily admit that the cost in both human and financial terms of allowing psychopathology to develop is intolerable, it is only reasonable to ask why public policy reflects so little concern with the area of prevention. Indeed the entire field of primary prevention has consistently been characterized more by rhetoric than by action. This fact is reflected in the funding patterns of federal and state governments, in the comparatively small (though growing) research efforts in the area, and in numerous aspects of our socioeconomic structure, which fosters rather than prevents the development of psychopathology.

Perhaps I owe you an apology for my emphasis on the difficulties that lie ahead of us. How much more gracious it would have been to open this conference on a note of brilliant elation. And yet if we do not acknowledge and examine the very real obstacles to developing a national public policy geared to primary prevention, we will be powerless to alter the current policy, dominated as it is by rhetoric, fragmented efforts, and underfunded programs.

I would like to enumerate some of the obstacles that lie ahead of us in this endeavor as I see them from my position as Commissioner of Mental Health of this state.

To begin with, there are some very real deficits in our understanding of both normal and pathological development. Our experimental investigations are continually beset by methodologic problems that are often intrinsic to our subject matter. The evolution of psychopathology in a given individual and the specific form it assumes are inevitably the complex result of many interacting factors. For this reason it is almost impossible at times to isolate and control the critical variables associated with any given effect, much less distinguish them from precipitating factors and contributing conditions. Moreover, the manifestations of the effects are often so distant in time from the relevant causes that one is faced with the task of inferring retrospectively the very data needing overt demonstration and examination. A propos of this, the need for long-term developmental studies is painfully obvious; but these are extremely difficult, very expensive, plagued with fundamental, ethical, and methodological problems, and generally unattractive to research granting agencies. As a result, very few studies have been initiated and even fewer have been completed. Complicating matters further has been the difficulty of quantification: crucial factors in the development of psychopathology must not only be isolated qualitatively, they must also be assessed quantitatively. In addition to the profound technical problems attendant on accomplishing this feat, researchers must confront the difficulties attributable to the Hawthorne Effect and the Heisenberg Principle, as well as facing the fact that the weight which must be assigned to critical causes cannot be viewed independently of the individual they impinge on. That is to say, the inherited and developmentally produced characteristics of the individual at any given time determine how and to what extent he will experience any subsequent influences. Obviously this extends to both quality and quantity.

For all the above reasons, and for many more, problems of evidence in the field have often appeared insuperable. They have made it difficult for mental health researchers to convince society that alteration of one set of variables will inevitably produce a demonstrable and salubrious change in another set. Precisely because it has been so difficult to gauge—much less replicate—the impact of any particular preventive strategy, a considerable degree of skepticism prevails about our capabilities in this area.

Such skepticism frequently greets a commissioner of mental health when he requests the legislature to provide resources for a particular primary prevention program. In the absence of convincing evidence to the contrary, legislators are unwilling to allocate funds to prevent further problems in the face of insufficient monies to solve present ones. It should be a source of comfort to researchers that well designed outcome studies can be extremely helpful to a commissioner when he approaches the legislature for funds. But the number of such studies is small, and the commissioner is often forced to acknowledge the collective ignorance that besets this area of mental health. Inevitably, public policy starkly reflects this ignorance and the skepticism it engenders.

We should not assume, nevertheless, that the deficits in our knowledge present the only—or even the most important—obstacles to widespread primary prevention efforts. At least as important is the profound ambivalence that we as a nation exhibit toward our children. The negative side of this ambivalence is most vividly expressed in the totally inadequate resources we expend on children, in the damaging practices of certain child-oriented institutions, and in specific properties of the legal system, which continues to sacrifice children's rights to the prerogatives of their parents. With respect to the provision of services, it is sad to note that in 1973 a mere 10 million dollars was allocated for mental health services to the population we euphemistically describe as our most precious resource. Compare this figure to the sum of 17 million dollars—the cost of a single bomber used in the Viet Nam war. The real tragedy about this 10 million dollars was that it was enough to buy us off, to quiet our protests, to give us the illusion of progress. Practically speaking, it wasn't even enough to begin to answer the needs of children in this country.

When the Joint Commission on the Mental Health of Children reviewed the problems and characteristics of the present service system, some unhappy conclusions emerged. First, the system tends to be oriented to the needs of professionals and institutions providing services rather than to the needs of children being served. Second, services tend to focus on correcting crisis situations rather than on altering the environmental conditions that cause such crises in the first place. Third, only a small fraction of the children in need are being served. Fourth, most programs for children who are being served receive so meager a budget that they are literally programed for failure at their outset. Fifth, programs labeled "innovative" are often only marginal upgradings of the existing system.

The ambivalence evidenced by these conclusions is further manifested in our legal system, which still fails to recognize the rights and needs of children. Mentally retarded children, for example, can still be placed in institutions of the most dreadful variety without any legal safeguards and without the requirement that all available alternatives must be exhausted before institutionalization is undertaken. Moreover, children who are placed in foster care by their biological parents are still subject to recall by the latter, perhaps years later, despite the deep attachments that may have developed between the children and their foster parents. Finally, in many states it is still left to the discretion of the court whether to appoint an attorney for a child embattled in a custody case.

These examples make it clear that especially where children are already disadvantaged or at high risk of pathological development, society tends to compound their problems by maintaining a laissez-faire attitude toward the development of its children, who are frequently sacrificed to the prerogatives of their parents. Needless to say, the profound ambivalence this reflects has important and obvious implications for the primary prevention of psychopathology, since children should be the natural beneficiaries of efforts expended in this direction. We are never going to reduce the incidence of psychopathology until we begin to acknowledge and alter the destructive fashion in which we often treat our children.

We come now to another important obstacle to developing a public policy oriented toward primary prevention: the socioeconomic structure of our society. It has been demonstrated that poverty, substandard housing, unemployment, and poor nutrition all appear to increase the risk of psychopathology (although in a highly complex fashion and through many intervening variables). That is to say, the incidence of disease and disability is by no means independent of the social and economic fabric of our society. Evidence can be seen in the high incidence of mild mental retardation, organic brain syndrome, and other kinds of psychopathology in those who live in greatest poverty. Over the last few years there have been many experimental attempts to counteract the pathogenic effects of poverty without dealing with the poverty itself. With few exceptions these attempts have been unsuccessful. Many disillusioned investigators have emerged from their experiences convinced that without alleviating the poverty itself, there is no chance of preventing its psychologically devastating effects.

Society would readily acknowledge the pathogenic effects of poverty; even so, little has been done to eradicate it, aside from the token and piecemeal initiatives undertaken by human service agencies. The efforts, and certainly the impulses, of these agencies have been heroic considering their inadequate funding, but they have generally managed only to cover the problems of poverty with a bandage rather than to cure them. From our perspective, their efforts represent one more example of society's attempt to accommodate itself to poverty rather than to root it out.

Why has nothing been done about this state of affairs? The answer is simple. The eradication of the poverty that plagues millions of our people would require a fundamental transformation of society, a significant redistribution of income and wealth among classes, and a substantial diversion of society's resources into social services. Treatment can be largely accommodated within the status quo; but prevention would shake the very foundations of our socioeconomic order, and as a nation we have not been willing to do this. Until we are, there will be no dramatic decline in the incidence of certain forms of psychopathology.

Given the uneven distribution of resources in our society, it is interesting to note that even the public resources which are allocated to the poor reflect a lack of concern with primary prevention. An example can be found in the relationship between the Medicaid program and welfare assistance for needy families with children. The latter is essentially a form of income maintenance. As mentioned earlier, there is good reason to assume that poverty and the risk of certain forms of psychopathology are closely related. Were an adequate level of income insured through welfare assistance, the need for mental health treatment under Medicaid would probably be reduced; but in many states the two programs are forced to compete for the same pot of money, and welfare assistance usually loses. The last few years have witnessed substantial growth in the Medicaid budget, but the purchasing power of the welfare budget has remained fairly static. There are two primary reasons for this state of affairs.

First, the transfer of money that takes place through the Medicaid program goes not to the poor themselves but to the professional and institutional providers responsible for their treatment. These providers have a decided stake in maintaining and increasing the Medicaid-reimbursed health care expenditures for the poor, and they use their considerable political influence to insure this result. The poor have no corresponding political advocate for maintaining their income. This year in Vermont, for example, we witnessed an increase in Medicaid reimbursement for poor patients in nursing homes, but no increase was granted by the legislature for Aid to Needy Families with Children.

Another reason why Medicaid expenditures tend to win out over resources for income maintenance is that sickness has always been more emotionally compelling than poverty in our society. Poverty tends to be viewed as one's own fault—a result of laziness, stupidity, one's evil ways, or the like—whereas sickness is regarded as an unfortunate circumstance that could befall anybody.

Efforts at primary prevention, then, often lose in their competition with secondary prevention at the public level; and the pattern replicates itself at the private and professional levels. This brings us to the fourth area I wish to discuss.

Mental health professionals as a group often have a minimum understanding of, and little commitment to, the need for primary prevention. This is hardly surprising considering that most of their formal education emphasizes techniques of treatment rather than principles of prevention. It is only natural, then, that this bias gets reflected in their professional lives, ideologic commitments, and allocation of time. Mental health professionals tend to view themselves as treaters of disease and disability rather than preservers and protectors of health. Moreover, and equally true, mental health providers have little financial incentive to spend their time on the primary prevention of psychopathology. Health insurance plans in general and mental health insurance plans in particular do not provide adequate reimbursement to the professional for time expended in activities of prevention, but only for time spent in the treatment of established pathological conditions. This is a critical problem: as long as preventive activities yield little financial reward, we will never see large-scale efforts in this direction. Patients are reimbursed upon developing illness and providers for treating it; and no one is reimbursed for preventing it.

Finally, I would like to speak about the difficult position in which commissioners of mental health frequently find themselves regarding the primary prevention of psychopathology. It is most unfortunate that such commissioners, who are theoretically able to articulate and act on the need for primary prevention, have little incentive or ability to do so. First, the commissioner often faces tremendous problems in the spheres of secondary and tertiary prevention; these are the most visible and compelling and are the ones he receives the most public pressure about. He is held responsible for the treatment of psychopathology but not for its prevention. He is never criticized because the incidence of depression, alcoholism, or suicide is increasing. Strong advocacy groups exist to express concern about problems which already exist and are perceived as compelling; but few constituencies are organized to support the prevention of the problems in the first place. Inadequate resources to implement strategies of prevention is the inevitable result. Second, some of the most effective programs of primary prevention may be those which do not officially fall within the sphere of the commissioner's responsibility—such programs as planned parenthood, day care, and income maintenance, among many others. A commissioner of mental health in fighting for his programs of secondary and tertiary prevention is often doing so at the expense of human service programs geared to primary prevention that fall outside his categorical sphere of responsibility. The ironic result is that the commissioner of mental health, though a sincere advocate of the need for primary prevention, often finds himself fighting against it through his actions. We are left with the paradox that a person who by virtue of his position could do a great deal to advance the cause of primary prevention can unwittingly become one of its foremost opponents.

Despite the seriousness of the political, economic, institutional and professional obstacles to developing public policy for primary prevention of psychopathology, there is much we can do to overcome them.

1. We must begin to change the orientation of our professional schools that are now geared to the techniques of treatment. Greater emphasis should be placed on child development, methods of consultation, and practical experiences to expose the student to the social and economic factors leading to the development of

psychopathology. Because the identification process in education is so critical, any substantive reorientation of professional schools may require the professors to invest more time in preventive activities.

2. We must increase our efforts to alter the institutions that impact so critically, and often so negatively, on our childrens' lives. Public education is an obvious focus for our concerted attention. The school system—with its captive audience, its tendency to induce strong transferential ties between teachers, and students, and the very central place it occupies in the life of the child and the community—is an ideal institution for promoting health and preventing disability. Unfortunately, however, the school system has tended to aggravate rather than alleviate children's problems in many ways, and we must help it to become more humane.

3. Human service constituencies must begin to view their separate interests as interdependent. Orientation toward treatment may be accommodated by various categorical efforts, but emphasis on prevention absolutely prohibits this. Advocates for separate human service programs must stop competing with each other and begin to combine their efforts if they are to make any real advances in the sphere of primary prevention.

Those dedicated to promoting mental health and preventing disability cannot afford to ignore the whole influence of the socio-economic environment. From this point of view there are very few social concerns outside our purview. We must in a number of ways participate in a sphere of responsibility from which we have traditionally excluded ourselves. Some have viewed social, economic, and environmental concerns as "not mental health," as if the latter had been somehow immutably defined. Some might say that in involving ourselves in social, economic, and political issues we have trespassed upon territories staked out by other groups. But I would urge that the very complexity of modern society has made it impossible to define simplistically precise boundaries between traditional territories of responsibility. We can no longer stand on the periphery of the stage commenting on political action like a Greek chorus. We must recognize that we own parts of this problem and begin to involve ourselves systematically in the broader issues of social policy in very pragmatic ways.

16

Primary Prevention: A View from the Federal Level

STEPHEN E. GOLDSTON

Since its inception the National Institute of Mental Health has carried out its legislative mandate to plan, direct, and coordinate the national effort to improve the mental health of the people of the United States by developing knowledge, manpower, and services to promote and sustain mental health, prevent severe mental illness, and treat and rehabilitate the mentally ill. Over the quarter century since 1948, NIMH has encouraged, supported, and developed a variety of imaginative and forward-looking programs.

With respect to primary prevention, however, NIMH's efforts have been—and remain—underdeveloped and unfocused; in fact, virtually no programs exist. An expert panel formed in late 1968 to advise NIMH along these lines found that "while many aspects of the total NIMH program may be viewed as related to primary prevention in general, typically what has prevailed has been more of a token investment than an adequate response to the challenge prevention presents." In view of this lack, it has been impossible to compose an inventory of NIMH's involvements in the area or to give precise information on the number of grants supported, the amount of funds allocated, and staff resources committed. Imprecise and impressionistic information must be substituted.

An informal inventory of NIMH's primary prevention activities that I undertook in 1972 led to the following observations. (a) The exact amount of grant money devoted to prevention could not be ascertained; I estimated that possibly $3 million was being spent for research. (b) About 60 research grants dealing to some degree with primary prevention were being supported. (c) A wide range and diversity of content characterized the projects. (d) A minute fraction of the research and evaluation funds in community mental health centers was being used for prevention studies. (e) Reflecting the views of mental health personnel in general, few NIMH staff members had any interest in primary prevention or grasped clearly the nature of prevention programming and techniques. There is little evidence to suggest that any of these conditions have been modified over the past few years.

Supported prevention projects as a group have been characterized by wide diversity, reflecting a general responsiveness to applications submitted as contrasted with a planned, programmed, federal effort to develop and fund a coordinated series of interrelated projects. The projects focused on such topics as designing and evaluating more satisfying housing environments; improving the climates of schools and day-care centers for early child care; developing community resources for the elderly; educating for marriage and enhancing marital relationships; preventing life crises by providing community supports, crisis management, and anticipatory guidance at transition points and in situational crises; early infant stimulation and cognitive development; affective education curricula development; prenatal parent education and family relations; alternative family styles; marriage and college life; life styles of teenage mothers; self-image and family dynamics in organ transplantation; and stepfathers and the mental health of their children.

Training programs dealing with prevention were few. By and large, curricula for training professional mental health workers contain no specific content on prevention. Some federal training grant funds, however, have supported unique and innovative projects that approach prevention through the technique of developing new kinds of manpower for nonclinical mental health work and providing mental health training for such target groups as child development specialists, school teachers and administrators, and clergy.

I also reviewed service programs, since federal agencies have provided construction and staffing for community mental health centers. Centers have generally demonstrated little interest in prevention, characterized as they are by traditional staffs and the limited scope of their programs. The neglect of prevention is reflected in an NIMH report on consultation and education (C&E) services provided by 400 operating federally funded community mental health centers during February 1974 (NIMH, 1975):

Measured in terms of total staff hours work in a sample week, consultation and education activities on the average (median) accounted for 5.2 percent of the total staff time. There is wide variation among individual centers—in 25 percent of the centers, consultation and education services accounted for 2.6 percent or less of the total hours worked in a sample week. At the other extreme consultation and education services represented 8.5 percent of the total hours worked in 25 percent of the centers.

According to the same report, "of the total consultation and education hours during February 1974, 44 percent was devoted to case consultation, 26 percent to staff development or continued education (other than inservice training for CMHC staff) and 30 percent was devoted to program-oriented consultation." That is to say, virtually one-half of the consultation time that should have been devoted to primary preventive activities was spent in clinical assessments or secondary prevention (early diagnosis and treatment).

Consultation and education, then, have generally accounted for around 5 percent of the time of community mental health center staff: the 5.2 percent during February 1974 reported above, and 4.9 percent according to data collected in February 1973 (NIMH, 1974). Allocation of funds runs parallel to expenditure of time: discussions with the NIMH biometry staff revealed that approximately 5 percent of centers' funds have been used for C&E services.

ATTITUDES AND PROGRAMS NEEDED FOR PRIMARY PREVENTION

Cited below are some unmet needs in preventive mental health programming at the federal level, many of which are identical (with minor variations) to those typically found in mental health agencies at the state and local levels.

(1) A commitment at the policy and operating levels to provide support, encouragement, resources, and sanction for prevention activities.

(2) A specific program focus with sufficient budgetary allocations and an organizational structure with visible responsibility and authority for programming in primary prevention.

(3) Reorientation of priorities so that planned active programming will replace reactive responsiveness to the field.

(4) No longer regarding mental health as separate and distinct

from somatic health. As a consequence of present policies and practices, mental health workers have abdicated responsibility for involvement in public health programs that have clear mental health components and implications—for example, maternal and child health services, nutrition and diet counseling, and family planning.

(5) Devoting resources to studying and devising means of helping people deal with real-life problems—those ever-occurring crises that require specific coping capacities and ego strengths in order to maintain health. We need to identify coping methods, develop educational programs, and find means and resources for helping people deal with crises throughout the life cycle.

(6) An information and retrieval system that identifies activities dealing with prevention.

(7) Inservice training to familiarize mental health workers with public health principles and epidemiology, to give them a better balance in their approaches and values between public health and community considerations and their accustomed clinical considerations.

(8) Strengthening consultation and education services within community mental health centers.

(9) Developing training programs in primary prevention among professional and paraprofessional groups at both the basic and the continuing-education levels.

(10) Providing resources to help states develop primary preventive programs within their departments of mental health. Currently, formal primary prevention programs at the state level exist only in Kentucky, Massachusetts, Michigan, and Ohio.

(11) Supporting research into new techniques and approaches in primary prevention.

(12) Developing publications about prevention activities for distribution to mental health programs across the nation.

Confronting these needs and working toward resolution of the inherent issues should be matters of high priority on the agenda of the mental health field at all levels.

PRESENT PROGRAM CONSIDERATIONS AND THEMES

During the past year substantive primary prevention programs have been developed at the federal level around two major themes of universal concern: death and life. Several key considerations have guided this work. First, a program has been defined as a planned effort to deal with various aspects of an identified major problem by means of a series of interrelated projects; a single isolated one-shot project is not a program. Second, within a public health context, each activity bears a relationship to another in terms of a shared conceptual framework, the types of populations involved, and the need to mobilize varied community resources. Third, although these efforts were performed at the federal level, an important measure of program success is the extent to which states and localities take on similar work; in this connection, community mental health facilities can adopt and adapt relevant aspects of the programs to their particular needs.

At the outset, no specifically designated funds were available to undertake most of the work cited; there was no administrative setup available for primary prevention (nor has any been established since); few, if any, precedents existed for the specific types of enterprises initiated; and only one staff member—myself—was working full time on primary prevention. In spite of these difficulties, we have proceeded to develop programs.

Death

In late 1973 representatives of the National Foundation for Sudden Infant Death, Inc. (NFSID) approached NIMH to request financial assistance for program efforts on the Sudden Infant Death Syndrome (SIDS). Annually, between 7,500 and 10,000 babies die from a real disease called the Sudden Infant Death Syndrome; the cause is unknown and death strikes quickly and silently; SIDS can be neither predicted nor prevented; and surviving parents and siblings react with a pervasive grief and guilt that often results in severe family dysfunction, divorce, and disability, including psychiatric sequelae (Bergman, 1969). Perceiving SIDS as a public health problem with pronounced mental health components, the NIMH staff devised the following framework for developing a program.

(1) Within a public health perspective, a primary prevention approach would be used in attempting to meet the mental health needs of surviving parents and siblings of an SIDS victim.

(2) SIDS program activities would be viewed as an opportunity

for initial explorations—as a prelude to major emphases—into the areas of death, dying, grief, bereavement, needs of surviving family members, and death education, including anticipatory guidance concerning death.

(3) SIDS program activities could demonstrate the feasibility and productivity of primary prevention approaches, and thereby encourage future programs focused on other specific life crises.

(4) Mental health personnel have a responsibility to work co-operatively with public health people on public health/mental health problems.

(5) Knowledge gained from the SIDS program could have major implications for future directions in the mental health field.

NIMH's first official SIDS activity was to award a contract to the NFSID for a two-year period commencing June 1974. The contract underwrites educational, counseling, and community organization activities in selected cities and counties aimed at strengthening existing community agencies and personnel (health departments and medical examiners or coroners' offices) to enable them to deal in an organized systematic fashion with the complex human problems associated with SIDS. Program strategies center on obtaining acceptance and implementation of the NFSID's recommended "minimum acceptable standard" for handling sudden unexpected infant deaths in all communities in the United States. The elements of this standard are:

1. Autopsies should be available on all children who die suddenly and unexpectedly and should be performed by qualified pathologists.

2. The term "sudden infant death syndrome" should be utilized as a cause of death on death certificates when appropriate.

3. Families should be notified by either telephone or letter of the autopsy results within twenty-four hours.

4. Follow-up counseling and information about SIDS and the characteristic grief reactions should be provided by a knowledgeable health professional.

The ultimate objective, toward which each element contributes, is to obviate the pervasive grief/guilt reactions. From this viewpoint, the NIMH and the NFSID are cooperating in a preventive psychiatry project within the framework of primary prevention, that is, attempting to reduce the likelihood of people becoming mentally ill or severely emotionally disturbed as a result of the life crisis occasioned by SIDS.

Shortly after the contract became operational, a program plan was promulgated to deal with the various mental health aspects of SIDS. Proposed activities included convening a national conference on SIDS and the outreach role that CMHC's might assume to provide counseling services for bereaved families; convening workshops involving educators in the various mental health professions, both basic professional education and continuing education, to discuss SIDS and to formulate suitable curricular sequences on SIDS and the counseling role of mental health workers; developing an annotated bibliography on the mental health aspects of SIDS and the counseling functions of mental health workers with respect to grief and bereavement; and providing support for research on such relevant issues as optimal forms of outreach by mental health workers to SIDS families, the role of the clergyman in providing counseling services to SIDS families, the effects of counseling on SIDS families, optimal forms of intervention for the surviving children in an SIDS family, the role of mutual-help groups in counseling SIDS families, strategies for articulating a health/mental health delivery system to provide counseling services to SIDS families, consulting strategies for workers providing counseling services, anticipatory guidance with respect to grief and bereavement, effective coping strategies for SIDS families and other bereaved families, crisis intervention and SIDS, and characteristics of families amenable to counseling and families rejecting counseling.

Unfortunately, the anticipated funds to initiate these activities were not forthcoming. Therefore, new strategies were developed to obtain necessary funds while remaining open and alert to emerging needs.

Interviews with SIDS parents presented first-hand opportunities to learn how surviving family members experience and cope with the loss of an infant. Three major observations emerged from discussions with bereaved family members:

(1) The mental health dimensions of SIDS are considerably greater than had been originally envisaged either by NIMH or NFSID.

(2) SIDS parents appear to have special difficulties in handling their infant's death vis-à-vis the surviving siblings; in addition, these parents have the same lack of information and the same anxieties about discussing death with children as do almost all parents in American society.

(3) Members of most bereaved families will not reach out for help from either a mental health facility or a private practitioner, partly because they are not aware that such resources exist, but largely because to do so carries a stigma. In addition, family members who reported that they did seek the assistance of mental health workers said they did not obtain meaningful help, in most instances because mental health workers are uninformed about SIDS in particular and about dealing with grief and bereavement in general. Lastly, mental health agencies are not organized to provide prompt effective service delivery to SIDS families.

These observations, along with knowledge gained from increasing involvement with the mental health issues of SIDS, have served to affirm the appropriateness and soundness of approaching the problem from a public health/mental health perspective. Basic to this perspective was the notion that the specific knowledge gained could be used to help all parents and children achieve a better understanding and acceptance of death as a part of the life process. Operationally, SIDS program activities have proven to be a vehicle for approaching the needs of larger populations.

Conceptually and in practice, two major program objectives on death emerged.

(1) To inform, educate, and involve mental health workers in activities related to the mental health aspects of SIDS. Four projects are included under this objective: (a) formulating guidelines for counseling SIDS families, identifying the needs of surviving siblings, and clarifying the role of the mental health consultant (these matters served as the agenda at the meeting of the Mental Health Advisory Committee to the NIMH/NFSID contract held in Kansas City, Missouri, on July 30, 1975; a report has been prepared; (b) developing and distributing a packet of mental-health-related SIDS literature to community mental health centers and other mental health constituencies; (c) conducting model seminars and workshops on the mental health aspects of SIDS for mental health workers (an initial effort was a statewide workshop held in Denver in July 1975); and (d) encouraging community

mental health centers to participate in emerging health service networks—that is, health/mental health service delivery systems—in order to provide a full range of services to surviving SIDS family members.

(2) To develop a primary prevention program focused on parent-child interactions around the life crisis of death. This objective will encompass the areas of death, dying, grief, bereavement, needs of surviving parents and children, and death education, including anticipatory guidance about death. Relevant projects include the following. (a) In cooperation with the National Institute of Child Health and Human Development (NICHD), a research planning workshop was held on May 29-30, 1975, on the theme "The Impact of Infant Death on Parents and Siblings." Participants from varied backgrounds explored and identified the research, training and service needs of family members surviving when an infant dies —from SIDS, prematurity, congenital malformation, or any other cause. A proceedings document will be available in the middle of 1977. (b) A work conference was convened on July 21-23, to focus on two aspects of the theme of parent-child communications about death: promoting death education as a part of parent education (that is, anticipatory guidance, death as a part of life) and helping parents to help their children understand and deal with death after a loss occurs. Mental health and behavioral specialists in the death area joined with communications experts to develop guidelines, identify priorities, and propose activities and approaches for public education as well as professional training. A proceedings monograph is in preparation. (c) Prior NIMH activities in related fields were reviewed in order to identify the state of existing knowledge and program gaps with particular emphasis on the subject of death-children-families.

In the immediate future, staff effort will be devoted to death area activities related to these two objectives. The emphasis on parent-child communications about death will be developed within the context of parent-child interaction in general, with one goal being to increase the present limited visibility and support for parent education efforts at the federal level. In addition, public education projects will be pursued to promote greater awareness about the characteristics of normal grief reactions as well as some of the harmful cultural myths relating to comforting the bereaved ("it was only a baby," "don't think about the past," and so on).

Mental health trainers will be encouraged to include content about death and the management of bereavement and grief within clinical training programs. Mental health service programs will be informed about the importance of preventive intervention by reaching out to families with young children when there has been a death in the family, particularly the death of a parent or a sibling. Such involvements should lead to identifying other unmet needs and subsequently to additional program developments. In time, the program scope may enlarge to include the concerns of dying patients as well as the needs of their families.

Paradoxically, the emphasis on death has as its major goal the promotion of mental health among the living, for to continue to deny the omnipresence of death and its consequences on survivors is to ignore a mental health issue of great and universal magnitude.

Life

Opportunities to develop primary prevention programs addressed to specific identifiable high risk groups exist at all points in the life cycle. Three such opportunities in which some program development has been initiated are described below.

Mental Health and Family Planning. A multitude of specific issues in family planning have obvious mental health relevance: the birth of unwanted and unloved children, illegitimacy, premarital pregnancy, intensification and perpetuation of poverty, postpartum psychosis, and excessive population growth (Schwartz, 1969). Beyond these issues, the fields of mental health and family planning have areas of mutual concern for which primary prevention approaches offer the most appropriate form of intervention; in this connection, Lieberman (1964) has referred to family planning as the most effective tool in preventive psychiatry.

The following three areas offer opportunities for primary preventive intervention. First, adequate preparation for parenthood would contribute toward sound mental health for both children and parents alike. Since planned parenthood suggests a thoughtful decision about whether, as well as when, to have children, primary prevention principles and objectives can be useful in family planning educational programs. Second, mental health professionals have an obligation to provide family planning services for their ambulatory or institutionalized patients; too often patients have returned to the community after a period of hospitalization only to be overwhelmed by an untimely and unwanted pregnancy. Third, providers of family planning services and mental health workers must be knowledgeable and at ease with all aspects of human sexuality and with the variety of interpersonal issues which arouse strong feelings toward subjects of such sensitive emotional importance.

In spite of the apparent shared interests and natural affinity of these two fields, little cooperative activity has been forthcoming. Indeed, in practice the relationship between them appears to be one of mutual neglect and seeming unawareness of their potential for contributing to each other. As a result, the public is the poorer. An early effort at exploring possible interdigitation between the two fields took place in January 1966 at a conference sponsored by NIMH in cooperation with the Population Crisis Committee. Among the key issues discussed were the relationship between family planning and mental health, the emotional impact of an unwanted child in a large family, the availability of meaningful studies, and the possibility of involving the newly emerging community mental health centers in matters of family planning. With respect to this latter point, Dr. Bertram S. Brown said:

> *In doing some staff work for this meeting, we did a rough survey to find out where there was active interdigitation of family planning services with mental health services. We found literally none. I am sure they do exist. I am sure there are some liaisons that exist between key individuals, but in terms of actual program administration, the linkages at the present time for practical purposes are non-existent in this country. (Population Crisis Committee, 1966)*

Five years later, in 1971, I myself tried to ascertain the nature and extent of linkages between community mental health centers and family planning services; the absence of any definitive information suggested that none existed in any formal sustained manner. In effect, the situation had not changed during the five-year interim period, which however was characterized by the proliferation of community mental health centers and of federally supported family planning services.

In 1974, at my instigation, funds were secured for a "speculative investigation" of the situation: to what extent were community mental health centers and family planning services interacting, and, in particular, were they providing primary preventive services to the total community they served? The study also explored reasons for the present status of such interactions and made recommendations on possible forms of collaboration.

Accordingly, we visited eleven cities having both a community mental health center and a family planning service to obtain information on the extent of the relationship between these two facilities. We found little evidence of collaboration in any form, whether focused on primary prevention or otherwise. Formal and informal patient referral patterns between services appeared to prevail in most of the communities; collaboration was minimal or nonexistent, however, with respect to interagency staff training, orientation of staff members, sharing of staffs, and other activities. Collaboration in any form was at best on an ad hoc basis.

We identified opportunities for collaborating to maximize the primary prevention potential:

1. Cross-Training of Staff. Mental health staffs could train family planning personnel in consultation and interviewing skills and in techniques for counseling in stress situations. Family planning workers, for their part, could share with mental health staffs their knowledge about the emotional dimensions and impact of sexuality and voluntary fertility control on normal populations.

2. Joint Planning. Mental health centers and family planning services working in cooperation could plan programs relating to such mutual concerns as the pregnant teenager, unwanted pregnancies, and the development of sex education programs.

3. Collaborative Community Education and Outreach. They could adopt each other's outreach techniques. For example, family planning workers have achieved some success in using media to gain community acceptance and to communicate their message but have had considerable difficulty gaining acceptance into school systems; the experience of mental health workers has been the reverse.

4. Joint Research. The myriad mutual concerns impinging on each field suggest abundant issues for research at the interface of mental health and family planning.

What this adds up to is the need to develop opportunities for family planning workers to become more aware of and sensitive to the mental health factors of their work, and for mental health personnel to learn about and deal with family planning concerns among the populations they serve. One starting point is to foster training efforts for mental health workers so that community mental health principles can be applied to such critical issues as the emotional aspects of contraception, subsequent children in families that have lost a child through death, and genetic counseling. The mental health/family planning interface offers a community setting for extending primary prevention services to normal populations in order to promote optimal human development.

New Mothers and Neonates. In an ingenious study of tremendous importance, Broussard (1966) has demonstrated that (1) television can be used as an effective means of providing anticipatory guidance to new mothers during the immediate postpartum period, and (2) this guidance effects the mother's perception of her new infant. Using specially devised inventories, Broussard obtained a measure of the mother's perception of her own baby as compared to the average baby. The data suggested that infants rated as less than average by their mothers at the end of the neonatal period (30 days after delivery) might represent a population at high risk for subsequent developmental and emotional difficulties during childhood.

Broussard conducted a blind follow-up study to test the hypothesis that there was a relationship between the mother's perception of her infant at one month of age and the child's subsequent emotional development. At age four and a half, 120 children were evaluated by two child psychiatrists who were unaware of the children's predictive risk rating. Among children whose mothers had a positive perception of them at one month of age, 20 percent were found to have emotional and developmental problems severe enough to require therapeutic intervention; among children viewed negatively at one month, however, intervention was indicated for 66 percent (Broussard, 1970, 1971). Broussard concluded (1972): "These findings appear to indicate that an intervention program which could modify the mother's perception of her newborn prior to one month of age could have a significant impact on the subsequent development of the child."

These research findings have become the basis for developing an intervention program focused on promoting positive perceptions of new mothers toward their infants as early as possible. One product of the program is to be a film on the emotional needs of the new mother, for viewing in hospitals during the immediate postpartum period. The purpose of the film is to direct the mother during this crisis period toward positive mental health by providing information, support, and anticipatory guidance which will (a) enhance the mother's healthy perceptions of both herself (in her new role) and her newborn infant, (b) promote the mother's sense of competence and confidence, (c) let her know the range of normal emotional reactions that follow pregnancy and delivery, and (d) comment on the effects of new parenthood on husband-wife relationships. As a companion piece to the film, a booklet will be distributed to new mothers to clarify, amplify, and reinforce the concepts presented in the film.

This film is perceived as the initial step in a program plan that encompasses the following proposed activities: (a) development of a training film for obstetrical/gynecological staffs in hospitals, aimed at maximizing their contribution toward promoting the new mother's sense of competence and self-esteem, (b) investigations into means of heading off postpartum stresses, and (c) establishing working relationships among federal mental health personnel and leadership in such key organizations as the American Academy of Pediatrics and the American College of Obstetrics and Gynecology, in order to deal with mental health issues of mutual concern that heretofore have not received the attention of all relevant professional groups.

Children in the Hospital. Building upon the identification of apparent gaps, steps are being taken to deal with the numerous issues surrounding the hospitalization of young children for either acute or chronic physical conditions. The key objectives are to prevent the occurrence of needless anxiety or emotional disturbance among young children during their period of hospitalization and to promote optimal personality growth and development during this time.

In the foreword to the publication "Red is the color of hurting" (Shore, 1971), Milton Senn stated:

It is shocking to learn, for example, that only 28 general hospitals out of a total of over 5,000 in the U.S.A. provide facilities for parents to stay overnight with their sick child. It is evident that many physicians, nurses, and hospital administrators still need to be convinced that changes are necessary and still need to be helped to see that good medical and nursing practices cannot be separated from good mental health.

Today there is still no accurate count of the number of hospitals providing overnight facilities for parents, but available information suggests they are the exception rather than the rule. One relatively simple form of primary preventive intervention is to provide such accommodations by changing hospital regulations. Successful intervention here could lead to related efforts on behalf of hospitalized children:

(a) Involving parents on a formal basis in the care, education, recreation, and psychological growth and development of their hospitalized children.

(b) Modifying hospital visiting hours on pediatric services so that parents have continuous access to their children.

(c) Eliminating hospital restrictions on age limits for visiting patients. All family members have a right to visit an ailing loved one; for young children the need for such contacts may often be crucial.

(d) Training hospital administrators, pediatricians, and pediatric nurses about the emotional needs of hospitalized children.

(e) Fostering widespread development of anticipatory guidance to prepare children for hospitalization as well as the experiences they are likely to encounter during hospitalization. Communications materials need to be prepared, evaluated, and distributed to hospitals.

PROPOSED PROGRAM AREAS FOR PRIMARY PREVENTION EFFORTS

Many virtually untapped areas are appropriate for primary prevention program development. Initial explorations confirm the merit of proceeding into the following areas pending the availability of resources:

1. Promoting the maternal-infant affectional bond and the early positive perceptions of the mother toward her infant. Building

upon the work reported by Marshall Klaus and his colleagues (1970, 1972), efforts would be taken to develop state-of-the art conferences, demonstrations, information dissemination, review of current hospital pediatric nursing, and administrative practices, linkages with relevant professional organizations, publications, films, and research.

2. The film for new mothers described above provides a basis for developing projects and procedures aimed at preventing postpartum disturbances by a series of interventions yet to be devised. Such work would offer invaluable opportunities for collaboration of mental health workers with obstetrics/gynecology specialists, hospital maternity staffs, the American Hospital Association, and other key groups.

3. Little is known about providing emotional support to children who "lose" a parent by divorce. Recent outstanding work on children's mourning reactions to the loss of a parent (Furman, 1974) suggest we should consider these findings in developing projects related to interventions with children of divorce. The broad focus of the work would be on the psychology of separation and loss and the effects on children and the total family unit.

4. The interface between the fields of nutrition and mental health suggest numerous opportunities for mental health input and interdisciplinary cooperation with respect to obesity, malnutrition, overnutrition, dieting, anorexia nervosa, the poor nutritional choices that characterize the American diet, and behavioral considerations in heart disease, cancer, and other physical conditions. The relationship between childhood hyperactivity and food additives will be a matter of increased concern to mental health workers.

5. Parent-child communications about death have been perceived programmatically as a first step toward concern with the entire area of death, dying, grief, and bereavement. As interventions are developed and tested out using available information, new knowledge must be generated to help people cope more effectively during this life crisis.

6. Concern with death has accentuated the need to promote a series of activities on parent-child communications in general. Programs and materials will be developed around parenting, relationship-building, and effective forms of parent education.

7. Mutual-help groups offer opportunities for meaningful assis-

tance to be provided to persons in need by others who have had similar experiences. The mental health dimensions of mutual-help groups will be explored, along with developing a curriculum for training mental health workers about the role of such groups in community human services delivery systems.

SUMMARY AND CONCLUSIONS

Above all, this chapter has attempted to demystify the confusion surrounding primary prevention by citing specific activities directed to specific high risk groups, based on specific scientific findings. In brief, the basic elements of a primary prevention program are identical with the features that should characterize any professional human service intervention effort:

1. Statement of the problem, identification of the target groups at risk, and specification of the goal(s) to be achieved.

2. Enumeration of specific techniques and strategies to be utilized.

3. Knowledge of and linkages with community resources needed.

4. Determination of measures to ascertain whether the goals have been reached.

A multitude of problem areas need to be investigated and all relevant scientific information must be applied to create active programs. Within a crisis theory/intervention model, an extensive life of life crisis points can be cited. Where one begins—that is, with what particular problem area directed to which specific high risk group—is a matter of local community needs and the perceptions of those involved, rather than of established professional procedures. But mental health workers and others who plan and implement primary prevention activities must have a scientific basis to go on; accordingly, they are urged to seek out research findings, and to act on the basis of what is known rather than on what logically seems to be valid and practical. Behavioral researchers are urged to focus their efforts on major life problems and means of intervention, and also to be responsible for explaining how their research results can be translated into action programs.

Mental health workers must move out from their relative isolation and put into action the principles of community mental health they articulate so vocally. Primary prevention offers a vehicle for doing this. Approaches and models for primary prevention work now exist, as does sufficient knowledge for developing programs. A key issue is whether mental health workers will continue to devote almost their total (already limited) resources to the casualties that appear at the mental health facility door, or whether they will give serious attention to the mental health of the entire population of a community. George Bernard Shaw is reputed to have said, "Principles without programs equal platitudes." Surely the principles are sound and the program models useful. The period of platitudes should have passed. Time will tell.

REFERENCES

Bergman, A. B., Pomeroy, M. A., and Beckwith, J. B. The psychiatric toll of the Sudden Infant Death Syndrome. *General Practitioner*, 1969, *40*, 99–105.

Broussard, E. R. Evaluation of anticipatory guidance counseling to primiparae using the medium of television. Paper presented at the American Public Health Association meeting, San Francisco, 1966.

Broussard, E. R., and Hartner, M. S. S. Maternal perception of the neonate as related to development. *Child Psychiatry and Human Development*, 1970, *1*, 16–25.

Broussard, E. R., and Hartner, M. S. S. Further considerations regarding maternal perception of the first born. In J. Hellmuth (Ed.), *Exceptional infant*, Vol. 2: *Studies in Abnormalities*. New York: Brunner/Mazel, 1971.

Broussard, E. R. Personal communication, June 22, 1972.

Furman, E. *A child's parent dies: Studies in childhood bereavement.* New Haven: Yale University Press, 1974.

Klaus, M., Kennell, J. H., Plumb, N., and Zuehlke, S. Human maternal behavior at the first contact with her young. *Pediatrics*, 1970, *46*, 187–192.

Klaus, M., Jerauld, R., Kreger, N. C., McAlpine, W., Steffa, M., and Kennell, J. H. Maternal attachment: Importance of the first post-partum days. *New England Journal of Medicine*, 1972, *286*, 460–463.

Lieberman, E. J. Preventive psychiatry and family planning. *Journal of Marriage and the Family*, 1964, *26*, 471–477.

Population Crisis Committee and the National Institute of Mental Health. *Family planning and mental health.* Washington, D.C., 1966.

Schwartz, R. A. The role of family planning in the primary prevention of mental illness. *American Journal of Psychiatry*, 1969, *125*, 125–132.

Shore, M. F. (Ed.). *Red is the color of hurting.* (Public Health Service Publication No. 1583.) Washington, D.C.: U.S. Government Printing Office, reprinted 1971.

VI
Improving the Quality of Life

Introductory Notes

The principal purpose of this first conference on the primary prevention of psychopathology was to focus on the variety of approaches to preventing the appearance of disturbed behavior through interventions affecting large numbers of people, and particularly persons at high risk. The picture would not be complete, however, without a look at the other side of the scientific coin. We felt obligated to call specific attention to the fact that there is more to life than the absence of pathology.

When Angus Campbell was chosen for the Distinguished Scientific Contribution Award by the American Psychological Association in 1974, his selection was based in part on his research on the quality of life. He agreed to present for our conference an early version of the address he was to deliver at the 1975 American Psychological Association Convention. That address, which appeared in the *American Psychologist* in February 1976, is reprinted here with the permission of Professor Campbell and the American Psychological Association.

According to his biography, Angus Campbell's career in social psychology was heavily influenced by his teacher, Kurt Lewin, with whom he worked at Stanford in the early 1930's. Campbell completed his dissertation at Stanford with E. R. Hilgard and, after World War II, went to the University of Michigan, where he was part of the group under Rensis Likert that set up the Institute for Social Research there. For twenty-five years he was Director of the Survey Research Center, and after Likert's retirement in 1970 he became Director of the Institute for Social Research. The work of the Center and the Institute is widely known for studies of race problems, political choice, and social accountability. During the past few years he has been immersed in the study of the quality of life.

The discussant of Professor Campbell's paper is Professor Emeritus Heinz Ansbacher, of the Department of Psychology at the University of Vermont, one of the foremost interpreters of the work of Alfred Adler. He and Dr. Rowena Ansbacher have collaborated over the years on a series of books and articles on Adler's work. They also jointly edit the *Journal of Individual Psychology* and they sponsor frequent workshops and conferences emphasizing Adlerian theory and practice.

17

Subjective Measures of Well-Being

ANGUS CAMPBELL
Discussant: HEINZ L. ANSBACHER

In 1798, Sir John Sinclair, writing in his Statistical Account of Scotland, described statistics in the following language:

> *The idea I annex to the term [statistics] is an inquiry into the state of a country, for the purpose of ascertaining the quantum of happiness enjoyed by its inhabitants, and the means of its future improvement.*

In the succeeding years, nations throughout the Western world have indeed been using statistics to assess the condition of their people; and as time has passed, the measures have become more inclusive, more sophisticated, and more important in their influence on public policy.

Our own country has certainly not been less energetic than others in this development. We now produce a flood of state and federal statistics that have come to be considered essential for the operation of a modern society. I do not believe it would be an exaggeration to say that the bulk of these data relate to the material aspects of American life—to income, expenditures and savings, the production and sales of goods and services, and various other marketplace transactions. If it is true that the basic purpose of collecting the data is to ascertain the "quantum of happiness" enjoyed by our inhabitants, clearly we have been defining happiness in monetary terms.

It is intriguing to speculate about why these monetary indicators have acquired the prestige they have in our society. Americans have a reputation of being a materialistic people, and it may be that our statistics simply reflect our values. This is a plausible hypothesis and may have some validity, although other societies whose market arrangements are very different from ours also pay close attention to these economic indicators.

I would suggest that an alternative way of explaining why these economic measures so dominate our national accounts is the simple fact that they are easy to count. Psychologists seldom have the experience of dealing with measures whose units are equal and interchangeable. Our data are not fungible; monetary data are. It is a tremendous advantage. We may well envy our colleagues who never worry about locating a zero point and who subject their data to all manner of manipulations with confident impunity. The attraction of these hard data that do not involve the kinds of measurement problems we are familiar with is easy to understand.

If these marvelously reliable data told us all we wanted to know about our society, we would not need to be concerned about measures of happiness and other aspects of life experience. The fact is, of course, that serious doubts have developed in this country whether we can depend exclusively on these economic measures as indicators of the goodness of life in our society. During the years since World War II we have experienced an unprecedented rise in national affluence, with a spectacular increase in average family income and an associated decline in the number of families below the poverty line. During the same period we have seen a phenomenal rise in the incidence of crime, an epidemic of various forms of public violence, a greatly increased use of drugs with associated drug abuse, a continuing increase in the number of fragmented families, a sharp drop in public confidence in elected officials, and what appears to be a substantial rise in social and political alienation. Dr. Pangloss himself would find it hard to believe that the quality of American life has been greatly enhanced during this period.

The Gross National Product—important as it undoubtedly is—is clearly not the ultimate criterion against which the quantum of happiness in this country can be assessed. Realization of this fact has given rise in recent years to an energetic search, both in this country and abroad, for a broader and more sensitive set of measures to provide a fuller description of people's lives. Described by Dudley Duncan (1969) as the social indicators "movement," the search entails developing new statistical series to monitor change in such areas of public life as education, health, employment, crime, victimization, political participation, and population growth and movement. Raymond Bauer's book, published in 1964, focused attention on this new development, and there has been increasing interest in both government and the universities since that time.

In 1974 the Office of Management and Budget issued a monograph entitled *Social Indicators, 1973*, which is the first attempt by a government agency to produce a comprehensive presentation of social statistics other than economic ones, and presumably this document will be updated and reissued at regular intervals.

Nearly all of these social indicators describe events, behaviors, or characteristics of individuals reported through governmental institutions of one sort or another; they do not depend on the individual's description of his own life. They might be called objective indicators. To these I would add those descriptions of the environment that report the extent of pollution in the air and water and the amount of disturbance of the natural order of things. These also, obviously, are objective indicators.

Statistics of this kind have value for a variety of purposes: to map variabilities within the population, to identify inequities, to anticipate public demand, to predict trends. They are also used to assess the quality of life. It is quite reasonably argued that the quality of life is enhanced as the level of education rises, the adequacy of medical care improves, the amount of substandard housing is reduced, and the purity of the air and water is increased.

If we believe that the quality of life lies in the objective circumstances of life, these measures will tell us all we need to know. But if we believe—as I assume most psychologists do—that the quality of life lies in the experience of life, then these are surrogate indicators. They describe the conditions of life which might be assumed to influence life experience, but they do not assess that experience directly.

To what extent can these objective measures be taken as valid indicators of the quality of life experience? The question is significant. To return to Sir John Sinclair's language, can we ascertain from an inquiry into the state of a country the quantum of happiness enjoyed by the inhabitants? I think it is apparent that for many economists, statisticians, politicians, and men of affairs in general the answer is "Yes," and they have not been greatly motivated to look beyond the repertoire of objective indicators for their evaluation of the state of public well-being. To a psychologist, however, the relationship between objective conditions and subjective experience must appear very imperfect. We have come to assume that there is a good deal of slippage between the world outside and the world inside. The degree and kinds of relationships between the characteristics of the external world and the quality of one's sense of well-being are facts to be demonstrated. Not many relevant facts are available to answer this question: but there are interesting fragments. National surveys show, for example, that during the period between 1957 and 1972, when most of the economic and social indicators were moving rapidly upward, the proportion of the population of this country who described themselves as "very happy" declined steadily, and this decline was greatest among the most affluent part of the population. A recent study (Schneider, 1975) has shown that in a comparison of thirteen American cities, the correlation between the objective characteristics of the cities and a measure of life satisfaction (reported from surveys of the residents of each city) was essentially zero. An elaborate comparison (Liu, 1973) of the quality of life in the fifty states on a broad battery of objective measures shows the eleven states of the Confederacy firmly entrenched at the bottom in every one of the ten dimensions of comparison. But when the people living in those southern states are asked to evaluate the quality of their lives, they are modestly but consistently more positive than people living in the other major regions of the country.

These data are certainly not comprehensive, and they are aggregative rather than individual, but they suggest what we would have suspected intuitively as psychologists: that if we wish to describe the quality of the life experience of the population, we will need measures different from those used to describe the objective circumstances in which people live. We will have to develop measures that go directly to the experience itself. These measures will surely not have the precision of indicators expressed in dollars, units of time, square feet, or degrees of temperature, but they will have the great advantage of dealing directly with what it is we want to know: the individual's sense of well-being.

Measuring human experience is of course what psychologists have always thought they did best, and countless psychologists have concerned themselves with the quality of life of individual patients. We have also devoted a great deal of attention to the psychological characteristics of undergraduate students. But it cannot be said that we have built a substantial body of research on the life experience of the general population. Partly because the population is so large, so dispersed, and so unwilling to make itself available at the researcher's convenience and partly because measures standardized on college students are often inappropriate for other people, and for other reasons as well, we have no archive of measurements of psychological well-being that we can set alongside the more familiar economic and social indexes..

There have been, of course, a number of pioneering attempts to develop measures to provide the kinds of data we are discussing. Three deserve mention. The first conceptualized well-being as a cognitive experience in which the individual compared his perception of his present situation to a situation he aspired to, expected, or felt he deserved. The discrepancy between his perceived life and his aspired-to life is expressed in a measure of satisfaction-dissatisfaction, and greater satisfaction is taken as an indicator of sense of well-being. Hadley Cantril is the name most commonly associated with this approach. During the early 1960's Cantril (1965) developed what he called his self-anchoring scale "to get an overall picture of the reality worlds in which people live," and he produced his incredible study of the aspirations and satisfactions of the people of thirteen different nations in 1965. You are also aware that the concept of satisfaction has been widely used in studying experience in specific life domains, especially work and marriage. There have been literally thousands of studies of satisfaction with work (Quinn, Staines, and McCullough, 1974) and probably a comparable number of studies of satisfaction with marriage. In calling these measures "cognitive" I do not wish to imply that they lack any "affective" component, but they appear to depend more on a basically intellective process than the other measures that have been used).

The second approach to large-scale studies of psychological well-being has emphasized the affective aspects of experience. Most prominent here have been the studies of Norman Bradburn, first with his studies of avowed happiness (Bradburn and Caplovitz, 1965) and then with the development of his "affect balance" scale (Bradburn, 1969). Bradburn was specifically concerned with "the subjective feeling states that individuals experience in their daily lives." He undertook to assess these states by enumerating particular positive and negative episodes that had occurred in his respondents' lives in the recent past. The procedure identified two measures of affect, positive and negative, which were somewhat surprisingly unrelated to each other. Though Bradburn's data were not precisely representative of the national population, they have since been replicated on national samples by Andrews and Withey (in press).

Finally, there have been a number of attempts to assess the experience of large populations by procedures deriving from psychiatric practice. Among the better known of the early studies were the Yorkville community mental health study (Rennie, 1952) and the Stirling County studies (MacMillan, 1957); the first national study was the Gurin, Veroff, and Feld (1960) project carried out for the Joint Commission on Mental Illness and Health. The latter study was primarily concerned with psychological and emotional stress and included a broad range of questions regarding symptoms, experiences, and general feelings. In general the measures appear to be more affective in quality than cognitive; the questions regarding general happiness in life tap what Bradburn calls positive affect, and the questions concerning worries, anxieties, and emotional crises reflect negative affect.

These three research strategies have been pursued independently of each other and with relatively little input from one to the other. The authors in each case were intent on ascertaining "the quantum of happiness enjoyed by [the nation's] inhabitants," and they identified the basic measures they developed as measures of happiness, using the term "happiness" as a synonym for "satisfaction" or "freedom from stress."

The attraction of the concept "happiness" is certainly great, coming as it does from the early Greek identification of happiness with the good life and having as it does almost universal currency as a recognized (if not uniquely important) component of the quality of life experience. It is one of those indispensable psychological concepts, like intelligence, morale, prejudice, and others, that have meaning to almost everyone but are difficult to define. Like those other concepts, it serves very well in everyday conversation but it proves too general when it is the subject of research inquiry. We find, for example, that satisfaction and happiness behave in different ways in the studies I have mentioned. Reported happiness is highest among young people and declines with age; general satisfaction is lowest among young people and increases with age. Happiness with marriage increases with level of education, but feelings of inadequacy as a marriage partner also increase with education. These measures are undoubtedly interrelated but, like the verbal and mathematical components of an intelligence test, they are not identical.

It would appear that we have come to the point where we must stop using the word "happiness" indiscriminately to refer to any aspect of experience we regard as positive and begin to work seriously on the problem of identifying the major dimensions of the experience of well-being, developing instruments to measure them, analyzing their relationships to each other, and building time-series that make it possible to study the nature of change.

My colleagues Philip Converse and Willard Rodgers and I have recently brought to completion a study intended to make a beginning on these objectives. The study was projected as the first in a series of national surveys that would monitor the quality of American life. It grew out of an earlier volume, *The Human Meaning of Social Change* (1972), which Converse and I had edited. Both that volume and the subsequent study were supported by the Russell Sage Foundation.

I propose to tell you only enough about our study to illustrate the kind of inquiry I think psychologists must inevitably become more concerned with. It was a study of the national population, based on a probability sample of all persons 18 years old and older living in private households in the 48 contiguous states. Representatives of the Institute for Social Research interviewed 2,164 women and men, using a structured questionnaire taken in the respondent's home and averaging about an hour and a quarter in length. We obviously did not have anybody on the couch, but as you know, a well-trained interviewer following a carefully developed schedule of questions can get a great deal of information out of a cooperative respondent in 75 minutes.

If we ask a person to describe his life, he will respond either in terms of his life as a whole or with a specific reference to the domains of life in which experience is segmented: work, marriage, housing, community, health, standard of living, and the like. We asked our respondents to undertake both of these forms of self-examination—to describe and assess their experience in 15 separate domains and respond to more general measures regarding their lives as a whole. I will not have time here to discuss any of the individual domain scores, but I want to say something about the three general measures of life experience we developed because I think they have promise. They will no doubt be improved in subsequent studies, but they appear to be solid enough to sustain the use we have made of them.

We were particularly concerned to obtain an assessment of satisfaction with life, an essentially cognitive measure. In earlier studies this has typically been accomplished by asking a single question, as in Cantril's (1965) self-anchoring format, for example. We asked such a question for purposes of continuity with the earlier studies, but we also developed an index composed of the satisfaction scores of 10 of the individual domains we asked about. This index correlated at nearly .70 with the single question and has a higher test-retest reliability. It is one of the three measures I will be talking about, the Index of Domain Satisfactions.

Our second measure was intended to give us a reading of the affective quality of life, directed more to the experience of pleasantness-unpleasantness than of satisfaction-dissatisfaction. We considered using the Bradburn Scale of Affect Balance for this purpose but chose instead to ask our respondents to react to a series of paired adjectives, describing their lives in positive or negative terms, presented in the semantic differential format. They were asked to describe their lives in general as falling at a point they chose in the space between interesting-boring, enjoyable-miserable, lonely-friendly, and the like. Factor analysis showed eight of these pairs carrying a substantial loading on the first factor and they became our Index of Positive Affect. It correlates about .5 with the Index of Domain Satisfactions.

Two of the adjective pairs in the total list did not appear to fit the structure of the eight used in the Index of Positive Affect but shared substantial weights in the second factor. These items—easy-hard and free-tied down—were combined with several questions concerned with sense of being rushed, worries about money, and worries of a broader character to form a scale we called the Index of Perceived Stress. These various questions do not interrelate as consistently as one might like and they seem to be more subject to variation over time than the other two measures; as an index, however, they move our data in interesting ways and appear to tap a different dimension of experience than the other two measures at the level of about .40.

Now let me return to my earlier question—what is the relationship of these subjective measures of well-being to the objective circumstances of life? How well could we have predicted from a knowledge of an individual's social and economic situation what

Table 1

Prediction of Measures of Sense of Well Being
from Characteristics of Individual's Situation

	Index of Satisfaction with Life Domains		Index of Positive Affect		Index of Perceived Stress	
	Eta	Beta	Eta	Beta	Eta	Beta
Life cycle	.26	.18	.24	.19	.27	.19
Urbanicity	.24	.19	.14	.14	.06	.06
Age	.22	.17	.08	.11	.31	.27
Race	.21	.10	.08	.06	.07	.04
Working or other	.17	.08	.18	.12	.22	.20
Family income	.14	.17	.18	.12	.10	.18
Occupation of head	.14	.11	.17	.06	.15	.14
Education	.10	.06	.10	.07	.08	.06
Religion	.09	.07	.11	.09	.05	.05
Sex	.02	.04	.02	.06	.04	.13
R =	.41		.33		.38	
R^2 =	.17		.11		.14	

his levels of satisfaction, positive affect, and perceived stress would be? You see in Table 1 the results of a Multiple Classification Analysis in which 10 situation variables are used simultaneously to explain the variance in each of the three subjective measures I have described. In none of the three cases do the 10 variables account for more than 17 percent of the variance. We must assume of course that there is a certain amount of error variance in these measures, contributed by inadequacies of measurement, but it would seem clear that there is a great deal about the way people describe their lives that cannot be predicted from this rather far-reaching information about the circumstances in which they live.

You will notice that the major contributor to the variance of the three measures of well-being is not income, as might have been anticipated. People in poverty are the most negative on all the measures and the affluent are most positive, but the overall relationships are rather modest. The more significant contributors are age and its related variable, life cycle, which combines age with the presence or absence of marriage and children. Even these relationships are not high; they are simply higher than those of other variables that might have been thought on common-sense grounds to carry greater weight in determining one's sense of well-being.

The pattern of relationships between the 10 situational variables and the Index of Domain Satisfactions is generally similar to the pattern of relationships to the other measures of well-being, but there are some obvious discrepancies in the case of individual variables. Age, for example, appears to contribute less to the Index of Positive Affect than it does to the other two measures. One assumes that these discrepancies reflect differences in the content of what the three indexes are measuring. We can identify these differences more effectively by comparing the responses given by contrasting population groups to each of the three subjective measures. This demonstration is carried out in Figure 1, where we have divided the total sample into the nine stages of the life cycle and plotted their scores on the three indexes. We see there that some groups have consistently high scores on all three measures—for example, men and women whose children are grown and who are themselves still married are consistently very positive. The empty nest appears to have a reputation it does not deserve. On the opposite side are divorced women, who are consistently very negative. More interesting for our present purposes are groups whose patterns are not consistent. Prominent among these are widowed men and women who, as we see, score well above average on the measure of domain satisfactions and report low levels of stress but are one of the most negative groups in their reports of positive affect. A second example is divorced men, who are very negative in their reports of domain satisfaction and positive affect but report less than average stress. Men who have never married, both those under 30 and those 30 and over, show the same irregular pattern. By contrast, young married women with a preschool age child report unusually high levels

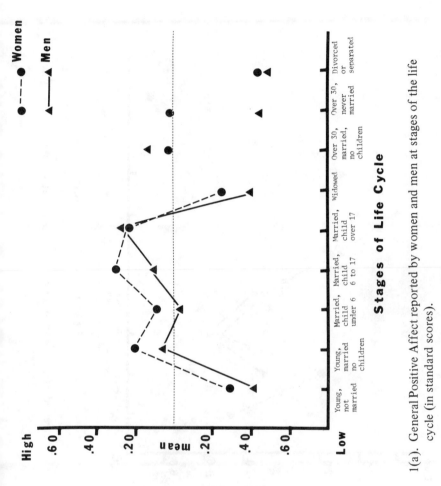

1(a). General Positive Affect reported by women and men at stages of the life cycle (in standard scores).

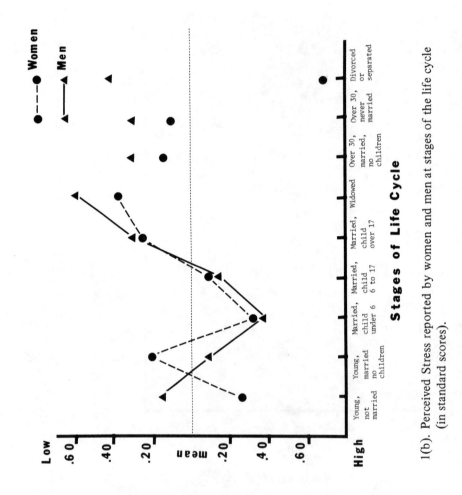

1(b). Perceived Stress reported by women and men at stages of the life cycle (in standard scores).

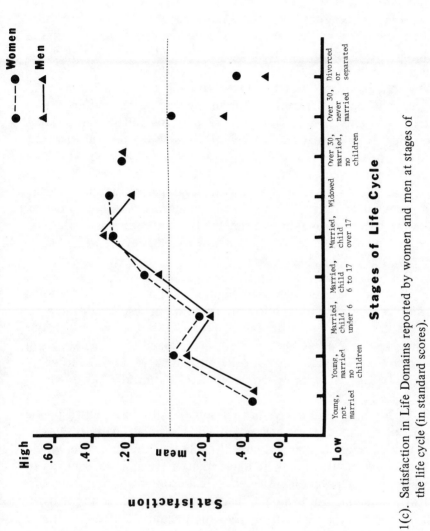

1(c). Satisfaction in Life Domains reported by women and men at stages of the life cycle (in standard scores).

of stress but approach the average on the measure of satisfaction and surpass it slightly on the measure of positive affect.

If we assume that these three measures are all tapping into that attribute of human experience called sense of well-being, or, more commonly, happiness, then we must conclude that this experience has more than one dimension. While the three measures we have developed are moderately related to each other, it is clear that people living in different life circumstances express different patterns of well-being and that these patterns reflect the peculiar quality of the situation they live in. It is surely not surprising to find, for example, that it is positive affect that is lacking in the lives of widows or that it is stress that characterizes the lives of mothers of young children. Our three measures, imperfect as they are, are in some degree tapping different dimensions of life experience. Certainly it is clear that by using the three measures separately we learn more about these people than we would have if we had combined them into a single index.

Despite the fact that the differences between the more discrepant of the life cycle groups shown in Figure 1 are not only significant in a sampling sense but quite substantial in terms of absolute differences, it is still true (as we saw in Table 1) that most of the variance in our three measures of well-being is left unexplained after we have taken account of life cycle and nine other situational variables. One would like very much to know where the explanation of this remaining variance lies.

Perhaps we might have gained some additional control of the missing variance if we had redefined our situational measures or extended their number. I doubt, though, that this maneuver would prove successful; I think it likely that the major determiners of well-being are psychological rather than economic or demographic. I would assume, for example, that the kinds of long-term predispositions making up the personality structure must contribute in some degree to the way people evaluate their lives. In fact, it might be argued that what we have been calling indicators of well-being are themselves measures of personality. Whatever the answer to that definitional problem may be, there are no doubt broad aspects of life cycle which one might expect would influence sense of well-being, achievement need, affiliative need, Friedman and Rosenman's Types A and B, and the like. If we were intent on explaining as much as possible of the variance in well-being, we would have to bring these variables into the equation.

It is also apparent that we would have to take account of the presence or absence of those various forms of interpersonal exchange that provide psychological support to people. The differences shown in Figure 1 in the levels of well-being reported by married people and those who are single, widowed, or divorced suggest the significance of social-emotional supportive relationships; and studies of organizations other than the family have demonstrated dramatic consequences, both psychological and physiological, when such support is not present (French, 1973; Gore, 1973). If we could draw on clinical experience to develop measures suitable for survey research to assess the quality of psychological support in people's lives, we should be able to account for some of the unexplained variance in our indicators of well-being.

Even if we had these data regarding personality predispositions and mechanisms of psychological support, however, our indicators of well-being would still vary in response to life events that occur episodically and sometimes unpredictably. The psychological gains and losses resulting from births, deaths, marriages, accidentsk illnesses, unemployment, and other such events clearly have the capacity to create short-term effects on the way a person evaluates his life. The events may be thought of as exogenous to a psychological explanation of well-being, but they clearly intrude into such a model and make it difficult to predict well-being from a knowledge of the more stable attributes of the person and his psychological situation.

If we return now to the quote from Sir John Sinclair with which I opened this commentary, we see that he described statistical inquiries as having the purpose of ascertaining not only "the quantum of happiness enjoyed by [the nation's] inhabitants" but also "the means of its future improvement." Let me conclude my remarks by considering the question of how a program of monitoring the psychological well-being of the population may be expected to lead to its enhancement.

The recent rush of interest in developing an expanded repertoire of social indicators has been accompanied by a certain enthusiasm for the potential and beneficial impact such data will have on public policy. It is argued reasonably enough that the availability of data describing the social situation of the population will enable public officials to make better-informed and more far-sighted decisions. The same argument might be made in justification of the kinds of subjective indicators we have been discussing.

Without challenging this argument, I would offer these amendments. First, I would recommend to my social science colleagues a certain modesty in their expectations regarding the consequences of introducing their data into the decision-making process. For reasons I will not review here, the results are seldom dramatic. Second, the most visible examples of social data that have had an immediate impact on policy come from studies which had restricted, well-defined, and immediate objectives. There is no doubt that research done to evaluate specific public programs, for example, can have direct and important payoff. Donald Campbell (1974) has been urging that an "experimenting society" will in the future make much greater use of this form of research than we do at present.

Finally, I would point out that indicator research is not experimental research and its utility is not likely to be as immediate or as explicit, although I believe that in the long run it will be more important. The monitoring of social and psychological indicators will produce the kind of information Biderman (1970) calls "enlightenment"—information that restructures the decision-maker's cognitive and affective map of society. This is likely to be a slow process. But we have witnessed in the last twenty-five years convincing examples of changing perceptions of social reality and consequent changes in social institutions and public behavior. Public policies toward our most basic social problems, poverty and racial segregation, have both changed dramatically during that time and there is no doubt in my mind that social science data have contributed significantly to the changes.

Quite aside from the contribution data from psychological indicators may make to public well-being through their influence on public policy, they will also have value as part of the matrix of information we need for an ultimate understanding of the nature of social change. We know far too little about the way new perceptions, beliefs, or values are germinated in some segment of society, how they are influenced by passing events, how they diffuse through the population generally, or how they are converted eventually into an institutional act. And we are just about as badly informed about the impact on public thinking and behavior once such an institutional act is taken. We lack the information necessary for a satisfactory theory of social change and we consequently do rather badly at predicting social change. It would be efficient, and rather elegant, if we could develop a theory which would tell us precisely what data would be necessary for its support, but this strategy does not seem to have carried us very far. Perhaps a more pragmatic procedure of intuitively feeling our way through successive waves of data will bring us to a theory that will tell us what we should have known in the first place.

REFERENCES

Andrews, F. M., and Withey, S. B. *Social Indicators of well-being*. New York: Plenum, in press.

Bauer, R. (Ed.). *Social indicators*. Cambridge, Mass.: M.I.T. Press, 1966.

Biderman, A. D. Information, intelligence, and enlightened policy: Function and organization of social feedback. *Policy Sciences*, 1970, *1*, 217–230.

Bradburn, N. M. *The structure of psychological well-being*. Chicago, Ill.: Aldine, 1969.

Bradburn, N. M., and Caplovitz, D. *Reports on happiness*. Chicago, Ill.: Aldine, 1965.

Campbell, A., and Converse, P. E. (Eds.). *The human meaning of social change*. New York: Russell Sage Foundation, 1972.

Campbell, D. *Getting ready for the experimenting society*. Address presented at the fall commencement of the University of Michigan, December 15, 1974.

Cantril, H. *The pattern of human concerns*. New Brunswick, N.J.: Rutgers University Press, 1965.

Duncan, O. D. *Toward social reporting: Next steps*. New York: Russell Sage Foundation, 1969.

French, R.F.P. Person role fit. *Occupational Mental Health*, 1973, *3* (1), 15-20.

Gore, S. *The influence of social support and related variables in ameliorating the consequences of job loss*. Unpublished doctoral dissertation, Department of Sociology, University of Pennsylvania, 1973. (Available from National Technical Information Service, Springfield, Virginia 22151.)

Gurin, G., Veroff, S., and Feld, S. *Americans view their mental health*. New York: Basic Books, 1960.

Liu, B.-C. *The quality of life in the United States: 1970*. Kansas City, Mo.: Midwest Research Institute, 1973.

MacMillan, A. M. The Health Opinion Survey: Technique for estimating prevalence of psychoneurotic and related types of disorder in communities. *Psychological Reports*, 1957, *3*, 325–339.

Quinn, R. P., Staines, G. L., and McCullough, M. R. *Job satisfaction: Is there a trend?* (Manpower Research Monograph No. 30). Washington, D.C.: U.S. Department of Labor, 1974.

Rennie, T. A. C. *The Yorkville Community Mental Health Research Study*. Paper presented at the annual conference of the Milbank Memorial Fund, New York City, November 1952.

Schneider, M. The quality of life in large American cities: Objective and subjective social indicators. *Social Indicators Research*, 1975, *1*, 495–509.

DISCUSSION BY HEINZ L. ANSBACHER

For the prevention of psychopathology, a conception of what one wants to attain in the positive sense—the opposite of psychopathology—certainly seems desirable. If we may define psychopathology simply as misery, its opposite would be happiness. But as Angus Campbell notes, "happiness," while serving perfectly well in everyday conversation, proves too general for research inquiry. Through the concept of "experience of well-being" he has provided a more sophisticated and better articulated equivalent of "happiness."

RECAPITULATION

From previous work Campbell found the experience of well-being to have three major dimensions:
1. Satisfaction with ten domains of life, an essentially cognitive quality. "I am satisfied with my work, my marriage, my housing, my community, my health, my standard of living, etc."
2. Experiencing pleasantness of life, an affective quality of life. "My present life is interesting, enjoyable, worthwhile, friendly, full, hopeful, rewarding, brings out the best in me."
3. Absence of perceived stress, what we might call an affective-physiological quality. "My present life is easy, not hard; I am free, not tied down; I do not feel rushed; I don't worry about money and other matters."
The present study is based on a nationwide survey of a sample of over 2100 men and women. For each of the above three dimensions of well-being an index of well-being was obtained and related to various objective circumstances of life.
The main results were derived from a breakdown of the index

data by nine stages of the life cycle, corresponding roughly to the age progression through life. For easy identification, we numbered the stages in our Figure 1 in the order in which they appear in Campbell's Figure 1, our order differing at one point from his.

The results reported by Campbell are essentially: "We see that some groups have consistently high scores on all three measures—for example, men and women whose children are grown and who are themselves still married. . . . On the opposite side are divorced women, who are consistently very negative" (p. 330). He notes further that age appears to contribute less to Index 2, pleasantness, than to Indexes 1 and 3, satisfaction and absence of stress. He also comments on inconsistencies in reference to life-cycle stages 6, 9, 8, and 4.

These results do not seem to give a very comprehensive picture, nor—because of the inconsistencies—a very satisfactory one.

RECASTING THE DATA

The limitations of Campbell's findings suggested to us a different approach to the data. We questioned the appropriateness of considering "absence of perceived stress" as a dimension of well-being Such reasoning is related to a tension-reduction theory of motivation, which today is seriously questioned.

Various studies argue against a drive or tension reduction theory. G. W. Allport (1955), for example, considered the "tension-reduction formula" to fall short of representing the nature of individual striving, in which characteristically "tension is maintained rather than reduced" (p. 49). "Salvation comes only to him who ceaselessly bestirs himself. . . . Propriate striving confers unity upon personality, but it is never the unity of . . . reduction of tension" (p. 67). Hans Selye (1956), physiologist and physician, declared: "Stress is part of life. It is a natural by-product of all our activities" (p. 299). "Complete rest is not good. . . . Stress, applied in moderation, is necessary for life" (p. 300). And then there is Alfred Adler (1935), who held that "Life (and all psychic expressions as part of life), moves ever toward 'overcoming,' toward perfection, toward superiority, toward success" (p. 68), implying the presence rather than the absence of stress as part of life.

Discussing the issue of tension reduction, Savatore R. Maddi

(1972) arrived at the conclusion that "not all behavior is oriented toward tension reduction, and some behavior may even be oriented toward tension increase" (p. 252). He finds that this favors the fulfillment model of personality in contrast to the conflict model.

With these considerations in mind, and hoping to obtain a clearer and more comprehensive picture, we replotted the data of Campbell's Figure 1 with the following changes.

1. The data of the two sexes were combined, since with only a few exceptions they were quite similar in all three dimensions of well-being. The one outstanding exception is the great difference in stress between divorced women and divorced men, Stage 9; in this instance we retained the separation of the results.

2. The order of life-cycle Stages 6 and 7 was reversed. This seemed logical, since the stages represent age progression through life and Stage 6 was last. Stage 7 might have been advanced an additional step. Stages 8 and 9 retained their end positions as they are of a different order, as will be explained below.

3. Most importantly, we plotted for the third dimension of well-being "perceived stress" rather than its opposite, "absence of perceived stress," as explained above. As "perceived stress," these data can actually no longer be considered a dimension of well-being.

4. The curves of all three dimensions were plotted on one figure to enable one to see their progression in relation to one another.

RESULTS AND DISCUSSION

Replotting the data resulted in Figure 1, which reveals several relationships that were previously hidden.

1. The curves for "positive affect" (A) and "satisfaction" (S) rise quite steadily from the low point at the beginning of the life cycle to later maturity (Stage 5), with A slightly ahead of S. The curves show only a minor reversal at Stage 3, where "perceived stress" (T) is extremely high. (More about this below.)

The increase in "positive affect" and "satisfaction" with the years is a comforting picture and quite in accord with what Maddi (1972) has described as a "fulfillment model" of personality (generally more optimistic) in contrast to a "conflict model" (generally more pessimistic). The prime exponent of the conflict model is Freud; but Murray, Sullivan, Rank, and Jung are also of this persuasion. The prime exponent of the fulfillment model is Adler,

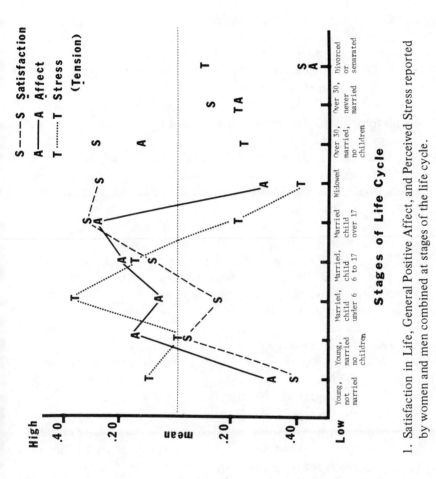

1. Satisfaction in Life, General Positive Affect, and Perceived Stress reported by women and men combined at stages of the life cycle.

while Robert White, Gordon Allport, and Fromm (and also Rogers and Maslow) are found here. Charlotte Bühler is also to be counted among the fulfillment theorists.

According to Maddi, "When they consider the entire life-span, fulfillment theorists think in terms of a fairly continual developmental process . . . considered to indicate . . . psychological growth" (p. 185). "Emphasis in ideal living is upon imaginativeness, spontaneity, individuality, self-reliance. . . . This emphasis contrasts sharply with that . . . found in the conflict model" (p. 185). One may well assume that such psychological growth also includes increase in "positive affect" and "satisfaction."

2. The A curve declines when there is no procreation (Stage 7, "no children") and declines sharply toward the last stage (Stage 6, "widowed"). The decline is even greater for the T curve where it begins also two stages earlier—"perceived stress" being apparently directly related to vitality (see below). By contrast, the S curve "satisfaction"—the cognitive quality of well-being—remains virtually at its height through Stages 7 and 6.

The "positive affect" (A) and "perceived stress" (T) curves correspond roughly to Bühler's (1959) "biological life curve" (p. 92). The T curve reflects the actual biological decline, and the A curve shows that life does indeed become less "interesting, enjoyable, full, and hopeful" when children are absent and with the inevitable, decline accompanying old age.

By contrast, the S curve—"satisfaction," the cognitive quality of well-being—remains almost at its peak through Stages 7 and 6. Apparently man becomes and remains cognitively reconciled with his situation even when the objective events sadden him. It reminds us of Nietzsche's concept of *amor fati*, about which he says: "My formula for the greatness of a human being is *amor fati*: that one wants nothing to be different . . . Not merely bear what is necessary . . . but love it" (Kaufmann, 1974, p. 283). Apparently man in general achieves some such greatness.

The fact that the S curve does not decline also supports Bühler's (1968) observation that "certain aspects of a person's psychological development take place independently of the biological part of his nature." Thus, "his creative mentality may still allow him to be mentally productive and to unfold new personality trends at an age when his physical self may already have deteriorated" (p. 16).

3. The curve of "perceived stress" (T) starts considerably higher

than the other two curves and reaches its peak at early maturity (Stage 3), whereas the other two curves do not reach their peaks until late maturity (Stage 5). From Stage 3 on, the T curve shows a steady decline to a point lower than the other two curves at any stage.

If we hold with Selye that "stress is part of life . . . a by-product of all our activities," we may say that "perceived stress" is high where vitality is high and declines steadily with declining vitality. An excess of stress is of course noxious. This may be approximated in Stage 3, where we find a simultaneous dip in "positive affect" and "satisfaction."

The high stress in youth again accords with Maddi's (1972) description of the fulfillment model of personality. In this model, "the more vigorous is the expression of the [great] force [in living], the greater is the experience of tension. . . . Although fulfillment positions do not strictly speaking assume that the person aims at the increase of tension per se, such increases are integrally a part of expressing the great force, and are not, in any case, particularly uncomfortable" (p. 183).

High stress early in life, Stage 1, suggests the "storm and stress" (*Sturm und Drang*) period, of which Charlotte Bühler (1959) writes: "Although not every generation of youths penetrates the society and culture of its time with storm and stress, one expects from healthy youth an active, aggressive going ahead" (p. 82).

4. Stages 1 to 6 represent a natural life-cycle progression. As for Stage 7 ("over 30, married, no children"), it seemed defensible to insert it in this sequence ahead of Stage 6, "widowed," because childlessness can in most cases be assumed to be due to natural causes or else to causes independent of interpersonal relationships with the other sex.

It is quite different from Stages 8 and 9 ("never married" and "divorced or separated"). These are not life-cycle stages but conditions of persons who were unable to find someone of the other sex to live with permanently, who were not willing to commit themselves to a person of the other sex, or who were unable to continue doing so.

Such people Adler called "failures" in love and marriage, one of the three "life tasks" or "life problems"—the other two being work and friendship. All three tasks are actually social and require social interest for a successful solution, and are thereby interrelated.

According to Adler (1931), "All failures—neurotics, psychotics, criminals, drunkards, problem children, suicides, perverts and prostitutes—are failures because they are lacking in . . . social interest. They approach the problems of occupation, friendship, and sex without confidence that they can be solved by cooperation" (p. 8). "These three problems are never found apart; they all throw crosslights on one another" (p. 241).

Regarding failure in love and marriage in particular, Adler (1929) observed: "When an individual's attitude towards love and marriage is hesitative, halting, or expectant, it indicates a general unpreparedness for social life, and we may safely infer a tendency to exclude a large part of the potentialities of life" (p. 49).

It is quite in accordance with such theory that persons belonging to Stages 8 and 9 having a hesitating attitude and a tendency to exclude a large part of life would be low in "perceived stress." But they are also low in "positive affect" and "satisfaction." Here their reduced social interest becomes effective. It is the opposite of the effect of a developed social interest by which "the feeling of worth and value is heightened, giving courage and an optimistic view, and there is a sense of acquiescence in the common advantages and drawbacks of our lot" (p. 79).

5. One great inconsistency remaining in this analysis of Campbell's data lies in the results on "perceived stress" from divorced or separated women (Stage 9). They are the most extreme of all 27 measures reported; they are in the opposite direction from those of the men; and their difference from the male scores is quite beyond the range of the remaining differences (over 1.10 standard scores, compared to a modal difference of less than .10 and two highest differences of approximately .45 standard scores). As a result of these figures, we used only the men's results and suggest that the women's results be studied further.

6. Regarding all these observations, we must firmly keep in mind that they refer only to averages, whose total range for all three curves separately extends over only .85 standard scores. The results can thus not be applied to individual cases.

SUMMARY AND CONCLUSIONS

Campbell's survey research study of the "experience of well-being" offers support to a "fulfillment model" theory of personality in that its data permit the following conclusions.

1. "Satisfaction with life," the cognitive aspect of well-being, or happiness, increases throughout the life cycle and remains high even at the stages where "experience of pleasantness," an affective component of happiness, declines.

2. "Perceived stress" is better understood as a concomitant of intensity of living than as a component of reduced well-being or unhappiness.

3. Persons who do not successfully meet or fulfill one of Alfred Adler's three life tasks, love and marriage (the other two being work and friendship) are likely to be low in psychological well-being.

The support offered by the data to a fulfillment model represents the significance of the study for primary prevention. The fulfillment model, being more optimistic than the conflict model (which is more pessimistic), would on an a priori or face-validity basis be the model of choice for the mental health field. We are mindful of the self-fulfilling prophecy phenomenon. The Campbell study now adds some empirical validity to the fulfillment model.

As practical implications of the study, the following suggest themselves.

1. In training mental health personnel, the fulfillment model should clearly be given preference over the conflict model, as doing justice to the data in addition to being more suitable to successful psychological intervention.

2. Regarding prevention specifically, training in parenthood and family education are indicated by the high point in "perceived stress" and dips in pleasantness and satisfaction in Stage 3. Where such measures are already in effect, they should be strengthened; where they are not, the need for them should be recognized and met.

3. The very low "experience of well-being" of divorced and separated persons suggests that failure in marriage may indeed be related to more general failure. The implication for prevention is training in skills that make for successful marriage, especially social interest—that is, an interest in the interests of the chosen person of the other sex.

REFERENCES

Adler, A. *Problems of neurosis*. New York: Harper Torchbooks, 1929, 1964.
Adler, A. *What life should mean to you*. New York: Capricorn Books, 1958.
Adler, A. Typology of meeting life problems (1935). In H. L. and R. R. Ansbacher (Eds.), *Superiority and social interest*. New York: Viking Press, 1973.
Allport, G. W. *Becoming: Basic considerations for a psychology of personality*. New Haven: Yale University Press, 1955.
Bühler, C. *Der menschliche Lebenslauf als psychologisches Problem*. 2d ed. Göttingen: Hogrefe, 1959.
Bühler, C. The general structure of the human life cycle. In C. Bühler and F. Massarick (Eds.), *The course of life: A study of goals in the humanistic perspective*. New York: Springer, 1968.
Kaufman, W. *Nietzsche: Philosopher, psychologist, antichrist*. 4th ed. Princeton: Princeton University Press, 1974.
Maddi, R. *Personality theories: A comparative analysis*. Rev ed. Homewood, Ill.: Dorsey Press, 1972.
Selye, H. *The stress of life*. New York: McGraw-Hill, 1956.

Bibliographical Essay

Introductory Notes

The Conference Committee decided to include as an Appendix the article on primary prevention written by Marc Kessler and George Albee, which appeared in the *Annual Review of Psychology*, 1975. This review provides an extensive bibliography of the field. Both Kessler and Albee are on the faculty of the Department of Psychology at the University of Vermont and both were active in planning the conference. A small number of stylistic changes have been made in the text and references. For reasons of economy, the citation system used in the original paper has been retained.

An Overview of the Literature
of Primary Prevention

MARC KESSLER AND GEORGE W. ALBEE

A quick glance at articles published over the years in the *Annual Review of Psychology* shows that many authors start out with disclaimers about the possibility of completing the task in the space assigned them by the editors. We are in this tradition. The editors asked for a chapter on Prevention of Mental Disorders. The review was to be accomplished in 25 pages (or less). Obviously, an impossible task. Preventive efforts have been divided by Caplan (71) into three separate major areas: primary prevention, secondary prevention, and tertiary prevention. As in conventional medicine, primary prevention is the steps taken to prevent the occurrence of a disease, secondary prevention is early treatment of the disease once it has occurred, and tertiary prevention is the attempt to minimize the long-term effects of the disease.

Recognizing the impossibility of the task of reviewing this tripartite field, and with the agreement of the editors, this chapter will be limited to an examination of primary prevention. Even here the literature is so enormous and amorphous as to defy adequate coverage. Our reading for a year leads us to the conclusion that practically every effort aimed at improved child rearing, increasing effective communication, building inner control and self-esteem, reducing stress and pollution, and the like—in short, everything aimed at improving the human condition, at making life more fulfilling and meaningful—may be considered to be part of primary prevention of mental or emotional disturbance. Legislators, social reformers, radicals, conservatives, and practically everyone else, propose solutions to human ills. The law requiring seat belts in automobiles which must be fastened before the car can function will clearly reduce the incidence of brain damage in thousands of people in the course of a year. Enforcing lower speed limits during the energy shortage has reduced the number of accidents and auto fatalities. Clearly this is primary prevention of emotional distress in persons not injured and in families of nonvictims.

The plan of this chapter is to provide a few guideposts through the maze of the vast literature on prevention. We start with definitions, or preconceptions, that people in the field bring to the area. Then we will examine some of the important models of the conditions that have been the targets for primary prevention. We will go on to discuss epidemiology and some of the social conflicts that may be generated by action programs. We will attempt to point out where efforts at primary prevention are being made and what the future may hold. Through all of this we will try to show the difficulties for scientific study inherent in the field, and we will make some attempts at clarifying the research problems.

The field of primary prevention is analogous in many ways to the great Okefenokee Swamp. Attractive from a distance and especially from the air, it lures the unwary into quagmires, into uncharted and impenetrable byways. There are islands of solid ground, sections of rare beauty, unexpected dangers, and violent inhabitants. If one explores, and survives, the area becomes compelling, even addictive. Meanwhile, the rest of the outside world goes on unconcerned and unaware. As we undertook the task of exploring this vast area we became more and more conscious of its size and of its undisciplined nature and the vagueness of the existing maps. Like many explorers we became a little crazy, somewhat monomaniacal. After this heady experience we still remain enchanted, although not overanxious to make the same trip again soon. This analogy, too, soon fails to represent reality. When reading through the literature on prevention we kept thinking of Raimy's (270) definition of psychotherapy as an "Unidentified technique applied to unspecified problems with unpredictable outcomes", . . . for which long and rigorous training is required (p. 3). In comparison with the field of primary prevention the field of psychotherapy is tough-minded and exact! Wherever we looked, whatever we read or heard, there were unexplored or unresearched hypotheses about primary prevention.

What is meant by primary prevention in the field of behavioral disorders? Most authors in this area have wrestled with attempts at definition, interspersed with more or less optimistic hopes for the future of primary preventive efforts (11, 28, 29, 33, 43, 45, 51, 73, 79, 86, 92, 94, 97, 106, 112, 124, 131, 134, 137, 140, 143, 151, 176, 177, 188, 201, 205, 206, 213, 215, 219, 220, 244, 262, 273, 274, 282, 283, 293, 294, 301, 303, 325, 329, 341, 342, 358, 368, 371). While Caplan (e.g. 69, 72) has written much recently to advance his own model of primary prevention, the mental hygiene movement has been around for a much longer period of time than he has, getting a tremendous impetus in the early part of this century (e.g. 43, 75). We are still experiencing a backlash against the extravagant claims of the "mental hygiene movement" started by Clifford Beers and others early in the century. This movement promised to eliminate most forms of mental and emotional distress through education—education of parents, education of children, teaching sound mental health principles to teachers, clergymen, and other significant influencers (99, 203, 211).

Currently there are several varying usages of the term primary prevention. A sampling of the terminology used in the literature may give an indication of the lack of consistency in the field. Wagenfeld (344) sees primary prevention as taking two basic forms: (a) intervention in life crises of individuals, and (b) altering the balance of physical, social, cultural, and psychosocial forces in the community. This is close to Caplan's position (e.g. 70). He says the primary prevention of mental disorders has a long-term goal of assuring continually adequate physical, psychosocial, and socio-cultural supplies, which both enable the individual to avoid stress and which increase the individual's capacity to withstand future stress. Definitions of primary prevention sometimes tend to be quite general. For example, Zax and Cowen (374) say that virtually all that is done to improve the lot of humans should be included. Or the definition can be very abstract. Roberts (283) lists three actions as preventive: (a) the removal of the noxious agent; (b) strengthening of the host to increase its resistance to noxious agents; or (c) preventing contact between the agent and the host. Bower (54) defines primary prevention as getting children through our health, family, and school institutions "smelling like a rose." Bower (51) has outlined a detailed action-oriented framework for accomplishing primary prevention. Without attempting to deal fully with his fairly complex model, we note that he believes primary prevention can be accomplished through medical, social, and psychological actions which must occur during prenatal, perinatal, and later periods of life in those areas of the normal social milieu like the school, and in employment settings, and by professionals (such as clergy, police, teachers) in institutions affecting people in trouble. He gives many examples of normal emotional hazards for which effective knowledge of preventive intervention exists and could be brought to bear. In his context primary prevention programs are "aimed at persons not yet separated from the general population and, hopefully, an intervention specific enough to be operationally defined and measured" (51, p. 837).

Given the large number of definitions of primary prevention, we were tempted to follow a suggestion of Wagenfeld (344). He suggested a return to the terminology everyone used before Caplan confused matters—namely, to discuss prevention, treatment, and rehabilitation. Prevention here means the prevention of the occurrence of mental disorders; treatment means intervention after the onset of the disorder; and rehabilitation means trying to reverse the damage and to rebuild the systems that have been disrupted by the disorder. Primary prevention is generally applied to groups or made available to everyone. It can be anything which prevents the occurrence of disorder. (Our conflict is that we gag on the word treatment as reflecting an inappropriate medical model.)

Problems of ideology often enter into attempts at defining primary prevention. There are political, social, and ethical implications when things are done to large groups (211). Elaine Cumming (98) divides mental health preventive efforts into two main strategies: (a) finding out what causes mental illness, then removing or preventing the cause, using malaria as her example; and (b) discovering the characteristics of immune or resistant populations and then making everyone else resemble them. She was quite aware of the ideological problems that might be involved in mental health preventive efforts. She quotes Bleuler, who, in talking about prevention of schizophrenia, said "the avoidance of masturbation, of disappointments in love, of strains or frights, are recommendations which can be made with a clear conscience, because these are things to be avoided in all circumstances" (98, p. 3). Not everyone today would agree.

The platforms of political parties, the writings of political theorists from Lenin and Mao, to Lincoln and Ghandi, to DeGaulle and Buckley, all claim as their major goal the improvement of the human condition, the creation of environments that will reduce or eliminate human misery and emotional distress for large groups of people and for future generations. The writings of the utopians from Plato to Skinner promise a more rational, orderly, and satisfying life for all, or nearly all. Philosophers, theologians, economists, and humanists have in common with politicians, environmentalists, and liberationists the goal of a better and more satisfying tomorrow. Few have any published data!

During the past year we found ourselves constantly writing references and ideas on scraps of paper and emptying our pockets each day of notes on the primary prevention relevance of childrens' group homes, titanium paint, parent-effectiveness-training, consciousness raising, Zoom, Sesame Street, the guaranteed annual wage, legalized abortion, school integration, limits on international cartels, unpolished rice, free prenatal clinics, antipollution laws, a yoghurt and vegetable diet, free VD clinics, and a host of other topics. Nearly everything, it appears, has implications for primary prevention, for reducing emotional disturbance, for strengthening and fostering mental health. And anyway, as Bleuler said, they are good things in themselves.

MODELS OF DISTURBANCE

Our problem, then, is to review a vast literature having to do with the prevention of conditions which are not clearly defined, which vary in rate enormously as a function of community tolerance for deviance, which change frequencies with changing social conditions, and which may not even exist as identifiable individual defects.

What order can we bring into the bewildering variety of efforts at primary prevention? A number of alternative approaches is available.

1. We could adopt a *developmental scheme*, examining efforts aimed at different developmental stages—efforts at genetic counseling (e.g. 229), marriage counseling (332), pregnancy planning (88, 182), prenatal care (290), good obstetrical care, parental assistance and guidance (38, 80, 175, 181), well-baby clinics and early identification and intervention (e.g. 53, 97, 272), preschool programs and enrichment programs (e.g. 14, 236, 318), foster home and group home care (87), early school intervention and mental hygiene

programs in the schools (e.g. 8, 13, 14, 50, 55, 93, 94, 336, 337, 346, 356, 378), sex education and human relations groups, the variety of crisis programs available (e.g. 16, 122, 154, 189, 223, 224, 309), and so on through the life span (15, 44, 152, 157, 159, 242, 339, 347) to the plethora of proposed support programs for the aged.

2. Or we could adopt a more usual scheme which separates the field into broad areas of preventive special focus: (a) preventing organic difficulties that cause emotional distress, such as untreated syphilis, lead poisoning, endocrinological malfunctioning, and brain injury; (b) attending to the psychodynamic problems that could be prevented through "mental hygiene education" of parents, teachers, and others; and (c) dealing with social problems which affect large numbers and which can be prevented only through efforts at changing the larger social environment. Sanford (301) gives a clear and concise overview of this particular logical division of effort (63).

3. Or we could examine the separate mental "diseases" or conditions which are to be prevented with reference to programs designed specifically for each: schizophrenia (32, 171, 291, 292), alcoholism (261), manic depressive disorder (87, 316), existential neurosis (222), juvenile delinquency (134, 135, 266, 286), addiction to drugs (39, 145, 316), mental deficiency (84, 156, 195, 267, 312), and so on.

4. Or we could argue that the prevention of mental "illness" or emotional distress is just a disguised form of the old medical model —that we are really distracted by the conventional wisdom of our time, and that we should focus on the development of competence, achievement, and self-actualization, and on positive mental health (e.g. 173).

Unwilling to adopt one of these models, and without space to consider them all, we will simply draw a rough map of the swamp as we see it—pointing to quagmires, putting in danger signs, and leaving much as terra incognita in the hope that other explorers will be tempted by the lure of the unknown and mysterious.

In any discussion of the field of primary prevention of disorders it early becomes imperative to define reliably the disorders that we are striving to prevent. Programs of prevention in our area also talk about the development of positive effects, about fostering "mental health" (173). Similar questions of definition can be asked about these conditions we are attempting to foster. If we cannot define mental illness reliably, how can we prevent it? (62, 355). If there is no such thing as mental illness, if there are only problems in living (334), then it may be foolish to talk about prevention in the usual sense. If there are such things as emotional distresses and behavioral disturbances which have antecedent causes, then our task is not meaningless at all. But before we become optimistic we must consider the ethical problems of trying to prevent "problems in living."

If mental disorders are primarily organic (279, 280, 313), if they are caused by a discoverable physical defect, the strategy for reducing the number of mentally disordered people then involves public health efforts of the sort that have been so successful in reducing the incidence of other widespread diseases (112, 113, 206, 221). If we are concerned only with prevention of the conditions which fit the diagnostic nomenclature of the *Diagnostic and Statistical Manual No. 2* (10)—persons who have been labeled schizophrenic, or neurotic, or brain damaged—then the problem, while still enormous, is of a finite order of magnitude. But if we define as emotionally disturbed those additional people who are prejudiced against other people because of their religion, age, or sex, then the number of disturbed people grows dramatically and the dimensions of the effort at prevention grow apace (1, 5-7).

Bower (51) cautions us:

> *A common conception of prevention often obfuscates thinking and action, namely, that little can be accomplished short of major social overhaul. Prevention of mental and emotional disorders is seen as the exclusive result of the abolition of injustice, discrimination, economic insecurity, poverty, slums, and illness. To seek less is to attempt to fell a giant sequoia with a toy axe* (p. 833).

Different behavioral models have led to the choice of different areas of investigation. The organicists frequently look at the molecular level for their explanations of behavior. Research has established the effects of genetic factors (103, 160, 295), nutritional factors (240), damage to the various parts and levels of the central nervous system, and other organic conditions which have measurable subsequent behavioral consequences (88, 248).

There can be no socially oriented prevention without the acceptance of psychological determinism. Psychological determinism holds that all behavior is caused by antecedent interpersonal conditions and events. The scientific problem is to identify the antecedent—consequent pattern of relationships in order to be able to explain, predict, and control events (192, 225, 276, 288, 289).

Many psychologists have focused on more molar events, particularly the experiences called conditioning and learning (e.g. 259). There is no question that human behavior is changed and modified as a consequence of experience. Sometimes both of these approaches are brought together into interactional studies. For example, there seem to be critical periods in the maturation of the human organism when exposure to particular learning experiences has the most definite and the strongest effects (see 306 for bibliography). When the organism is ready it can learn, but no amount of practice before this time has much effect, and practice subsequent to the critical period (306) has less effect. Proponents of the "psychogenic hypothesis" have argued that the most critical period for the learning of emotional reactions is during infancy and early childhood. This hypothesis suggests that the formation of adult personality is very largely the consequence of the emotional conditions during the early formative critical periods. This observation is both obvious to most clinicians and difficult to prove scientifically. Clinicians tend to accept it unquestioningly, as a result of their experience, and scientists tend to question it because it is unsubstantiated by unambiguous research findings (179, 247, 280, 372).

Not all investigators accept the psychogenic hypothesis. For example, Rimland (280) says, "I predict that research will ultimately show psychosocial influences to have minor—if any—relevance in causing the limited disorders called 'neuroses' and even less relevance in causing severe disorders known as psychoses" (p. 704). Hebb (155) supports this position: "there are no data to prove that . . . there is a class of 'functional' mental illness that is produced by emotional disturbance alone." Frank (125) concluded that no factors of parent-child interaction could be found to be unique in any diagnostic groups, nor to distinguish these groups from controls (p. 191).

Much of this iconoclasm will sound strange to clinicians with the social-developmental-dynamic orientation. Every graduate student in psychology has been exposed to the "classic" works of people like Spitz (331), Goldfarb (138, 139), and Bowlby (58).

The message transmitted by these different investigators has to do with the importance of early experiences of "mothering," of the affectional ties between infant and caregiver, and of the terribly damaging later consequences of inconsistency, of placing infants in institutions and other settings where their affectional needs were not satisfied. Recently a widely quoted study by Heston (158) presented another side of the picture. Heston found that when infants who had been born to schizophrenic mothers were placed for adoption within a matter of days after birth, their subsequent rate for schizophrenia was considerably greater than the rate for a control group born to nonschizophrenic but emotionally disturbed mothers in the same institutions. Both kinds of studies have been criticized for methodological deficits and both must be viewed with some caution because, as is so often the case, the respective investigators believed they would find the results they did.

It should be noted that critics of the psychogenic hypothesis do not say that childhood experiences do not cause later problems; rather they say that the relationship has not been proved. One has the feeling that they believe organic explanations ultimately will be sufficient. If this were really true, our task would be easy, for it is in the complex area of social, cultural, and familial causation that we have our greatest confusion and complexity. In order to substantiate the "psychogenic hypothesis" it would be necessary to demonstrate with a high order of reliability a clear relationship between specific and objectively identifiable early forms of emotionally distressing experiences and subsequent behavioral disturbances. It would also be useful to show that most persons whose early experiences were free of such disturbances developed into normal adults. It would also be desirable to show that persons with exceptionally warm and supportive early experiences were, as a group, relatively successful and creative in addition to being free of pathological symptoms. Because of the enormously complicated problems of stretching a research effort over the long years between the possible cause and the later effects, clear relationships are difficult to establish with scientific precision. This difficulty is even greater than in other areas of prevention in medical epidemiology. because of the problems of definition described above.

There are a few longitudinal studies of humans, and many with animals, which seem to support conventional clinical observations. Thus, for example, Bayley (25) reports strong negative association between maternal hostility during the early years of the child's life and measured intelligence more than 30 years later, and positive association between ratings of maternal affection during the early years and intelligence in middle age (26). There are other studies which deal with various psychological and social factors in the development of mental disturbances which are relevant to the psychogenic hypothesis (20, 66, 102, 104, 119, 125, 126, 141, 161, 165, 166, 169, 170, 191, 232, 246, 251, 260, 275, 286, 306, 326, 353).

The major strategies of primary prevention depend for their relevance and effectiveness on the truth of this proposition—that early happenings have later consequences, especially that emotional damage to the child is reflected in its adult disturbance. There is no argument in the organic area. Organic damage is the easiest to measure. Lead poisoning from the ingestion of lead paint, for example, produces measurable changes in the blood and damage to the brain, with long-term consequences for the child's ability to learn and to behave normally (214). German measles during the first 3 months of pregnancy can produce irreversible retardation in the child. Chromosomal anomalies can lead to Down's Syndrome and to other structural mental diseases. Blood changes, chromosomal anomalies, disturbed reflexes, and other factors are all objective and measurable in the infant and young child. They usually are associated with conditions that bring the infant or young child to a medical setting where records are made and observations are quantified and stored (250, 251). Later investigators can go back and find these objective records and correlate them with current problems.

The situation gets much more complicated when we search for relationships between social experiences during early life and later behavior. These relationships are more difficult to establish because of the more difficult problem of measurement. In the case of psychological influences—social experiences and events—no such permanent records are likely to have been made. The ambivalent alternation of affection and rejection by the mother, the child's experience of being left frequently with a negligent baby sitter, the effects of the sudden withdrawal of love and attention at the time of arrival of a new sibling—where are these events recorded, and how are they retrieved? Three recent volumes on life history research in psychopathology go a long way toward summarizing the scattered evidence of these and related relationships (276, 288, 289).

Yet much of our clinical experience suggests the powerful long-term effects of damaging emotional experiences which have occurred early in the life of individuals. Almost inevitably the evidence is less reliable than the evidence for organic factors. In the absence of well-documented longitudinal studies with follow-up observations, we must rely on retrospective studies with all of the methodological problems they entail.

The psychogenic hypothesis seems often to elicit strong feelings of opposition from those hardnosed scientists who like to deal only with "facts" and objective measurements. The evening that Freud announced to the Viennese Neurological Society that all adult neuroses, in his experience, could be traced to early sexual trauma, the reaction of his audience was either skeptical or hostile (178). Audience reaction continues to reflect these feelings. As evidence of the weakness of the psychogenic hypothesis, the organicists point to the fact that some children from the most emotionally deprived and difficult backgrounds often grow up to be apparently well-adjusted and well-balanced adults. It is interesting in this respect to note the fact that only one person in 20 with untreated syphilis develops the mental illness we call general paresis. This low rate in no way invalidates the certainty of organic connection between syphilis and paresis.

Clearly, the "psychogenic hypothesis" held by a majority of present-day clinicians seems to have had its primary origin in the work of Freud. Everyone who has studied Freud's work is familiar with his attempts at relating adult disturbance to childhood experience. Yet Lemkau (204), making a careful search of all Freud's writings (including writing to a number of Freudian scholars) in quest of some indication of Freud's specific ideas on prophylaxis, concluded that Freud made no specific mention of the subject.

Lemkau (204) does attempt to summarize Freud's work as it relates to primary prevention with propositions such as the following. All behavior is caused, and causes may be modified in such a way that undesirable behavior is avoided. Emotional reactions follow a maturational process which is orderly and predictable and to some extent controllable. Human development involves stress, and excessive stress is unfortunate, but consequences could be prevented by the control of excessive stress; personality is markedly influenced by emotional relationships, particularly with parents; and finally, cultural factors have significant effects on the individual's adjustment. Although Freud never examined the specific implications of these relationships for prevention, a great many persons influenced by his work have attempted to apply the principles in the area of prevention (301).

Sanford (301) discusses those followers of Freud, especially his daughter Anna Freud, who have been interested in the application of psychoanalytic knowledge to prevention. The coincidence of social cataclysms (the Russian Revolution, the Great Depression) with the development of analytic theory resulted in a school of socially oriented analysts. The most notable instigator of psychological and social theories relevant to prevention was Alfred Adler. Adler (3) argued for the development through education of social responsibility (also see Ansbacher and Ansbacher 12).

But psychodynamic theories are not the only source of the psychogenic hypothesis. Darwin (75) had shattered the illusion of the fixity of the species, advancing the idea of the modifiability of every species, including the human. Clifford Beers wrote his book in 1908, and the mental hygiene movement sprang out of the ready *zeitgeist*. William James and Adolf Meyer were influenced by Beers, influenced him in turn, and helped spread the idea that "mental disease" could be prevented if the human environment was improved.

Bloom (43) quotes Meyer as follows: "Communities have to learn what they produce in the way of mental problems and waste of human opportunities, and with such knowledge they will rise from mere charity and mere mending, or hasty propaganda, to well balanced early care, prevention and general gain of health" (p. 1).

The point is that efforts at primary prevention must stress the temporal order of social cause and effect. If an effect is to be prevented, experiences that precede the phenomenon must somehow be controlled in order to prevent its occurrence. In the field of mental health, one of the major clinical hypotheses involves the long-term effect of the infant's and child's experiences on adult personality and the causation of personality disturbance. If the evidence is accepted that certain experiences in early childhood have positive or negative effects on adult functioning, then efforts at prevention should attempt to maximize the early positive experiences and minimize or eliminate the negative experiences. Evidence supporting these relationships is so voluminous as to defy sum-marization. In both infrahuman and human subjects careful re-search studies have demonstrated the power of early positive and negative experience on adult experience (note the earlier refer-ences).

Important sources of documentation of the "psychogenic hypo-thesis" have come from both human and controlled animal laboratory studies (61, 192, 199, 335, and others). The work of Harlow (153) is well known in this context. Severe and patho-logical adult behavior follows from the absence of adequate mothering of monkey infants; lack of love is permanently damaging without the restorative effect of peer group play. Such laboratory studies are difficult to duplicate in the human arena. One of the most convincing was the observation of Skeels (321-323), who documented the remarkable improvement in a group of very young children who were labeled retarded and who made dramatic and unexpected intellectual and emotional progress when "adopted" by a group of older retarded girls in an institution in Iowa. Most of these children, Skeels showed, reached a normal level of intelligence and on being placed in adoptive families grew up to be normal, healthy, emotionally stable adults in contrast to those left in institutions.

The important point is that unless the "psychogenic hypothesis" is an accurate reflection of the true state of affairs, there is no basis for efforts at primary prevention which focus on the social and emotional experiences of children. To argue that the nature and quality of early experience has little effect on the development of adult personality, and especially disturbed personality, would make unnecessary all of the elaborate attempts at protecting infants and young children from psychological damage. Orphanages and foundling homes have been replaced by more carefully designed systems of foster home placement of children. Attention to the psychological and emotional needs of children is based on repeated clinical reports of the damage done by cold and impersonal han-dling (e.g. 57, 331).

On the other hand, if we do accept the psychogenic hypothesis, then efforts at primary prevention, in addition to being concerned with prevention of organic and physical damage, must also be directed at the social and emotional experience of children. This effort will lead social scientists directly into social and political action in the attempt to shape social conditions in ways that directly or indirectly affect the security and emotional responses of parents and children.

Both approaches to primary prevention (preventing or eliminating organic damage due to defective genes, disease, toxins, and accidents, and prevention of damaging emotional experiences) ultimately lead to some interference with individual freedom. In the extreme, primary preventive efforts might be expected to lead eventually to such practices as social control of child bearing, with licenses issued only to persons genetically sound; prenatal tests which could result in therapeutic abortions; and sperm and ova banks (33). Similarly, efforts at primary prevention could ultimately lead especially to nursery and child rearing institutions where the negative effects of emotionally immature parents could be avoided.

Given a lack of coherent understanding of what it really is that we are trying to prevent, perhaps the most compelling reason for continuing the efforts of prevention is cited in Bloom's paper on the medieval miasma theory (41). Miasma theory held that soil polluted with waste products of any kind gave off a miasma into the air which caused many major diseases. Bloom goes on to say that current theories of prevention may appear to be patterned after the model first proposed by the miasmatists. In spite of the groundless basis for miasma as cause, the attempts of the sanitarians did have the effect of reducing the rate of infectious diseases. Perhaps in our current attempts at social overhaul, sweeping clean with a wide broom will be efficacious only because we may inadvertently hit the appropriate dirt.

EPIDEMIOLOGY AND ECOLOGY

It is public health dogma that no widespread human disease is ever brought under control by the treatment of afflicted individuals. Smallpox was not conquered by treating smallpox patients; neither was treatment of the individual the answer to typhoid fever, polio, or measles. Every plague afflicting humankind has been controlled when discovery of the cause led to taking effective steps to remove it. This process is primary prevention. We vaccinate all children and adults so that they will not contract smallpox. We give children polio viruses that have been killed or attenuated for the same reason, and we give them measles vaccine, and we put fluorides into their drinking water to prevent dental caries. There are at least two approaches to establishing the research base for preventive efforts in mental health. The first is to study the possible biological, psychological, and sociological factors in the origins of disorders discussed above under the headings of bio-genesis and psychogenesis. A second is to study the pattern of distribution of disturbances in the population: epidemiology.

According to Gruenberg (149), epidemiology "includes a study of the factors that determine the patterns of disease occurrence and how the factors can be modified to eliminate the disease from the population." He goes on to say:

Epidemiological analysis follows a fairly simple pattern. A factor, f, is suspected of playing a role in the production of a disease, d; populations having much more f are examined to see if they have more d than populations having little f; through inferences based on all relevant knowledge and on theories derived from clinical familiarity with the disease, the investigators obtain a picture of the chain of circumstances that leads to the occurrence of the disease; finally, crucial links in the chain are attacked experimentally. The relationships are often highly indirect and highly complicated but this general strategy has succeeded in bringing many animal and plant diseases under control. (149, p. 2)

Obviously this approach to the study of mental disorders has its problems. One is the absence of any objective means of identifying the presence of the "disease." It is relatively easy to study the epidemiology of diabetes, or bone fractures, or murder, because each provides objective data to be counted. The effectiveness of a prevention program can be measured by looking at changes in rates. But if we have no reliable way of identifying the phenomenon, the problem of measuring change becomes insurmountable (105, 114, 115). Mental illness usually involves a social judgment about behavior, a social decision to call the behavior deviant or sick. Barbara Wooten (367) has discussed this problem at some length. She says:

. . . anti-social behavior is the precipitating factor that leads to mental treatment. But at the same time the fact of the illness is

366   Marc Kessler and George W. Albee

*itself inferred from this behavior; indeed it is almost true to say
that the illness is the behavior for which it is also the excuse. But
any disease, the morbidity of which is established only by the
social failure that it involves, must rank as fundamentally different from those with which the symptoms are independent of
social norms.*

The rate of mental conditions obviously is a function not only
of the frequency of the "pathological" behavior but also of the
community's tolerance for the behavior. Thus, San Francisco has
been called "the tolerant city" because much wider ranges of
deviant behavior are tolerated by the citizenry. This would tend
to decrease the rate of reported disturbance there in comparison
with what the rate might be in other cities, except perhaps that
the tolerance may also serve to attract a wider range and larger
number of deviant persons to the more tolerant environment.

Primary prevention may demand various kinds of social action
to reduce the subsequent rate of disturbance. Paradoxically, and
perhaps only in the case of mental disorders, increasing community toleration also has the effect of reducing the rates. Sexual
behavior which is forbidden by law in certain states or countries,
and which leads to severe penalties if discovered, may well be
tolerated in other states or countries. Where homosexuality was
once punished as a monstrous deviation it now has been decrim-
inalized in parts of the world if occurring between consenting
adults. A newly formed Association of Gay Psychologists is working to increase public understanding and tolerance of this sexual
choice. A recent vote of the American Psychiatric Association has
removed homosexuality as a disease entity from the diagnostic and
statistical manual. (This is a fascinating use of democracy rather
than science in the description and definition of "disease.") Similar
changes in attitudes have occurred toward consumption of pornog-
raphy, and the result is a change in reported rates of consumption
independent of a change in the actual rate of the behavior.

One obvious way, then, to reduce the rate of mental disorders
in the population would be to change the definition of what constitutes mental disorder. We could either sharply limit the use of
the term "mental illness" to the most obviously and seriously disturbed people, or we could broaden the definition to include mild
disturbances to which everyone is subjected (268). Either change

would have immediate effects on rates and would be reflected in our epidemiological studies. Inasmuch as public attitudes about mental disorder tend to be more tolerant (S. Starr in 177) than the views of the experts, it is possible to manipulate data on rates by manipulating the groups that make the definition. It is possible to manipulate opinions about mental illness through various kinds of instruction, information, and personal contact (110, 241, 249). The extensive literature concerning both public attitudes and professional attitudes has been reviewed recently by Judith Rabkin (268).

Reviewing the earlier literature on the epidemiology of mental illness, Plunkett and Gordon (263) suggested that its value is more potential than actual. Sources of data were examined and found wanting. The inability of the field of psychiatry to develop a meaningful and reliable classification system was identified as a major problem. Plunkett and Gordon set forth a preliminary research plan for well-controlled field experiments to identify and codify causal factors in such problems as suicide, alcoholism, postpartum psychoses, and psychosomatic disturbances. Because each of these conditions offers some hope for objective, reliable identification, their distribution in the population might be measured as a first step toward discovering causal factors. But these authors, both experienced epidemiologists, were less than sanguine about our chances for the meaningful study of the other so-called mental illnesses.

In any attempt to weigh the success of efforts at primary prevention, one is faced with examining programs that are aimed at conditions of uncertain identification, and of unknown distribution, in an area where objectivity is lacking or may be unobtainable (e.g. 115, 116).

In spite of the difficulties involved in the epidemiological approach in this area, a number of studies have been conducted. Gruenberg (149, 150), Hollingshead and Redlich (162), Langner and Srole (197-199, 333), Leighton (200), Pasamanick (257), and Zusman (381) have all reported epidemiological data on general populations. An excellent review and critique of problems in this field is by Miller and Mishler (232).

Epidemiology has also been applied to such specialized populations as elementary school children (83, 127, 133), native Americans on reservations (315, 316), and of course to those afflicted with many specific disorders. An excellent example of the latter is the work of Calahan (65) on alcoholics.

One of the earliest epidemiological studies of mental disturbances and mental retardation was the "Jarvis Report"—the *Report of the Commission on Lunacy and Idiocy in Massachusetts, 1855* (174). In this classic study Jarvis was convinced by his data of the intimate relationship between pauperism and insanity. Clearly there were more insane persons among the poor, and especially among those who were paupers. One hundred years later Ryan (297) reported high rates of untreated or neglected disturbance among the poor. Multiproblem families, together with the children of the poor, and the elderly had the highest rates of disturbance. Most of the recent epidemiological research reports the same finding (e.g. 104, 126, 162, 167-170, 228, 232, 277, 348, 370).

The critical problem is "attribution of cause." Does poverty cause in a direct or indirect way the high rate of mental disturbance among the poor? Does poverty cause high rates of crime, alcoholism, drug addiction, and related indices of social pathology? Or perhaps both poverty and various forms of pathological behavior might be due to some common underlying defect. Jarvis (and more recent conservatives) hold the latter view. Jarvis saw poverty as

An inward principle, enrooted deeply within the man, and running through all his elements . . . and hence we find that, among those whom the world calls poor, there is less vital force, a lower tone of life, more ill health, more weakness, more early death, a diminished longevity. There is also less self respect, more idiocy and insanity and more crime than in the independent.

These "diseases" of poverty and lunacy were traceable to an "imperfectly organized brain and feeble mental constitution" (114, pp. 45, 52-56). It is instructive to remember that the foreign insane paupers whom Jarvis considered defective were the immigrant Irish, whose descendants have long since disappeared into middle class respectability and whose rates of mental disturbance have dropped dramatically in the intervening century. It is instructive also to note that each succeeding wave of immigrants to the inner city—the Scandinavians, the eastern European Jews, the southern Italians, and most recently the Chicanos, Puerto

Ricans, and blacks–have taken their place among the Class Five poor and have shown high rates of social pathology during the time that they occupy the low rung on the social ladder. It seems reasonable to argue that if both poverty and a high rate of social pathology were due to some common defect, genetic or constitutional, the rates for these groups would not decline precipitously as they achieve economic security. Such evidence is difficult to document statistically, but circumstantially at least we would argue that the predominant weight of evidence supports the position that poverty causes social disability rather than both being a result of some inherent common defect (298, 299).

Much of this literature has been reviewed recently by Elizabeth Taylor Vance (343). She surveys the widespread efforts in conceptualizing the dimension *social competence–social disability*, which she sees as the major continuum for a wide variety of such syndromes as process schizophrenia, antisocial behavior, and cognitive deficit. In her thorough review she suggests that "there is much evidence to suggest that the extrinsic conditions in contemporary life that seem most conducive to the development of syndromes of social disability converge in the environmental correlates of urban poverty. Social disability would appear to be a dynamic and organic outcome of such conditions" (p. 508).

The clear implication is that individual therapy will be helpless to break the cycle. Rather, "the traditional activities of the clinician must be modified in the direction of greater involvement in the developmental, environmental and social context of the individual. On the other hand, an intimate knowledge and conceptualization of human behavior and development should guide the shaping of community psychology activity" (p. 508).

In this regard, primary prevention of mental disorders is frequently claimed as "belonging" to community psychology, a new applied specialty field.

Many persons date the beginning of community psychology with the Boston (Swampscott) Conference of 1965 (34). There, a group of persons dissatisfied with the traditional and reactive role of clinical psychology invented or appropriated the term "community psychology" to designate a new specialty more interested in prevention than in psychotherapy and rehabilitation. Community psychology deals with social systems, programmed interventions, and the planning of environments. It aims at enhancing human competency and adheres to an ecological rather than a psycho-analytic model.

Cowen (92), in his *Annual Review* article on community psychology in 1973, suggested that attempts at splitting review articles in this field into (a) intervention in psychopathology and (b) prevention of mental disorders, leads to all kinds of conceptual difficulties. He suggested that eventually community intervention chapters might begin to fuse with prevention chapters. Searching through all the articles in the *Community Mental Health Journal* that dealt with "prevention," "preventing," or "prevent" he was frustrated to find that only some 3 percent dealt with these topics. In his search of the *Coordinate Index Reference Guide to Community Mental Health* (136) he found only 2 percent of the references classified under "primary prevention." He came to the disheartening conclusion that the social-community intervention area has largely ignored primary prevention and has failed to develop a research base.

Ecological variables recently have come to be seen as possible contributing factors in the development of mental disorder (63, 107, 108, 128). Epidemiologists have long appreciated the complexity of ecological systems producing health and disease. Their insights are applicable to some rather serious mental disturbances which may not be diseases at all but conditions which are a result of complex ecological systems. A characteristic of ecological systems is that disturbance in one place at one time may set off a complex chain of events leading to consequences only dimly and distantly perceived. Thus the spraying of orchards in Minnesota with biocides may affect the oyster beds in Louisiana, with long-range consequences to the health of children eating oysters from these beds. Many years later a senator from Louisiana may die of a coronary, partly because of damage done by her childhood eating habits and food intake. But the chain is not so simple and direct. The prosperity of the Minnesota apple growers may have stimulated the production of beef in Iowa, making pork cheaper in Louisiana during the young adulthood of the coronary victim . . . and so on and on. Similar complex chains certainly exist in the mental health field so that we should not be surprised to discover that only relatively modest research efforts have been made, and great controversy and disagreement exist, to tease out cause and effect relationships. Three recent volumes on life history research examine some of these research questions (276, 288, 289; see also 59, 60).

In the complex "web of causation" is entangled a swarm of effects. Married persons in general have a smaller chance of developing a mental disturbance than single persons. Elderly persons who are living with a spouse have a strikingly lower rate of hospitalization for mental conditions than solitary elderly folk (172). Children from intact families have lower rates than children from broken homes (254-256, 286). Even more complex societal variables enter into the web of causation. Persons living in preindustrial societies reportedly are rarely affected with manic depressive psychosis (235, 360), nor are they subject to the classical Victorian neuroses that Freud spent his life studying. The sexually repressed Victorians, on the other hand, developed high rates of depression and symptom neurosis when as children they were taught to inhibit sexual thoughts, feelings, and behavior in order to struggle upward into the middle class, taking the route of either education or capital accumulation. In the old industrial societies like England and the United States the symptom neuroses are declining in frequency, but there is a dramatic rise in existential anxiety and the existential neurosis (Who am I? What is the purpose of my existence? What does it all mean?).

Actually a number of social changes that have been adopted without consideration of their ultimate benefits in preventing mental disturbance may prove to have significant mental health implications. The discovery and widespread use of controlled methods of contraception should reduce the number of unwanted children. As these children often experience rejection and a resulting emotional deprivation that leads to behavioral disturbances, reducing their number should reduce disturbance rates. The widespread use of compulsory seat belts in automobiles and the development of other safety devices, including padded dashboards and inflation devices, should reduce significantly the number of brain injuries suffered in auto accidents, with the resulting prevention of mental disorders associated with laceration and trauma to the brain. Reducing the amount of carbon monoxide and lead in the air our city children breathe should also have the effect of reducing the amount of cellular damage to the central nervous system and its consequences.

One recent review (76) of ecological stress examined a whole range of genuine environmental stresses—radiation, laser beams, insecticides, noise pollution, air pollution, temperature extremes, driving problems, and overcrowding (31, 36, 85, 194, 245, 359, 362). These all have been shown to affect mental health in some way, and therefore their distribution and control should concern those in primary prevention.

We do not know enough yet about all the possible effects of these and other contaminants, but the evidence that does exist suggests unfortunate behavioral consequences on animals and children. Unhappily, Dubos (107-109) has pointed out that the worst of the environment pollution contaminants are still to come. He cites English studies that demonstrate an apparently permanent malfunctioning of children reared under high pollution conditions.

Psychologists have been interested in the study of stress for many years. Now, the last decade has seen an increased concern with an ecological approach that examines the complexities of interacting factors in the environment inducing stress in the individual and thereby affecting mental health (141). Primary prevention in the mental health field ordinarily connotes prevention of psychological problems. But a voluminous body of evidence also indicates that the stresses of complex societies lead to disorders labeled *psychosomatic.* For example, a spate of recent books examines the relationship between life stress and coronary heart disease. The literature on stress inducing hypertension, duodenal ulcers, and other physical symptoms is enormous and obviously beyond the space limits of this chapter (87, 117, 230, 253, 269, 357, 364, 374).

The new approach to the impact of environmental factors on the development of mental disorders opens yet another alleyway in the maze of factors that must be studied and accounted for in attempting to organize the field of primary prevention. For those interested in pursuing further studies we can suggest the references cited above, as well as the National Institute of Mental Health's *Bibliography: Epidemiology of Mental Disorders: 1966-1968* (381), which lists some 170 titles concerning the design and implementation of studies, over 500 articles on the etiology of mental disease, close to 400 on rates, and about 250 on the characteristics of "diseased populations." (See also 60, 101, 141, 361.)

PRIMARY PREVENTION PROGRAMS

The social-developmental psychological hypothesis concerning the origins of mental disorders has led to many programs and proposals that have as their focus either broad or specific disorders. The programs range all the way from the general education programs of the mental hygiene movement that started with the work of Adolf Meyer and Clifford Beers to more specific programs of early intervention cited, for example, by Bower, Rolf, Zax and Cowen, Kelly, and Garmezy (56, 130, 185, 291, 338, 376). The question that we must address briefly is how primary preventive efforts are to take place. Knowing as much or as little as we do, what is to be done? The National Association for Mental Health (238) has prepared one of the most specific blueprints for action in primary prevention. It gives actual steps to be taken by citizens' groups in their community to achieve prevention of later emotional disturbance. The NAMH proposal focuses specifically on prenatal and perinatal conditions as areas where definite action should be taken. The time from conception to 6 months after birth was chosen as the action period. Among the actions recommended are prenatal and perinatal care affecting the expecting mother and the developing fetus, ways of coping with life crisis situations affecting the mother particularly, the development of better parenting skills, the modification of the social system that may be expected to be a source of stress if unmodified (welfare, medical care, day care), and the insurance of adequate medical care for mother and infant following birth.

There is no dearth of other suggestions concerning how primary preventive programs should be carried out (202, 226, 338). Caplan (73), for example, discusses those preventive programs that focus on strengthening physical and social resources: efforts to prevent prematurity; providing appropriate nutrition to children with a genetic metabolic defect such as phenylketonuria; requiring iodized salt in areas where iodine supplies may be inadequate; preventing psychosis due to pellagra; acting to prevent lead poisoning in slum children; providing opportunities for cognitive enrichment for preschool children through the educational system. Caplan goes on to examine other psychosocial resources and suggests that efforts should be directed to maintaining a healthy family environment; to special intervention at the illness, hospitalization, or death of the mother; to providing homemaker services when needed and in-hospital care by the mother when the child is hospitalized. He also suggests applying crisis intervention as a preventive effort, as well as education of caregivers, mental health consultation, and personal preparation for healthy crisis coping through education and anticipatory guidance (see also 24, 30, 68, 217, 369, 371).

Bloom (43) suggested three action tactics: crisis intervention; anticipatory guidance, including, for example, meetings between clergymen and engaged parishioners or between social workers and groups of new parents; and consultation. Eisenberg (111) called for preventive programs to include family planning, good health care and decent housing, adequate unemployment compensation and job training for displaced workers, case work service to minimize family breakdown, effective substitute care for homeless children, enriched school programs, recreational facilities, vocational training, and other services.

The National Institute of Mental Health (239, 241, 243, 244) has proposed a program of mental health prevention which is educational rather than clinical in conception, with a goal to increase the individual's capacity for improving the quality of his life. It calls for a developmental approach, including efforts to improve early child development and to increase parental competence, then focusing on mental health aspects of public school education and on adolescence. It also considers special needs of high risk groups, including high risk pregnancies requiring better prenatal care. Socialization training, development of competence, and improved self-esteem are included in the plan.

Kelly (184, 185) talks of three types of therapeutic programs. (a) The clinical approach focuses on changes in individuals or small groups; it radiates its effects to others as one of the indirect results of the services offered. (b) Systematic changes in organizations are aimed at helping the organizations deal with future crises. (c) Community organization techniques focus on mobilizing community resources for community action. Kelly gives examples of each of these approaches.

Poser (265) suggests an approach to prevention based on the principles of learning. He suggests that mechanisms involving remedial learning techniques such as desensitization, flooding, and aversive conditioning be used to immunize subjects against later encounters with crisis. He suggests that primary prevention might best be achieved by the deliberate exposure of susceptible high risk individuals to learning experiences that are spontaneously encountered by most normal individuals.

Smith (327) suggests that a real attempt should be made to identify those inevitable crisis or life stress events viewed as critical to the mental health of individuals. Then we should help or teach the individuals to deal effectively with those crises. Early intervention at the school or preschool level is really geared toward the prevention of disorders which occur later in life: ten, fifteen, even twenty years after the time of the intervention. Evaluative programs should engage in long-term follow-up to ascertain the effectiveness of the program study. Unfortunately, this kind of long-term follow-up has not been characteristic of most studies in the mental health field. Exceptions are the Berkeley Growth Studies (25, 26), Project Talent, and the studies cited in Rolf et al. (276, 288, 289). Future preventive approaches to mental disorder must provide the necessary long-term funding for follow-up measures.

The above are just a sample of the discussion in the literature of general strategies for the prevention of mental disorders. What about more specific programs? We will mention some representative current approaches to the prevention of mental disorders, without attempting to evaluate the adequacy of these approaches.

PROGRAMS

The aim of preventive techniques in social planning is to use the social system to strengthen adaptive behaviors. Preventive approaches have been attempting to use major components of the social system, including the family, the schools, the world of work, and the community.

There have been a number of fairly specific targets for preventive efforts. The family, for example, has been a focus through attempts at parental education, early family intervention as preschool intellectual training (e.g. 21, 47, 78, 80, 120, 272, 284, 319, 320), work on training parents as therapists (e.g. 305), programs in the school (49, 52, 90, 91, 93, 94, 96, 97, 144, 304), such programs in compensatory education as the Headstart Program, and the special programs for low-income and minority groups (81, 82, 86,

90, 181, 189, 258, 278, 304, 381) and for the community (2, 9, 27, 35, 118, 121, 148, 164, 183, 189, 190, 212, 218, 237, 264, 281, 311, 328, 349, 352, 354).

One major focus for attempts at intervention and prevention is children at an early age. This area has been given special attention in the recent past. Both the Group for the Advancement of Psychiatry (147) and the Joint Commission on the Mental Health of Children (176) have focused on this important area and have pointed to the serious lack of mental health programs for childdren, not only primary but also secondary and tertiary programs. There are a number of current programs aimed at children (4, 17, 37, 40, 61, 74, 129, 142, 175, 181, 193, 272, 307, 317, 318, 340, 345, 351); Bolman reviews a number of them (46).

The important role of the school in preventing mental disorders and promoting competence has been discussed for a number of years (61, 163, 176, 177). There is a growing number of programs in school settings to develop the competencies of school children and to prevent the educational and learning difficulties that can lead to further emotional and social maladjustment. It is noteworthy that some of the programs are in the main geared not toward the prevention or amelioration of emotional disorders but, in many instances, toward developing competence in the individuals. Many authors feel these are interdependent (13, 72, 89-97, 132, 144, 180, 216, 300, 373, 375, 376).

Bolman has reviewed programs for the family and general programs (47, 48). Other program reports include those by Rees (271), Robertson (284), Ryan (296), Skeels and Skodak (321-324), and Slobin (325). There is some question whether crisis intervention and suicide prevention is primary or secondary prevention. Rather than go into a detailed review of these areas we list a number of references for those who are interested (18, 19, 100, 122, 154, 189, 208-210, 223, 233, 285, 309, 310, 314, 315, 350, 363).

A major question to be addressed concerns the efficacy of primary preventive programs. Do they work? Much has been written about the evaluation of primary preventive efforts (42, 123, 130, 207, 231, 234, 252, 287, 288, 291, 308), and these references should be consulted for detailed information concerning evaluation research. The work of Campbell and Stanley (67) stands out as one of the definitive studies in the field of evaluative research. It takes into account the realistic constraints that are found in doing action-oriented research in a number of fields, and its guidance is quite applicable to the field of primary prevention.[2]

SUMMARY AND CONCLUSIONS

Primary prevention in many areas may require social and political changes to improve the quality of life (302). Bower and others suggest that a lack of progress in the area of prevention may be traced to specific social resistance to the changes that would be required to actually make a difference. A major source of resistance is to the idea that real prevention must make major social system changes. It is true that many observers of our social pathology argue that patchwork solutions will not do, and that the whole structure of our polluted, industrialized, overpopulated, overenergized, overcrowded sexist and racist society breeds such massive human injustice and distress that the only hope for prevention is for major social reorganization. To prevent mental and emotional disorders, it is argued, we must abolish such injustices as unemployment, bad housing, social discrimination, personal insecurity, and poverty. As a consequence of the threat all of this holds to the status quo, the Establishment does little to encourage or support efforts at primary prevention in the social sphere because it believes (with some justification) that it would be funding programs aimed at a major redistribution of its power. Money is generally available for biomedical research on the search for the individual defect, but social programs are more often suspect (6, 186, 187).

2. Since completing this chapter, we have seen additional reviews of the field of primary prevention which cover the subject, or parts of it, in much greater detail than we have been able to do in the space available to us. The interested reader is referred to these publications: (a) R. F. Muñoz and J. G. Kelly, The prevention of mental disorders, in C. Cofer, ed., *Programmed Learning Aid Series*, Richard Irwin Co. (in press); (b) J. Monahan, The prevention of violence, in J. Monahan, ed., *Community Mental Health and the Criminal Justice System*, New York, Pergamon, 1974; and (c) A. Binder, J. Monahan, and M. Newkirk, Diversion from the juvenile justice system and the prevention of delinquency, in the volume cited in (b).

A second force operating to resist efforts at primary prevention is our societal commitment to privacy and to personal freedom of choice, "the right and privilege of each person, and family, in a free society to mind his own business and have others mind theirs" (51). Even such relatively simple matters as the fluoridization of the water supply and the requirement of vaccination against polio and smallpox—clear as is the research evidence which supports these practices—elicit widespread resistance and public debate. To urge even more drastic invasions of privacy, to propose the more emotion-laden kinds of intervention believed by many to have profound preventive implications for mental health, is to call out even more violent resistance. Sex education, growth groups, consciousness raising, parent effectiveness training, and day care are programs that make many members of our society tremble with anger (64).

Society is ambivalent enough about requiring people whose behavior is already disturbed to undergo compulsory therapeutic procedures. Profound philosophic questions are involved in programs like behavioral modification aimed at improving the mental functioning. But society is highly ambivalent about utilizing some of these same techniques to intervene in the lives of individuals, especially children, who have not yet shown any kind of behavioral disturbance. Even when the approach is to prevent the development of later antisocial behaviors, as the implications in the work of the Gluecks (134, 135), for example, there is a great deal of concern over the rights of individuals to be let alone.

We assume that both childhood experiences and societal rules are important determinants of later behavioral adjustment or disturbance. It has been noted that two of the most important activities engaged in by members of our society legally require no training or demonstrated ability—that of governing and that of raising children—and that any laws proposed in either area would be quickly rejected as a serious curtailment of freedom.

The explanatory models we use to account for mental disorder have profound implication for choosing our strategies for primary prevention. Most true diseases can be brought under control with relatively little disturbance to the existing social order. These are the familiar public health methods. The requirement of vaccination against smallpox implies some degree of coercion; the treatment of public water supplies with antibacterial agents to prevent disease, and with fluorides to prevent tooth decay, are public health measures adopted without the individual consent of the people affected. Most rational observers would agree that such preventive measures involve little threat to the social order. It is when we get to efforts at preventing mental disorder and emotional distress that real ethical problems begin to appear. To get really involved in primary prevention of emotional disturbance often suggests social and political change quite far removed from the conventional conservatism characteristic of middle class professionals. Here is another interesting paradox. Those persons most likely to understand the relationship between social problems like poverty, unemployment, discrimination, and prejudice and resulting high rates of mental disorder and distress, are members of the professions who work most closely with these "mental cases." Yet members of professions —in large measure because of the nature of their professional training—are selected to be relatively conscience-laden, upwardly mobile, politically conservative-to-liberal, but certainly not revolutionary, social change agents. In addition, they tend to be the most informed and therefore the most logical ones to be concerned about individuals' rights. Too often they remain silent.

We can say with Bloom (41) that the most compelling reason for continuing efforts at prevention is suggested by the success of the miasmatists. Cleaning up the waste turned out to be the way to prevent disease. Elements of the theory were wrong but the results were right.

It is tempting to search for a simple formula to cover all of the complexities of environmental stress causing disruptive behavior and emotional problems. It is tempting to suggest an extension to the human environment of Lord Acton's (23) dictum: "Power tends to corrupt—absolute power corrupts absolutely." Everywhere we looked, every social research study we examined, suggested that major sources of human stress and distress generally involve some form of excessive power. The pollutants of a power-consuming industrial society; the exploitation of the weak by the powerful; the overdependence of the automotive culture on powerful engines (power-consuming symbols of potency); the degradation of the environment with the debris of a comfort-loving impulse-yielding society; the power struggle between the rich consuming nations and the exploited third world; the angry retaliation of the impoverished and the exploited; on a more personal level the exploitation of women by men, of children by adults, of the elderly by a youth-worshiping society—it is enough to suggest the hypothesis that a dramatic reduction and control of power might improve the mental health of people. It is a tempting oversimplification, a hypothesis we will not propose seriously, but one that we recommend for quiet contemplation. We have found it particularly satisfying under relaxed environmental conditions—in a rowboat on a quiet Vermont lake on a sleepy summer day just before the fish begin to bite.

References

1. Abell, P., McNeil, E., and Powell, B. Prejudice and the helping relationship: One method for increasing awareness. *American Journal of Orthopsychiatry*, 1973, *43*, 254.
2. Aberle, D. F. Introducing preventive psychiatry into a community. *Human Organization*, 1950, *9*, 5–9.
3. Adler, A. *The education of children*. New York: Greenberg, 1930.
4. Ahmad, M., and Simmons, E. A comprehensive child guidance service (an initial survey of North Wales Child Guidance Clinics). *Acta Paedopsychiatrica*, 1972, *39*, 92–98.
5. Albee, G. W. Emerging concepts of mental illness and models of treatment: The psychological point of view. *American Journal of Psychiatry*, 1969, *125*, 870–876.
6. Albee, G. W. Who shall be served? *Professional Psychology*, 1969, *1*, 4–7.
7. Albee, G. W. The uncertain future of clinical psychology. *American Psychologist*, 1970, *25*, 1071–1080.
8. Allinsmith, W., and Goethals, G. W. *The role of schools in mental health*. New York: Basic Books, 1962.
9. Altrocchi, J., and Eisdorfer, C. Apprentice-collaborator field training in community psychology: The Halifax County program. In I. Iscoe and C. C. Spielberger (Eds.), *Community psychology: Perspectives in training and research*. New York: Appleton-Century-Crofts, 1970.
10. American Psychiatric Association. *Diagnostic and statistical manual of mental disorders*. Washington, D.C.: APA, 1969.
11. American Public Health Association, Program Area Committee on Mental Health. *Mental disorders: A guide to control methods*. New York: American Public Health Association, 1962.
12. Ansbacher, H. L., and Ansbacher, R. R. (Eds.). *The individual psychology of Alfred Adler*. New York: Basic Books, 1956.
13. Anthony, E. J. Primary prevention with school children. See Ref. 22, 1971, 131–158.

14. Arnold, R., Perlman, M., McQueeney, D., and Gordan, D. Nature of mental health consultation to preschool problems. *American Journal of Orthopsychiatry*, 1973, *43*, 220.
15. Ashman, G. R., Dowles, W. E., Ron, W. D., and Agranoff, B. Case finding and interviewing methods for a preventive occupational psychiatry programme. *Proceedings of the Third World Conference on Psychiatry*. Toronto: Toronto University Press, 1963.
16. Augenbaum, R. J., and Augenbaum, F. D. Brief intervention as a preventive force in disorders of early childhood. *American Journal of Orthopsychiatry*, 1967, *37*, 697–702.
17. Baer, C. J. The school of progress and adjustment of underage and overage students. *Journal of Educational Psychology*, 1958, *49*, 17–19.
18. Bagley, C. Evaluation of a suicide prevention scheme by an ecological method. *Social Science and Medicine*, 1968, *2*, 1–14.
19. Bagley, C. An evaluation of agencies concerned with the prevention of suicidal behaviors. *Life Threatening Behavior*, 1971, *1*, 33–50.
20. Bandura, A., and Walters, R. H. *Social learning and personality development*. New York: Holt, Rinehart and Winston, 1963.
21. Bard, M., and Berkowitz, B. Training police as specialists in family crisis intervention: A community psychology action program. *Community Mental Health Journal*, 1967, *3*, 315–317.
22. Barten, H. H., and Bellak, L. (Eds.), *Progress in community mental health*, Vol. 2. New York: Grune and Stratton, 1972.
23. Bartlett, J. *Familiar quotations: A collection of passages, phrases, and proverbs traced to their sources, in ancient and modern literature*, 663. Boston: Little, Brown (13th ed.), 1955.
24. Barton, D., and Abram, H. S. Preventive psychiatry in the general hospital. *Comprehensive Psychiatry*, 1971, *12*, 330–336.
25. Bayley, N. Behavioral correlates of mental growth: birth to 36 years. *American Psychologist*, 1968, *23*, 1–17.
26. Bayley, N., and Shaefer, E. S. Correlation of maternal and child behaviors with the development of mental abilities. *Monographs of the Society for Research on Child Development*, 1964, *29*, 97.
27. Becker, R. E. The organization and management of community mental health services. *Community Mental Health Journal*, 1972, *8*, 292–302.
28. Beier, E. G. Preventive measures in the mental health area: Some theoretical considerations on justification and a fantasy about the future. In C. Frederich (Ed.), *Future of psychotherapy*. Boston: Little, Brown, 1969.
29. Beiser, M. Primary prevention of mental illness: general vs. specific approaches. See Ref. 282, 1968, 84–91.
30. Belknap, I. *Human problems of State mental health hospitals*. New York: McGraw Hill, 1965.
31. Bell, G., and MacGreevey, P. *Behavior and environment: A bibliography of social activities in urban space*. University of Pittsburgh Department of Urban Affairs, 1969.

32. Bellak, L. (Ed.) *Schizophrenia: A review of the syndrome.* New York: Logos, 1958.
33. Bellak, L. *Handbook of community psychiatry and community mental health.* New York: Grune and Stratton, 1964.
34. Bennett, C. C. et al. (Eds.) *Community psychology: A report of the Boston Conference on the Education of Psychologists for Community Mental Health.* Boston University Press, 1966
35. Bennett, W. H. *Community Mental Health Services based on established health unit offices.* Pilot project report from the Muskoka-Parry Sound Health Unit. Ontario Ministry of Health Meeting with Medical Officers of Health, Toronto, 1972.
36. Beranek, L. L. Noise. *Scientific American*, 1966, *215*, 66–76.
37. Berlin, I. N. Prevention of mental and emotional disorders of childhood. See Ref. 366, 1972, 1088–1109.
38. Berlin, I. N., and Berlin, R. Parents' role in education as primary prevention. *American Journal of Orthopsychiatry*, 1973, *63*, 221.
39. Bernstein, A., Epstein, L. J., Lennard, H. R., and Ransom, D. C. The prevention of drug abuse. See Ref. 137, 1972, 439–47.
40. Birch, H. G., and Gussow, J. D. *Disadvantaged children: Health, nutrition and school failure.* New York: Harcourt, 1970.
41. Bloom, B. L. The "medical model," miasma theory, and community mental health. *Community Mental Health Journal*, 1965, *1*, 333–338.
42. Bloom, B. L. The evaluation of primary prevention programs. See Ref. 281, 1968, 117–35.
43. Bloom, B. L. Strategies for the prevention of mental disorders. See Ref. 283, 1971, 1–20.
44. Bloom, B. L. A university freshman preventive intervention program: report of a pilot project. *Journal of Consulting and Clinical Psychology*, 1971, *37*, 235–242.
45. Blostein, S. Prevention in mental health: selected annotated bibliography. *Canadian Mental Health*, 1969, *17*, Suppl.
46. Bolman, W. M. An outline of preventive psychiatric programs for children. *Archives of General Psychiatry*, 1967, *17*, 5–8.
47. Bolman, W. M. Preventive psychiatry for the family: theory, approaches and programs. *American Journal of Psychiatry*, 1968, *125*, 458–472.
48. Bolman, W. M., and Westman, J. C. Prevention of mental disorder: An overview of current programs. *American Journal of Psychiatry*, 1967, *123*, 1058–1068.
49. Bower, E. M. Primary prevention in a school setting. See Ref. 69, 1961, 353–77.
50. Bower, E. M. The modification, mediation and utilization of stress during the school years. *American Journal of Orthopsychiatry*, 1964, *34*, 667-674.
51. Bower, E. M. Primary prevention of mental and emotional disorders. A conceptual framework and action possibilities. See Ref. 196, 1965, 1–9.
52. Bower, E. M. Preventive services for children. In B. L. Bloom and D. P. Buck (Eds.), *Preventive services in mental health programs.* Boulder, Colo.: Wiche, 1967.

53. Bower, E. M. *Early identification of emotionally handicapped children in school.* Springfield, Ill.: Thomas, 1969.
54. Bower, E. M. Slicing the mystique of prevention with Occam's razor. *American Journal of Public Health,* 1969, *59,* 478–484.
55. Bower, E. M. K.I.S.S. and Kids: A mandate for prevention. *American Journal of Orthopsychiatry,* 1972, *42,* 556–565.
56. Bower, E. M. Primary prevention of mental and emotional disorders. *American Journal of Orthopsychiatry,* 1963, *33,* 832–848.
57. Bower, E. M., Shellhamer, T. A., and Dailey, J. M. School characteristics of male adolescents who later became schizophrenic. *American Journal of Orthopsychiatry,* 1960, *30,* 712–729.
58. Bowlby, J., and Ainsworth, M. *Maternal care and mental health.* World Health Organization. Geneva: Penguin, 1964.
59. Brown, G. W., Harris, T. O., and Peto, J. Life events and psychiatric disorders. Part 2: nature of causal link. *Psychological Medicine,* 1973, *3,* 159–176.
60. Brown, G. W., Sklair, F., Harris, T. O., and Birley, J. L. T. Life events and psychiatric disorders. Part 1: Some methodological issues. *Psychological Medicine,* 1973, *3,* 74–87.
61. Brownbridge, R., and Van Vleet, P. (Eds.) *Investment in prevention: The prevention of learning and behavior problems in young children.* San Francisco: Pace I.D. Center, 1969.
62. Buell, B. Is prevention possible? *Lindemann Memorial Lecture.* National Conference on Social Welfare. New York: Community Research Association, 1969.
63. Byers, R. K. Lead poisoning: review of the literature and report on 45 cases. *Pediatrics,* 1959, *23,* 585–603.
64. Cain, A. The perils of prevention. *American Journal of Orthopsychiatry,* 1967, *37,* 640–642.
65. Cahalan, D. *Problem drinkers.* San Francisco: Jossey-Bass, 1970.
66. Calhoun, J. B. Population density and social pathology. *Scientific American,* 1962, *206,* 139–148.
67. Campbell, D. T., and Stanley, J. C. *Experimental and quasi-experimental designs for research.* Chicago: Rand McNally, 1966.
68. Caplan, G. Practical steps for the family physician in the prevention of emotional disorders. *Journal of the American Medical Association,* 1959, *170,* 1497–1506.
69. Caplan, G. *Prevention of mental disorders in children.* New York: Basic Books, 1961.
70. Caplan, G. Opportunities for school psychologists in the primary prevention of mental disorders in children. *Mental Hygiene,* 1963, *47,* 525–539.
71. Caplan, G. *Principles of preventive psychiatry.* New York: Basic Books, 1964.
72. Caplan, G. The role of pediatricians in community mental health (with particular reference to primary prevention of mental disorders in children). See Ref. 33, 1964, 287–99.

73. Caplan, G., and Grunebaum, H. Perspectives on primary prevention: a review. *Archives of General Psychiatry*, 1967, *17*, 331–346.
74. Caplan, G., and Lebovici, S. (Eds.) *Adolescence: Psychosocial perspectives.* New York: Basic Books, 1969.
75. Caplan, R. *Psychiatry in the community in 19th century America.* New York: Basic Books, 1969.
76. Carson, D. H., and Driver, B. L. A summary of an ecological approach to environmental stress. *American Behavioral Scientist*, 1966, *10*, 8–11.
77. Carter, J. W. (Ed.) *Research contribution from psychology to community mental health.* New York: Behavioral Publications, 1968.
78. Cary, A., and Reveal, M. Prevention and detection of emotional disturbances in preschool children. *American Journal of Orthopsychiatry*, 1967, *37*, 719–724.
79. Chalke, F. C. R., and Day, J. J. (Eds.) *Primary prevention of psychiatric disorders.* Toronto: University of Toronto Press, 1968.
80. Charny, I. Parental intervention with one another on behalf of their child: a breakthrough tool in preventing emotional disturbance. *Journal of Contemporary Psychotherapy*, 1972, *5*, 19 ff.
81. Christmas, J. J. Sociopsychiatric rehabilitation in a black urban ghetto. 1. Conflicts, issues and directions. *American Journal of Orthopsychiatry*, 1969, *39*, 651–661.
82. Christmas, J. J. Philosophy and practice of socio-psychiatric rehabilitation in economically deprived areas. See Ref. 22, 1972, 159–74.
83. Clarfield, S. An analysis of referral problems and their relation to intervention goals in a school based preventive mental health program. *Dissertation Abstracts International*, 1973, *33*, 6072.
84. Clarke, A. D. B. Prevention of subculture subnormality: problems and prospects. *British Journal of Subnormality*, 1973, *19*, 7–20.
85. Cohen, A. *Noise and psychological state.* National Center for Urban Industrial Health, U.S. Public Health Service, Cincinnati, Ohio, 1968.
86. Cohen, R. E. Principles of preventive mental health programs for ethnic minority populations: the acculturation of Puerto Ricans to the United States. *American Journal of Psychiatry*, 1972, *128*, 1529–1533.
87. Coleman, J. C., and Broen, W. E. *Abnormal psychology and modern life.* (4th Ed.) Glenview, Ill.: Scott Foresman, 1972.
88. Colman, A. D., and Colman, L. L. *Pregnancy—The psychological experience.* New York: Heider and Heider, 1971.
89. Committee on Preventive Psychiatry of the Group for the Advancement of Psychiatry. *Promotion of mental health in the primary and secondary schools: An evaluation of four projects.* Topeka, Kans.: Group for the Advancement of Psychiatry, 1951.
90. Cowen, E. L. Emergent approaches to mental health problems. An overview and directions for future work. See Ref. 96, 1967, 389–455.
91. Cowen, E. L. Mothers in the classroom. *Psychology Today*, 1969, *2*, 36–39.
92. Cowen, E. L. Social and community interventions. *Annual Review of Psychology*, 1973, *24*, 423–472.

93. Cowen, et al. A preventive mental health program in the school setting: description and evaluation. *Journal of Psychology*, 1963, *56*, 307-356.
94. Cowen, E. L., Dorr, D., Izzo, L. D., Madonia, A., and Trost, M. A. The primary mental health project: A new way to conceptualize and deliver school mental health service. *Psychology in the Schools*, 1971, *8*, 216-225.
95. Cowen, E. L., Dorr, D., Trost, M. A., and Izzo, L. D. A follow-up study of maladapting school children seen by non-professionals. *Journal of Consulting Psychology*, 1972, *36*, 235-238.
96. Cowen, E. L., Gardner, E. A., and Zax, M. (Eds.) *Emergent approaches to mental health problems.* New York: Appleton-Century-Crofts, 1967.
97. Cowen, E. L., and Zax, M. Early detection and prevention of emotional disorder: conceptualization and programs. See Ref. 77, 1968, 46-59.
98. Cumming, E. Unsolved problems of prevention. *Canadian Mental Health*, 1968, Suppl. 56.
99. Davis, J. A. *Education for positive mental health.* Reprint 88 National Opinion Research Center, University of Chicago Press, 1963.
100. Decker, J. B., and Stubblebine, J. M. Crisis intervention and prevention of psychiatric disability: A follow-up study. *American Journal of Psychiatry*, 1972, *129*, 725-729.
101. Defense Documentation Center. *Environmental effects on behavior: A report bibliography.* Alexandria, Va.: Defense Documentation Center, 1970.
102. Deutsch, M., Katz, I., and Jensen, A. R. (Eds.) *Social class, race and psychological development.* New York: Holt, Rinehart and Winston, 1968.
103. Dobzhansky, T. Genetics and the diversity of behavior. *American Psychologist*, 1972, *27*, 523-530.
104. Dohrenwend, B. P., and Dohrenwend, B. S. *Social status and psychological disorder.* New York: Wiley, 1969.
105. Dohrenwend, B. P., Egri, G., and Mendelsohn, F. S. Psychiatric disorder in general populations: A study of the problem of clinical judgment. *American Journal of Psychiatry*, 1971, *127*, 1304-1312.
106. Dorr, D. An ounce of prevention. *Mental Hygiene*, 1972, *56*, 25-27.
107. Dubos, R. Environmental determinants of human life. In D. C. Glass (Ed.), *Environmental influences.* New York: Russell Sage Foundation, 1968.
108. Dubos, R. *So human an animal.* New York: Scribner, 1968.
109. Dubos, R. We can't buy our way out. *Psychology Today*, 1970, *3*, 20, 22, 86-87.
110. Edwards, J. E., Penick, E. C., and Suway, B. Evaluating the use of television in community mental health education. *Hospital and Community Psychiatry*, 1973, *24*, 771-772.
111. Eisenberg, L. Possibilities for a preventive psychiatry. *Pediatrics*, 1962, *30*, 815-828.
112. Eisenberg, L. Preventive psychiatry. *Annual Review of Medicine*, 1962, *13*, 343-360.

113. Eisenberg, L. Preventive psychiatry—if not now, when. *World Mental Health*, 1963, *19*, 48–64.
114. Elkind, H. B. The epidemiology of mental disease. *American Journal of Psychiatry*, 1927, *6*, 623–640.
115. Elkind, H. B. Is there an epidemiology of mental disease? *American Journal of Public Health*, 1938, *28*, 245–250.
116. Emerson, H. Epidemiology a possible resource in preventing mental disease. In F. R. Moulton (Ed.), *Mental Health*. American Association for the Advancement of Science, 1969.
117. Engel, G. L., and Adler, R. Psychological factors in organic disease. *Mental Health Progress Report*, U.S. Department of Health, Education, and Welfare, 1967, 1–23.
118. Epps, R., et al. *A community concern*. Springfield, Ill.: Thomas, 1965.
119. Eysenck, H. J., and Rachman, S. *The causes and cures of neurosis*. London: Routledge and Kegan Paul, 1965.
120. Fabian, A. The disturbed child in the ghetto day care center: The role of the psychiatric consultant. *American Academy of Child Psychiatry Journal*, 1972, *11*, 467–491.
121. Fairweather, G. *Methods for experimental social intervention*. New York: Wiley, 1967.
122. Farbern, N. *Bibliography on suicide and suicide prevention*. Public Health Service Publication 1979. Washington, D.C.: Superintendent of Documents, 1969.
123. Flanagan, J. C. Evaluation and validation of research data in primary prevention. *American Journal of Orthopsychiatry*, 1971, *41*, 117–123.
124. Foley, A. R., and Gorham, C. S. W. Toward a new philosophy of care: perspectives on prevention. *Community Mental Health Journal*, 1973, *9*, 99–107.
125. Frank. G. H. The role of the family in the development of psychopathology. *Psychological Bulletin*, 1965, *64*, 191–205.
126. Fried, M. *Social problems and psychopathology*. Group for the Advancement of Psychiatry *Symposium*, 1964, *10*, 403–446.
127. Fuller, G., and Friedrich, D. Predicting potential school problems. *Perceptual and Motor Skills*, 1973, *37*, 453–454.
128. Galle, O. R., Groue, W. R., and McPherson, J. M. Population density and pathology: What are the relations for man? *Science*, 1972, *176*, 23–30.
129. Garber, N. Pediatric child psychiatry collaboration in a health maintenance organization. *American Journal of Psychiatry*, 1973, *130*, 1227.
130. Garmezy, N. Vulnerability research and the issue of primary prevention. *American Journal of Orthopsychiatry*, 1971, *41*, 101–116.
131. Glidewell, J. C. *Issues in community psychology and preventive mental health*. New York: Behavioral Publications, 1971.
132. Glidewell, J. C., Gildea, M. C. L., and Kaufman, M. K. The preventive and therapeutic effects of the school mental health programs. *American Journal of Community Psychology*, 1973, *1*, 295–329.

133. Glidewell, J. C., and Swallow, C. S. *The prevalence of maladjustment in elementary schools: A report prepared for the Joint Commission on the Mental Health of Children.* Chicago: University of Chicago Press, 1969.

134. Glueck, S., and Glueck, E. T. *Delinquents in the making: Paths to prevention.* New York: Harper, 1952.

135. Glueck, S., and Glueck, E. *Family environment and delinquency.* Boston: Houghton Mifflin, 1962.

136. Golann, S. E. (Ed.) *Coordinate index reference guide to community mental health.* New York: Behavioral Publications, 1969.

137. Golann, S. E., and Eisdorfer, C. *Handbook of community mental health.* New York: Appleton-Century-Crofts, 1972.

138. Goldfarb, H. The effects of early institutional care on adolescent personality. *Child Development*, 1943, *14*, 213–223.

139. Goldfarb, H. Effects of psychological deprivation in infancy and subsequent stimulation. *American Journal of Psychiatry*, 1945, *102*, 18–33.

140. Goslin, D. (Ed.) *Handbook of socialization theory and research.* New York: Rand McNally, 1969.

141. Green, C. S. *Psychological stress and mental dysfunction.* Chicago: Crerar Library, 1969.

142. Greenberg, J. Differential prediction of reading failure at the first grade level: The goal, prevention. *American Journal of Orthopsychiatry*, 1973, *43*, 223–224.

143. Greenblatt, M., et al. *The prevention of hospitalization.* New York: Grune and Stratton, 1963.

144. Griffin. C. L., and Reinhorz, H. Z. Prevention of the 'failure syndrome' in the primary grades: Implications for intervention. *American Journal of Public Health*, 1969, *59*, 2029–2034.

145. Grinspoon, L. *Marihuana reconsidered.* Cambridge, Mass.: Harvard University Press, 1971.

146. Group for the Advancement of Psychiatry. *Psychopathological disorders in childhood: Theoretical considerations and a proposed classification.* New York: G.A.P. Rep. 62, 1953.

147. Group for the Advancement of Psychiatry. *Crisis in child mental health: A critical assessment.* G.A.P. Rep. 82, 1970.

148. Group for the Advancement of Psychiatry. *The dimensions of community psychiatry.* New York: G.A.P. Rep. 69, Vol. 6, 1968.

149. Gruenberg, E. M. The epidemiology of mental disease. *Scientific American*, 1954, *190*, 38–42.

150. Gruenberg, E. M. Epidemiology of mental disorders. *Milbank Memorial Fund Quarterly*, 1957, *35*, 107–126.

151. Gruenberg, E. M. The prevention of mental disorders. *Journal of Chronic Diseases*, 1959, *9*, 187–198.

152. Gump, L. R. The application of primary preventive mental health principles to the college community. *Community Mental Health Journal*, 1973, *9*, 133–142.

153. Harlow, H. F., and Harlow, M. Learning to love. *American Scientist*, 1966, *54*, 244–272.
154. Haughton, A. Suicide prevention program in the U.S.: An overview. *Bulletin of Suicidology*, 1968, *7*, 25–29.
155. Hebb, D. O. *Organization of behavior*. New York: Wiley, 1949.
156. Heber, R., and Stevens, H. A. (Eds.) *Mental retardation: Review of research*. Chicago: University of Chicago Press, 1964.
157. Herzberg, F. *Work and the nature of man*. Cleveland: World Publishing Co., 1966.
158. Heston, L. L. Psychiatric disorders in foster home reared children of schizophrenic mothers. *British Journal of Psychiatry*, 1966, *112*, 819–825.
159. Hilleboe, H. E. Preventing future shock: Healthy development in the 60's and imperatives for the 70's. Eleventh Bronfman Lecture. *American Journal of Public Health*, 1972, *62*, 136–145.
160. Hirsch, J., and Hostetter, R. C. Behavior genetics. In P. London and D. Rosenhan (Eds.), *Foundations of abnormal psychology*, New York: Holt, Rinehart, and Winston, 1968.
161. Hoffman, M., and Hoffman, L. *Review of child development research*, Vol. I. New York: Russell Sage Foundation, 1964.
162. Hollingshead, A. B., and Redlich, F. C. *Social class and mental illness*. New York: Wiley, 1968.
163. Hollister, W. Issues for school mental health. *North Carolina Journal of Mental Health*, 1966, *2*, 42 ff.
164. Hornstein, H. A., Bunker, B. B., Burke, W. W., Glindes, M., and Lewicki, R. J. (Eds.) *Social intervention: A behavioral science approach*. New York: Free Press, 1973.
165. Hunt, J. McV. *Intelligence and experience*. New York: Ronald, 1961.
166. Hunt, J. McV. Toward the prevention of incompetence. See Ref. 77, 1968, 19–45.
167. Hunt, J. McV. Poverty versus equality of opportunity. In V. L. Allen (Ed.), *Psychological factors in poverty*. Chicago: Markham, 1970.
168. Hunter, R. C. A., Rassell, J. A., Goldberg, B., Kral, V. A., and Lamberti, A. Primary prevention of specific disorders: Neurotic states; suicide; brain damage and retardation, in genetic psychiatry; delinquency. See Ref. 282, 1968, 98–110.
169. Hurley, R. *Poverty and mental health: A causal relationship*. New York: Random House, 1969.
170. Huttman, E. D. *Public housing: The negative psychological effects on family living*. Presented at American Orthopsychiatric Association, 1971.
171. Jackson, D. D. *The etiology of schizophrenia*. New York: Basic Books, 1960.
172. Jaco, E. G. *The social epidemiology of mental disorders*. New York: Russell Sage Foundation, 1960.
173. Jahoda, M. *Current concepts of positive mental health: A report to the Staff Director, Jack R. Ewalt*. New York: Basic Books, 1958.

174. Jarvis Report 1855. *The report of the Commission on Lunacy and Idiocy in Massachusetts.* Cambridge: Harvard University Press, 1971.
175. Johnson, D. L., et al. The Houston Parent-Child Development Center: A Parent Education Program for Mexican-American Families. Mimeo: University of Houston.
176. Joint Commission on the Mental Health of Children. *Crisis in child mental health: Challenge for the Seventies.* Hagerstown: Harper and Row, 1970.
177. Joint Commission on Mental Illness and Health. *Action for mental health.* New York: Basic Books, 1961.
178. Jones, E. *Life and works of Sigmund Freud.* Vols. 1, 2, 3. New York: Basic Books, 1953.
179. Kagan, J. Personality development. In P. London and D. Rosenhan (Eds.), *Foundations of abnormal psychology.* New York: Holt, Rinehart, and Winston, 1968.
180. Kantor, M. B., Gildea, M. C. L., and Glidewell, J. C. Preventive and therapeutic efforts of maternal attitude change in the school setting. *American Journal of Public Health,* 1969, *59,* 490–502.
181. Karnes, M. B., Studley, W. M., Wright, W. R., and Hodgins, A. S. An approach for working with mothers of disadvantaged pre-school children. *Merrill-Palmer Quarterly of Behavior and Development,* 1968, *14,* 174–184.
182. Kawi, A. A., and Pasamanick, B. Associations of factors of pregnancy with development of reading disorders in childhood. *Society for Reading Disorders and Child Development.* Yellow Springs, Ohio, 1959.
183. Kellam, S. G., and Schiff, S. K. The Woodlawn mental health center: A community mental health model. *Social Service Review,* 1966, *40,* 255–263.
184. Kelly, J. G. Towards an ecological conception of preventive interventions. See Ref. 77, 1968, 76–99.
185. Kelly, J. G. The quest for valid preventive interventions. In C. D. Spielberger (Ed.), *Current topics in clinical and community psychology,* Vol. 2. New York: Academic Press, 1970.
186. Keniston, K. How community mental health stamped out the riots, 1968–1978. In B. Denner and R. H. Price (Eds.), *Community mental health: Social action and reaction.* New York: Holt, Rinehart, and Winston, 1973.
187. Kennedy, J. F. *Message from the President of the United States relative to Mental Illness and Mental Retardation.* House Document No. 58, 88th Congress, 1st session, 1965, Washington, D. C.: Government Printing Office.
188. Kiesler, F. Programming for prevention. *North Carolina Journal of Mental Health,* 1965, *1,* 3–17.
189. Kiev, A. New directions for suicide prevention centers. *Life Threatening Behavior,* 1972, *2,* 189–193.
190. Kirk, E. W. Group practice of psychology: A community model. *Dissertation Abstracts International,* 1973, *33,* 3310.

191. Kirk, S., and Weiner, B. (Eds.) *Behavioral research on exceptional children.* Washington, D.C.: Council on Exceptional Children, 1963.
192. Kohlberg, L., LaCross, J., and Ricks, D. The predictability of adult mental health from childhood behavior. See Ref. 366, 1972, 1217–1284.
193. Kraft, I. Prevention mental ill health in early childhood. *Mental Hygiene,* 1964, *48,* 414–423.
194. Kryter, K. D. Psychological reactions to aircraft noise. *Science,* 1966, *151,* 1346–1355.
195. Kuman, B. H. *Mental retardation: Some recent developments in the study of causes and social effects of this problem.* New York: Pergamon, 1968.
196. Lambert, N. M. (Ed.) *The protection and promotion of mental health in schools,* 1–9. Bethesda, Md.: U.S. Department of Health, Education, and Welfare, Public Health Service Publication 1226, 1965.
197. Langner, T. S., Herson, J. H., Greene, E. T., Jameson, J. D., and Goff, J. Children of the city: Affluence, poverty, and mental health. In V. L. Allen (Ed.), *Psychological factors in poverty.* Chicago: Markham, 1970.
198. Langner, T. S., and Michael, S. T. *Life stress and mental health.* New York: Macmillan, 1963.
199. Langner, T. S., and Michael, S. T. *Life stress and mental health: II. The midtown Manhattan study.* New York: Free Press, 1963.
200. Leighton, A. H. *My name is legion, Stirling County study,* Vol. 1. New York: Basic Books, 1959.
201. Leighton, A. H. Some notes on preventive psychiatry. *Canadian Psychiatric Association Journal,* 1967, *12,* 43N–52.
202. Lemert, E. M. *Human deviance, social problems and social control.* Englewood Cliffs, N.J.: Prentice-Hall, 1967.
203. Lemkau, P. V. *Mental hygiene in public health.* New York: McGraw-Hill, 1955.
204. Lemkau, P. V. Freud and prophylaxis. *Bulletin of the New York Academy of Medicine,* 1956, *32,* 887–893.
205. Lemkau, P. V. Prospects for the prevention of mental illness. *Mental Hygiene,* 1966, *53,* 172–179.
206. Lemkau, P. V. Prevention in psychiatry. *British Journal of Social Psychiatry,* 1968, *2,* 127–133.
207. LeRiche, W. H. Preventive programmes in mental diseases: Their evaluation. See Ref. 282, 1968, 69–83.
208. Lester, D. The evaluation of suicide prevention centers. *International Behavioral Science,* 1971, *3,* 40–47.
209. Lester, D. The myth of suicide prevention. *Comprehensive Psychiatry,* 1972, *13,* 555–560.
210. Lester, D. The prevention of homicide. *Crisis Intervention,* 1972, *4,* 105–111.
211. Levine, M., and Levine, A. *A social history of the helping services.* New York: Appleton-Century-Crofts, 1970.

212. L'Hote, M. On an experience of primary prevention in a community service. *Psychiatrie l'Enfant*, 1971, *14*, 283–309.
213. Linderman, E. Current concept of prevention in mental health. See Ref. 330, 1964.
214. Lin-Fu, J. S. *Lead poisoning in children*. U.S. Department of Health, Education, and Welfare, Children's Bureau Publication No. 452. Washington, D.C.: Superintendent of Documents, 1967.
215. Lombroso,C. *Crime: Its causes and remedies*. Boston: Little Brown, 1911.
216. Long, B. E. Behavioral science for elementary school pupils. *Elementary School Journal*, 1970, *70*, 253–260.
217. Luban-Plozza, B. Preventive medical and psychosocial aspects of family practice. *Psychiatry in Medicine*, 1972, *3*, 327–332.
218. Lubchansky, I. L. Social psychiatry: Contents and form of an experience. *Acta Psiquiatricia y Psicologia de America Latina*, 1972, *18*, 154–159.
219. Malmquist, C. P. Preventive psychiatry—present status and future. *Minnesota Medicine*, 1960, *42*, 333–343.
220. Malmquist, C. P. Preventive psychiatry—present status and future. *Minnesota Medicine*, 1961, *43*, 237–243.
221. Martin, J. P. Conquest of general paresis. *British Medical Journal*, 1972, *3*, 159–160.
222. Maslow, A. H. *Toward a psychology of being*. Princeton: Van Nostrand, 1962.
223. McGee, R. Evaluation of crisis intervention programs and personnel: A summary and critique. *Life Threatening Behavior*, 1972, *2*, 168–182.
224. McKerracher, D. G., Griffin, J. D., and Szyrynski, V. Some methods of primary prevention: The general medical practitioner; public education and school procedures; crisis theory and preventive interaction. See Ref. 282, 1968, 145–168.
225. Mellsop, G. W. Psychiatric patients seen as children and adults: Childhood predictions of adult illness. *Journal of Child Psychology and Psychiatry*, 1972, *13*, 91–101.
226. *Mental disorders: A guide to control methods*. New York: American Public Health Association, 1962.
227. Meyers, J. K., and Bean, L. C. *A decade later: A follow-up of social class and mental illness*. New York: Wiley, 1968.
228. Meyers, J. K., and Roberts, B. H. *Family and class dynamics in mental illness*. New York: Wiley, 1959.
229. Mikkelson, M., and Stene, J. Genetic counseling in Down's Syndrome. *Human Heredity*, 1970, *20*, 457–464.
230. Milgram, S. The experience of living in cities. *Science*, 1970, *167*, 1461–1468.
231. Miller, K. S. Research training in community mental health. In I. Iscoe and C. D. Spielberger (Eds.), *Community psychology: Perspectives in training and research*. New York: Appleton-Century-Crofts, 1970.
232. Miller, S. M., and Mishler, E. G. Social class, mental illness and American psychiatry: An expository review. *Milbank Memorial Fund Quarterly*, 1959, *37*, 174–199.

233. Murphy, G. E. Clinical identification of suicidal risk. *Archives of General Psychiatry*, 1972, *27*, 356–359.
234. Murphy, G. E. Prevention of mental disorder: Some research suggestions. *Journal of Hillside Hospital*, 1960, *9*, 146.
235. Murphy, H. B. M., Wittkower, E. D., and Chance, N. A. Crosscultural inquiry into the symptomatology of depression: A preliminary report. *International Journal of Psychiatry*, 1967, *3*, 6–15.
236. Murphy, L. B., and Chandler, C. A. Building foundations for strength in the preschool years: Preventing developmental disturbances. See Ref. 137, 1972, 303–330.
237. Nangeroni, A. Social action in preventive psychiatry. *Canadian Mental Health*, 1968, *15*, 19–24.
238. National Association for Mental Health. *Primary prevention of mental disorders in prenatal and perinatal periods—action guidelines.* 1973, 1–25.
239. National Institutes of Health. Report of meeting on primary prevention, December 1968.
240. National Institutes of Health. *The effects of diet and nutrition on learning.* Bethesda, Md.: National Institutes of Health, 1970.
241. National Institutes of Health. *Promoting mental health.* Report of the Primary Prevention Panel to the Director, National Institute of Mental Health, 1970.
242. National Institutes of Mental Health. *A selected bibliography on occupational mental health.* Rockville, Md.: National Clearinghouse for Mental Health Information. Public Health Service Publication 1338, 1965.
243. National Institutes of Mental Health. *The protection and promotion of mental health in schools.* Mental Health Monograph 5, 1968.
244. National Institutes of Mental Health. *Consultation in mental health and related fields: A reference guide.* Public Health Service Publication 1920, 1969.
245. National Research Council, Committee on Biologic Effects of Atmospheric Pollutants. *Lead: Airborne in perspective.* Washington, D.C.: National Academy of Science, 1972.
246. Newman, M. B., and San Martino, M. The child and the seriously disturbed parent: Treatment issues. *Journal of the American Academy of Child Psychiatry, 12*, 162–181.
247. Newton, G., and Levine, S. (Eds.) *Early experience and behavior.* Springfield, Ill.: Thomas, 1968.
248. Noyes, A., and Kolb, L. C. *Modern clinical psychiatry.* Philadelphia: Saunders, 1968.
249. Ohio Department of Mental Health and Mental Retardation, Columbus. Gold Award: Television as a tool in primary prevention. *Hospital and Community Psychiatry*, 1973, *24*, 691–694.
250. Ojemann, R. H. (Ed.) *Four basic aspects of preventive psychiatry.* Report, 1st Institute for Preventive Psychiatry. Iowa City: University of Iowa Press, 1959.

251. Ojemann, R. H. (Ed.) *Recent contributions of biological and psychosocial investigations to preventive psychiatry.* Proceedings, 2nd Institute for Preventive Psychiatry. Iowa City: University of Iowa Press, 1959.
252. Ojemann, R. H. *Recent research looking toward preventive intervention.* Iowa City: University of Iowa, 1961.
253. Ojemann, R. H. (Ed.) *Recent research on creative approaches to environmental stress.* Proceedings, 4th Institute for Preventive Psychiatry. Iowa City: University of Iowa Press, 1963.
254. O'Neal, P., and Robins, L. N. The relation of childhood behavior problems to adult psychiatric status: A 30 year follow up of 150 subjects. *American Journal of Psychology,* 1958, *114,* 961–969.
255. O'Neal, P., and Robins, L. N. Childhood patterns predictive of adult schizophrenia: A 30 year follow up. *American Journal of Psychiatry,* 1958, *15,* 385–391.
256. O'Neal, P., and Robins, L. N. Relations of childhood behavior problems to adult psychiatric status. In H. C. Quay (Ed.), *Children's behavior disorders.* Princeton: Van Nostrand, 1968.
257. Pasamanick, B. (Ed.) *Epidemiology of mental disorders.* Washington, D.C.: American Association for the Advancement of Science, 1959.
258. Peck, H. B., Kaplan, S. R., and Roman, M. Prevention, treatment and social action: A strategy of intervention in a disadvantaged urban area. *American Journal of Orthopsychiatry,* 1966, *36,* 57–69.
259. Phillips, L. The competence criterion for mental health programs. *Community Mental Health Journal,* 1967, *3,* 73–76.
260. Phillips, L., and Zigler, E. Social competence: The action-thought parameter and vicariousness in normal and pathological behaviors. *Journal of Abnormal and Social Psychology,* 1961, *63,* 137–146.
261. Plaut, T. F. A. Prevention of alcoholism. See Ref. 137, 1972, 421–438.
262. Plog, C. S., and Edgerton, W. B. (Eds.) *Changing perspectives in mental illness.* New York: Holt, Rinehart, and Winston, 1969.
263. Plunkett, R. J., and Gordon, J. E. *Epidemiology and mental illness.* New York: Basic Books, 1960.
264. Poorkaj, H., and Boccelman, C. The impact of community volunteers on delinquency prevention. *Sociology and Social Research,* 1973, *57,* 335–341.
265. Poser, E. G. Toward a theory of behavioral prophylaxis. *Journal of Behavior Therapy and Experimental Psychiatry,* 1970, *1,* 39–45.
266. Powers, E., and Witmer, H. *An experiment in the prevention of delinquency.* New York: Columbia University Press, 1951.
267. President's Task Force on Mentally Handicapped. *President's Task Force, Action Against Mental Disability.* Washington, D.C.: Government Printing Office, 1970.
268. Rabkin, J. Opinions about mental illness: Review of the literature. *Psychological Bulletin,* 1972, *77,* 153–171.
269. Rahe, R. H., and Holmes, T. H. Life crisis and major health change. *Psychosomatic Medicine,* 1966, *28,* 774.

270. Raimy, V. *Training in clinical psychology.* New York: Prentice Hall, 1950.
271. Rees, S. C., and Doan, H. McK. An evaluation of a pilot treatment for infants and mothers (Mimeo). West End Creche, Toronto, Canada, 1973.
272. Reid, H., Brown, E., Hansen, Y., and Sperber, Z. Preventive interventions for the very young: An infant consultation service interweaves service, training, and research. *American Journal of Orthopsychiatry,* 1973, *43*, 246–247.
273. Reiff, R. Mental Health manpower and institutional change. *American Psychologist,* 1966, *21*, 540–548.
274. Reiff, R. Mental Health manpower and institutional change. See Ref. 96, 1967, 74–88.
275. Ribble, M. *Rights of infants.* New York: Columbia University Press, 1943.
276. Ricks, D. F., Thomas, A., and Roff, M. *Life history research in psychopathology,* Vol. 3. Minneapolis: University of Minnesota Press, 1974.
277. Riessman, F., Cohen, J., and Perl, A. (Eds.) *Mental health of the poor.* New York: Free Press, 1964.
278. Riessman, F., and Hallowitz, E. The neighborhood service center: An innovation in preventive psychiatry. *American Journal of Psychiatry,* 1967, *123*, 1408–1412.
279. Rimland, B. *Infantile autism.* New York: Appleton-Century-Crofts, 1964.
280. Rimland, B. Psychogenesis versus biogenesis: The issues and the evidence. See Ref. 262, 1969, 702–735.
281. Roberts, L. M., Greenfield, N. S., and Miller, M. H. (Eds.) *Comprehensive mental health.* Madison: University of Wisconsin Press, 1968.
282. Roberts, C. A. *Primary prevention of psychiatric disorders.* Clarence Hincks Memorial Lecture, 1967. University of Toronto Press, 1968.
283. Roberts, C. A. Psychiatric and mental health consultation. *Canadian Journal of Public Health,* 1970, *51*, 17–24.
284. Robertson, B. Primary prevention: A pilot project. *Canadian Mental Health,* 1968, *15*, 20–22.
285. Robins, E., Murphy, G. E., Wilkinson, R. H., Gassner, S., and Kayes, J. Some clinical considerations in the prevention of suicide based on a study of 134 successful suicides. *American Journal of Public Health,* 1959, *49*, 888–899.
286. Robins, L. N. *Deviant children grown up.* Baltimore: Williams and Wilkins, 1966.
287. Roen, S. R. Evaluative research and community mental health. In A. E. Bergin and S. L. Garfield (Eds.), *Handbook of psychotherapy and behavioral change: An empirical analysis.* New York: Wiley, 1971.
288. Roff, M., and Ricks, D. F. (Eds.) *Life history research in psychopathology.* Minneapolis: University of Minnesota Press, 1970.
289. Roff, M., Robins, L. N., and Pollack, M. *Life History research in psychopathology,* Vol. 2. Minneapolis: University of Minnesota Press, 1972.

290. Rogers, M. E., et al. Prenatal and perinatal factors in the development of childhood behavior disorders. *Psychiatrica Neurologica Scandinavica*, 1966, Suppl. 102.

291. Rolf, J. E., and Harig, P. T. Etiological research in schizophrenia and the rationale for primary intervention. *American Journal of Orthopsychiatry*, 1974, *44*, 538-584.

292. Romano, J. (Ed.) *Origins of schizophrenia.* New York: Excerpta Medica Foundation, 1967.

293. Rosenblum, G. (Ed.) *Issues in community psychology and preventive mental health.* New York: Behavioral Publications, 1971.

294. Rosenblum, G. Mental health retools for the 70's. *Massachusetts Journal of Mental Health*, 1972, *2*, 5-16.

295. Rosenthal, D., and Kety, S. S. (Eds.) *The transmission of schizophrenia.* Elmsford, N.Y.: Pergamon, 1968.

296. Ryan, W. Preventive services in the social context: Power, pathology and prevention. In *Preventive services in mental health programs, Proceedings of a mental health institute, Salt Lake City*, 49-60. Boulder, Colo.: Western Interstate Commission on Higher Education, 1967.

297. Ryan, W. *Distress in the city.* Cleveland: Case Western Reserve University Press, 1969.

298. Ryan, W. *Blaming the victim.* New York: Random House, 1971.

299. Ryan, W. Emotional disorder as a social problem: Implications for mental health programs. *Journal of Orthopsychiatry*, 1971, *41*, 638-645.

300. Sandler, I. N. Characteristics of women working as child aides in a school-based preventive mental health program. *Journal of Consulting and Clinical Psychology*, 1972, *39*, 56-61.

301. Sanford, N. The prevention of mental illness. See Ref. 365, 1965, 1378-1400.

302. Sanford, N. Is the concept of prevention necessary or useful? See Ref. 137, 1972, 461-471.

303. Sarason, I. G. *Abnormal psychology.* New York: Appleton-Century-Crofts, 1972.

304. Sarason, S. B., Levine, M., Goldenberg, I. I., Cherlin, D. L., and Bennett, E. M. *Psychology in community settings.* New York: Wiley, 1966.

305. Scarr-Salapatek, S. Race, social class and I.Q. *Science*, 1971, *174*, 1285-1295.

306. Schecter, M. D. Prevention in psychiatry: Problems and prospects. *Child Psychiatry and Human Development*, 1970, *1*, 68-82.

307. Schulhofer, E. Short term preparations of children for separation, divorce, and remarriage of parents. *American Journal of Orthopsychiatry*, 1973, *43*, 248-249.

308. Schuman, L. M. Research methodology and potential in community health and preventive medicine. *Annals of the New York Academy of Sciences*, 1963, *107*, 557-569.

309. Schwartz, S. L. A review of crisis intervention programs. *Psychiatric Quarterly*, 1971, *45*, 498-508.

310. Seiden, R. Suicide and public health: A brief appraisal. *Life Threatening Behavior*, 1972, *2*, 99–103.
311. Selig, A. L. Prevention of mental illness and community organization. A review and annotated bibliography. *Journal Supplement Abstract Service*, 1973, MS 369.
312. Sergovich, F. R. Cytogenetic practise in a mental retardation clinic. *Canadian Psychiatric Association Journal*, 1967, *12*, 35–52.
313. Sheldon, W. H., and Stevens, S. S. *The varieties of temperament: A psychology of constitutional differences.* New York: Harper, 1942.
314. Shneidman, E. S. Prevention of suicide: A challenge for community science. See Ref. 137, 1972, 449–460.
315. Shore, J. H., Bopp, J. F., Waller, T. R., and Dawes, J. W. A suicide prevention center on an Indian reservation. *American Journal of Psychiatry*, 1972, *128*, 1086–1091.
316. Shore, J. H., Kinzie, J. D., Hampton, J. L., and Pattison, E. M. Psychiatric epidemiology of an Indian village. *Psychiatry*, 1973, *36*, 70–81.
317. Shrier, D., and Lourman, S. Psychiatric consultation at a day care center. *American Journal of Orthopsychiatry*, 1973, *43*, 394–400.
318. Shure, M., Spivak, G., and Gordon, R. Problem solving thinking: A preventive mental health program for preschool children. *Reading World*, 1972, *11*, 259–273.
319. Signell, K. A. Kindergarten entry: A preventive approach to community mental health. *Community Mental Health Journal*, 1972, *8*, 60–70.
320. Silver, A. A., and Hagin, R. A. Profile of a first grade: A basis for preventive psychiatry. *Journal of the American Academy of Child Psychiatry*, 1972, *11*, 645–674.
321. Skeels, H. M. Effect of adoption of children from institutions. *Children*, 1965, *12*, 33–34.
322. Skeels, H. M. Adult status of children with contrasting early life experiences. *Monographs of the Society for Research on Child Development*, 1966, *31*, 1–65.
323. Skeels, H. M. Headstart on Headstart: 30 year evaluation. *5th Annual Distinguished Lectures in Special Education: Summer Session, 1966.* Los Angeles: University of Southern California School of Education, 1967.
324. Skodak, M., and Skeels, H. M. A final follow-up study of 100 adopted children. *Journal of General Psychology*, 1949, *75*, 85–125.
325. Slobin, M. S. A resource center for primary prevention in mental health. Cleveland State University Department of Psychology (mimeo), 1972.
326. Smith, M. B. Competence and socialization. In J. A. Clausen (Ed.), *Socialization and society.* New York: Little, Brown, 1968.
327. Smith, W. G. Critical life-events and prevention strategies in mental health. *Archives of General Psychiatry*, 1971, *25*, 103–109.
328. Sobey, F. *Nonprofessional revolution in mental health.* New York: Columbia University Press, 1970.
329. Soddy, K., and Ahrenfeldt, R. H. *Mental health and contemporary thought*, Vol. 2. London: Tavistock, 1967.

330. Spiegel, A. (Ed.) *The mental health role of settlement and community centers.* NIMH Technical Assistance Project, 1964.
331. Spitz, R. Anaclitic depression: An inquiry into the genesis of psychiatric conditions in early childhood. *Psychoanalytic Study of the Child,* 1946, *2,* 313–342.
332. Spoon, D., and Southwick, J. Promoting mental health through family life education. *Family Coordinator,* 1972, 279–286.
333. Srole, L., Langner, T. S., Michael, S. T., Opler, M. K., and Rennie, T. A. C. *Mental health in the metropolis: The midtown Manhattan study,* Vol. I.
334. Szasz, T. *The myth of mental illness.* New York: Hoeber-Harper, 1961.
335. Szurek, S. *Antisocial child: His family and his community.* Palo Alto, Calif.: Science and Behavior Books, 1969.
336. Trost, M. A. The child aide mental health program. *Mental Health in the Classroom,* 7, 1968.
337. Trost, M. A. The preventive role of social work in a school setting. *Child Welfare,* 1968, *47,* 397–404, 425.
338. Treisman, M. Mind, body and behavior: Control systems and their disturbances. In P. London and D. Rosenhan (Eds.), *Theory and research in abnormal psychology.* New York: Holt, Rinehart, and Winston, 1969.
339. Tureen, L., and Wortman, M. A program sponsored by a labor union, for treatment and prevention of psychiatric conditions. *American Journal of Orthopsychiatry,* 1965, *35,* 594–597.
340. Udry, J. R., and Morris, N. M. S spoonful of sugar helps the medicine go down. *American Journal of Public Health,* 1971, *61,* 776–785.
341. VanAntwerp, M. Primary prevention: A challenge to mental health associations. *Mental Hygiene,* 1970, *54,* 453–456.
342. VanAntwerp, M. The route to primary prevention. *Community Mental Health Journal,* 1971, 7, 183–188.
343. Vance, E. T. Social disability. *American Psychologist,* 1963, *28,* 498–511.
344. Wagenfeld, M. O. The primary prevention of mental illness. *Journal of Health and Social Behavior,* 1972, *13,* 195–203.
345. Walder, W. M., Cohen, S. I., and Daston, P. G. *Teaching parents and others principles of behavior control for modifying the behavior of children.* Report to U.S. Office of Education, Washington, D.C., 1967.
346. Walker, L. The school psychologist as a preventive mental health consultant. *Dissertation Abstracts International,* 1973, *33,* 5024.
347. Waxer, P., and White, R. Introducing psychological consultation to a university community. *Canadian Psychology,* 1973, *14,* 256–265.
348. Weinberg, A. A. Mental ill-health, consequent to migration and loneliness, and its prevention. *Psychotherapy and Psychosomatics,* 1967, *15,* 69.
349. Weinberg, S. K. Part VIII: Prevention of disordered behavior and mental health. "Community Psychiatry." *The sociology of mental disorders.* Chicago: Aldine, 1967.
350. Weiner, S. Effectiveness of a suicide prevention program. *Mental Hygiene,* 1969, *53,* 357–363.

398   Marc Kessler and George W. Albee

351. Wellington, J. Mothers' day out: Description of a program for the psychologist consultant to parents and their pre-school children. *Proceedings of the 81st Annual Convention of the American Psychological Association*, 1973, *8*, 963.
352. W.I.C.H.E. *Preventive services in mental health programs*. Proceedings of the Mental Health Institute, Boulder, Colorado, 1967.
353. White, R. W. Motivation reconsidered: The concept of competence. *Psychological Review*, 1959, *66*, 297–333.
354. Whitlock, G. *Preventive psychology and the church*. Westminster Press, 1973.
355. Whittington, H. G. *Is prevention of mental illness possible?* Chicago: Florence Crittenton Association of America, 1967.
356. Wiener, G., Andrews, S. R., Blumenthal, J., and Rabinowitz, M. *New Orleans Parent Child Development Center* (mimeo), 1973.
357. Wilkinson, R. Some factors influencing the effect of environmental stressors upon performance. *Psychological Bulletin*, 1969, *72*, 260–272.
358. Williams, R. D. (Ed.) *The prevention of disability in mental disorders*. Washington, D.C.: U.S. Department of Health, Education, and Welfare Publication 924, 1962.
359. Wilner, D. M., Walkley, R. P., Pinkerton, T. C., and Tayback, M. *The housing environment and family life: A longitudinal study of the effects of housing on morbidity and mental health*. Baltimore: Johns Hopkins, 1962.
360. Wittkower, E. D., and Fried, S. Some problems of transcultural psychiatry. *International Journal of Social Psychiatry*, 1958, *3*, 245–252.
361. Wohlwill, J. F. The emerging discipline of environmental psychology. *American Psychologist*, 1970, *25*, 303–312.
362. Wohlwill, J. F., and Carson, D. H. Environment and behavioral science: Retrospect and prospect. In J. F. Wohlwill and D. H. Carson (Eds.), *Environment and the social sciences: Perspectives and applications*. Washington, D.C.: American Psychiatric Association, 1972.
363. Wold, C. A two year follow up of suicide prevention center patients. *Life Threatening Behavior*, 1973, *3*, 171–183.
364. Wolff, H. S. Life stress and bodily disease: A formulation. In *Proceedings of the Association for Research in Nervous and Mental Disease*, Vol. 29. Baltimore: Williams and Wilkins, 1950.
365. Wolman, B. (Ed.) *Handbook of clinical psychology*. New York: McGraw-Hill, 1965.
366. Wolman, B. (Ed.) *Manual of child psychopathology*. New York: McGraw-Hill, 1972.
367. Wooten, B. *Social science and social pathology*. London: Allen and Unwin, 1959.
368. World Health Organization Technical Report Series 9. Mental Health: Report of the First Session of the Expert Committee. Geneva: World Health Organization, 1950.
369. World Health Organization Technical Report Series 134. The psychiatric hospital as a center for preventive work in mental health: Fifth Report

of the Expert Committee on Mental Health. Geneva: World Health Organization, 1957.

370. World Health Organization Technical Report Series 185. Epidemiology of Mental Disorders: Eighth Report of the Expert Committee on Mental Health, Geneva: World Health Organization, 1960.

371. Wortiz, S. B. General topics. *Year book of neurology, psychiatry and neurosurgery*. Chicago: Year Book Medical Publications, 1968.

372. Yarrow, L. S. Maternal deprivation: Toward an empirical and conceptual re-evaluation. *Psychological Bulletin*, 1961, *58*, 459–490.

373. Zax, M. A teacher-aide program for preventing emotional disturbance in primary grade school children. *Mental Hygiene*, 1966, *50*, 406–414.

374. Zax, M., and Cowen, E. L. *Abnormal psychology: Changing conceptions*. New York: Holt, Rinehart, and Winston, 1972.

375. Zax, M., and Cowen, E. L. Early identification and prevention of emotional disturbance in a public school. See Ref. 96, 1967, 331–351.

376. Zax, M., and Cowen, E. L. Research on early detection and prevention of emotional dysfunction in young school children. In C. D. Spielberger (Ed.), *Current topics in clinical and community psychology*, Vol. 1. New York: Academic, 1969.

377. Zax, M., and Specter, G. A. *An introduction to community psychology*. New York: Wiley, 1974.

378. Zax, M., and Specter, G. A. Primary prevention in the schools. See Ref. 377, 1974, pp. 147–172.

379. Zubin, J., and Freyhan, F. A. Social psychiatry. *Proceedings of the 57th Annual Meeting of the American Psychological Association*. New York: Grune and Stratton, 1968.

380. Zusman, J., and Davidson, D. L. *Practical aspects of mental health consultation*. Springfield, Ill.: Thomas, 1972.

381. Zusman, J., Hannon, V., Locke, B. Z., and Geller, M. *Bibliography: Epidemiology of mental disorders: 1966–1968*. National Institute of Mental Health, National Clearinghouse for Mental Health Information Publication 5034, 1970.

Index of Names

Numbers in parentheses indicate the location of a chapter in this volume.
Italicized numbers indicate the location of a name in a list of references.

Index of Subjects